TAKING SIDES

Clashing Views on Controversial Political Issues

7th edition

Printed on Recycled Paper

Clashing Views
on Controversial
Political Issues

7th edition

**Edited, Selected,
and with Introductions by**

George McKenna
City College, City University of New York

and

Stanley Feingold
Westchester Community College

The Dushkin Publishing Group, Inc.

In memory of Hillman M. Bishop and Samuel Hendel, masters of an art often neglected by college teachers: teaching.

Taking Sides ® is a registered trademark of The Dushkin Publishing Group, Inc.

Library of Congress Catalog Card Number: 90-81837

Manufactured in the United States of America

Seventh Edition, Third Printing

ISBN: 0-87967-926-3

PREFACE

In the first edition of *Taking Sides* we wrote:

> The purpose of this book is to make a modest contribution toward the revival of political dialogue in America. What we propose to do is to examine some leading issues in American politics from the perspective of sharply opposed points of view. We have tried to select authors who argue their points vigorously but in such a way as to enhance our understanding of the issue.
>
> For each issue we have selected a pair of essays, one pro and one con. We hope the reader will examine each position carefully and then take sides.

The success of the past six editions has encouraged us to remain faithful to our original objectives, methods, and format. We believe in public dialogue. We are convinced that the best way to guard against narrow-mindedness and fanaticism is to bring opposing views together and let them clash. We hope that students who confront lively and thoughtful statements from opposing sides on contemporary political issues will be stimulated in their own critical thinking about American government and politics. We are convinced that a healthy, stable democracy requires a citizenry that considers such questions as, What are the highest priority issues the government should address? What attitudes should Americans take toward their government? To what extent, if any, does government need to be changed? We are convinced that a healthy, stable democracy requires a citizenry that considers these kinds of questions and participates—however indirectly—in answering them. The alternative is apathy, passivity, and, sooner or later, the rule of tyrants.

For every debate, we have chosen what we believe are appropriate and well-reasoned statements by committed advocates of each side of the debate. If the argument contains an element of passion as well as reason (and most do!), it is passion with substance, not empty rhetoric. That is a distinction the student of American politics cannot afford to ignore.

However, we do not consider all points of view to be equal. On the contrary, we encourage our readers to become partisans, as long as they support their positions with logic and facts, make reasonable replies to opposing arguments, and are willing to revise their views if they are proven wrong.

Changes to this edition We have considerably revised this seventh edition. There are five completely new issues: *Should the Federal Courts Be Bound by the "Original Intent" of the Framers?* (Issue 8); *Do People Have a Right to Burn the American Flag?* (Issue 12); *Should Drugs Be Legalized?* (Issue 14); *Should the United States Support* Perestroika *in the Soviet Union?* (Issue 18); and

Should Idealism Be the Basis of American Foreign Policy? (Issue 19). We have also—in response to numerous requests from users of this book—reinstated two issues from earlier editions that we had dropped from the sixth edition: *Should Pornography Be Protected as Free Speech?* (Issue 13); and *Should Abortion Be Considered a Basic Right?* (Issue 16). In restoring them, however, we have used new, up-to-date sources. Indeed, with many issues that we have decided to keep, we have changed one or more of the selections in order to keep the arguments current and relevant. In all there are 22 new selections in this edition. We have also revised the introductions and postscripts where it was necessary.

A word to the instructor An *Instructor's Manual with Test Questions* (multiple-choice and essay) is available through the publisher. A general guidebook, called *Using Taking Sides in the Classroom,* which discusses methods and techniques for integrating the pro/con approach into any classroom setting, is also available.

Acknowledgments We received many helpful comments and suggestions from our friends and readers across the United States and Canada. Their suggestions have markedly enhanced the quality of this edition of *Taking Sides* and are reflected in the seven totally new issues and the updated selections.

Our thanks go to those who responded with suggestions for the seventh edition: Michael J. Adelman, Ohio University; Paul Barton-Kriese, Indiana University East; Anthony Brunello, Eckerd College; Charles Burke, Baldwin-Wallace College; William Burris, Guilford College; Robert Cassier, Santa Barbara City College; William M. Downer, Thiel College; Ernest Giglio, Lycoming College; Ruth Grubel, University of Wisconsin; David Hunter, University of Georgia; Fredric Lamb, University of Oklahoma; Jasper M. Licalzi, Jr., Temple University; William V. Moore, College of Charleston; Theodore R. Mosch, University of Tennessee; Chester Rhoan, Chabot College; Richard Riley, Baylor University; Milburn J. Stone, Rhode Island College; Elliot Tenofsky, Linfield College; Craig Wheeland, Villanova University; and J. Williams, Principia College.

We also appreciate the spontaneous letters from instructors and students who wrote to us with comments and observations. We wish to acknowledge the support given to this project by Rick Connelly, president of The Dushkin Publishing Group. We are grateful as well to Mimi Egan, program manager, for her very able editorial supervision. Needless to say, the responsibility for any errors of fact or judgment rests with us.

George McKenna
City College, City University of New York

Stanley Feingold
Westchester Community College

CONTENTS IN BRIEF

CONTENTS

Political scientist Thomas R. Dye believes that power in America is wielded by only a handful of people. Sociologist Andrew M. Greeley argues that there is no single, established center of power in America and draws upon the behavior of the system as evidence.

Professors Benjamin Ginsberg and Martin Shefter contend that political parties have declined and that elections leave many controversial issues unresolved. They argue that a political stalemate would result from the likelihood of a Democratic Congress and a Republican president. Professor Everett Carll Ladd counters that the party system is not vulnerable to special interests, that it is appropriate for America's constitutional system, and that it has the endorsement of the American people.

Common Cause president Fred Wertheimer argues that PACs exert too much influence over the electoral process, allowing special interests to have access to elected officials at the expense of the national interest. Political analyst Herbert Alexander insists that PACs have made significant contributions to the American political system.

William Rusher, a media analyst and former publisher of the *National Review*, argues that the media are biased against conservatives and that news coverage promotes liberal opinions. Professors Edward Herman and Noam Chomsky critique the mass media from the perspective of the left and find the media to be a "propaganda mill" in the service of the wealthy and powerful.

Journalist Gregg Easterbrook believes that before Congress can lead the nation, it must be able to lead itself, and it has notably failed to do so. Professor Gary Orfield argues that Congress does a good job of reflecting the attitudes and trends of the electorate as a whole.

Lawyer Theodore B. Olson contends that Congress is restricting powers that should be wielded by the president. Historian Robert Nisbet counters that American democracy is threatened by the unchecked growth of presidential power.

Editor Barry Crickmer argues that the interests of citizens and consumers could be better served by the forces of the profit motive than by goverment intervention. Professor Susan Tolchin and journalist Martin Tolchin contend that without vigorous regulation businesses will destroy the environment and endanger lives in their single-minded pursuit of profit.

Educator and former Court of Appeals judge Robert H. Bork argues that the original intent of the framers of the Constitution can and should be upheld by the federal courts, because not to do so is to have judges perform a political role they were not given. Professor Leonard W. Levy believes that the "original intent" of the framers cannot be found, and, given these changing times, it could not be applied in dealing with contemporary constitutional issues.

Retired Supreme Court justice William Brennan argues that flag-burning deserves protection under the First Amendment, which safeguards freedom of speech. Supreme Court chief justice William Rehnquist counters that flag-burning is not speech but an inarticulate, vicious act, unworthy of protection under the First Amendment.

Lawyer Donna Demac contends that, with the exception of child pornography, the cure of censorship is worse than the disease of pornography, whose social harm is unproven. President of Focus on the Family James Dobson is ardently opposed to pornography. He believes pornography humiliates and exploits women and children and is unprotected by the First Amendment.

Legalizing drugs would help put the criminal drug dealers out of business while protecting the rights of adults to make their own choices, contends educator Ethan Nadelmann. Political scientist James Q. Wilson argues that drug legalization would vastly increase the use of dangerous drugs along with the social problems that are created by such usage.

Political scientist Charles Murray is convinced that the best welfare policy, at least for able-bodied working-age people, is no welfare support by the government. Professor William Julius Wilson argues that welfare policy has *not* contributed to economic decline for the poor; what has had an effect on poverty rates are social changes leading to a sharp rise in black male unemployment.

The decision to have an abortion is a moral choice, argues writer Mary Gordon. She feels women are capable of making this choice, based on such considerations as poverty, wanting a child, and the woman's age and circumstances. Cardinal John O'Connor contends that whatever a woman's convictions or circumstances may be, abortion of a fetus amounts to killing an unborn child and is therefore unacceptable.

Edd Doerr, executive director of Americans for Religious Liberty, believes that public schools, like other public institutions, should promote and reflect shared values, leaving religious instruction and celebration to the home and place of worship. George Goldberg, a writer and lawyer, holds that government may not favor one religion over another, but school prayer and the teaching of religion are permissible as long as all religions are accorded equal treatment.

Samuel P. Huntington argues that American decline is exaggerated, temporary, and reversible. America possesses the major sources of national power, Huntington says, and therefore has the capacity to renew itself.

INTRODUCTION

Labels and Alignments
in American Politics
George McKenna
Stanley Feingold

With the approach of the 1992 presidential election, we hear more and more talk about the political views of candidates. Attempts are made to categorize them under such headings as "liberal," "conservative," "right," and "left." Liberals are supposed to be more "left" than conservatives, who are placed somewhere on the "right," although there are those on the extreme left and extreme right who are neither liberal nor conservative but "radical." Few, however, would really want to be called radical; those on the outer edges of the left prefer to be called "progressive," while extreme rightists find other names to characterize themselves; in the media they are usually tagged as "extremists." Then there are those who want to avoid any fixed identification with the left or the right, and they often resort to terms like "pluralist" to identify themselves. "Moderate" is another label usually coveted by American politicians; it has a nice sound.

Is there more than just sound to terms like liberal, conservative, radical, progressive, moderate, extremist, and pluralist? Do these terms have any meaning? They may be useful as terms of art or rhetoric, but do they help us citizens and voters understand opposing views on the major issues that face America today? We believe that they do, but that they must be used thoughtfully. Otherwise, the terms may end up obscuring or oversimplifying positions. Our purpose in this Introduction is to explore the basic, core meanings of the terms in order to make them useful to us as citizens.

LIBERALS VERSUS CONSERVATIVES: AN OVERVIEW

Let us examine, very briefly, the historical evolution of the terms *liberalism* and *conservatism*. By examining the roots of these terms, we can see how these philosophies have adapted themselves to changing times. In that way, we can avoid using the terms rigidly, without reference to the particular contexts in which liberalism and conservatism have operated over the past two centuries.

Classical Liberalism
The classical root of the term liberalism is the Latin word *libertas*, meaning "liberty" or "freedom." In the early nineteenth century, liberals dedicated

themselves to freeing individuals from all unnecessary and oppressive obligations to authority—whether the authority came from the church or the state. They opposed the licensing and censorship of the press, the punishment of heresy, the establishment of religion, and any attempt to dictate orthodoxy in matters of opinion. In economics, liberals opposed state monopolies and other constraints upon competition between private businesses. At this point in its development, liberalism defined freedom primarily in terms of freedom *from*. It appropriated the French term *laissez-faire*, which literally means "leave to be." Leave people alone! That was the spirit of liberalism in its early days. It wanted government to stay out of people's lives and to play a modest role in general. Thomas Jefferson summed up this concept when he said, "I am no friend of energetic government. It is always oppressive."

Despite their suspicion of government, classical liberals invested high hopes in the political process. By and large, they were great believers in democracy. They believed in widening suffrage to include every white male, and some of them were prepared to enfranchise women and blacks as well. Although liberals occasionally worried about "the tyranny of the majority," they were more prepared to trust the masses than to trust a permanent, entrenched elite. Liberal social policy was dedicated to fulfilling human potential and was based on the assumption that this often-hidden potential is enormous. Human beings, liberals argued, were basically good and reasonable. Evil and irrationality were believed to be caused by "outside" influences; they were the result of a bad social environment. A liberal commonwealth, therefore, was one that would remove the hindrances to the full flowering of the human personality.

The basic vision of liberalism has not changed since the nineteenth century. What has changed is the way it is applied to modern society. In that respect, liberalism has changed dramatically. Today, instead of regarding government with suspicion, liberals welcome government as an instrument to serve the people. The change in philosophy began in the latter years of the nineteenth century, when businesses—once small, independent operations—began to grow into giant structures that overwhelmed individuals and sometimes even overshadowed the state in power and wealth. At that time, liberals began reconsidering their commitment to the *laissez-faire* philosophy. If the state can be an oppressor, asked liberals, can't big business also oppress people? By then, many were convinced that commercial and industrial monopolies were crushing the souls and bodies of the working classes. The state, formerly the villain, now was viewed by liberals as a potential savior. The concept of freedom was transformed into something more than a negative freedom *from*; the term began to take on a positive meaning. It meant "realizing one's full potential." Toward this end, liberals believed, the state could prove to be a valuable instrument. It could educate children, protect the health and safety of workers, help people through hard times, promote a healthy economy, and—when necessary—force business to act more humanely and responsibly. Thus was born the movement that culminated in New Deal liberalism.

New Deal Liberalism
In the United States, the argument in favor of state intervention did not win a truly popular constituency until after the Great Depression of the 1930s began to be felt deeply. The disastrous effects of a depression that left a quarter of the work force unemployed opened the way to a new administration—and a promise. "I pledge you, I pledge myself," Franklin D. Roosevelt said when accepting the Democratic nomination in 1932, "to a new deal for the American people." Roosevelt's New Deal was an attempt to effect relief and recovery from the Depression; it employed a variety of means, including welfare programs, public works, and business regulation—most of which involved government intervention in the economy. The New Deal liberalism relied on government to liberate people from poverty, oppression, and economic exploitation. At the same time, the New Dealers claimed to be as zealous as the classical liberals in defending political and civil liberties.

The common element in *laissez-faire* liberalism and welfare-state liberalism is their dedication to the goal of realizing the full potential of each individual. Some still questioned whether this was best done by minimizing state involvement or whether it sometimes requires an activist state. The New Dealers took the latter view, though they prided themselves on being pragmatic and experimental about their activism. During the heyday of the New Deal, a wide variety of programs were tried and—if found wanting—abandoned. All decent means should be tried, they believed, even if it meant dilution of ideological purity. The Roosevelt administration, for example, denounced bankers and businessmen in campaign rhetoric but worked very closely with them while trying to extricate the nation from the Depression. This set a pattern of pragmatism that New Dealers from Harry Truman to Lyndon Johnson emulated.

Progressive Liberalism
Progressive liberalism emerged in the late 1960s and early 1970s as a more militant and uncompromising movement than the New Deal had ever been. Its roots go back to the New Left student movement of the early 1960s. New Left students went South to participate in civil rights demonstrations, and many of them were bloodied in confrontations with southern police; by the mid-1960s they were confronting the authorities in the North over issues like poverty and the Vietnam War. By the end of the decade, the New Left had fragmented into a variety of factions and had lost much of its vitality, but a somewhat more respectable version of it appeared as the New Politics movement. Many New Politics crusaders were former New Leftists who had traded their jeans for coats and ties; they tried to work within the system instead of always confronting it. Even so, they retained some of the spirit of

he New Left. The civil rights slogan "Freedom Now" expressed the mood of the New Politics. The young university graduates who filled its ranks had come from an environment where "non-negotiable" demands were issued to college deans by leaders of sit-in protests. There was more than youthful arrogance in the New Politics movement, however; there was a pervasive belief that America had lost, had compromised away, much of its idealism. The New Politics liberals sought to recover some of that spirit by linking up with an older tradition of militant reform, which went back to the time of the Revolution. These new liberals saw themselves as the authentic heirs of Tom Paine and Henry David Thoreau, of the abolitionists, the radical populists, the suffragettes, and the great progressive reformers of the early twentieth century.

While New Deal liberals concentrated almost exclusively on bread-and-butter issues such as unemployment and poverty, the New Politics liberals introduced what came to be known as social issues into the political arena. These included: the repeal of laws against abortion, the liberalization of laws against homosexuality and pornography, the establishment of affirmative action programs to ensure increased hiring of minorities and women, and passage of the Equal Rights Amendment. In foreign policy too, New Politics liberals departed from the New Deal agenda. Because they had keener memories of the unpopular, and (for them) unjustified war in Vietnam than of World War II, they became doves, in contrast to the general hawkishness of the New Dealers. They were skeptical of any claim that the United States must be the leader of the free world, or, indeed, had any special mission in the world; some were convinced that America was already in decline and must learn to adjust accordingly. The real danger, they argued, came not from the Soviet Union but from the mad pace of our arms race with the Soviets, which, as they saw it, could bankrupt the country, starve our social programs, and culminate in a nuclear Armageddon.

New Politics liberals were heavily represented at the 1972 Democratic national convention, which nominated South Dakota senator George McGovern for president. By the 1980s, the New Politics movement was no longer new, and many of its adherents preferred to be called progressives. By this time their critics had another name for them: radicals. The critics saw their positions as inimical to the interests of the United States, destructive of the family, and fundamentally at odds with the views of most Americans. The adversaries of the progressives were not only conservatives but many New Deal liberals, who openly scorned the McGovernites.

This split still exists within the Democratic party, although efforts have been made to compromise the difference, as the Democrats did in 1988 by pairing Michael Dukakis, whose Massachusetts supporters were generally on the progressive side of the party, with New Dealer Lloyd Bentsen as his running mate. In 1992, Democrats will again seek the right formula, or the right ticket, for holding together the two different kinds of liberalism that coexist (sometimes uneasily) in their party.

Conservatism

Like liberalism, conservatism has undergone historical transformation in America. Just as early liberals (represented by Thomas Jefferson) espoused less government, early conservatives (whose earliest leaders were Alexander Hamilton and John Adams) urged government support of economic enterprise and government intervention on behalf of privileged groups. By the time of the New Deal, and in reaction to the growth of the welfare state since that time, conservatives have argued strongly that more government means more unjustified interference in citizens' lives, more bureaucratic regulation of private conduct, more inhibiting control of economic enterprise, more material advantage for the less energetic and less able at the expense of those who are prepared to work harder and better, and, of course, more taxes—taxes that will be taken from those who have earned money and given to those who have not.

Contemporary conservatives are not always opposed to state intervention. They may support larger military expenditures in order to protect society against foreign enemies. They may also allow for some intrusion into private life in order to protect society against internal subversion and would pursue criminal prosecution zealously in order to protect society against domestic violence. The fact is that few conservatives, and perhaps fewer liberals, are absolute with respect to their views about the power of the state. Both are quite prepared to use the state in order to further *their* purposes. It is true that activist presidents such as Franklin Roosevelt and John Kennedy were likely to be classified as liberals. However, Richard Nixon was also an activist, and, although he does not easily fit any classification, he was far closer to conservatism than to liberalism. It is too easy to identify liberalism with statism and conservatism with anti-statism; it is important to remember that it was liberal Jefferson who counseled against "energetic government" and conservative Alexander Hamilton who designed bold powers for the new central government and wrote: "Energy in the executive is a leading character in the definition of good government."

Neoconservatism and the New Right

Two newer varieties of conservatism have arisen to challenge the dominant strain of conservatism that opposed the New Deal. Those who call themselves (or have finally allowed themselves to be called) neoconservatives are recent converts to conservatism. Many of them are former New Deal Democrats, and some like to argue that it is not they who have changed; it is the Democratic party, which has allowed itself to be taken over by advocates of progressive liberalism. They recognize, as did the New Dealers, the legitimacy of social reform, but now they warn against carrying it too far and creating an arrogant bureaucracy. They support equal opportunity, as they always did, but now they underscore the distinction between equal opportunity and equality of result, which they identify as the goal of affirmative action programs. Broadly speaking, neoconservatism shares with the older variety of conservatism a high respect for tradition and a view of human nature that some would call pessimistic. Neoconservatives, like all conservatives, are also deeply concerned about the communist threat to America. They advise shoring up America's defenses and resisting any movement that would lead the nation toward unilateral disarmament.

A more recent and more politically active variant of conservatism is called the New Right. Despite the semantic resemblance between New Right and neoconservatism, the two differ in important ways. Neoconservatives are usually lapsed liberals, while New Rightists tend to be dyed-in-the wool conservatives—though ones who are determined to appeal to wider constituencies than did the Old Right. Neoconservatives tend to be academics, who appeal to other similar elites through books and articles in learned journals. The New Right aims at reaching grass-roots voters through a variety of forums, from church groups to direct-mail solicitation. Neoconservatives customarily talk about politico-economic structures and global strategies; New Rightists emphasize the concerns of ordinary Americans, what they call family issues—moral concerns such as abortion, prayer in public schools, pornography, and what they consider to be a general climate of moral breakdown in the nation. These family issues are very similar to the social issues introduced into the political arena by the advocates of progressive liberalism. This should not be surprising, since the rise of the New Right was a reaction to the previous success of the progressive movement in legitimizing its stands on social issues.

Spokesmen for progressive liberalism and the New Right stand as polar opposites: The former regard abortion as a woman's right; the latter see it as legalized murder. The former tend to regard homosexuality as a life-style that needs protection against discrimination; the latter are more likely to see it as a perversion. The former have made an issue of their support for the Equal Rights Amendment; the latter includes large numbers of women who fought against the amendment because they believed it threatened their role identity. The list of issues could go on. The New Right and the progressive liberals are like positive and negative photographs of America's moral landscape. For all their differences however, their style is very similar. It is heavily laced with moralistic prose; it tends to equate compromise with selling out; and it claims to represent the best, most authentic traditions of America. This is not to denigrate either movement, for the kinds of issues they address are indeed moral issues, which do not generally admit of much compromise. These issues cannot simply be finessed or ignored, despite the efforts of conventional politicians to do so. They must be aired and fought over, which is why we include some of them, such as abortion (Issue 16) and church-state relations (Issue 17), and flag burning (Issue 12), in this volume.

RADICALS, REACTIONARIES, AND MODERATES

The label reactionary is almost an insult, and the label radical is worn with pride by only a few zealots on the banks of the political mainstream. A reactionary is not a conserver but a backward-mover, dedicated to turning the clock back to better times. Most people suspect that reactionaries would restore us to a time that never was, except in political myth. For many, the repeal of industrialism or universal education (or the entire twentieth century itself) is not a practical, let alone desirable, political program.

Radicalism (literally meaning "from the roots" or "going to the foundation") implies a fundamental reconstruction of the social order. Taken in that sense, it is possible to speak of right-wing radicalism as well as left-wing radicalism—radicalism that would restore or inaugurate a new hierarchical society as well as radicalism that calls for nothing less than an egalitarian society. The term is sometimes used in both of these senses, but most often the word radicalism is reserved to characterize more liberal change. While the liberal would effect change through conventional democratic processes, the radical is likely to be skeptical about the ability of the established machinery to bring about the needed change and might be prepared to sacrifice "a little" liberty to bring about a great deal more equality.

Moderate is a highly coveted label in America. Its meaning is not precise, but it carries the connotations of sensible, balanced, and practical. A moderate person is not without principles, but he or she does not allow principles to harden into dogma. The opposite of moderate is extremist, a label most American political leaders eschew. Yet, there have been notable exceptions. When Arizona senator Barry Goldwater, a conservative Republican, was nominated for president in 1964, he declared: "Extremism in defense of liberty is no vice! . . . Moderation in the pursuit of justice is no virtue!" This open embrace of extremism did not help his electoral chances; Goldwater was overwhelmingly defeated. At about the same time, however, another American political leader also embraced a kind of extremism, and with better result. In a famous letter written from a jail cell in Birmingham, Alabama, the Reverend Martin Luther King, Jr., replied to the charge that he was an extremist not by denying it but by distinguishing between different kinds of extremists. The question, he wrote, "is not whether we will be extremist but what kind of extremist will we be. Will we be extremists for hate, or will we be extremists for love?" King aligned himself with the love extremists, in which category he also placed Jesus, St. Paul, and Thomas Jefferson, among others. It was an adroit use of a label that is usually anathema in this country.

PLURALISM

The principle of pluralism espouses diversity in a society containing many interest groups and in a government containing competing units of power.

This implies the widest expression of competing ideas, and in this way, pluralism is in sympathy with an important element of liberalism. However, as Madison and Hamilton pointed out when they analyzed the sources of pluralism in the *Federalist* commentaries on the Constitution, this philosophy springs from a profoundly pessimistic view of human nature, and in this respect it more closely resembles conservatism. James Madison, possibly the single most influential member of the convention that wrote the Constitution, hoped that in a large and varied nation, no single interest group could control the government. Even if there were a majority interest, it would be unlikely to capture all of the national agencies of government—the House of Representatives, the Senate, the presidency and the federal judiciary—each of which was chosen in a different way by a different constituency for a different term of office. Moreover, to make certain that no one branch exercised excessive power, each was equipped with "checks and balances" that enabled any agency of national government to curb the powers of the others. The clearest statement of Madison's, and the Constitution's, theory can be found in the fifty-first paper of the *Federalist*:

> It may be a reflection on human nature that such devices should be necessary to control the abuses of government. But what is government itself, but the greatest of all reflections on human nature? If men were angels, no government would be necessary.

This pluralist position may be analyzed from different perspectives. It is conservative insofar as it rejects simple majority rule: yet it is liberal insofar as it rejects rule by a single elite. It is conservative in its pessimistic appraisal of human nature; yet pluralism's pessimism is also a kind of egalitarianism, holding as it does that no one can be trusted with power and that majority interests no less than minority interests will use power for selfish ends. It is possible to suggest that in America pluralism represents an alternative to both liberalism and conservatism. Pluralism is anti-majoritarian and anti-elitist and combines some elements of both.

SOME APPLICATIONS

Despite our effort to define the principal alignments in American politics, some policy decisions do not neatly fit into these categories. Readers will reach their own conclusions, but we may suggest some alignments to be found here in order to demonstrate the variety of viewpoints.

The conflicts between neoconservatism and liberalism are expressed in the opposed approaches of Linda Rocawich and James Q. Wilson to the question of crime (Issue 9). Wilson proceeds from a conservative view of human nature (a view that liberals call pessimistic and conservatives call realistic) to the conclusion that the best approach to crime fighting would combine swift and sure punishment for crime with a social environment that emphasizes such virtues as self-restraint. Rocawich, who has a more optimistic view of human nature, thinks that compassion and rehabilitation are better than prisons as means of reducing crime. More difficult to classify is the issue of whether the government regulates too much (Issue 7). Susan and Martin Tolchin's critique of deregulation is compatible with either New Deal or progressive liberalism, but Barry Crickmer's case against regulation is reminiscent of classical liberalism, or libertarianism.

Walter Berns's defense of the death penalty (Issue 10: *Is Capital Punishment Justified?*) is almost a purely conservative position. Like other conservatives, Berns is skeptical of the possibilities of human perfection and therefore regards retribution—"paying back" a murderer instead of trying to "reform" him—as a legitimate goal of punishment. Issue 11, on affirmative action, has become a litmus test of the new "progressive" liberalism. The progressives say that it is not enough for our laws to become color-blind or gender-blind; they must now reach out to remedy the ills caused by racism and sexism. But conservatives and some New Deal liberals oppose affirmative action, which they regard as a new form of discrimination.

Former federal Court of Appeals judge Robert Bork's case (in Issue 8) for using "original intent" as the basis of constitutional interpretation is a classic conservative argument, seeking as it does to extract from the thought of the Constitution's founders some authentic guide for interpreting the Constitution today. Professor Leonard Levy's criticism of this approach is liberal in its insistence that the Constitution's meaning must change with the times. In issue 13, James C. Dobson's argument for strict enforcement of antipornography laws is conservative, with a distinctly "New Right" flavor; his argument is that pornography threatens family and society. On the other side of the issue, Donna Demac formulates her argument in liberal terms: even pornographers are entitled to liberty of expression. The arguments in the flag-burning case (Issue 12) fall into the same pattern, with Chief Justice Rehnquist arguing that our nation has a right to preserve its unique symbol of unity against desecration and Justice Brennan contending that even ugly acts of symbolic speech must be protected by the First Amendment.

Issues 18 and 20—which address the question of aid to the Soviets and the argument over whether the United States is declining—have at various times divided liberals and conservatives. As far back as the 1940s, liberals pressed for aid to the Soviets (military aid during World War II and economic aid in its aftermath) and conservatives resisted it. In Issue 18, historian John Lewis Gaddis renews the liberal argument for aid, while the anonymous "Z" warns us to stay clear of the Soviet Union during this tumultuous period. As for the issue of U.S. decline, liberals have tried, since the end of the 1960s, to demonstrate that excessive military commitments threaten America's economic well-being, which is historian Paul Kennedy's argument in Issue 20; conservatives have questioned this argument and the facts used to back it up, much as political scientist Samuel Huntington does in the same issue.

This book contains a few arguments that are not easy to categorize. The issue of drug legalizations (Issue 14) often divides liberals and conservatives (liberals for legalization, conservatives against it), but it does not always divide so neatly. Conservative editor and writer William F. Buckley favors drug legalization, while progressive liberal Reverend Jesse Jackson opposes it. The arguments here are usually pragmatic ones: Is it really possible, without incurring excessive social costs, to succeed in banning drugs? Such arguments often cut across liberal-conservative lines, although in our selections, political scientist James Q. Wilson, who opposes drug legalization, seems more conservative in his political orientation than does Ethan Nadelmann, who favors legalization. The abortion issue (Issue 16) also has unpredictable aspects. Archbishop John O'Connor, who makes the case against legalized abortion in this issue, has joined other bishops and cardinals in adopting liberal positions on issues such as social welfare, military cutbacks, and opposition to capital punishment. Other pro-lifers, such as columnist Nat Henthoff, are even more outspokenly liberal, while some prominent conservatives, such as Arizona senator Barry Goldwater, come down squarely on the pro-choice side. It is not clear that the abortion issue fits very easily into liberal-conservative compartments.

The same must be said of Issue 19, realism versus idealism in foreign policy. The temptation is to say that the realist is conservative and the idealist liberal. Realism in foreign policy proceeds from a view of human nature similar to that of conservatism: in both cases the view is that self-interest—of nations as well as individuals—is an unvarying law which must constantly be kept in mind. Liberals are more inclined toward belief in change and in a more optimistic view of our nature. But in our selections, historian Arthur Schlesinger, Jr., makes the case for realism, and Schlesinger certainly belongs in the liberal camp. No doubt much depends on the kind of realism and idealism being considered. Schlesinger worries about the idealists who set off on crusades against "evil" in the world, and he probably has in mind some of the Reagan conservatives of the early 1980s who wanted to roll back the Soviet "empire" (although the logic of Schlesinger's argument could also apply to zealots on the left). Stanley Kober, on the other hand, makes the case for a certain kind of liberal idealism based not upon anticommunism but human rights.

Obviously one's position on the issues in this book will be affected by circumstances. However, we would like to think that the essays in this book are durable enough to last through several seasons of events and controversies. We can be certain that the issues will survive. The search for coherence and consistency in the use of political labels underlines the options open to us and reveals their consequences. The result must be more mature judgments about what is best for America. That, of course, is the ultimate aim of public debate and decision-making, and it transcends all labels and categories.

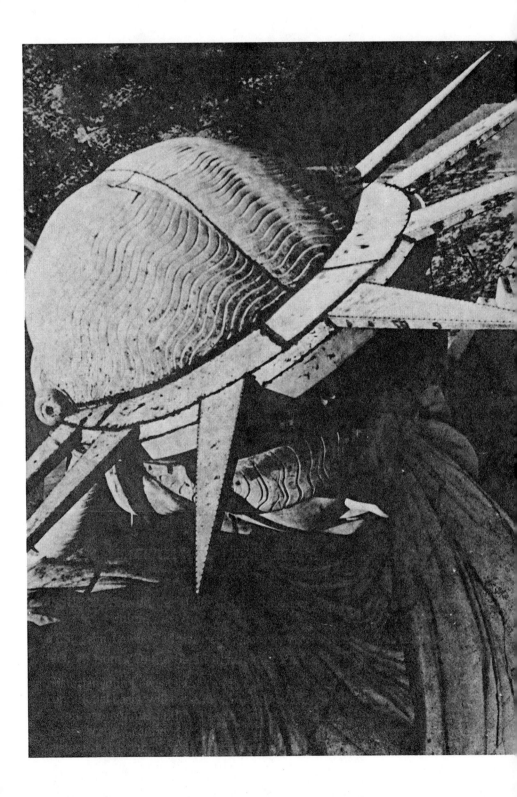

Statue of Liberty/Library of Congress

PART 1

Democracy and the American Political Process

Democracy *is derived from two Greek words,* demos *and* kratia, *and means "people's rule." The issue today is whether the political realities of America conform to the ideal of people's rule. Are the people really running the country? Or is it run by elites who are not accountable to the people? Socialists say that big business runs the economy and controls the political agenda. Is that a fair charge, or is it based on simplistic premises? Political party reformers have tried to encourage greater participation by voters, but critics charge that the parties are losing their power and influence. Another issue generating controversy is the power of pressure groups, particularly that of political action committees (PACs). Are these groups undermining people's rule, or are they helping to make democracy work? Finally, in this section, we address the issue of the news media's role in the governmental process.*

Is America Ruled by an Elite?

Have American Political Parties Lost Their Power?

Do Political Action Committees Undermine Democracy?

Do the News Media Have a Liberal Bias?

ISSUE 1

Is America Ruled by an Elite?

YES: Thomas R. Dye, from *Who's Running America: The Conservative Years* (Prentice-Hall, 1986)

NO: Andrew M. Greeley, from *Building Coalitions* (Franklin Watts, 1974)

ISSUE SUMMARY

YES: Political scientist Thomas R. Dye emphasizes the power wielded by a handful of people in America.
NO: Sociologist Andrew M. Greeley believes that there is no single, established center of power and points to the behavior of the system as evidence.

The U.S. Constitution was framed behind closed doors in 1787, and since that time there have been periodic charges that America is controlled, or is in imminent danger of being controlled, by a power elite. All representative government is necessarily government by elites (that is, small, select ruling groups), but those who raise the specter of a power elite are charging that America is run by an *unrepresentative* elite—one that is unaccountable to the majority of voters. Almost invariably it is added that this elite is not only political but economic as well. Although all industrial societies have gradations of wealth, the system of democracy is supposed to counter the weight of money with the weight of numbers. The basic contention of the elite theorists, then, is not simply that there are rich and poor in America but that the very rich—or a small elite working in league with them—are making all the crucial decisions.

Fear of elitism has had a long history in America. Richard Henry Lee, one of the signers of the Declaration of Independence, spoke for many anti-federalists (who opposed ratification of the Constitution) when he warned that the proposed charter shifted power away from the people and into the hands of the "aristocrats" and "moneyites," those who "avariciously grasp at all power and property." Long after these fears were more or less quieted, there still remained a residue of suspicion that the wealthy were manipulating the machinery of government for their own purposes. Before the Civil War, Jacksonian Democrats charged Eastern merchants and bankers with usurping the power of the people. After the Civil War, a number of radical parties and movements revived this theme of anti-elitism. The rise of industrial monopolies, an apparent increase in political corruption, and economic hardship for Western farmers brought about the founding of the People's Party at the beginning of the 1890s. The Populists, as they were more commonly called, wanted economic and political reforms aimed at transferring power away from the rich and back to "the plain people." The populist assumption was that ordinary people had once possessed sovereign power in America but that it had slipped away from them.

Since the 1930s, American radicalism has been more influenced by Marxism than by populism. Like populists, Marxists emphasize the domination of America by the rich; unlike populists, Marxists do not look back with nostalgia on some golden age of democracy in America. Marxists believe America has always been dominated by the wealthy, although the domination has taken different forms at different times. Marxists also stress the class basis of domination. Instead of seeing elitism as a conspiracy of a few evil men, Marxists view it more impersonally, as a tendency inherent in capitalism.

One of the best-developed arguments disputing the populist-Marxist thesis that America is ruled by an unrepresentative elite is the argument of *pluralism*. Pluralists readily admit that there are many elites in our society. That is precisely their point: because America contains so many groups, each has a tendency to counterbalance the power of the others. Thus, they believe, no group or coalition of groups can become the establishment in America.

Arguing against the pluralist thesis in favor of the elitist thesis is political scientist Thomas R. Dye, who suggests that power in America is largely concentrated in a handful of people. Andrew Greeley, a priest and sociologist who teaches at the University of Arizona, argues the pluralist position in the following debate on elitism.

YES

Thomas R. Dye

ELITISM IN A DEMOCRACY

Great power in America is concentrated in a tiny handful of people. A few thousand individuals out of 238 million Americans decide about war and peace, wages and prices, consumption and investment, employment and production, law and justice, taxes and benefits, education and learning, health and welfare, advertising and communication, life and leisure. In all societies—primitive and advanced, totalitarian and democratic, capitalist and socialist—only a few people exercise great power. This is true whether or not such power is exercised in the name of "the people." . . .

In a modern, complex industrial society, power is concentrated in large institutions: corporations, banks, utilities, insurance companies, broadcasting networks, the White House, Congress and the Washington bureaucracy, the military establishment, the prestigious law firms, the large investment houses, the foundations, the universities, and the private policy-planning organizations. The people at the top of these institutions—the presidents and principal officers and directors, the senior partners, the governing trustees, the congressional committee chairpersons, the secretaries, the senior advisers, the Supreme Court justices, the four-star generals and admirals—are the objects of our study. . . .

. . . The duality of leadership is reminiscent of the medieval dualism between church and state. . . .

Business and financial leaders in America are *not* simply one interest group among many, as portrayed in most "pluralist" writing. These leaders themselves make decisions about "who gets what when and how." Studies of power in society must include economic power.

THE CONCENTRATION OF ECONOMIC POWER

Economic power in America is highly concentrated. Indeed, only about 4,300 individuals—two one-thousandths of 1 percent of the population—exercise formal authority over half of the nation's industrial assets, over half of all banking assets, over half of all assets in communications, transportation, and utilities, and over two-thirds of all insurance assets. These individuals are the presidents, officer-directors, and directors of the largest corporations in these fields. The reason for this concentration of power in the hands of so few people is found in the concentration of industrial and financial assets in a small number of giant corporations. The following statistics can only suggest the scale and concentration of modern corporate enterprise in America.

There are about 200,000 *industrial corporations* in the United States with total assets in 1983 of about $1.6 trillion. The 100 corporations listed in Table 1.1 control 58.2 percent ($939 billion) of all industrial assets. The five largest industrial corporations—Exxon, General Motors, IBM, Mobil, and Texaco—control 13 percent of all industrial assets.

The concentration of resources among a relatively few industrial corporations is slowly increasing over time. In a 34-year period, the proportion of all industrial assets controlled by the top 100 corporations grew as follows:

1950	39.8%
1955	44.3%
1960	46.4%
1965	46.5%
1970	52.3%
1976	54.9%
1980	55.0%
1983	58.2%

. . . Economic power in America is highly concentrated. A small number of corporations control over half the nation's industrial assets; half of all assets in communications, transportation, and utilities; nearly two-thirds of all banking assets, and two-thirds of all insurance

assets. This concentration of economic power is increasing gradually over time, as the nation's largest corporations gain ever larger shares of total corporate assets.

Power over corporate assets rests in the hands of about 4,300 presidents and directors. These directors, not the stockholders or employees, decide major policy questions, choose the people who will carry out these decisions, and even select their own replacements. However, most of these presidents and directors have climbed the corporate ladder to their posts. These "managers" owe their rise to power to their skill in organizational life, and to their successful coping with the new demands for expertise in management, finance, technology, and planning. Individual capitalists are no longer essential in the formation of capital assets. Most industrial capital is raised either within the corporation itself or from institutional borrowing.

It is true that the Rockefellers, Fords, DuPonts, Mellons, and other great entrepreneurial families still exercise great power over corporate resources. But a majority of the directors of family-dominated firms have been brought in from outside the family; and only about 150 of the 500 largest corporations are family-dominated.

Corporate leadership is very stable over time. Turnover among top managers is low, and the nation's largest corporations have the power and resources to protect their dominant positions. . . .

Governmental power may be even more concentrated than corporate power in America. One indicator of its growing concentration is the increasing proportion of the gross national product produced by government. All governmental expenditures now account for one-third of the GNP, and *federal* expenditures ac-

Table 1.1

The 100 Largest Industrial Corporations (Ranked by Assets)

Rank	Corporation	Assets ($ billions)	Cumulative Percent*
1	Exxon	$62.9	3.9
2	General Motors	45.7	6.7
3	IBM	37.2	9.0
4	Mobil	35.1	11.2
5	Texaco	27.2	12.9
6	Standard Oil (Indiana)	25.8	14.5
7	du Pont	24.4	16.0
8	Standard Oil of California	24.0	17.5
9	Ford Motor	23.9	19.0
10	General Electric	23.3	20.4
11	Atlantic Richfield	23.3	21.9
12	Shell Oil	22.2	23.2
13	Gulf Oil	21.0	24.5
14	U.S. Steel	19.3	25.7
15	Tenneco	18.0	26.8
16	Standard Oil (Ohio)	16.4	27.9
17	ITT	14.0	28.7
18	Phillips Petroleum	13.1	29.5
19	Sun	12.5	30.3
20	Dow Chemical	12.0	31.1
21	Occidental Petroleum	11.8	31.8
22	Eastman Kodak	10.9	32.5
23	Getty Oil	10.4	33.1
24	Union Carbide	10.3	33.7
25	Union Pacific	10.2	34.4
26	R. J. Reynolds Industries	9.9	35.0
27	Philip Morris	9.7	35.6
28	Xerox	9.3	36.2
29	Unocal	9.2	36.7
30	AT&T Technologies	9.1	37.3
31	Control Data	8.8	37.8
32	United Technologies	8.7	38.4
33	Westinghouse Electric	8.6	38.9
34	Proctor & Gamble	8.1	39.4
35	Allied	7.6	39.9
36	Boeing	7.5	40.4
37	Caterpillar Tractor	7.0	40.8
38	Chrysler	6.8	41.2
39	Monsanto	6.4	41.6
40	Avco	6.4	42.0
41	Aluminum Co. of America	6.3	42.4
42	Amerada Hess	6.2	42.8
43	Diamond Shamrock	6.0	43.1
44	Goodyear	6.0	43.5
45	Weyerhauser	5.9	43.9
46	Deere	5.9	44.3
47	Minnesota Mining & Manufacturing	5.8	44.6
48	International Paper	5.6	45.0
49	Dart & Kraft	5.4	45.3

count for nearly two-thirds of all government expenditures.

Running for office is not the same as running a government. Presidents must depend on "serious men" to run government. Skill in campaigning does not necessarily prepare individuals for the responsibility of governing. Key government executives must be recruited from industry, finance, the law, the universities, and the bureaucracy itself. These "serious men" do not appear to differ much in background or experience from Republican to Democratic administrations.

While a significant number of top politicians have inherited wealth and power, most have climbed the ladder from relative obscurity to political success. Among current leaders, Kennedy and Bush inherited great wealth and power, but Reagan, Mondale, Hart, and Kemp all climbed to prominence from very modest backgrounds. Most politicians are lawyers but not top corporate or professional lawyers.

The "military-industrial complex"—the Defense Department, the corporations with large military contracts, and members of Congress with defense-oriented constituencies—is an important influence in Washington, but defense spending is only 6 percent of the nation's GNP and only a few corporations are dependent upon defense contracts. Defense spending declined to less than 25 percent of the federal budget in the 1970s and only recently climbed to 30 percent. Military leadership does not enjoy the same prestige as in the years after World War II. Military leaders are more likely to come from middle- and lower-class backgrounds than other leaders.

Congress seldom initiates programs, but rather it responds to the initiatives of the President, the executive departments,

influential interest groups, and the mass media. Power *within* Congress is concentrated in the House and Senate leadership and in the chairperson and ranking minority members of the standing committees. Compared to other national elites, congressional leaders appear localistic. Their claim to national leadership must be safely hedged by attention to their local constituencies. Members of Congress are frequently recruited from very modest, middle-class backgrounds.

The Supreme Court is the most elitist branch of government. Its nine members are not elected, and they serve life terms. They have the authority to void the acts of popularly elected Presidents and Congresses. It was the Supreme Court, rather than the President or Congress, that took the lead in eliminating segregation from public life, ensuring voter equality in representation, limiting the powers of police, and declaring abortion to be a fundamental right of women. Although most Justices have been upper class in social origin, their appointment has generally been related to their political activities rather than to their experience in the law.

THE NEWSMAKERS

Television is the major source of information for the vast majority of Americans, and the people who control this flow of information are among the most powerful in the nation. Indeed, today the leadership of the mass media has successfully established itself as equal in power to the nation's corporate and governmental leadership.

The rise of the mass media to a position of preeminence among institutions of power is a relatively recent phenomenon. It is a direct product of the development of a national television communications network extending to nearly every home in America. (In 1952, only 19.9 percent of all American homes had television sets, compared to 99.8 percent in 1972).[1] Newspapers had always reported wars, riots, scandals, and disasters, just as they do today. But the masses of Americans did not read them—and fewer still read their editorials. But television reaches the masses: it is really the first form of *mass* communication devised. It also presents a *visual* image, not merely a printed word. . . .

The prime-time programmers—the television producers, production company executives, and network vice-presidents responsible for program selection—are the most liberal segment of the nation's elite.[2] Almost all are from the big cities of the east and west coasts. Almost all are white males. A majority are Jewish. They are well-educated, and extraordinarily well-paid, and independent or Democratic in their politics. They are *not* radicals or socialists: almost all believe that "people with ability should earn more," and most support free enterprise and oppose government ownership of the economy. However, these television programmers are very critical of government and business; they believe strongly that society is unfair to women, blacks, and minorities; and they are socially very liberal, in terms of their views on abortion, homosexuality, and adultery.

More importantly, perhaps, the programmers believe that they have a responsibility to change America's views to fit their own. They believe that television should "promote social reform." (Fully two thirds of the programmers interviewed agreed with this definition of their role in society.) "This is perhaps the single most striking finding in our study.

According to television's creators, they are not in it just for the money. They also seek to move their audience toward their own vision of the good society."[3]

We live in terms of the stories we tell—stories about what things exist, stories about how things work, and stories about what to do. . . . Increasingly, media-cultivated facts and values become standards by which we judge.[4] Much of our learning is subconscious. We learn how New York cab drivers live from *Taxi*, how Texas oil families live from *Dallas*, how waitresses live from *Alice*, and so on. If these televised images are inaccurate, we end up with wrong impressions of American life. If television shows emphasize sex and violence, we come to believe that there is more sex and violence in America than is actually the case.

Occasionally, voices are raised against sex and violence on prime-time television. In 1981, fundamentalist religious groups threatened to boycott the products of companies that advertised on shows that included sex, violence, or profanity. The networks promptly labeled the proposed boycott an infringement of their freedom of the press. But the advertisers listened. Proctor and Gamble, the nation's largest single advertiser, announced that it would withdraw its ads from shows with "gratuitous sex, violence, and profanity." Religious groups claimed a temporary victory and dropped their proposed boycott. Network television may "clean up its act" for a season, but in the long run it can be expected to broadcast whatever it believes will attract viewing audiences.

For millions of Americans, television is a way of keeping in touch with their environment. Both entertainment and advertising provide model ways of life.

People are shown products, services, and life styles that they are expected to desire and imitate. By creating these desires and expectations, the media help to define how Americans should live. . . .

The people who control the flow of information in America are among the most powerful in the nation. Television network broadcasting is the first form of truly *mass* communication; it carries a visual image with emotional content as well as information. Television news reaches virtually everyone, and for most Americans it is the major source of information about the world.

The power of mass media is primarily in agenda-setting—deciding what will be decided. The media determine what the masses talk about and what elite must decide about. Political issues do not just "happen." The media decide what are "issues," "problems," even "crises," which must be acted upon.

Control of the television media is highly concentrated. Three private corporations (CBS, NBC, and ABC) determine what the people will see and hear about the world; they feed 800 local TV stations that account for 80 percent of the news and entertainment broadcasts. Most of the nation's 1,748 daily newspapers receive their news from AP and/or UPI wire services. The ten largest newspaper chains account for one third of the total newspaper circulation in the country.

Those at the top of the mass media include both inheritors and individuals who worked their way up the management ladder. Among the media elite are the heads of CBS, NBC, and ABC; the *New York Times; Washington Post—Newsweek;* Time, Inc.; and the ten largest newspaper chains.

The mass media must attract large audiences to sell to advertisers. The principal source of bias in the news originates from the need to capture large audiences with drama, action, and confrontation. The result is an emphasis on "hard" news—unfavorable stories about prominent people and business and government. However, media attention to scandal, abuse, violence, and corruption has not always produced liberal reformist values. Many scholars believe it has produced "television malaise"—distrust, cynicism, and disaffection from public affairs caused by negative reporting on American life. This reporting may also be contributing to the public's decline in confidence in the media.

The media elite is the most liberal segment of the nation's elite. While this elite supports the free enterprise system and reward based on merit, it favors government intervention to reduce income differences and aid women, blacks, and minorities. News executives claim only to "mirror" reality, yet at the same time they take credit for civil rights laws, ending the Vietnam War, and expelling Richard Nixon from the White House. Primetime programming executives are even more liberal in their views, and they acknowledge that their role is to "reform" society. . . .

WHO'S RUNNING AMERICA? SUMMARY OF FINDINGS

Concentration of Institutional Resources

. . . The nation's resources are concentrated in a relatively small number of large institutions. Half of the nation's industrial assets are concentrated in 100 manufacturing corporations; half of U.S. banking assets are concentrated in the 50 largest banks; and half of our assets in transportation, communications, and utilities are concentrated in just 50 corporations. Two-thirds of the nation's insurance assets are concentrated in 50 companies; 50 foundations control 40 percent of all foundation assets; 25 universities control 50 percent of all private endowment funds in higher education; 3 network broadcasting companies control 90 percent of the television news; and 10 newspapers chains account for one-third of the nation's daily newspaper circulation. It is highly probable that 30 Wall Street and Washington law firms exercise comparable dominance in the legal field; that 15 Wall Street investment firms dominate decision-making in securities; and that a dozen cultural and civic organizations dominate music, drama, the arts, and civic affairs. Federal government alone now accounts for 21 percent of the gross national product and two-thirds of all government spending. More importantly, concentration of resources in the nation's largest institutions in increasing over time.

Individual Versus Institutional Resources

The resources available to individuals in America are infinitesimal in comparison with the resources available to the nation's largest institutions. Personal wealth in itself provides little power; it is only when wealth is associated with top institutional position that it provides the wealth-holder with any significant degree of power.

Managerial elites are gradually replacing owners and stockholders as the dominant influence in American corporations. Most capital investment comes from retained earnings of corporations and bank loans, rather than from individual investors.

Nonetheless, personal wealth in America is unequally distributed: the top fifth of income recipients receive over 40 percent of all income, while the bottom fifth receives about 5 percent. This inequality is lessening very slowly over time, if at all.

The Size of the Nation's Elite

Approximately 6,000 individuals in 7,000 positions exercise formal authority over institutions that control roughly half of the nation's resources in industry, finance, utilities, insurance, mass media, foundations, education, law, and civic and cultural affairs. This definition of the elite is fairly large numerically, yet these individuals constitute an extremely small percentage of the nation's total population—less than three-thousandths of 1 percent. However, this figure is considerably larger than that implied in the "power elite" literature.

Perhaps the question of hierarchy or polyarchy depends on whether one wants to emphasize numbers or percentages. To emphasize hierarchy, one can comment on the tiny *percentage* of the population that possesses such great authority. To emphasize polyarchy, one can comment on the fairly large *number* of individuals at the top of the nation's institutional structure; certainly there is room for competition within so large a group.

Interlocking Versus Specialization

Despite concentration of institutional resources, there is clear evidence of specialization among institutional leaders. Eighty-five percent of the institutional elites identified in our study were "specialists," holding only one post of the 7,300 "top" posts. Of course, many of these individuals held other institutional positions in a wide variety of corporate, civic, and cultural organizations, but these were not "top" positions as we defined them. Only 15 percent of our institutional elites were "interlockers" holding more than one top post at the same time.

However, the multiple "interlockers"—individuals with six or more top posts—not surprisingly turned out to be "giants" in the industrial and financial world. Another finding is that there was a good deal of "vertical" overlap—top position-holders who have had previous experience in other top corporate, governmental, and legal positions—more so than there is "horizontal" (concurrent) interlocking. Over one-quarter of governmental elites have held high corporate positions, and nearly 40 percent of the corporate elites have held governmental jobs. Yet even this "vertical overlapping" must be qualified, for most of the leadership experience of corporate elites was derived from *corporate* positions, and most of the leadership experience of governmental elites was derived from *government and law.*

There are, however, important concentrations of combined corporate, governmental, and social power in America. Large corporations such as AT&T have many interlocking director relationships with industrial corporations, banks, utilities, and insurance companies. There are identifiable groupings of corporations by interlocking directorships; these groupings tend to center around major banks and regions of the country. In addition, there is concentration of power among the great, wealthy, entrepreneurial families—the Rockefellers, Mellons, DuPonts, Fords. One of the most important of these concentrations is in the Rockefeller family group, which has an extensive network in industrial, financial, political, civic, educational, and cultural institutions.

Inheritors Versus Climbers

There is a great deal of upward mobility in American society, as well as "circulation of elites." We estimate that less than 10 percent of the top corporate elites studied inherited their position and power; the vast majority climbed the rungs of the corporate ladder. Most governmental elites—whether in the executive bureaucracy, Congress, or the courts—also rose from fairly obscure positions. Elected political leaders frequently come from parochial backgrounds and continue to maintain ties with local clubs and groups. Military leaders tend to have the largest percentage of rural, southern, and lower-social-origin members of any leadership group.

Separate Channels of Recruitment

There are multiple paths to the top. Our top elites were recruited through a variety of channels. Governmental leaders were recruited mainly from law and government; less than one in six was recruited from the corporate world. Military leaders were recruited exclusively through the military ranks. Most top lawyers rose through the ranks of the large, well-known law firms, and mass media executives were recruited primarily from newspaper and television. Only in the foundations, universities, and cultural and civic associations was the formal leadership drawn from other sectors of society.

Social Class and Elite Recruitment

Individuals at the top are overwhelmingly upper- and upper-middle-class in social origin. Even those who climbed the institutional ladder to high position generally started with the advantages of a middle-class upbringing. Nearly all top institutional elites are college-educated, and half hold advanced degrees. Elite are notably "Ivy League": 54 percent of top corporate leaders and 42 percent of top governmental leaders are alumni of just 12 well-known private universities. Moreover, a substantial proportion of corporate and government leaders attended one of just 30 private "name" prep schools.

Very few top corporate or governmental elites are women, although more women are now being appointed to top corporate boards. A greater number of women serve in top positions in the cultural world, but many of these women do so because of their family affiliation.

It is clear that very few blacks occupy any positions of authority in the institutional structure of American society. We estimate that in 1980 only about ten blacks served as directors of the nation's corporations, banks, or utilities.

Corporate elites are somewhat more "upper-class" in origin than are governmental elites. Governmental elites had slightly lower proportions of private prep school types and Ivy Leaguers than corporate elites, and governmental elites were less eastern and urban in their origins than corporate elites. Governmental leaders in our study had more advanced professional degrees (generally law degrees) than did corporate elites.

Conflict and Consensus Among Elites

Elites in all sectors of American society share a consensus about the fundamental values of private enterprise, limited government, and due process of law. Moreover, since the Roosevelt era, elites have generally supported liberal, public-regarding, social welfare programs—including social security, fair labor standards, unemployment compensation, a graduated income tax, a federally aided welfare system, government regulation of public utilities, and countercyclical fiscal and monetary policies. Elite consensus also includes a desire to end minority discrimination—and to bring minority Americans into the mainstream of the political and economic system. Today's liberal elite believes that it can change people's lives through the exercise of governmental power—eliminate racism, abolish poverty, uplift the poor, overcome sickness and disease, educate the masses, and generally *do good*.

While American politics continue in this liberal tradition, there has been a growing disillusionment among elites with government interventions in society, and a reaffirmation of the role of the home, the community, and the free market in shaping society. The "neoconservatives" are still liberal and public, regarding in their values, but inflation, Watergate, civil unrest, and Vietnam have combined to dampen their enthusiasm for large, costly government programs. Even among "neoliberals" there is a realization that many old liberal programs and policies are inadequate to society's needs today, and they are committed to a search for "new ideas" to foster economic growth and cure society's ills.

Elite from all sectors of society (even leaders of blacks, women, and youth) believe in equality of opportunity rather than absolute equality. Elites throughout American history have defended the principle of merit. Absolute equality, or "leveling," has always been opposed by the nation's leadership.

Elite disagreement does occur *within* this consensus over fundamental values.

However, the range of disagreement is relatively narrow and tends to be confined to means rather than ends. Specific policy disagreements among various elite groups occur over questions such as the oil depletion allowance, federal versus state and local control of social programs, tax reform, specific energy and environmental protection proposals, and specific measures for dealing with inflation and recession.

NOTES

1. *Statistical Abstract of the United States, 1973*, p. 693.

2. See Linda S. Lichter, S. Robert Lichter, and Stanley Rothman, "Hollywood and America: The Odd Couple," *Public Opinion*, December/January 1983, pp. 54–58.

3. *Ibid.*, p. 58.

4. George Gerbner, "Cultural Indicators," *Journal of Communications*, Summer 1978, p. 176. Also cited by Graber, p. 122.

NO

Andrew M. Greeley

BUILDING COALITIONS

It is important that all of us who are concerned about politics realize that only on occasion can we legitimately blame a vague and shadowy "them" for our problems. Admittedly, it would be much easier if we could; then we could just sweep "them" out of office and replace them with some of "us." But one of the melancholy results of a democratic society in which power is widely diffused is that "they" turn out in the final analysis to be "we." . . .

There is a good deal to be said for the elitist viewpoint, and anyone who approaches American society with the naive notion that power is equally distributed in the population and that mere persuasive argumentation will mobilize the power in favor of social change is simply asking for trouble.

1. Some people have more power than others. The president of General Motors, for example, is likely to have more influence on decisions that are made in Washington than the assembly-line worker. The archbishop of Chicago is likewise going to have greater impact on what the Catholic Church does than the parish priest. Compared to Mayor Daley or County President George Dunne or Governor Walker or the president of the Chicago Board of Trade or of Marshall Field and Company or the *Chicago Sun-Times* I am relatively powerless about what happens in my native city. Indeed, a member of the United Steelworkers of America probably has more power than I do, because he is at least able to bring pressure on city events through his union that I am not able to bring because I lack some sort of intermediate pressure group standing between me and the city.

2. Because of the way power is distributed in American society, certain groups of men, either because of their position or because of the support they can command from large organizations, can have decisive power on specific issues, no matter what anyone else thinks. While it is rare that the combination of these powerful men can override the strongly felt convictions of a majority of the population, it is generally unnecessary for them to try. On most issues the majority of the population is relatively indifferent. Thus if the *Chicago Tribune* determines that there is to be a lakefront exposition hall named after their late beloved publisher, it is likely to succeed because it

needs only the support of a few city leaders, and opposition to it is likely to be limited to a small segment of the population. A majority of Chicagoans probably don't care much one way or the other about the lakefront hall; if asked, they may be vaguely for it. It will be virtually impossible for the opposition to organize massive antagonism toward the idea among the general population.

3. Some extremely critical decisions are made in American society by a handful of men. For example, the decision to go ahead with the Bay of Pigs invasion and the subsequent decision to respond to the Russian intrusion of missiles into Cuba by a blockade were made by a handful of men in secret. So too, apparently, have most of the decisions in the Indochina war been made by a small group operating in secret. These men obviously do not make their decisions in complete isolation from the pressures of the wishes and opinions of the rest of society, and they also eventually run the risk of being ejected from political office if what they do displeases at least a majority of those who vote in an election. Nevertheless, most of us do not have much power in the making of foreign policy. Our influence on foreign policy is limited to what the political leadership thinks our limits of hostile response are and to our plebiscite on election day.

4. Well-organized pressure groups do exercise an influence on American society all out of proportion to the size of their membership and the representativeness of their opinions. Even though there is strong national support for gun control legislation, for example, the National Rifle Association has been successful in limiting gun control laws and in punishing senators who have dared to push too vigorously against the association. This is but one example of an incredible number of pressure groups that zealously watch social events to make sure that the well-being of their members—judged, of course, by the professional staff of the organization—is not harmed by what goes on among the political leaders.

5. David Riesman and others have called these pressure groups (which run all the way from the United States Catholic Conference to the National Education Association and include the United Steelworkers of America, the American Chamber of Commerce, and a vast variety of other thoroughly reliable and respectable institutions) "veto groups," that is, their power is most effective in preventing things from happening than in causing them to happen. The American Medical Association, for example, has effectively vetoed national health insurance for several decades, but it has not displayed much power in getting positive legislation for its own benefit. The veto groups may occasionally join forces with one another and rally around some common cause, but under normal circumstances they are much better at saying no than at saying yes.

6. But when all these concessions are made to the accuracy of the elitist analysis, one is still faced with the fact that they miss the most critical obstacle to social reform in the United States, and that obstacle is not the existence of an establishment but the relative nonexistence of one. To put the matter somewhat differently, it is the lack of concentration of power that is the real obstacle to social reform.

Let us take two examples. First of all, if there were an establishment of business, military, intellectual, and political leaders who did in fact exercise political control over the country, they would have gotten us out of the Vietnam war long before they did. The war was bad for business, bad for education, bad for government, bad for everyone in sight. It combined inflation with recession, alienated the youth, split the college campuses wide open, and had a rending effect on the whole fabric of American society. Furthermore, American business did not profit from the war, American political leaders did not profit from it (they generally lost elections because of it), and the American people, whose sons were killed, did not profit from it. Almost all the influential national journals were against it, and even the military muttered that it was trapped into the war by intellectual advisors of the president against their better judgment. Nevertheless, though it may have been desirable for all concerned to get us out of the war, there never existed a powerful establishment that could convene itself and announce that the war was over. The young people who vigorously demonstrated against the war were frustrated and angry because they could not communicate with the establishment to make it end the war. They might have considered the possibility that if there were an establishment, it certainly would have ended the war. The reason they can't communicate with an establishment is that there isn't one.

One can also take it as well established that the best way to cope with housing pressures in America's large cities is to distribute substantial segments of the black population in the suburban fringe that rings these large cities. Political leaders, business leaders, research experts, community leaders, virtually everyone would agree that the desegregation of the sub-

urbs is absolutely essential for coping with problems of urban housing. Yet there does not exist in American society a group of men powerful enough to enforce such a decision over the collective opposition of all the suburban veto groups. If there were an establishment with a base of power, we would certainly have blacks in the suburbs.

The implication of the previous paragraph is that an establishment should be capable of benign as well as malign activity. Many benign actions would be very much in the self-interest of any establishment worthy of the name. That these benign things do not get done is, I think, conclusive evidence that, alas, there is no establishment. Things would be much simpler and neater if there were.

Implicit in radical criticism of the establishment is the strategy that argues that if one replaced the existing establishment with a new one composed of radical elitists and representing "the people," then one could institute benign social reforms. Professor [C. Wright] Mills* was quite explicit about that. He did not so much advocate the abolition of power elite as making it responsible— responsible to intellectuals. But obviously it could not be made responsible to all intellectuals, so Mills decided that the power elite should be responsible to those intellectuals who happened to have the same ideas on foreign policy that he did. The power elite, in other words, will become "responsible" when it is willing to do what C. Wright Mills and his colleagues tell it to do. On the whole, I am not sure I would have liked to be governed by Professor Mills or any

*Late professor of sociology at Columbia University and author of The Power Elite (Oxford, 1956).—Eds.

of his successors. I very much doubt that we could have worked out an arrangement whereby they would have been willing to stand for reelection. It would be interesting to see what those critics of the establishment would do if they became it. They would discover, of course, as do all government leaders, how limited their powers really are. They would probably suspect some sort of conspiracy on the part of shadowy forces still existing in the society bent on frustrating their noble plans. Like most other Jacobins before them, they would probably use force to destroy the conspiracy, only to discover that even force has its limitations as a means of effective government.

The most important obstacle to social change in the United States, then, is not the concentration of power but its diffusion. If power was concentrated sufficiently, those of us who wish for change would merely have to negotiate with those who hold the power and, if necessary, put pressure on them. But power is so widely diffused that, in many instances, there is no one to negotiate with and no one on whom to put pressure. American society has been organized from the beginning around two premises: (1) "the central guiding trend of American constitutional development has been the evolution of a political system in which all the active and legitimate groups in the population can make themselves heard at some crucial stage in the process of decision."* The second principle is a corollary of the first: (2) The larger society cannot ignore for very long what a given group considers to be its fundamental self-interest. No group, in

*Robert A. Dahl, *Preface to Democratic Theory* (Chicago: University of Chicago Press, 1956), p. 137.

other words, can be expected to assume the role of the permanent loser. . . .

One can fault this system of pluralism in two respects. First, one can say that it has failed according to its own principles; that certain disadvantaged groups are not given an adequate hearing or that society does not recognize its obligation to facilitate the development of political power in these groups. The criticism is certainly a valid one. The very nobility of the political ideal implied in American pluralism makes departures from it unfortunate and ugly, but if this is the only criticism one has to make, then the strategy is obvious: one must bargain to persuade the rest of society that its consensus must be broadened sufficiently to admit these other groups as valued and equal participants in the enterprise.

The second criticism is that given the complexities and difficulties of the modern world, the diffusion of power that exists in American society is dangerously inefficient. If one has to bargain with Polish surgeons, Latvian truckdrivers, red-necked farmers, Irish politicians, conservative black clergymen, Jewish garment makers, Swedish computer operators, Texas oil barons, Portuguese fishermen from Fall River, and cattle ranchers from Montana in order to win support for absolutely imperative social changes, then these changes will be delayed, perhaps for too long, while the evil and injustice continues. It is demeaning, degrading, and immoral to have to bargain for the elimination of clear and obvious injustice. Racism is obscene, war is obscene; both should go away without our having to bargain on the subject. A political system that distributes power so that bargaining is necessary to eliminate obscene immorality is in itself not merely inefficient but immoral. It is not proper that those who are moral and wise should be forced to negotiate with those who are immoral and stupid.

This is a logically and consistently coherent case; in effect, it advocates the abolition of the pluralistic bargaining, coalition-forming polity that we currently have. It advocates taking the slack out of the political system and placing it in the hands of a ruling elite that would be both virtuous enough and powerful enough to accomplish quickly those social changes deemed urgent or imperative. One supposes that a strong case can be made for issues like pollution, population control, and racial injustice not to be made subject to the bargaining process, that wise and virtuous ruling elites should enforce by legislation and by police power, if necessary, the regulations that cope with these problems. The issues are so critical that there is no time to bargain with those whose intelligence and sensitivity is so deficient that they cannot see how imperative it is that action be taken with utmost speed. One can, I say, make a convincing case for such a political system, but let it be clear that it is an elite-establishmentarian system with a vengeance, that it bears no similarity to what normally has been considered democracy, that it is completely at odds with the American political tradition, and completely objectionable to most Americans. . . .

If this model of American society is correct, the appropriate political strategy for those who wish to accomplish social change is not to tear down the establishment but rather to seek allies to form coalitions of various individuals and groups with some commonality of interest. These coalitions will represent an amassing of power that will be stronger than the power of those whose behavior we think is socially injurious. Thus, for example, a coalition was finally put together to force both safety and antipollution devices on the American automobile industry. It took a long time to put such a coalition together—indeed, much too long. Coalitions must be formed more rapidly if we are going to be able to cope with the critical problems that constantly arise in advanced industrial societies. The alternative to winning allies for one's cause is to impose it on the majority of one's fellow citizens whether they like it or not. Not only would this mean the end of political freedom, but it also might be extremely risky, because once we have begun to impose our will as a minority we run the risk that they may start counting noses and in full realization of our minority position, impose their will on us.

There was one thing clear in the summer and fall of 1972. Practitioners of the New Politics were as capable of misusing power as were the "corrupt bosses" whom they supposedly replaced. It did not, however, appear that they were substantially superior to the bosses in their capacity to use power intelligently. Indeed, a persuasive case could be made that as power brokers, the New Politicians were as inept as they were at everything else. Those who wish to rebuild the Democratic coalition can ill afford to be naive about the position of power in American society. Neither can they afford the naivete of raging against mythical dragons like "the establishment." There may well be certain concentrations of power in American society that the reconstructed Democratic coalition will want to break up, but it must first amass for itself a sufficient concentration of political power to be able to have a reasonable chance of winning an election and implementing its program. The builders of the new Democratic coalition must understand what their predecessors of 1972 apparently did not: One builds political power not by excluding people but by including them.

POSTSCRIPT

Is America Ruled by an Elite?

The arguments of both Dye and Greeley raise questions. Greeley freely acknowledges that America is a society with gradations of power. Just as a parish priest does not have the same power as a bishop, so an ordinary citizen is less powerful than a political officeholder, or the assembly-line worker at General Motors less powerful than the corporate president. Does Greeley mean to suggest that hierarchy is inherent in all political relationships? What, then, becomes of the concept of popular sovereignty? As for Dye, he may have successfully demonstrated that there are economic elites, media elites, and political elites, but has he demonstrated that they are all the same elites. If they are different—and if they compete with each other on important issues—then perhaps his "elite" thesis is not so different after all from Greeley's.

The literature of political science and sociology contains many confrontations between elite-theory and pluralism. In his refutation of elite-theory, Greeley makes reference to C. Wright Mills's *The Power Elite* (Oxford, 1956), which is a classic statement of elite-theory. G. William Domhoff's *Who Rules America Now?* (Prentice-Hall, 1983) is a well-documented book about elitism. As for pluralism, Greeley cites with approval Robert Dahl and David Riesman. Dahl's *Preface to Democratic Theory* (University of Chicago Press, 1969) and *Who Governs?* (Yale, 1961) are elaborate defenses of the pluralistic thesis. Reisman's *The Lonely Crowd* (Yale, 1961) deals with a number of aspects of American society, including what he calls "veto groups." Political scientist

Michael Parenti has written an American government textbook, *Democracy for the Few* (St. Martin's, 1980), based on the thesis that our politics and government are dominated by rich corporate elites.

One way of evaluating the pluralist and elitist perspectives on who rules America would be to study them in terms of concrete examples. We might ask, for example, what significant events have occurred in America over the past twenty years. The list would probably have to include the civil rights revolution, the Vietnam War, the rise (or reappearance) of feminism, the exposure and repercussions of Watergate, and the passage of the 1986 tax reform law. Were all these the work of one elite "establishment" or did they result from an interaction of groups in the political arena?

ISSUE 2

Have American Political Parties Lost Their Power?

YES: Benjamin Ginsberg and Martin Shefter, from *Politics by Other Means: The Declining Importance of Elections in America* (Basic Books, 1990)

NO: Everett Carll Ladd, from "Party Reform and the Public Interest," in A. James Reichley, ed., *Elections American Style* (Brookings Institution, 1987)

ISSUE SUMMARY

YES: Professors Benjamin Ginsberg and Martin Shefter believe that parties have declined because elections do not decide many controversial issues and that political stalemate results from the likelihood of a Democratic Congress and Republican president.

NO: Professor Carll Ladd maintains that America's party system is appropriate for its constitutional system, that the party system is not more vulnerable to special interests, and that the American people approve of it.

Unlike party systems in most countries, America's two-party system has been more local than national. In the past, local party machines and bosses chose candidates for elective office, dispensed the patronage that officeholders could dispense to the party faithful, conducted the campaigns, and got out the vote. Local parties even performed social services, such as providing access to government agencies, dealing informally with minor law infractions, and helping the poor. People tended to identify themselves, their families, regions, and ethnic groups with one of the major parties.

The party system reflected the constitutional system. Federalism gave much power and control over elections to the states, and the separation of powers between Congress and the president discouraged the creation of ideological parties standing for clearly defined and opposed goals. The party system worked well, until welfare policies displaced its social function, television rendered its old-style campaigning obsolete, and the political traumas of Vietnam, Watergate, and the Iran-Contra affair created public disillusionment with politics and parties.

One-third of all adult Americans call themselves independent and refuse to identify with either party. That proportion is even higher among young voters. Half of all adult Americans did not vote in the 1988 presidential election, and the proportion of nonvoters is even higher in state and local elections.

When both parties overhauled their national presidential nominating conventions, a significant effort was made to increase voter involvement. In a series of procedural reforms, largely inspired by the bitter and violent Democratic convention in 1968, both parties moved in the direction of selecting nearly all convention delegates in state primaries and caucuses in which all enrolled party members (and sometimes any registered voter) could participate. The system has stimulated great involvement on the part of particular interests, but less than half of those voting in the general election have taken the trouble to vote to choose delegates, and an even smaller number vote in local primaries.

Taken together, the sharp declines in party campaigning, party loyalty, and voting have been seen by some commentators as signs of a decline in the power of political parties. If party loyalty diminishes, more candidates will run independent campaigns. Does it matter? Yes, if parties still play irreplaceable roles in recruiting candidates and running campaigns. Yes, if a consequence of voter disillusionment is a shrinking electorate. And yes, if parties become so devoid of issue orientation that no partisan coherence can be found to unite party members in Congress.

Perhaps, to paraphrase Mark Twain, the report of the demise of America's major parties is premature. As defenders of party vitality point out, parties raise and spend most of the money in elections and influence the selection of candidates for races other than the presidency. Everett Carll Ladd believes that, on balance, the American party system works and Americans have cause to be satisfied with it. Benjamin Ginsberg and Martin Shefter argue that the decline of the party system is accelerating and will be difficult to reverse.

YES

Benjamin Ginsberg
and Martin Shefter

PARTY DECLINE AND ELECTORAL DEADLOCK

Most analyses of American politics assume the primacy of elections. But elections are political institutions, and their significance cannot be taken for granted. The role played by elections has varied over time, and these shifts must be understood in the same terms as changes in the role and power of other institutions. Over the course of American history, political actors have undertaken to transfer decision making on a number of major issues from the electoral to other arenas, such as administrative agencies, the courts, and, in the Civil War, the battlefield. Indeed, forces defeated at the polls have not been averse to using other institutions they control to nullify electoral results. For example, during the late nineteenth and early twentieth centuries, middle- and upper-class "reformers" in American cities were at times able to use state legislative investigations, newspaper exposés, and judicial proceedings to drive from office the machine politicians whom they were unable to defeat through the ballot box.

The declining significance of elections in contemporary America is a product of the electoral deadlock that has developed in the United States over the past quarter century. The duration and scope of this deadlock are without precedent in American history. For eighteen of the twenty-two years between 1968 and 1990, neither the Republican nor the Democratic party was able simultaneously to control the presidency and both houses of Congress. Moreover, for twelve of the eighteen years that the Republicans controlled the White House during this period, the Democrats held majorities in both the House and the Senate.

This deadlock is linked to the decay of America's traditional partisan and electoral institutions. That decay began in the Progressive era, accelerated with the events surrounding the presidencies of Franklin D. Roosevelt and Lyndon Johnson, and has resulted in the virtual destruction of local party organizations and a sharp decline in voting turnout rates. Of course, the

Democratic and Republican parties still exist. But they have essentially become coalitions of public officials, office seekers, and political activists; they lack the direct organizational ties to rank-and-file voters that had formerly permitted parties to shape all aspects of politics and government in the United States.

The decay of party organization is a major theme in analyses of contemporary American politics. Political scientists have attributed to it declines in voter turnout, increased electoral volatility, and a diminution in the accountability of public officials to voters. But in focusing on the effects of the decline of party *within* the electoral arena, analysts have paid insufficient heed to its implications for the relationship *between* elections and other political institutions.

Generally speaking, strong party organizations enhance the significance of elections, while declines in party strength reduce the importance of electoral processes. Inasmuch as their influence derives from the electoral arena, political parties are the institutions with the largest stake in upholding the principle that power should be allocated through elections. Thus, a diminution of party influence and an increase in the power of other political agencies is likely not only to reduce the relevance of elections for governmental programs and policies but also to allow electoral results themselves to be circumvented, resisted, or even reversed by forces that control powerful institutions outside the electoral realm.

In contemporary American politics, party decline has fostered a stalemate in the national electoral arena and encouraged contenders for power to look elsewhere for weapons to use against their political foes. This deadlock has stemmed from the differential impact of

the decay of political parties, and the decline of electoral turnout that has resulted from it, on congressional and presidential elections. With party decline, personal organization and name recognition have become critical in low-visibility elections such as those for the House of Representatives. In a variety of ways, Democratic candidates have gained an advantage in these realms. Republicans have the advantage in high-visibility presidential contests, where issues and ideology are of prime importance. The decay of political parties has reduced voter turnout, especially among low- and moderate-income groups, resulting in a heavily middle-class electorate—44 percent of those voting in the 1988 presidential election had family incomes above $35,000 a year—increasingly concerned with its tax burden. GOP presidential candidates have been able to appeal more effectively than their Democratic opponents to this predominantly middle-class electorate.

In congressional elections, the first advantage that the Democrats derive from party decline and low levels of turnout has to do with incumbency. The growth of split-ticket voting that has accompanied party decline enables incumbents to build personal bases of support for themselves and to retain their seats even when the other party's presidential candidate sweeps their district. Moreover, the ability of incumbents to draw upon the resources of the federal government for electoral purposes is an especially important factor when only 35 percent of the eligible electorate votes. The overwhelming advantage House and, to a lesser extent, Senate incumbents have come to enjoy has contributed to the Democrats' ability to perpetuate the congressional majorities they first built during the 1930s and renewed in their 1964 and 1974 electoral landslides.

Because of the resignation, retirement, and death of incumbents, three to four dozen congressional seats become vacant in each election year. However, the Democrats maintain an advantage in races for open seats, winning roughly 60 percent of these contests in recent years. One reason Democrats have been able to do so well is that they have a stronger base in state and local government. This base gives the Democrats an advantage in the drawing of congressional district lines. It also provides them with a pool of experienced and visible elected officials available to compete for open House and Senate seats.

Another source of the Democrats' advantage in congressional elections is their ability to draw upon the support of thousands of individuals who are affiliated with local governments and nonprofit organizations and who are prepared to work for candidates committed to domestic programs and expenditures. This support grows more valuable as party organizations and voting turnout decline.

In the presidential arena, by contrast, the decline of party organization and voter turnout has weakened the Democrats and strengthened the Republicans. Groups committed to higher levels of domestic spending and other liberal causes play a major role as campaign workers and contributors, caucus participants, and primary voters in the Democratic presidential nominating process. With the collapse of party organization, Democratic candidates for the White House have become heavily dependent upon these groups to conduct and finance their primary campaigns. The appeals that candidates must make to compete successfully for the party's pres-

idential nomination, however, often undermine their chances in the general election by permitting the GOP to portray them as being too liberal. Such portrayal can be extremely damaging in presidential general elections. Here ideology and national issues play a much larger role than in congressional contests, where voters are mainly concerned with protecting narrower interests.

The issue of race confronts Democrats with a particularly acute version of this problem. Black voters overwhelmingly favor the Democrats, and that party's presidential candidates have become heavily dependent upon this support in general elections. In fact, the Democrats have received more than 20 percent of their votes from blacks in recent presidential contests. Though there is little danger that these voters will defect to the Republicans, the Democratic party's chances of victory in presidential races can be seriously impaired if blacks do not come to the polls in large numbers. To maintain high levels of black voter turnout, the Democrats must focus on such issues as civil rights and social programs. Unfortunately for the Democrats, these appeals have alienated large numbers of blue-collar white voters in the North and South who, since the 1960s, have become increasingly dissatisfied with the party's stands on racial questions.

The Democrats' dilemma has been exacerbated by the growing political prominence of Jesse Jackson, who has energized and won the ardent support of millions of black Americans. Jackson's influence over the black electorate has enabled him to demand, as a condition for his urging blacks to vote, that the Democrats accord him a prominent role and focus on issues of concern to his constituency. To the extent that they meet these demands, the Democrats risk losing even more support among those whites who are wary of the party's stance on race. In 1984, the Democratic presidential nominee Walter Mondale was impaled on one horn of this dilemma when he aggressively courted black voters and lost substantial support among these whites.

In 1988, Michael Dukakis sought both to placate Jackson at the Democratic national convention and at the same time to avoid the appearance of having made substantial concessions to him. This effort was doomed to failure, and Dukakis found himself caught on both horns of the Democrats' racial dilemma. Many whites, believing that the Democrats had once again shown too much concern for blacks, supported the Republicans. Blacks, for their part, were convinced that Dukakis had not been sufficiently attentive either to Jackson or to their political interests more generally—convictions that Jackson did little to dispel. As a result, black voter turnout dropped from its 1984 level. This combination of white defection and black nonparticipation was a central factor contributing to Dukakis's defeat in the 1988 presidential election.

The only way the Democrats can overcome their racial impasse is to develop issues and programs that attract voters across racial lines, most likely by devising programs that appeal to blacks and whites on the basis of common economic concerns. Such a strategy was employed by nineteenth-century European social democratic parties, which succeeded in uniting workers by imbuing them with a common class identification.

The ability of the Democrats to employ a social democratic strategy is limited, however, by the reality that low levels of voter mobilization leave America with an overwhelmingly middle-class electorate, which is unlikely to be sympathetic to such appeals. Proposals from Jesse Jackson and others that the Democratic party take steps to register and mobilize large numbers of new minority and low-income voters have met with a cool response from many established party leaders and public officials. They fear that a massive influx of new voters might further heighten the party's racial dilemma, drive middle-class voters into the Republican camp, and threaten the party's control of offices it currently holds. Without significant expansion of the electorate, however, efforts to win elections by uniting white and black voters are not likely to succeed.

These factors help to explain why the Republicans prevailed in five of six presidential elections between 1968 and 1988, while the Democrats continued to dominate House elections and usually won control of the Senate during these same years. In effect, the decay of America's traditional electoral structures has permitted each of the major contenders for power to establish an institutional stronghold from which it cannot easily be dislodged through electoral means. . . .

ELECTORAL MOBILIZATION AND GOVERNMENTAL POWER

The relationship between political patterns and governmental effectiveness is a complex one. Practices that severely undermine governmental capacities in some settings may not in others—witness the ability of Japan to thrive despite widespread political corruption. But, in the United States and elsewhere, political patterns have at times emerged that have seriously inhibited governments from pursuing collective purposes. For example, in Israel during the late 1980s, electoral stalemate between the Labor and Likud parties paralyzed the government. This stalemate prevented the government from responding effectively to uprisings in the occupied territories and to diplomatic initiatives by the Palestine Liberation Organization, thereby threatening the relationship with the United States, which is a necessary condition for Israel's very survival.

Similar examples can be found in American history. In the United States during the early 1930s, prevailing political patterns led the government to pursue policies that exacerbated rather than ameliorated the Depression. A particularly notable example is the Smoot-Hawley tariff of 1930. The logrolling practices that at the time characterized the formulation of trade policy in the U.S. Congress led to the adoption of the highest tariffs in American history. This precipitated foreign retaliation, a virtual collapse of international trade, and helped turn what could have been an ordinary cyclical downturn into the most severe economic crisis of the modern era. Even more striking than the events of the early 1930s were those preceding the Civil War. Political paralysis during the Buchanan administration prevented the government from responding to its own dismemberment as southern states seceded from the Union.

Historically, efforts to overcome political patterns that undermine governmental effectiveness have taken one of two forms in the United States: political demobilization or mobilization. Demobilization involves attempts to free government from "political interference" by insulating decision-making processes, restricting political participation, or both.

Mobilization consists of efforts by one or another contender for power to overcome political stalemate and governmental paralysis by bringing new voters into the electorate and winning over some of the opposition's supporters. In this way, a party can overwhelm its opponents in the electoral arena and take full control of the institutions of government. Such a strategy also provides a party with a mass base of support that can enable it to confront and prevail over entrenched social and economic interests.

Demobilization and insulation were the paths followed by institutional reformers in the United States during the Progressive era. The Progressives, who spoke for a predominately middle-class constituency, sought to cope with the problems of turn-of-the-century America by strengthening the institutions of national, state, and local government. Progressives undertook to strengthen executive institutions by promoting civil service reform, creating regulatory commissions staffed by experts, and transferring fiscal and administrative responsibilities from elected to appointed officials. In addition, asserting that the intrusion of partisan considerations undermined governmental efficiency, the Progressives attacked state and local party organizations. They sponsored legislative investigations of ties between party leaders and businessmen and the criminal prosecution of politicians they deemed to be corrupt. The Progressives also supported the enaactment of personal registration requirements for voting that served to reduce turnout among the poorly educated, immigrant, nonwhite, and working-class voters who had provided party organizations with their mass base. Partly as a result of these measures, voter participation rates in the

United States fell by nearly thirty percentage points during the first quarter of the twentieth century, a decline from which they never fully recovered.

In the short run, the Progressive strategy of administrative reform did help to enhance governmental capacities in the United States. Government agencies penetrated by parties and rife with patronage are not well suited to performing the functions of a modern state. However, politicians are not in a position to prevail over entrenched social and economic forces when they lack the support of an extensive and well-organized mass constituency. In the long run, the Progressive strategy of insulation and demobilization undermined the strength of American government relative to powerful interests in civil society and helped to produce the low rates of voter turnout that contribute to political stalemate in the United States today.

The second strategy—political mobilization—was used most effectively in the United States by the administrations of Abraham Lincoln and Franklin D. Roosevelt. To fight the Civil War and break the power of Southern slaveholders, the Lincoln administration vastly expanded the scope of the American national state. It raised an enormous army and created a national system of taxation, a national currency, and a national debt. The extensive organizing and extraordinary popular mobilization that brought the Republicans to power in 1860 enabled them to raise more than two million troops, to sell more than $2 billion in bonds to finance the military effort, and to rally popular support for the war. The higher levels of party organization and political mobilization in the North than in the South, as much as the superiority of Northern industry, help explain the triumph of the Union cause in the Civil War.

The Roosevelt administration permanently transformed the American institutional landscape, creating the modern welfare and regulatory state. The support which the administration mobilized through party organizations and labor unions helped it contend with opposition to its programs both inside and outside the institutions of government. A marked increase in electoral turnout, a realignment of some existing blocs of voters, and a revitalized Democratic party apparatus provided Roosevelt with the enormous majorities in the Electoral College and Congress that allowed him to secure the enactment of his programs. Worker mobilization through unions and strikes forced businessmen to accept the new pattern of industrial relations the administration was seeking to establish.

DEMOBILIZATION VERSUS MOBILIZATION IN CONTEMPORARY POLITICS

The dangers facing the United States in the 1990s are not as immediate as those that the nation confronted on the eve of the Civil War or in the aftermath of the 1929 stock market crash. Nevertheless, America's political processes impede governmental responses adequate to the challenges that the nation faces. This impediment is contributing to the difficulties now confronting America in the international economic arena.

Of the political expedients adopted and the solutions proposed in recent years for the nation's problems, the majority follow the first of the aforementioned paths—that of political insulation and demobilization. Thus, the often-proposed constitutional amendment requiring a balanced budget would deprive elected officials of discretion over fiscal policy. The bipartisan commissions—increasingly used to overcome governmental stalemate—represent an attempt to insulate government decisions from political pressure. And there are clear demobilizing implications in recent calls for the Democratic party to distance itself from racial minorities so as to become more competitive in presidential elections.

Whatever advantages might be derived from such expedients in the short run, they raise issues of democratic legitimacy and, as the experience of Progressivism suggests, in the long run they are likely to weaken government. The founders of the American republic recognized that a strong national government could not be built in the United States on a narrow popular base. As James Wilson observed at the Constitutional Convention of 1787, "raising the federal pyramid to a considerable altitude" required giving it "as broad a base as possible."

It is precisely the narrow base of the "federal pyramid" that underlies governmental disarray in the United States today. As we have suggested, . . . the decay of American electoral democracy—particularly the destruction of party organizations and erosion of voter turnout—has contributed to electoral deadlock and the consequent emergence of alternative forms of political struggle. This pattern of politics undermines governmental institutions and further discourages voter participation. In its origins, character, and consequences, America's postelectoral political order is linked to low levels of popular participation in politics.

America's current political and governmental disarray is unlikely to be overcome as long as the electoral deadlock of the past quarter century persists. Breaking this deadlock would probably require one or the other party to engage in political mobilization. The probability that this path will be taken, however, is not great.

NO

Everett Carll Ladd

PARTY REFORM AND THE PUBLIC INTEREST

The prevailing view in American political science since the Second World War has been that presidential leadership is insufficient without disciplined parties. In 1950, for example, the Committee on Political Parties of the American Political Science Association issued its call for a system of stronger parties able to meet the national need "for more effective formulation of general policies and programs and for better integration of all of the far-flung activities of modern government."[1]

The American system's dispersion of authority has often been faulted for retarding political accountability and popular control. Giving the public effective means of control over a big, complex government is difficult, yet vital in any country that takes democracy seriously. A century ago, Wilson lamented that "the average citizen may be excused for esteeming government at best but a haphazard affair upon which his vote and all of his influence can have but little effect. How is his choice of a representative in Congress to affect the policy of the country as regards the questions in which he is most interested?"[2]

Contemporary American political science for the most part sees the strengthening of parties as essential for extending popular control over government and ensuring greater responsiveness of public institutions to popular wishes. Only strong parties can so organize issues that the public can speak effectively on them. If they make elected officials in some sense collectively rather than individually responsible to the electorate, parties greatly expand the public's capacity to reward and punish.

Similarly, stronger and more disciplined parties have been seen as an important but elusive potential antidote to extreme congressional individualism and the opening it offers the swarm of special interests. The 1950 APSA report made this case. "The value of special-interest groups in a diversified society . . . should be obvious," its authors argued. "But organized interest groups cannot do the job of the parties. Indeed, it is only when a working formula of the public interest in *general* character is made manifest by the

From Everett Carll Ladd, "Party Reform and the Public Interest," in A. James Reichley, ed., *Elections American Style* (Brookings, 1987). Copyright © 1987 by the Brookings Institute. Reprinted by permission. Some notes omitted.

parties in terms of coherent programs that the claims of interest groups can be adjusted on the basis of political responsibility. . . . [The proliferation of interest groups and the extension of their sway] makes necessary a reinforced party system that can cope with the multiplied organized pressures."[3]

Strong parties are needed not only to curb special interest influence by forcing them "to pick on people their own size" but also to help the underorganized many have their proper say in competition with the highly organized few. E. E. Schattschneider gave classic statement to this argument: "The flaw in the pluralist heaven is that the heavenly chorus sings with a strong upper-class accent."[4] . . .

Surely the American governmental system, built upon federalism and separation of powers, does greatly divide and disperse political authority. Indeed, in the parliamentary sense of the term, the United States really does not have a *government* at all. The president has significant authority, but he and his executive subordinates are rightly called the *administration*, not the *government;* Congress's role is so great that it would have to be part of the government for there to be a government. In this dispersed and decentralized scheme, barriers aplenty are erected to coherent, centrally developed policies. And interest groups are indeed presented with multiple points of access at all levels. It is very messy, and presidents are not alone in finding it frustrating.

The American governmental order has dictated a special type of party system. Given federalism, the parties historically were organized on state lines, and even when individual state parties were robust and disciplined the national party system remained fragmented. Given

separation of powers, the case for party discipline evident in parliamentary systems could never be made, and party factions had a variety of bases from which to maintain their independence. Given the extreme individualism that has always distinguished American political culture, calls for greater collective party authority have rarely struck a responsive chord among the public, and succeeding waves of "reform" have had the principal result of further extending political individualism. The "reforms" of the 1960s and early 1970s in Congress, for example, left individual members even more advantaged vis-à-vis the House and Senate leadership.

All in all, today's party system does not reduce the effects of the constitutionally dictated separation of powers: rather it reflects them and, in so doing, magnifies them. American political parties are not well equipped for developing comprehensive policy positions, presenting them to the electorate, and seeing them through into legislated programs that might be voted up or down in the next election.

DISTINCTION BETWEEN CHANGE AND REFORM

. . . No one who pays close attention to politics would dismiss out of hand every call for change in our parties and elections system. I do maintain, however, that the more substantial recently proposed changes fail to show real promise of making things better by such national-interest standards as more responsive democratic government and wiser long-term policies.

I should acknowledge that my current judgment in this regard differs to some extent from that of times past. I have always been skeptical about claims that proposed changes should be readily recognized as reforms. Often, the changes do not in fact make things better—and within a few years of their enactment the cry is raised loudly that the reforms must themselves be reformed. Nonetheless, I did at one time accept much of the argument in favor of stronger parties and an improved presidential nominating process. With regard to the latter, I offered my own elegant blueprint for change, which included a bigger role for party and elected officials in conjunction with a single, nationwide presidential primary.[5] While I remain comfortable with much of the earlier analysis, I think I yielded too readily to the underlying notion that successful institutional tinkering is easily conceived.

Tinkering

Proposed changes differ as to their comprehensiveness. Some are potentially far-reaching, such as arguments for strengthening the national parties. Others are much more limited, such as proposals for altering the schedule of presidential primaries. My concern with the latter sort of proposals is in part the familiar one about unintended consequences—that they often result in two steps forward and two steps back, or sometimes two-and-one-half steps back. They advocate change that has merit but also disadvantages. . . .

Major Surgery

The American system in its entirety—including the separation of powers and the decentralized, undisciplined party system established within it—undoubt-

edly makes more difficult the enactment of programs that reflect some centrally inspired coherence. Even when a president wins a handsome public endorsement, he must immediately grapple with a fiercely independent Congress in which members of his own party as well as the opposition resist him at critical junctures. Compared with parliamentary systems with relatively disciplined parties, our system is surely disjointed and at times even incoherent.

Given that in other systems party factions have gained working control of the government and managed to enact their programs with less compromise and adjustment than is typically required in the United States, one must question whether the biases of the American system should be seen as disadvantageous. Arthur Schlesinger, Jr., argues that the key problem evident in the making of public policy in the United States is not that we are unable to enact a set of elegant programs because of the system of dispersed authority. "Our problem . . . is that we do not know what to do. . . . If we don't know what ought to be done, efficient enactment of a poor program is a dubious accomplishment—as the experience of 1981 demonstrates. [Schlesinger was critical of various economic proposals that the Reagan administration advanced and Congress enacted.] What is the great advantage of acting with decision and dispatch when you don't know what you are doing?"[6]

Schlesinger points out that as early as a century ago foreign visitors to the United States were leveling much the same criticisms of the American system as are made today. In *The American Commonwealth*, Lord Bryce summarized the British view that the American system was virtually incapable of settling major national questions. "An Englishman is disposed to ascribe these failures to the fact that as there are no leaders, there is no one responsible for the neglect of business, the miscarriage of bills, the unwise appropriation of public funds. 'In England,' he says, 'the ministry of the day bears the blame of whatever goes wrong in the House of Commons. Having a majority, it ought to be able to do what it desires.' "[7]

Bryce also reported the response that he encountered among American political leaders. They insisted that Congress had not settled a number of major national questions not because of defects in institutional structure "but because the division of opinion in the country regarding them has been faithfully reflected in Congress. The majority has not been strong enough to get its way; and . . . no distinct impulse of mandate towards any particular settlement of these questions has been received from the country. It is not for Congress to go faster than the people. When the country knows and speaks its mind, Congress will not fail to act." Schlesinger endorses this general argument. "When the country is not sure what ought to be done, it may be that delay, debate and further consideration are not a bad idea. And if our leadership is sure what to do, it must in our democracy educate the rest—and that is not a bad idea either."[8]

Admittedly, this argument has a large subjective component. It is distrustful of the notion that an ascendant political faction is likely to be the repository of special wisdom and insight on what programs will best advance certain ends. Schlesinger seems to have come to this perspective as a result of his disagreement with certain Reagan administration policies. I find a recurring experience:

the errors of a great many ascendant factions in many different governmental contexts have demonstrated that barriers to clear control of the government are generally conducive to sound long-term policy in the national interest.

When reasonably broad agreement is reached on a course of action, the American system seems perfectly capable of coherent and expeditious responses, even on complex policy questions. The Tax Reform Act of 1986 is a case in point. The conventional wisdom before its enactment was that it presented precisely the kind of situation where special interests inevitably dominate—a hyper-individualistic Congress wholly incapable of fending off special interest pleas, combined with complex, and hence invisible to the general public, tax code provisions. Yet no such thing happened. When substantial intellectual and political agreement was reached on the wisdom of a general course of change in tax policy, that change was swiftly and coherently established. (Whether we will live to regret it is, of course, another matter.)

Any governmental or electoral system can at times yield policy that passes muster by standards of enduring national interests—and similarly any can fail to do so. Judgments as to the adequacy of a particular system are inevitably colored by one's view of their recent yield. A case in point is the criticism of the British system advanced by some American political scientists, notably Pendleton Herring and Don K. Price, at the end of the 1930s. Leon Epstein notes that both Herring and Price thought that "Britain's disciplined party leadership had produced bad policy results during the 1930s, at the very time that American presidential leadership appeared to have been relatively successful."[9]

Herring's observations are worth considering as one contemplates whether our own system needs more party discipline and centralization. In Britain, Herring argued, "it is the whole tendency of the system that distinctive parties govern the nation in accordance with the class basis upon which their strength is organized. . . . The isolation of classes into separate parties prevents that modification of extreme points of view that is possible when different elements join in compromise. . . . One party machine rules while the opposition elements stand aside and hope for mistakes that will oust those in power." Herring found the American presidential system with its weak parties and dispersed power more attractive. "The chief executive is forced to seek middle ground. He cannot depend on his own party following. His measures are often supported by minority party members. The separation of executive and legislative branches gives both Congress and the president an opportunity to appeal to the voters."[10]

Epstein suggests that American political science has suffered from its infatuation through much of this century with its idealized picture of a British "responsible-party" system.[11] Shaken from their attraction to some degree by developments in the 1930s and again by recent British experience in formulating public policy, political scientists still have not sufficiently examined questions of the institutional capacity of the British system for encouraging sound broad-based policies. My own limited examination suggests that every party system in the advanced industrial democracies is a complex mix that reflects both the strengths and the weaknesses of the larger political-institutional system of which it is a part. Cross-national borrowing is a dubious venture.

DOES THE U.S. SYSTEM ADVANTAGE SPECIAL INTERESTS?

The United States has a plethora of interest groups intruding into the governmental process at all levels. Moreover, the number of groups operating at the national level has burgeoned over the last quarter century. From these developments it has been easy to reach the conclusion that the American system has given special interests a unique and excessive opportunity to shape policy.

Jack L. Walker challenges the view, however, that the explosion of interest group activity has anything to do with the characteristics of the American parties and the election system. The factors he cites for the expansion of group activity are: (1) long-term increases in the level of education of the population, providing a large pool of skills on which various citizen movements can draw; (2) development of inexpensive yet sophisticated methods of communication; (3) a period of social protest beginning with the civil rights demonstrations of the early 1960s, which called many established practices into question and provided a strong stimulus for change; (4) the creation of massive new governmental programs; (5) subsequent efforts by governmental agencies and foundations to encourage links among the providers and consumers of the new programs; and (6) defensive response by groups that felt threatened by new regulatory legislation in areas like consumer protection, occupational health and safety, and environmentalism.[12]

A great number of developments outside the parties and election system have encouraged groups to organize, set up Washington offices, and try to bend programs and policies more to their wishes.

It might still be true that the American electoral system gives unusual opportunities to special interests; but upon examination this claim appears unsubstantiated. The experience of Western democracies indicates that different electoral and governmental systems stimulate different forms of interest group intervention; it does not establish that more centralized systems fare better in resisting special interests.

In France, notes Frank L. Wilson, "with deputies voting en bloc according to their parties' decisions, interest groups might be expected to redirect their pressure from the individual deputy to the party, but there is no evidence that this shift took place. Instead, interest groups redirected their activities toward influencing government and the bureaucracy."[13] Over half of the interest group leaders Wilson interviewed said that their groups rarely or never contacted the parties as such. These officials described contacts with ministers and civil servants as by far their most effective means of action; parliamentary lobbying ranked near the bottom of the list. Interest group interventions in France look different from those in the United States, but are not less influential.

In Britain decisionmaking is highly centralized in the government and in the parties. As a result, compared with the United States, parliamentary lobbying is relatively limited, though far from nonexistent. However, when interest groups form strong bonds with tightly disciplined parties in this centralized decisionmaking environment, the influence of these special interests over government policy may dwarf that achieved by their counterparts in the United States. No interest group or collection of groups has influence over the Democratic or Republican parties comparable with that of the labor movement over the Labor party in Britain. The British system may have special difficulty in responding to more general interests because of the extent of group involvement in party decision-making.

Elected officials of both parties of the United States routinely do business with a great variety of different interest groups. The reverse is true: most groups consider it in their interest to maintain access to people on both sides of the aisle and in the various sectors where decisions are made. The main result seems to be that groups rarely dominate any broad sector of national policy, although they may exercise great influence in narrower policy sectors where "iron triangle" relationships apply.

DOES THE SYSTEM DIMINISH PUBLIC CONTROL?

Calls for "reform" aimed at more disciplined and "responsible" parties have typically assumed that the public is frustrated by the wide dispersion of power in which no faction is able to gain clear control of "the government" and see its programs comprehensively enacted. The exact opposite seems to be the case. When public opinion polls ask Americans what they think about a system in which Republicans control the presidency and the Democrats control Congress, they invariably indicate their satisfaction.

Examining public opinion on many of the large contemporary issues, one gets a better sense of why divided control may not appear to Americans as either confusing or threatening. Again and again one finds a public that is highly ambivalent. For example, *Public Opinion* magazine has reviewed the opinions of Americans on various "role of government" questions. Over the last two decades the public has been continuously pulled in two directions. On the one hand, Americans make expansive claims for services of all sorts, many of which they expect the government to provide. On the other hand, they see government as intrusive, clumsy, and problem-causing. Those who have wanted to cut back on domestic government have naturally chosen to emphasize the public's dissatisfaction with government's size and scope; those who want more government intervention stress the public's appetite for services.[14] The fact is that both dimensions have been prominent in American thinking over the last two decades; the story is the tension between the two viewpoints, not their resolution to the left or right or between the parties.

Given these ambivalent feelings, fractured party control may be seen as a highly effective vehicle of popular control. If the public has not made up its mind in what direction it wants to go or, more precisely, has decided it does not want to go consistently in any direction, what better vehicle than a system in which a loosely disciplined Democratic majority pushes one way through Congress and a loosely disciplined Republican coalition pushes the other way through the executive? An ambivalent public's control of policy is enhanced by a system of dispersed authority. Frustration seems to reside more with certain party elites than with the general public.

The relationship of a party system to the promotion of broad national interests will never be demonstrated with the final precision of Pythagorean theorem. There are too many slippery concepts, too many sources of variation in end results.

Nonetheless, it is striking that over the past century, in which the American system of dispersed authority has been so much lamented, so little real evidence has been accumulated to support the argument that party discipline and centralized policymaking actually serve the national interest. Special interests do not appear less influential in parliamentary systems with disciplined parties. Centralized systems of policymaking show no signs of being able to regularly produce sounder results. The American public shows satisfaction, not frustration, with the system in which no party faction can dominate the course of public policy. The basic case for extensive reform of the American party system simply has not been established.

NOTES

1. American Political Science Association, *Toward a More Responsible Two-Party System*, supplement to *American Political Science Review*, vol. 44 (September 1950), p. 16.
2. Wilson, *Congressional Government*, pp. 331–32.
3. APSA, *Toward a More Responsible Two-Party System*, p. 19.
4. E. E. Schattschneider, *The Semisovereign People: A Realist's View of Democracy in America* (Holt, Rinehart, and Winston, 1960), p. 35.
5. Everett Ladd, "A Better Way to Pick Our Presidents," *Fortune*, May 5, 1980, pp. 132–42.
6. Arthur M. Schlesinger, Jr., "Leave the Constitution Alone," in Donald L. Robinson, ed., *Reforming American Government* (Westview Press, 1985), p. 53.
7. James Bryce, *The American Commonwealth*, vol. 1 (Macmillan, 1918), pp. 153–54.
8. Schlesinger, "Leave the Constitution Alone," p. 54.
9. Leon D. Epstein, "What Happened to the British Party Model?" *American Political Science Review*, vol. 74 (March 1980), p. 10; Don K. Price, "The Parliamentary and Presidential Systems," *Public Administration Review*, vol. 3 (Autumn 1948), pp. 317–34; and Pendleton Herring, *Presidential Leadership* (Farrar and Rinehart, 1940), especially pp. 128–46.
10. Herring, *Presidential Leadership*, pp. 129–30.
11. Epstein, "What Happened to the British Party Model?"

12. Jack L. Walker, "The Origins and Maintenance of Interest Groups in America," *American Political Science Review*, vol. 77 (June 1983), p. 397.

13. Frank L. Wilson, "French Interest Group Politics: Pluralist or Neocorporatist?" *American Political Science Review*, vol. 77 (December 1983), p. 905.

14. For data on the public's conflicting views of government, see *Public Opinion*, vol. 9 (March–April 1987), pp. 21–33.

POSTSCRIPT

Have American Political Parties Lost Their Power?

Both Ginsberg and Shefter, as critics of the party system, and Ladd, in defense of it, agree on the continued likelihood of divided national government; that is, having a Democratic Congress and a Republican president. The House of Representatives has had a Democratic majority for all but four of the sixty years from 1933 through 1992. The Senate has had a Democratic majority for all but ten years in the same period. Yet, we have had a Republican president for twenty of the twenty-four years from 1969 through 1992. What explanations do the authors give for this remarkable contrast? Why do they disagree in their assessment of it?

Points raised in these readings arise again later. Consider Ladd's conclusion that America's parties are not more vulnerable than other systems to special interests in connection with another issue in this volume: *Do Political Action Committees Undermine Democracy?* Compare Ladd's conclusion also with Ginsberg and Shefter's observation that elections do not decide all issues in the issue which asks: *Should the Federal Courts Be Bound by the "Original Intent" of the Framers?*

George E. Reedy, in *The Twilight of the Presidency: From Johnson to Reagan* (New American Library, 1987), mourns what he calls "the end of the party line." Martin P. Wattenberg, in *The Decline of American Parties 1952–1984* (Harvard, 1986), examines the forces that he claims have made parties increasingly irrelevant. A series of essays that display guarded optimism about the future of the major parties can be found in Joel L. Fleishman, ed., *The Future of American Political Parties: The Challenge of Governance* (Prentice-Hall, 1982). Leon Epstein, author of *Political Parties in the American Mold* (University of Wisconsin, 1986), rejects both decline and realignment, arguing that the major parties are both adaptable and valuable.

ISSUE 3

Do Political Action Committees Undermine Democracy?

YES: Fred Wertheimer, from "Campaign Finance Reform: The Unfinished Agenda," *Annals of the American Academy* (July 1986)

NO: Herbert E. Alexander, from "The Case for PACs," *A Public Affairs Council Monograph*

ISSUE SUMMARY

YES: Common Cause president Fred Wertheimer argues that PACs exert too much influence over the electoral process, allowing special interests to get the ear of elected officials at the expense of the national interest.

NO: Political analyst Herbert Alexander insists that PACs have made significant contributions to the American political system.

Half a century ago, American folk humorist Will Rogers observed that it took a lot of money even to *lose* an election. What would Will Rogers say if he were alive today?

The cost of television as a medium of communication and persuasion has greatly increased the expenditures in election campaigns. In 1984, campaign expenditures for the presidential election totaled $325 million, $50 million more than in the previous election. The cost of campaigning for Congress is also rising dramatically. Campaign spending on House and Senate races totaled $450 million in 1986, more than double the amount spent in 1978. Money, said a prominent California politician, is the "mother's milk of politics."

More controversial than the amount of money spent in politics is its source. Political action committees have become a major factor in financing American election campaigns. PACs (as they are called) have proliferated in recent years, with more than one hundred new special-interest groups being founded each year. It is estimated that there are now more than 4,100 PACs, representing almost every conceivable political interest.

By raising money from political sympathizers, association members, and public solicitations, PACs have provided the funds with which candidates reach the public. It is estimated that PACs spent more than $80 million on campaigns in 1982, when there was no presidential election. In 1984 at least ten incumbent senators (in both parties) received more than $300 thousand in PAC money. Some members of Congress have taken no chances on winning an existing PAC's approval and have created their own. The Congressional Club, founded by Republican senator Jesse Helms of North Carolina, raised nearly $5 million in 1983 alone.

Legislators are divided on the influence of PACs. Democratic representative Barney Frank of Massachusetts has said: "You can't take thousands of dollars from a group and not have it affect you." But Republican congressman Henry Hyde offers a different perspective. "The more PACs proliferate," he says, "the less influence any individual PAC has. . . . Their influence is diminished by their proliferation."

Critics argue that PAC money in recent years probably influenced congressional votes on bills to maintain high dairy price supports and to defeat legislation that would have required warranties on used cars. On the other hand, defenders of PACs maintain that they are less interested in influencing members of Congress opposed to their point of view than in electing new members who are sympathetic.

PACs are not a new phenomenon. Pressure groups, or factions, as founding father James Madison called them, have always been part of the political process. To eliminate them would be to destroy liberty itself. What Madison hoped for was the broadest participation of interest groups, so that compromises among them would result in an approximation of the national interest.

Has this happened? In the following selections, Fred Wertheimer, president of Common Cause, a self-styled citizens' lobby, argues that the opposite has occurred. In his view, the proliferation of PACs has given special interests the power to override the national interest. Disputing this view is political analyst Herbert Alexander, who points out a number of significant contributions PACs have made to the American political system.

YES

CAMPAIGN FINANCE REFORM:
THE UNFINISHED AGENDA

Our democracy is founded on the concept of representation. Citizens elect leaders who are given responsibility to weigh all the competing and conflicting interests that reflect our diversity and to decide what, in their judgment, will best advance the interests of the citizenry.

It is obviously a rough system. It often does not measure up to the ideal we might hope to attain. But we continue to place our trust in this system because we believe our best chance at governing ourselves lies in obtaining the best judgment of elected representatives.

Unfortunately, that is not happening today. We are not obtaining the best judgment of our elected representatives in Congress because they are not free to give it to us. As a result of our present congressional campaign financing system—and the increasing role of political action committee (PAC) campaign contributions—members of Congress are rapidly losing their ability to represent the constituencies that have elected them.

We have long struggled to prevent money from being used to influence government decisions. We have not always succeeded, but we have never lost sight of the goal. Buying influence violates our most fundamental democratic values. We have long recognized that the ability to make large campaign contributions does, in fact, make some more equal than others. . . .

CONGRESSIONAL CAMPAIGN FINANCING

The last decade of congressional campaign financing has been marked by an exponential increase in the number of PACs formed by corporations, labor unions, trade associations, and other groups. In 1974 there were 608 PACs. Today there are more than 4000.

This explosion in PACs can be traced to congressional action—and inaction—in 1974. Ironically, at the very time when members of Congress were acting to clean up presidential elections, they opened the door for PACs to

From Fred Wertheimer, "Campaign Finance Reform: The Unfinished Agenda," *Annals of the American Academy* (July 1986). Copyright © 1986 by Fred Wertheimer. Reprinted by permission of Sage Publications, Inc., and the author.

enter the congressional arena in an unprecedented way. The key to the PAC explosion was a provision attached to the 1974 law by labor and business groups, over the opposition of Common Cause and other reform advocates, that authorized government contractors to establish PACs. In addition, by creating public financing for presidential campaigns, but not for congressional races, the 1974 amendments focused the attention and interest of PACs and other private campaign donors on Congress.

The resulting growth in PACs was no accident, and it certainly was not a reform. The growth of PACs, moreover, is certainly no unintended consequence of the 1974 law—the provision was included to protect and enhance the role of PACs in financing campaigns, and it has.

This tremendous increase in the number of PACs has not resulted in balanced representation in Washington. As Senator Gary Hart, Democrat of Colorado, has told the Senate:

It seems the only group without a wellheeled PAC is the average citizen—the voter who has no special interest beyond low taxes, an efficient government, an honorable Congress, and a humane society. Those are the demands we should be heeding—but those are the demands the PACs have drowned out.

In fact, the increasing number of PACs has largely served to increase the ability of single interests to bring pressure to bear on a congressional candidate or a member of Congress. There are more than 100 insurance company PACs, more than 100 PACs sponsored by electric utilities, and more than 300 sponsored by labor unions. Representative David Obey, Democrat of Wisconsin, has observed that frequently in Washington:

an issue affects an entire industry and all of the companies and labor unions in that industry. . . . When that occurs, [and] a large number of groups which have made substantial contributions to members are all lobbying on the same side of an issue, the pressure generated from those aggregate contributions is enormous and warps the process. It is as if they had made a single, extremely large contribution.

The increase in the number of PACs, not surprisingly, has also produced a tremendous increase in PAC contributions to congressional candidates. In 1974, PACs gave $12.5 million to congressional candidates. By the 1984 elections, their contributions had exceeded $100 million, an eightfold increase in ten years.

PAC money also represents a far more important part of the average candidate's campaign funds than it did ten or so years ago. In 1974, 15.7 percent of congressional candidates' campaign money came from PACs; by the 1984 election, that proportion had increased to 30 percent.

Yet these numbers only begin to tell the story. The increased dependence on PAC contributions has been greatest for winners, those individuals who serve in Congress and who cast votes that shape our daily lives. In the Ninety-ninth Congress (1985–86), over 150 House members received 50 percent or more of their campaign funds from PACs, including 20 of the 27 committee chairs and party leaders. House winners in the 1984 election received an average of 41 percent of their campaign dollars from PACs. Of all winning House candidates in the 1974 election, only 28 percent received one-third or more of their campaign funds from PACs. By 1984, that figure had grown to 78 percent.

For senators, PAC contributions are also becoming a more important source of campaign dollars. Senators elected in 1976 received a total of $3.1 million from PACs; Senate winners in the 1984 election raised $20 million from OACs. In the 1984 elections, 23 winning Senate candidates raised more than $500,000 each from PACs.

Some have suggested that the growth in PACs is an important new form of citizen involvement in the political process. Yet PAC participation is often likely to be more of an involvement in the corporate process or the union process or the trade association process than it is in the political process. University of Minnesota professor Frank J. Sorauf has noted:

> To understand political participation through PACs, we need also to note the nature of the participation. Some of it is not even political activity; buying a ticket in a raffle, the proceeds of which go to a PAC, a party, or a candidate, does not qualify as a political act by most standards. Even the contributory act of writing a check or giving cash to a PAC is a somewhat limited form of participation that requires little time or immediate involvement; in a sense it buys political mercenaries who free the contributor from the need to be personally active in the campaign. It is one of the least active forms of political activity, well suited to the very busy or to those who find politics strange, boring, or distasteful.

In fact, the growth of PACs and the increased importance of PAC money have had a negative effect on two different parts of the political process—congressional elections and congressional decision making. First, PAC money tends to make congressional campaigns less competitive because of the overwhelming advantage enjoyed by incumbents in PAC fund-raising. The ratio of PAC contributions to incumbents over challengers in 1984 House races was 4.6 to 1.0; in the Senate, incumbents in 1984 enjoyed a 3.0 to 1.0 advantage in PAC receipts. On the average, 1984 House incumbents raised $100,000 more from PACs than did challengers. This $100,000 advantage was true even in the most highly competitive House races, those in which the incumbent received 55 percent or less of the vote. In these races, incumbents received an average of over $230,000 from PACs; their challengers received less than $110,000. The advantage enjoyed by incumbents is true for all kinds of PAC giving—for contributions by labor groups, corporate PACs, and trade and membership PACs.

Second, there is a growing awareness that PAC money makes a difference in the legislative process, a difference that is inimical to our democracy. PAC dollars are given by special interest groups to gain special access and special influence in Washington. Most often PAC contributions are made with a legislative purpose in mind. The late Justin Dart, former chairman of Dart Industries, once noted that dialogue with politicians "is a fine thing, but with a little money they hear you better." Senator Charles Mathias, Republican of Maryland, has stated:

> An official may not change his or her vote solely to accommodate the views of such contributors, but often officials, including myself, will agree to meet with an individual who made a large contribution so the official can hear the contributor's concerns and make the contributor aware these concerns have been considered. . . . Since an elected

official has only so much time available, the inevitable result of such special treatment for the large contributor is that other citizens are denied the opportunity they otherwise would have to confer with the elected official.

Common Cause and others have produced a number of studies that show a relationship between PAC contributions and legislative behavior. The examples run the gamut of legislative decisions, including hospital cost containment, the Clean Air Act, domestic content legislation, dairy price programs, gun control, maritime policies, and regulation by the Federal Trade Commission of professional groups or of used-car sales.

PAC gifts do not guarantee votes or support. PACs do not always win. But PAC contributions do provide donors with critical access and influence; they do affect legislative decisions and are increasingly dominating and paralyzing the legislative process.

In the last few years, something very important and fundamental has happened in this country—and that is the development of a growing awareness and recognition of the fact that the PAC system is a rotten system that must be changed. We know that concern is growing when Irving Shapiro, former chairman and chief executive officer of duPont and the former chairman of the Business Roundtable, describes the current system of financing congressional campaigns as "an invidious thing, it's corrupting, it does pollute the system." . . .

CONCLUSION

In the spring of 1973, Common Cause chairman John Gardner told the Senate Commerce Committee that "there is nothing in our political system today that creates more mischief, more corruption, and more alienation and distrust on the part of the public than does our system of financing elections. Despite major progress in improving the presidential campaign-financing system, that observation remains true today with regard to the congressional campaign-financing system. As former Watergate special prosecutor and current Common Cause chairman Archibald Cox has observed, inaction has resulted in "a Congress still more deeply trapped in the stranglehold of special interests which threatens to paralyze the process of democratic government." Congress needs to complete the reforms begun in the wake of Watergate by fundamentally transforming its own campaign-financing system and by making other adjustments needed to preserve the integrity of presidential public financing, campaign reporting requirements, and limitations on contributions by individuals and PACs.

A consensus has been reached in this country that PACs are inimical to our system of representative government. The question now remaining is whether that public consensus can be translated into congressional action.

No solution that may be adopted will be final and perfect. We will always need to reevaluate and adjust any campaign finance system. The presidential public financing system demonstrates the need for periodic adjustments. But more important, the experience of presidential public financing shows us that fundamental improvement in our campaign finance laws is indeed attainable.

We can and must have a better system for financing congressional campaigns. Representative government is at stake.

NO

Herbert E. Alexander

THE CASE FOR PACs

Seen in historical perspective, political action committees represent a functional system for political fund raising that developed, albeit unintentionally, from efforts to reform the political process. PACs represent an expression of an issue politics that resulted from attempts to remedy a sometimes unresponsive political system. And they represent an institutionalization of the campaign fund solicitation process that developed from the enactment of reform legislation intended to increase the number of small contributors.

Despite the unforeseen character of their development, PACs have made significant contributions to the political system:

1. *PACs increased participation in the political process.* The reform efforts that spawned PACs were designed to allow more voices to be heard in determining who will become our nation's elected officials. Thanks in part to PACs, that goal has been achieved.

Although it is difficult to determine how many individuals now participate in the political process through voluntarily contributing to political action committees, some useful information is available. The survey of company PACs by Civic Service, Inc., found that in the 1979–1980 election cycle more than 100,000 individuals contributed to the 275 PACs responding to the survey, and that the average number of donors to those PACS was 388. By extrapolation, it appears that all corporate PACs active in the 1979–1980 cycle received contributions from at least 210,000 individuals.

The largest conservative ideological group PACs, which rely on direct mail solicitations, received about 1.3 million contributions in 1979–1980, though individuals may well have contributed to more than one of those groups. It is difficult to estimate the total number of persons who gave to professional and membership association PACs, though information about specific groups is available. For example, an official of the National Association of Realtors PAC estimated that his group had 80,000 contributors in 1979, 87,000 in 1980, 92,000 in 1981 and about 95,000 in 1982. It is more difficult still to estimate the number of contributors to labor PACs, although here, too, information is available regarding specific groups. According to a National

From Herbert E. Alexander, "The Case for PACs," a Public Affairs Council monograph. Copyright © 1983 by the Public Affairs Council. Reprinted by permission.

Education Association official, for example, the NEA PAC received donations from about 600,000 persons in the 1979–1980 election cycle.

Surveys taken between 1952 and 1976 indicate that from 8 to 12 percent of the total adult population contributed to politics at some level in presidential election years, with the figure standing at 9 percent in 1976. According to a survey by the Center for Political Studies at the University of Michigan, however, 13.4 percent of the adult population—about 17.1 million persons—gave to candidates and causes during the 1979–1980 election cycle. Survey data suggest that the increase registered in 1980 is due to the increased number of persons giving to interest groups. Of those surveyed, 6.8 percent gave to candidates, 3.8 percent gave to parties, and 6.8 percent gave to interest groups. Since those figures add up to well over 13.4 percent, it is obvious that a significant number of persons contributed in two or all three categories.

2. *PACs allow individuals to increase the impact of their political activity.* PACs and their interest group sponsors not only encourage individual citizens to participate in the electoral process, they provide them with a sense of achievement or effectiveness that accompanies taking part in political activity with like-minded persons rather than merely acting alone.

3. *PACs are a popular mechanism for political fund raising because they respect the manner in which society is structured.* Occupational and interest groups have replaced the neighborhood as the center of activities and source of values and the ideologically ambiguous political parties as a source of political action. Individuals seem less willing to commit themselves to the broad agenda of the parties; they are interested mainly in single issues or clusters of issues. PACs, organized on the basis of specific occupational or socioeconomic or issue groupings, allow individuals to join with others who share their values and interests and to undertake action to achieve the political goals they perceive as most important to them.

4. *PACs and the interest groups they represent serve as a safeguard against undue influence by the government or by the media.* By energetically promoting their competing claims and views, such groups prevent the development of either a single, official viewpoint or a media bias. They demonstrate the lively pluralism so highly valued and forcefully guaranteed by the framers of the Constitution.

5. *PACs have made more money available for political campaigns.* By helping candidates pay the rising costs of conducting election campaigns, PACs help to assure the communication of the candidates' views and positions and thus to clarify campaign issues. They also encourage individuals without wealth to run for office.

6. *PACs have contributed to greater accountability in election campaign financing.* Corporations are legitimately concerned about public policy, but prior to the FECA they were uncertain about the legality of providing financial support to candidates who would voice their concerns. That many corporations resorted to subterfuges to circumvent the law is common knowledge. By sanctioning the use of PACs by corporations, the law has replaced the undisclosed and often questionable form of business participation in politics with the public and accountable form practiced by corporate and other business-related PACs today. However much money now is derived from corporate PACs, it is not clear that corporate PAC money today is greater proportionally than was business-derived money when

there were no effective limits on giving and when disclosure was less comprehensive.

HOW PACSs CAN RESPOND

PACs enjoy a growing constituency, but, in view of current anti-PAC publicity and endeavors, PAC supporters must engage in a concerted educational effort regarding their methods and goals if PACs are to avoid being restricted in their ability to participate in the political process. That effort should include, certainly, responding with specific and accurate information to criticisms made of PACs and making plain the many values PACs bring to the political process.

Educational efforts also might include using the methods of PAC opponents to the advantage of the PAC movement. For example, PAC opponents frequently correlate PAC contributions and legislative outcomes and conclude that the contributions resulted in specific legislative decisions. PAC critics publicized widely the fact that maritime unions contributed heavily to some members of the House Merchant Marine Committee who favored a cargo preference bill introduced in 1977 and supported by the unions. They implied the committee members were influenced by the contributions to report out a favorable bill. PAC supporters did little to discover and publicize the committee members' other sources of funds. The American Medical Association Political Action Committee, for example, contributed to every incumbent on the House Committee, yet AMPAC and the medical practitioners who support it had no vested interest in the cargo preference bill or in other legislation considered by the committee. Nor was much publicity given to the fact that the two committee members who received the greatest financial support from the unions represented districts in which there is a significant amount of port activity and that consequently they would understandably be responsive to maritime interests.

When critics use simplistic correlations to demonstrate undue PAC influence on the decisions of legislators, PAC supporters should endeavor to present the whole campaign finance picture: What percentage of the legislators' campaign funds came from the interest group or groups in question? Did those groups also contribute to other legislators whose committee assignments gave them no formative role in legislation of particular interest to the groups? Did groups with no special interest in the legislation in question contribute to the legislators dealing with it at the committee or subcommittee level? What factors in the legislators' home districts or states might have influenced the legislators' decisions? What non-monetary pressures were brought to bear on the legislators?

It also might be useful for PAC supporters to publicize "negative correlations," which would demonstrate that PAC contributions often do not correlate with specific legislative decisions.

PAC supporters also should question the unarticulated assumptions at the basis of much of the anti-PAC criticism.

• Money is not simply a necessary evil in the political process. By itself money is neutral; in politics as in other areas its uses and purposes determine its meaning.

• There is nothing inherently immoral or corrupting about corporate or labor contributions of money, any more than any other private contribution of funds.

• All campaign contributions are not attempts to gain special favors; rather, contributing political money is an important form of participation in a democracy.

• Money is not the sole, and often not even the most important, political resource. Many other factors affect electoral and legislative outcomes. (At the close of the 97th Congress, for example, an immigration reform bill that reportedly had widespread support in the House and the Senate died because of the effective lobbying efforts of employees, labor unions and minorities who believed they would be adversely affected by it; few, if any, campaign contributions were involved in the effort to forestall the legislation.)

• Curbing interest group contributions will not free legislators of the dilemma of choosing between electoral necessity and legislative duty. Even if PACs were eliminated, legislators would still be confronted with the sometimes conflicting demands between doing what will help them remain in office and serving what they perceive as the public good.

• A direct dialogue between candidates and individual voters without interest group influence is not possible in a representative democracy. Politics is about people, their ideas, interests and aspirations. Since people seek political fulfillment partly through groups, a politics in which supportive groups are shut out or seriously impaired is difficult to conceive.

There is danger, clearly, in our pluralistic society if groups are overly restricted in their political activity. It is useful to recall that five of the most significant movements of the last two decades—the civil rights movement, the Vietnam peace movement, the political reform movement, the women's rights movement, and the movement toward fiscal restraint—originated in the private sector, where the need for action was perceived and where needed interest organizations were established to carry it out. *These movements would not have taken place if like-minded citizens had not been permitted to combine forces and thereby enhance their political power.*

One hundred and fifty years ago, de Tocqueville recognized that in America "the liberty of association [had] become a necessary guarantee against the tyranny of the majority." The freedom to join in common cause with other citizens remains indispensable to our democratic system. The pursuit of self-interest is, as Irving Kristol has pointed out, a condition, not a problem.

POSTSCRIPT

Do Political Action Committees Undermine Democracy?

Interestingly, both Alexander and Wertheimer couch their arguments in terms of democratic values: open government, fairness to all, and popular participation. Alexander claims that PACs bring a wide variety of groups into the political process, give new groups a chance to be heard, and let corporations openly contribute funds instead of resorting to back-channel routes. Wertheimer pins much of his argument on the need for equality in the democratic process, and he worries that PACs make some voters "more equal" than others.

Edward Roeder has edited a useful directory of PACs that supplies information about their sources, their funds, and whom they support. See his *PACs Americana: The Directory of Political Action Committees and Their Interests*, 2nd ed. (Sunshine Service, 1986). Larry Sabato's *PAC Power* (Norton, 1984) is a comprehensive overview of PACs: what they are, how they operate, and their impact. Frank J. Sorauf's *What Price PACs?* (Priority Press, 1985) studies PAC financing and its implications today. For an excellent general study of interest groups, including PACs, see Graham K. Wilson's *Interest Groups in the United States* (Clarendon Press, 1981).

Other countries succeed in setting strict limits on campaign spending. Can we do it without inhibiting political expression? Should we substitute public financing of congressional elections? Or do we accept PACs as a vigorous expression of political freedom? In short, do PACs undermine or do they underline democracy?

ISSUE 4

Do the News Media Have a Liberal Bias?

YES: William A. Rusher, from *The Coming Battle for the Media: Curbing the Power of the Media Elite* (Morrow, 1988)

NO: Edward S. Herman and Noam Chomsky, from "Propaganda Mill," *The Progressive* (June 1988)

ISSUE SUMMARY

YES: Media analyst William Rusher argues that the media are biased against conservatives and that news coverage promotes liberal opinions.
NO: Professors Edward Herman and Noam Chomsky critique the mass media from the perspective of the left and find the media to be a "propaganda mill" in the service of the wealthy and powerful.

"A small group of men, numbering perhaps no more than a dozen 'anchormen,' commentators and executive producers . . . decide what forty to fifty million Americans will learn of the day's events in the nation and the world." The speaker was Spiro Agnew, vice president of the United States during the Nixon administration. The thesis of Agnew's speech, delivered to an audience of midwestern Republicans in 1969, was that the television news media are controlled by a small group of liberals who foist their liberal opinions on viewers under the guise of "news." The upshot of this control, said Agnew, "is that a narrow and distorted picture of America often emerges from the televised news." Many Americans, even many of those who were later shocked by revelations that Agnew took bribes while serving in public office, agreed with Agnew's critique of the "liberal media."

Politicians' complaints about unfair news coverage go back much further than Spiro Agnew and the Nixon administration. The third president of the United States, Thomas Jefferson, was an eloquent champion of the press, but after six years as president, he could hardly contain his bitterness. "The man who never looks into a newspaper," he wrote, "is better informed than he who reads them, inasmuch as he who knows nothing is nearer to truth than he whose mind is filled with falsehoods and errors."

The press today is much different than it was in Jefferson's day. The press then was a "mom-and-pop" operation. Newspapers were pressed in hand-operated frames in many little printing shops around the country; everything was local and decentralized, and each paper averaged a few hundred subscribers. Today, newspaper chains have taken over most of the once-independent local newspapers. The remaining independents rely heavily on national and international wire services. Almost all major magazines have national circulations; some newspapers, like *USA Today* and the *Wall Street Journal*, do too. Other newspapers, like the *New York Times* and the *Washington Post*, enjoy nationwide prestige and help set the nation's news agenda. Geographical centralization is even more obvious in the case of television. About 70 percent of national news on television comes from three networks whose programming originates in New York City.

A second important difference between the media of the eighteenth century and the media today has to do with the ideal of "objectivity." In past eras, newspapers were frankly partisan sheets, full of nasty barbs at the politicians and parties they didn't like; they made no distinction between "news" and "editorials." The ideal of objective journalism is a relatively recent development. It traces back to the early years of the twentieth century. Disgusted with the sensationalist "yellow journalism" of the time, intellectual leaders urged that newspapers cultivate a core of professionals who would concentrate on accurate reporting and who would leave their opinions to the editorial page. Journalism schools cropped up around the country, helping to promote the ideal of objectivity. Although some journalists now openly scoff at it, the ideal still commands the respect—in theory, if not always in practice—of working reporters.

The two historical developments, news centralization and news professionalism, play off against one another in the current debate over news "bias." The question of bias was irrelevant when the press was a scatter of little independent newspapers. If you didn't like the bias of one paper, you picked another one—or you started your own, which could be done with modest capital outlay. Bias started to become an important question when newspapers became dominated by chains and airwaves by networks, and when a few national press leaders like the *New York Times* and the *Washington Post* began to emerge. When one news anchor can address a nightly audience of 25 million people, the question of bias is no longer irrelevant.

But *is* there bias? If so, *whose* bias? These are the central questions. Defenders of the press usually concede that journalists, like all human beings, have biases, but they deny that they carry their biases into their writing. Journalists, they say, are professionals, trained to bring us news unembellished by personal opinion. They conclude that bias is in the eye of the beholder: left-wingers think the press is conservative, right-wingers call it liberal; both are unhappy that the press isn't biased in *their* direction.

Both the left and the right disagree. The left considers the press conservative because it is tied in with big business, indeed *is* a big business. The right insists that the bias of the press is overwhelmingly liberal because most reporters are liberal. In the following selections, Professors Noam Chomsky and Edward Herman develop a critique of the media from a "left" perspective, and media analyst William Rusher argues that the media are biased against conservatives.

YES

William A. Rusher

THE COMING BATTLE FOR THE MEDIA

It is the conviction of a great many people, not all of them conservative by any means, that news presentation by the media elite is heavily biased in favor of liberal views and attitudes.

It is important, right at the outset, to specify precisely what is being objected to. This is a free country, and journalists are every bit as entitled to their private political opinions as the rest of us. But the average newspaper or television news program, and certainly those we have categorized as the "media elite," purport to be offering us something more than the personal opinions of the reporter, or the chief editor, or even the collective opinions of the journalistic staff. In one way or another, to one extent or another, they all profess to be offering us the "news"—which is to say, an account of as many relevant events and developments, in the period in question, as can be given in the space or time available. Moreover, in offering this account, the media we are discussing implicitly claim to be acting with a reasonable degree of objectivity. Their critics sharply challenge that claim.

But just how much objectivity is it reasonable to expect? The question is more complicated than it may at first appear. There is a school of thought— popular, perhaps naturally, among a certain subcategory of journalists themselves—that a journalist is, or at least ought to be, a sort of vestal virgin: a chalice of total and incorruptible objectivity. But this, of course, is non- sense, and is certainly not expected by any reasonable person.

Journalists too are, after all, sons and daughters of Adam. Their conception was far from immaculate; they share our taint of Original Sin. They were born into our common society, received the same general education we all received, and had roughly the same formative experiences. How likely is it that, simply by choosing to pursue a career in journalism, they underwent some sort of miraculous transformation, to emerge shriven and pure, purged of all bias and dedicated henceforth solely to the pursuit of the unvarnished Truth? . . . Just how does one go about demonstrating that the media elite are, in the matter of their private opinions, overwhelmingly partial to liberal policies and liberal political personalities? A general impression, based on familiarity with their work-product as on display in the *New York Times* or the *Washington Post*, in *Time* or *Newsweek*, or on the evening news programs of one or another of the major networks, is absolutely worthless. You will be told that your perception is distorted by your own partiality to conservative policies and personalities. You will be assured that the liberals complain just as loudly as conservatives about maltreatment by the media (though on inspection it turns out to be the harder left—e.g., Alexander Cockburn—that complains; liberals typically, and understandably, complain very little about distortion by the media elite). You will be referred to news stories in which there was no liberal bias, and to news presentations well and truly balanced—shining exceptions that merely emphasize the rule.

There is, in fact, only one way to ascertain with precision anyone's political leaning, inclination, or prejudice, and that is to interview him or her in depth. Moreover, if the intention is to evaluate the opinions of an entire group, the sample interviewed must be large enough to be dependably representative. Fortunately there have recently been several conscientious surveys of the political views of America's media elite, and the results are thoroughly unambiguous. . . .

[A] remarkable survey, whose results were published in 1981 . . . was conducted in 1979 and 1980 by two professors of political science—S. Robert Lichter of George Washington University and Stanley Rothman of Smith College—as part of a larger inquiry into the attitudes of various elites, under the auspices of the Research Institute on International Change at Columbia University. The survey itself was supervised by Response Analysis, a survey research organization.

Lichter and Rothman began by defining the following organizations as America's "most influential media outlets": three daily newspapers—the *New York Times*, the *Washington Post*, and the *Wall Street Journal*; three weekly newsmagazines—*Time*, *Newsweek*, and *U.S. News and World Report*; the news departments of four networks—CBS, NBC, ABC, and PBS; and the news departments of certain major independent broadcasting stations.

Within these organizations they then selected at random, from among those responsible for news content, individuals to be approached for interviews. In the print media, these included "reporters, columnists, department heads, bureau chiefs, editors and executives responsible for news content." In the electronic media, those selected included "correspondents, anchormen, producers, film editors and news executives." . . .

It transpires that, of those who voted in these elections at all (and this was 82 percent in 1976, when all but the youngest among those interviewed in 1979–80 would have qualified), *never less than 80 percent of the media elite voted for the Democratic candidate.* . . .

Like many American liberals, the media elite accept the essential free-enterprise basis of the United States economy, but they are devoted to welfarism. Over two thirds (68 percent) believe "the government should substantially reduce the income gap between the rich and the poor," and nearly half (48 percent) think the government should guarantee a job to anyone who wants one.

On sociocultural issues, the media elite's support for liberal positions is overwhelming. Ninety percent believe it is a woman's right to decide whether or not to have an abortion. A solid majority (53 percent) can't even bring itself to affirm that adultery is wrong.

There is far more to the Lichter-Rothman survey than the above brief sample of its findings, but the basic thrust of the study is unmistakable: America's media elite are far to the left of American public opinion in general on the great majority of topics. . . .

THE EFFECT ON THE "NEWS"

Proving statistically that the media's demonstrated liberalism influences their handling of the news is no simple matter. The media clearly aren't going to do us the favor of admitting it, and the formidable human capacity for self-delusion makes it likely that many members of the media don't even realize it, at least not fully. A good many of them undoubtedly think their selection and treatment of stories is governed solely by their acute "news sense," where any objective observer would detect bias. And even when a member of the media knows full well that his handling of news stories is influenced by his biases, he is naturally prone to minimize that influence and make excuses for the residue.

Adding to the difficulty is the fact that evidence of bias, liberal or otherwise, is almost inevitably somewhat subjective. One man's "bias" is another man's "robust journalism," etc. Obvious as the bias may be to many thoughtful people, how can one nail it down?

One of the earliest and still one of the best efforts to do so was made by Edith Efron in her book *The News Twisters* (Nash, 1971). It is said that medieval philosophers had a high old time arguing

over how many teeth a horse has, until some spoilsport ended the game by going out and actually counting them. That was essentially Efron's solution, too. . . .

[Rusher quotes extensively from Efron's discussion of her methodology. She counted the number of words used in prime-time TV news programs that could be classified "for" and "against" the three major candidates for president in 1968: Alabama governor George Wallace (running as an independent), Democrat Hubert Humphrey, and Republican Richard Nixon. —Eds.]

Efron then sets forth, in bar-graph form, the total number of words spoken for and against the three presidential candidates on the three major networks during the period under study. In the case of George Wallace, the result was as follows:

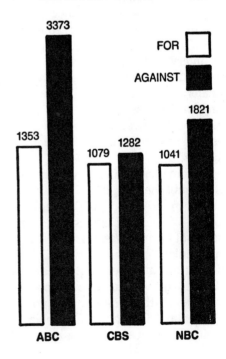

THE EFFECT ON THE "NEWS"

FOR □

AGAINST ■

ABC: 1353 (FOR), 3373 (AGAINST)
CBS: 1079 (FOR), 1282 (AGAINST)
NBC: 1041 (FOR), 1821 (AGAINST)

In the case of Hubert Humphrey, the graph looked like this:

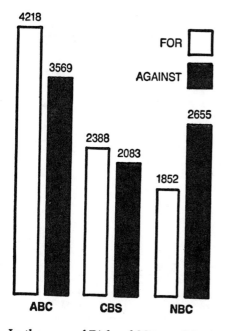

In the case of Richard Nixon, this was the result:

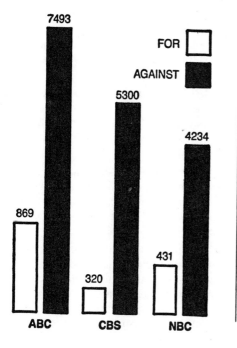

Now, how can the statistics regarding Nixon be interpreted, save as a product of bias? Bear in mind that this was long before Watergate—indeed, that in the next election (1972) Nixon would be re-elected by a landslide. Yet in 1968 the words spoken *against* Nixon on ABC (the network with the smallest imbalance in this respect) outnumbered the words spoken *for* him by nearly nine to one. At NBC the negative proportion was almost ten to one. At CBS it actually exceeded sixteen to one. . . .

Maura Clancey and Michael Robinson conducted another comprehensive study of the media's bias in reporting the "news," in connection with the 1984 presidential election, under the auspices of George Washington University and the American Enterprise Institute. . . .

Clancey and Robinson summed up their findings as follows:

There may be some questions about the validity of our measure, but there can be no question about the lopsidedness of what is uncovered. Assuming that a piece with a positive spin equals "good press," and assuming that negative spin equals "bad press," Ronald Reagan and George Bush proved overwhelmingly to be the "bad press" ticket of 1984. Figure 1 [see next page] contains the number of news seconds we scored as good press or bad press for each of the candidates. Ronald Reagan's bad press total was *ten times greater* than his good press total. (7,230 seconds vs. 730). In other words, his "spin ratio" was ten-to-one negative.

George Bush had a spin ratio that defied computation—1,500 seconds of "bad press" pieces and zero seconds of good press.

Walter Mondale and Geraldine Ferraro, on the other hand, had slightly *positive* spin ratios—1,970 seconds of

Figure 1

News seconds

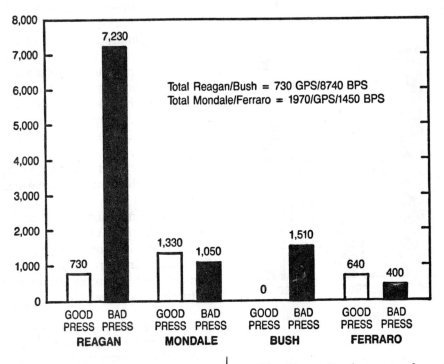

Total Reagan/Bush = 730 GPS/8740 BPS
Total Mondale/Ferraro = 1970/GPS/1450 BPS

good press about themselves as people or potential leaders, and 1,450 seconds of bad press. Given what we know about the bad news bias of television, the fact that anyone, let alone any ticket, got more positive spin than negative is news indeed.

But Clancey and Robinson are not even prepared to concede that their own lopsided results in 1984 conclusively demonstrated a liberal bias on the part of the media. On the contrary, they suggest, "liberal bias is not the only explanation, or even the best."

Instead, they posit the existence of what they call "the four I's"—non-ideological reasons for the bad press admittedly accorded Reagan and Bush in 1984. These are:

"Impishness"—a human tendency to want to turn a walkaway into a horse race "to keep one's own work interesting."

"Irritation"—annoyance at what the media perceived as Reagan's glib one-liners and his alleged "Teflon coating" (i.e., his seeming invulnerability to criticism).

"Incumbency"—a sense that the media have "a special mission to warn Americans about the advantages any incumbent has," especially when he is winning big.

"Irrevocability"—the feeling that a double standard is justified because 1984 was the last time Reagan would ever face the electorate. Under those circumstances, giving him a bad press became "a near-messianic mission."

Defenders of the media may well wonder whether pleading them guilty to the above unpleasant set of impulses would actually constitute much of an improvement over admitting that they have a liberal bias. But they can be spared that painful decision, because "the four I's" simply don't survive careful inspection. In pure theory they might explain the media's astonishing bias against Reagan in 1984, but not one of them applies to the equally well-established instance of bias discussed earlier: the media's treatment of Nixon in the 1968 campaign.

That campaign was no "walkaway" for Nixon; it was one of the closest presidential elections in United States history—43.4 percent for Nixon, 42.7 for Humphrey, and 13.5 for Wallace. And Nixon was certainly no Reagan, either in his mastery of glib one-liners or in possessing a "Teflon coating." Moreover, he was not the incumbent, or even the nominee of the incumbent's party. And 1968 was *not* the last time Nixon could or would face the electorate. Yet the media gave him the same biased treatment that Reagan received in 1984. The conclusion is unavoidable that the media's conduct had the same basis in both cases: a liberal bias neatly congruent with the demonstrated liberal preferences of the overwhelming majority of the media elite.

NO

Edward S. Herman
and Noam Chomsky

PROPAGANDA MILL

It is a primary function of the mass media in the United States to mobilize public support for the special interests that dominate the Government and the private sector.

This is our conclusion after years of studying the media. Perhaps it is an obvious point—but the common assumption seems to be that the media are independent and committed to discovering and reporting the truth. Leaders of the media claim that their news judgments rest on unbiased, objective criteria. We contend, on the other hand, that the powerful are able to fix the premises of discourse, decide what the general populace will be allowed to see, hear, and think about, and "manage" public opinion by mounting regular propaganda campaigns.

We do not claim this is all the mass media do, but we believe the propaganda function to be a very important aspect of their overall service.

In countries where the levers of power are in the hands of a state bureaucracy, monopolistic control of the media, often supplemented by official censorship, makes it clear that media serve the ends of the dominant elite. It is much more difficult to see a propaganda system at work where the media are private and formal censorship is absent.

This is especially true where the media actively compete, periodically attack and expose corporate and governmental malfeasance, and aggressively portray themselves as spokesmen for free speech and the general community interest. What is not evident (and remains undiscussed in the media) is the severely limited access to the private media system and the effect of money and power on the system's performance.

Critiques of this kind are often dismissed by Establishment commentators as "conspiracy theories," but this is merely an evasion. We don't rely on any kind of conspiracy hypothesis to explain the performance of the media; in fact, our treatment is much closer to a "free-market" analysis.

Most of the bias in the media arises from the selection of right-thinking people, the internalization of preconceptions until they are taken as self-

From Edward S. Herman and Noam Chomsky, "Propaganda Mill," *The Progressive* (June 1988). Adapted from *Manufacturing Consent: The Political Economy of the Mass Media* by Edward S. Herman and Noam Chomsky (Pantheon Books, 1988). Copyright © 1988 by Edward S. Herman and Noam Chomsky. Reprinted by permission of Pantheon Books, a division of Random House, Inc.

evident truths, and the practical adaptation of employees to the constraints of ownership, organization, market, and political power.

The censorship practiced within the media is largely self-censorship, by reporters and commentators who adjust to the "realities" as they perceive them. But there are important actors who do take positive initiatives to define and shape the news and to keep the media in line. This kind of guidance is provided by the Government, the leaders of the corporate community, the top media owners and executives, and assorted individuals and groups who are allowed to take the initiative.

The media are not a solid monolith on all issues. Where the powerful are in disagreement, the media will reflect a certain diversity of tactical judgments on how to attain generally shared aims. But views that challenge fundamental premises or suggest that systemic factors govern the exercise of State power will be excluded.

The pattern is pervasive. Consider the coverage from and about Nicaragua. The mass media rarely allow their news columns—or, for that matter, their opinion pages—to present materials suggesting that Nicaragua is more democratic than El Salvador and Guatemala; that its government does not murder ordinary citizens, as the governments of El Salvador and Guatemala do on a routine basis; that it has carried out socioeconomic reforms important to the majority that the other two governments somehow cannot attempt; that Nicaragua poses no military threat to its neighbors but has, in fact, been subjected to continuous attack by the United States and its clients and surrogates, and that the U.S. fear of the Nicaraguan government is based more on its virtues than on its alleged defects.

The mass media also steer clear of discussing the background and results of the closely analogous attempt of the United States to bring "democracy" to Guatemala in 1954 by means of a CIA-supported invasion, which terminated Guatemalan democracy for an indefinite period. Although the United States supported elite rule and organized terror in Guatemala (among many other countries) for decades, actually subverted or approved the subversion of democracy in Brazil, Chile, and the Philippines (again, among others), is now "constructively engaged" with terror regimes around the world, and had no concern about democracy in Nicaragua so long as the brutal Somoza regime was firmly in power, the media take U.S. Government claims of a concern for "democracy" in Nicaragua at face value.

In contrast, El Salvador and Guatemala, with far worse records, are presented as struggling toward democracy under "moderate" leaders, thus meriting sympathetic approval.

IN CRITICIZING MEDIA BIASES, WE OFTEN draw on the media themselves for at least some of the "facts." That the media provide some information about an issue, however, proves absolutely nothing about the adequacy or accuracy of media coverage. The media do, in fact, suppress a great deal of information, but even more important is the way they present a particular fact—its placement, tone, and frequency of repetition—and the framework of analysis in which it is placed. That a careful reader looking for a fact can sometimes find it, with diligence and a skeptical eye, tells us nothing about whether that fact received the attention and context it deserved, whether it was intelligible to most readers, or whether it was effectively distorted or suppressed.

The standard media pattern of indignant campaigns and suppressions, of shading and emphasis, of carefully selected context, premises, and general agenda, is highly useful to those who wield power. If, for example, they are able to channel public concern and outrage to the abuses of enemy states, they can mobilize the population for an ideological crusade.

Thus, a constant focus on the victims of communism helps persuade the public that the enemy is evil, while setting the stage for intervention, subversion, support for terrorist regimes, an endless arms race, and constant military conflict—all in a noble cause. At the same time, the devotion of our leaders—and our media—to this narrow set of victims raises public patriotism and self-esteem, demonstrating the essential humanity of our nation and our people.

The public does not notice media silence about victims of America's client states, which is as important as the media's concentration on victims of America's enemies. It would have been difficult for the Guatemalan government to murder tens of thousands over the past decade if the U.S. press had provided the kind of coverage it gave to the difficulties of Andrei Sakharov in the Soviet Union or the murder of Jerzy Popieluszko in Poland. It would have been impossible to wage a brutal war against South Vietnam and the rest of Indochina, leaving a legacy of misery and destruction that may never be overcome, if the media had not rallied to the cause, portraying murderous aggression as a defense of freedom.

Propaganda campaigns may be instituted either by the Government or by one or more of the top media firms. The campaigns to discredit the government of Nicaragua, to support the Salvadoran elections as an exercise in legitimizing democracy, and to use the Soviet shooting down of the Korean airliner KAL 007 as a means of mobilizing support for the arms buildup were instituted and propelled by the Government. The campaigns to publicize the crimes of Pol Pot in Cambodia and the allegations of a KGB plot to assassinate the Pope were initiated by the *Reader's Digest*, with strong follow-up support from NBC television, *The New York Times*, and other major media companies.

Some propaganda campaigns are jointly initiated by the Government and the media; all of them require the media's cooperation.

THE MASS MEDIA ARE DRAWN INTO A SYMbiotic relationship with powerful sources of information by economic necessity and reciprocity of interest. The media need a steady, reliable flow of the raw material of news. They have daily news demands and imperative news schedules. They cannot afford to have reporters and cameras at all places where important stories may break, so they must concentrate their resources where significant news often occurs, where important rumors and leaks abound, and where regular press conferences are held.

The White House, the Pentagon, and the State Department are central nodes of such news activity at the national level. On a local basis, city hall and the police department are regular news beats for reporters. Corporations and trade groups are also regular and credible purveyors of stories deemed newsworthy. These bureaucracies turn out a large volume of material that meets the demands of news organizations for reliable, scheduled flows. They also have the great merit of being recognizable and credible because of their status and prestige.

Another reason for the heavy weight given to official sources is that the mass media claim to be "objective" dispensers of the news. Partly to maintain the image of objectivity, but also to protect themselves from criticism of bias and the threat of libel suits, they need material that can be portrayed as presumptively accurate. This also reduces cost: Taking information from sources that may be presumed credible reduces investigative expense, whereas material from sources that are not *prima facie* credible, or that will draw criticism and threats, requires careful checking and costly research.

The Government and corporate bureaucracies that constitute primary news sources maintain vast public-relations operations that ensure special access to the media. The Pentagon, for example, has a public-information service that involves many thousands of employees, spending hundreds of millions of dollars every year and dwarfing not only the public-information resources of any dissenting individual or group but the aggregate of *all* dissenters.

During a brief interlude of relative openness in 1979 and 1980, the U.S. Air Force revealed that its public-information outreach included 140 newspapers with a weekly total circulation of 690,000; *Airman* magazine with a monthly circulation of 125,000; thirty-four radio and seventeen television stations, primarily overseas; 45,000 headquarters and unit news releases; 615,000 hometown news releases; 6,600 news media interviews; 3,200 news conferences; 500 news media orientation flights; fifty meetings with editorial boards, and 11,000 speeches. Note that this is just the Air Force. In 1982, *Air Force Journal International* indicated that the Pentagon was publishing 1,203 periodicals.

To put this into perspective, consider the scope of public information activities of the American Friends Service Committee and the National Council of the Churches of Christ, two of the largest nonprofit organizations that consistently challenge the views of the Pentagon. The Friends' main office had an information services budget of less than $500,000 and a staff of eleven in 1984–1985. It issued about 200 press releases a year, held thirty press conferences, and produced one film and two or three slide shows. The Council of Churches office of information has an annual budget of about $350,000, issues about 100 news releases, and holds four press conferences a year.

Only the corporate sector has the resources to produce public information and propaganda on the scale of the Pentagon and other Government bodies. These large actors provide the media with facilities and with advance copies of speeches and reports. They schedule news conferences at hours geared to news deadlines. They write press releases in usable language. They carefully organize "photo-opportunity" sessions.

In effect, the large bureaucracies of the powerful subsidize the mass media, and thereby gain special access. They become "routine" news sources, while non-routine sources must struggle for access and may be ignored.

Because of the services they provide, the continuous contact they sustain, and the mutual dependency they foster, the powerful can use personal relationships, threats, and rewards to extend their influence over the news media. The media may feel obligated to carry extremely dubious stories, or to mute criticism, to avoid offending sources and disturbing a close relationship. When one depends on authorities for daily news, it is difficult to call them liars even if they tell whoppers.

Powerful sources may also use their prestige and importance as a lever to deny critics access to the media. The Defense Department, for example, refused to participate in discussions of military issues on National Public Radio if experts from the Center for Defense Information were invited to appear on the same program. Assistant Secretary of State Elliott Abrams would not appear on a Harvard University program dealing with human rights in Central America unless former Ambassador Robert White were excluded. Claire Sterling, a principal propagandist for the "Bulgarian connection" to the plot to assassinate the Pope, refused to take part in television programs on which her critics would appear.

The relation between power and sourcing extends beyond official and corporate provision of news to shaping the supply of "experts." The dominance of official sources is undermined when highly respectable unofficial sources give dissident views. This problem is alleviated by "coopting the experts"—that is, putting them on the payroll as consultants, funding their research, and organizing think tanks that will hire them directly and help disseminate their messages.

The process of creating a body of experts who will confirm and distribute the opinions favored by the Government and "the market" has been carried out on a deliberate basis and a massive scale. In 1972, Judge Lewis Powell, later elevated to the Supreme Court, wrote a memo to the U.S. Chamber of Commerce in which he urged business "to buy the top academic reputations in the country to add credibility to corporate studies and give business a stronger voice on the campuses."

During the 1970s and early 1980s, new institutions were established and old ones reactivated to help propagandize the corporate viewpoint. Hundreds of intellectuals were brought to these institutions, their work funded, and their output disseminated to the media by a sophisticated propaganda effort.

The media themselves also provide "experts" who regularly echo the official view. John Barron and Claire Sterling are household names as authorities on the KGB and terrorism because the *Reader's Digest* has funded, published, and publicized their work. The Soviet defector Arkady Shevchenko became an expert on Soviet arms and intelligence because *Time*, ABC television, and *The New York Times* chose to feature him despite his badly tarnished credentials. By giving these vehicles of the preferred view much exposure, the media confer status and make them the obvious candidates for opinion and analysis.

Another class of experts whose prominence is largely a function of their serviceability to power consists of former radicals who have "come to see the light." The motives that induce these individuals to switch gods, from Stalin (or Mao) and communism to Reagan and free enterprise, may vary, but so far as the media are concerned, the ex-radicals have simply seen the error of their ways. The former sinners, whose previous work was ignored or ridiculed by the mass media, are suddenly elevated to prominence and anointed as experts.

MEDIA PROPAGANDA CAMPAIGNS HAVE generally been useful to elite interests. The Red Scare of 1919–1920 helped abort the postwar union-organizing drive in steel and other major industries. The Truman-McCarthy Red Scare of the early 1950s helped inaugurate the Cold War and the permanent war economy, and also weakened the progressive coalition that had taken shape during the New Deal years.

The chronic focus on the plight of Soviet dissidents, on enemy killings in Cambodia, and on the Bulgarian Connection helped weaken the Vietnam Syndrome, justify a huge arms buildup and a more aggressive foreign policy, and divert attention from the upward distribution of income that was the heart of the Reagan Administration's domestic economic program. The recent propaganda attacks on Nicaragua have averted eyes from the savageries of the war in El Salvador and helped justify the escalating U.S. investment in counterrevolution in Central America.

Conversely, propaganda campaigns are *not* mobilized where coverage of victimization, though it may be massive, sustained, and dramatic, fails to serve the interests of the elite.

The focus on Cambodia in the Pol Pot era was serviceable, for example, because Cambodia had fallen to the communists and useful lessons could be drawn from the experience of their victims. But the many Cambodian victims of U.S. bombing *before* the communists came to power were scrupulously ignored by the U.S. press. After Pol Pot was ousted by the Vietnamese, the United States quietly shifted its support to this "worse than Hitler" villain, with little or no notice in the press, which once again adjusted to the official political agenda.

Attention to the Indonesian massacres of 1965–1966, or to the victims of the Indonesian invasion of East Timor since 1975, would also be distinctly unhelpful as bases of media campaigns, because Indonesia is a U.S. ally and client that maintains an open door to Western investment. The same is true of the victims of state terror in Chile and Guatemala— U.S. clients whose basic institutional structure, including the state terror system, were put in place by, or with crucial assistance from, the United States.

No propaganda campaigns are mounted in the mass media on behalf of such victims. To publicize their plight would, after all, conflict with the interests of the wealthy and powerful.

POSTSCRIPT

Do the News Media Have a Liberal Bias?

As the opposing arguments in this section indicate, we can find critics on both the left and the right who agree that the media are biased. What divides such critics is the question of whether the bias is left-wing or right-wing. Defenders of the news media may seize upon this disagreement to bolster their own claim that "bias is in the eye of the beholder." But it could also mean that the news media are unfair to both sides. If that were true, however, it would seem to take some of the force out of the argument that the news media have a distinct ideological tilt.

Edward Jay Epstein's *News From Nowhere* (Random House, 1973) remains one of the great studies of the factors that influence television news shows. A study by S. Robert Lichter et al., *The Media Elite* (Adler and Adler, 1986), tends to support Rusher's contention that the media slant leftward, whereas Ben Bagdikian's *The Media Monopoly* (Beacon Press, 1983) lends support to Chomsky and Herman. David Halberstam's *The Powers That Be* (Knopf, 1979), a historical study of CBS, the *Washington Post*, *Time* magazine, and the *Los Angeles Times*, describes some of the political and ideological struggles that have taken place within major media organizations.

Edward Jay Epstein's book, previously cited, uses as an epigraph a statement by Richard Salant, president of CBS News in the 1970s: "Our reporters do not cover stories from *their* point of view. They are presenting them from *nobody's* point of view." Most probably, Salant had not intended to be facetious or ironic, but the statement so amused Epstein that he parodied it in the title of his book: *News From Nowhere*!

PART 2

The Institutions of Government

The Constitution provides for three governing bodies: the president, Congress, and the Supreme Court. Over the years our government has generated another organ with a life of its own: the bureaucracy. In this section, we examine issues that concern all the branches of government (executive, legislative, and judicial). Many of these debates are contemporary manifestations of issues that have been argued since the country was founded.

Is Congress Too Weak?

Has the Power of the Presidency Been Eroded?

Does the Government Regulate Too Much?

Should the Federal Courts Be Bound by the "Original Intent" of the Framers?

ISSUE 5

Is Congress Too Weak?

YES: Gregg Easterbrook, from "What's Wrong With Congress?" *The Atlantic* (December 1984)

NO: Gary Orfield, from *Congressional Power: Congress and Social Change* (HBJ, 1975)

ISSUE SUMMARY

YES: Journalist Gregg Easterbrook believes that before Congress can lead the nation, it must be able to lead itself, and it has notably failed to do so.

NO: Professor Gary Orfield argues that Congress does a good job of reflecting the attitudes and trends of the electorate as a whole. If Congress seems unresponsive, he says, it is not the fault of the institution but a comment on the priorities of the country at the moment.

Democratic President Harry Truman castigated a "do-nothing" Republican Congress, and Republican president Ronald Reagan criticized an obstructionist Democratic House of Representatives. Presidents often find Congress to be, if not too strong, at least too independent. President George Bush, like his predecessor, has urged that the president be given an "item veto," the power to veto sections of a proposed law, an authority that would weaken Congress and strengthen the president.

Champions of Congress, on the other hand, deplore the absence of sufficient power to keep the president in line. Extensive congressional hearings on the Watergate and Iran-Contra scandals challenged the unchecked (and what they claimed was the unconstitutional) exercise of presidential power, but they failed to lead to any real enlargement of congressional power.

Can Representative Government Do the Job? was the title of a thoughtful 1945 book, and more than four decades later many Americans remain uncertain about the answer to that question.

There is a widespread belief that Congress is a clumsy, unwieldy institution. The structure of Congress impresses (or depresses) its critics as being a horse-and-buggy vehicle in a jet age. Power is fragmented among many committees in the absence of national parties, which might impose discipline on legislators and coherence on legislation. Within the committees, the chairmen have the power; until recently, chairmen were chosen strictly on the basis of seniority (length of service) rather than for their leadership abilities. Woodrow Wilson called America "a government by the chairmen of standing committees of Congress." Although much power has since shifted to the president, congressional chairmen remain subject to few checks.

Perhaps the decline of Congress in this century is partly due to its outmoded structure, but it is easy to see how the two world wars, the Korean and Vietnam wars, and the Great Depression, as well as other issues that transcend national boundaries, contributed to the decline. Increasingly, we have looked to the president rather than to Congress for inspiration, initiative, and leadership. The president, after all, is an individual, and we can personalize his power; we can identify him and identify *with* him, while Congress remains a faceless abstraction.

The president can act with a promptness and decisiveness that the two houses and their 535 members cannot. He alone is nationally elected and may, therefore, come closer to being a tribune of the people. He alone possesses the power of life and death as the negotiator of international relations and commander in chief of the armed forces.

It was not surprising, therefore, that liberals looked to the president for the bold action that was not forthcoming from a lethargic and leaderless Congress. But many who had supported presidential dominance eventually ended up warning against the "Imperial Presidency" as a result of Watergate, the Iran-Contra scandal, the abuse of power, the evidence of unnecessary presidential secrecy and calculated deceit, and a new awareness of unchecked presidential decision-making.

The fear that presidential power may be abused has kindled the hope that representative government can be improved. Toward that end, the seniority system (at least for Democrats) is no longer a certain route to committee chairmanships. The requirement of open committee meetings and increased access to once-confidential files has increased public (particularly the press's) scrutiny of governmental behavior. Congress has set up its own budget committees, and the War Powers Act was designed to inhibit presidential war making in the absence of a congressional declaration of war.

Despite these reforms, there has been harsh public and press criticism of Congress for raising its pay; for accepting large contributions from and lobbying on behalf of now bankrupt and often corruptly run savings and loan associations and political action committees; and for the kind of unethical behavior that led to the resignation of the Speaker of the House of Representatives. There have also been investigations of members of both houses of Congress.

Perhaps, as Gary Orfield suggests, what is necessary is not technical reform but political will—that is, a public desire to have Congress exercise its power more vigorously. If the national legislature is less liberal than some reformers wish it might be, Orfield argues, it is because the American people by and large want it that way. Gregg Easterbrook is convinced that Congress is too weak. He would enhance legislative power by reforming the fragmentation of legislative power, the inability to modernize the budget process, and the proliferation of lobbies.

YES

Gregg Easterbrook

WHAT'S WRONG WITH CONGRESS?

Representative Michael Synar, of Oklahoma, swears that this actually happened: He was addressing a Cub Scout pack in Grove, Oklahoma, not far from his home town of Muskogee. Synar asked the young boys if they could tell him the difference between the Cub Scouts and the United States Congress. One boy raised his hand and said, "We have adult supervision."

Is anyone in charge on Capitol Hill? October's two-week-long melodrama over shutting down the government was not an isolated instance. Recently Congress voted for a $749 billion package of tax cuts, and only a few months later was locked in debate over a constitutional amendment for a balanced budget. The House voted in favor of Ronald Reagan's plan to almost double the number of nuclear warheads in the U.S. arsenal, and not long after voted in favor of the nuclear freeze. Only once in the past six years has Congress finished the budget appropriations before the beginning of the fiscal year; many spending bills have not been completed until months after the spending they supposedly control has begun. Long periods of legislative stalling are followed by spasms in which bills are passed with wild abandon, and these often contain "unprinted amendments" whose contents congressmen have never had an opportunity to read. Many provisions of "tax leasing" became law that way, as, in 1981, did the phone number of a woman named Rita. Rita's number had been scribbled in the margin of the only copy of an amendment being voted on, and the following day it was duly transcribed into the printed copy of the bill.

"The system is a mess, and what's amazing is how many members of Congress are fully aware that the system is a mess," says Alan Dixon, a senator from Illinois. Congress has, of course, seemed out of control at many points in the past. During the late 1930s, as signs of war grew, Congress was synonymous with irresponsibility; during the McCarthy era, with cowardice. In 1959 it ground to a halt over the minor issue of Dwight Eisenhower's nomination of Lewis Strauss as secretary of commerce and the even less important issue of an Air Force Reserve honorary promotion for the actor Jimmy Stewart. Through the 1960s it huffed and puffed about the Vietnam

From Gregg Easterbrook, "What's Wrong with Congress?" *The Atlantic* (December 1984). Copyright © 1984 by Gregg Easterbrook. Reprinted by permission of the author.

War, but never failed to approve funds for the fighting. In 1972, after hours of acrimonious debate, it voted to raise the federal debt ceiling for a single day. A degree of built-in vacillation was part of the Founding Fathers' plan for the legislature. But have recent changes in the structure both of U.S. politics and of Congress as an institution pushed Congress across the fine line separating creative friction from chaos?

"Congress today is a totally different institution from what it was when I arrived, in 1961," says Morris Udall, of Arizona, one of the House's senior members. "The magnitude of change is no illusion." The end of the seniority system; the arabesque budget "process" and other time-consuming new additions like the War Powers Act; the transformation from party loyalty to political-action-committee (PAC) loyalty; the increased emphasis on media campaigning; the vogue of running against Washington and yet being a member of the Washington establishment; the development of ideological anti-campaigns; a dramatic increase in congressional-subcommittee power and staff size, and a parallel increase in the scope and intensity of lobbying—all are creations of the past fifteen years. Some have served to make the nation's legislature more democratic and to improve its contact with the public. Others have made congressmen more frantic and timorous. But every change has in some respect caused Congress to become more difficult to run. Right now there isn't anyone in charge, and there may never be again.

EVERYWHERE A MR. CHAIRMAN

Hardly anyone laments the dismantling of the seniority rules—not even people like Udall, who would benefit if the old system still existed. From roughly the turn of the century until 1975 rank was based solely on how many years a member had been in Congress. The chairman of a committee could create or disband subcommittees, choose the subcommittee chairmen (often choosing himself), dictate when the subcommittees held hearings and whether bills were "referred" to them, hire the committee staff, and exert total control over when the committee itself would hold hearings or report bills to the floor. All these powers rested exclusively with twenty to twenty-five men in each chamber; others in Congress would wield power only by outvoting the senior members on the floor, and then only when the senior members permitted such votes to occur.

Seniority had long been considered unassailable, for the reason that senior members would use their powers to block any reform. But by the late 1960s the resistance of the southern committee chairmen to the obvious need for civil-rights reform had eroded seniority to the point at which challenges became possible. Every two years, as a new Congress was convened and new internal rules were passed, younger members would press for further concessions. "In 1971 we managed to pass a resolution saying that seniority would not be the sole criterion for chairmanship and that there ought to be a vote," Udall explains. "It was vaguely worded and we didn't try to take the issue any further. In 1973 for the first time, we held such votes. Every chairman was retained, but it established the precedent—that there had to be a vote. Then in 1975 we won."

It was a pivotal year for the structure of Congress. Ninety-two new representatives, mostly Democrats—the "Class of

'74"—had been elected to the House in the wake of Watergate. Government institutions in general were in a state of low regard. Conservative southerners had been shamed by how long they had stood by Richard Nixon; and two powerful old-school committee chairmen, Wilbur Mills, of the Ways and Means Committee, and Wayne Hays, of the House Administration Committee, were going off the deep end. The Class of '74 provided the extra margin of votes needed to end seniority in the House. Three entrenched chairmen — Wright Patman, of the Banking Committee, F. Edward Hebert, of Armed Services, and W. R. Poage, of Agriculture—were overthrown. More significant in the long run, a "subcommittee bill of rights" was passed. Essentially, subcommittees won the right to hold hearings on any subject at any time. Committee members would be able to "bid" for subcommittee chairmanships; full committee chairmen could no longer control these slots or hold more than one subcommittee chairmanship themselves. Each subcommittee chairman would get funds for at least one staff aide who would work for him personally, not for the committee. The total number of subcommittees would be expanded. A similar though more genteel sequence of change took place in the Senate.

The autocracy of the chair broken, Congress was transformed from an institution in which power was closely held by a few to an institution in which almost everyone had just enough strength to toss a monkey wrench. In 1964 there were forty-seven meaningful chairmanships available in the House and Senate. Between the dispersion of subcommittee posts and the increase in the total number of committees and subcommittees, 326 Mr. Chairman positions were avail-able in 1984. Allowing for those who hold more than one chairmanship, 202 of Congress's 535 members—38 percent—are now in charge of something.

More than any other factor, the deregulation of subcommittees has increased Congress's workload and decreased its cohesion. In 1970, before the change, congressional committees held an average of twenty-three meetings a day, and it remains at that level today. Senators now average twelve committee and subcommittee assignments each. With the trend toward "government in the sunshine" the number of closed committee hearings has dropped substantially—from 35 percent of all hearings in 1960 to seven percent in 1975. This serves the public's right to know but also increases the amount of time congressmen spend posturing for public consumption instead of saying what they think, which is practical only in closed hearings. The subcommittee bill of rights established "multiple referral," under which several subcommittees could consider the same bill or topic. The result is increased redundancy, more speechifying, and almost unlimited potential for turf fights.

According to John Tower, chairman of the Senate Armed Services Committee, "Our committee spends a large proportion of its time trying to fend off competition from other committees and monitoring what the other committees are doing." In the Senate the Armed Services, Appropriations, Governmental Affairs, Budget, Foreign Relations, and Veterans' Affairs committees all have an interest in military legislation; subcommittees of the same committee may also have overlapping jurisdictions, such as the Arms Control and European Affairs subcommittees of Foreign Relations. Multiple subcommittees each with multiple jurisdictions are a primary cause of the dizzy progression of non-events in Congress. Headlines like SENATE MOVES TO BAN IMPORTS and HOUSE HALTS FUNDS often refer to subcommittee actions that will be modified many times before they take effect or, more likely, vanish without a trace. Some sort of milestone was achieved last June when both the International Economic Policy Subcommittee of the Senate Foreign Relations Committee and the International Trade Subcommittee of the Senate Finance Committee held hearings covering the same topic—Japanese auto imports—on the same day, at the same time, with many of the same witnesses.

Driving the systsem is the unleashed desire of congressmen to be in command of something—anything. Culture shock for new congressmen arriving in Washington can be severe. Having just won a grueling electoral test and bearing the status of big wheels at home, in Washington they discover that they are among thousands of potentially important people competing for influence and attention. Young congressmen also find themselves assigned to cramped, dingy offices with Naugahyde furnishings and no majestic view of the Capitol dome. The yearning for a Washington badge of recognition and the additional perquisites that would make Capitol Hill life what they imagined it to be can set in almost immediately.

A chairmanship is particularly important because television is permitted in hearing rooms. Almost from the onset of television, congressmen have realized the promotional potential of the carefully scripted hearing: the McCarthy and Kefauver hearings of the 1950s, which were among the first "television events," made their eponyms famous.

Fame may be an elusive goal, but publicity is not. The proliferation of networks and newscasts meshes perfectly with the proliferation of Capitol Hill hearings. Congress itself is difficult for television to cover, because no single person is in charge and few actions are final. A well-done hearing, in contrast, has a master of ceremonies, a story line, and an easily summarized conclusion when a witness commits a gaffe, announces a "policy shift," or clashes angrily with committee members. Hearings, unlike floor action, also allow congressmen to introduce props—the masked witness being a perennial favorite, piles of money or gimmicks like chattering teeth being reliable avenues to television coverage.

Once created, a subcommittee takes on a life of its own, if for no other reason than that the staff must justify its existence. In 1970 the House Committee on the District of Columbia had fifteen staff members; today it has thirty. The Senate Rules Committee had thirteen staff members in 1970 and today has twenty-seven. The House Appropriations Committee has more than twice as many staff members as it had in 1970, and the Merchant Marine and Fisheries Committee's staff has risen from twenty-one to eighty-nine. Debra Knopman, a former staff aide to Senator Daniel Moynihan, says, "The staffs are so large everybody wants to have his say and leave his own little stamp. Pretty soon the weight of people wanting attention becomes greater than the force moving the legislation, and the whole thing grinds to a halt." . . .

THE BUDGET THAT WOULDN'T DIE

The way Congress spends money was converted into a "process" with the passage, in 1974, of the Congressional Budget and Impoundment Control Act. Its immediate purpose was to prevent Richard Nixon from "impounding," or refusing to spend, money that Congress had appropriated. But the Budget Act also had a long-term goal: solving a structural defect in Congress's spending machine.

Before 1974 the House and Senate each had three kinds of committees involved with the budget: authorizing, appropriating, and revenue. The authorizing committees, like Agriculture, Transportation, Energy, and Interior, are the most familiar; they "authorize" federal activity by writing legislation in their subject areas. But though they can start or end programs, they cannot approve expenditures—only the two appropriating committees can do that. Since the amount spent on a program usually determines that program's effect on policy, the potential for overlapping and disputation is boundless. Neither authorizing nor appropriating committees, meanwhile, have the power to raise the money that backs up the checks—only the Finance Committee, in the Senate, and the Ways and Means Committee, in the House, do. Because of this separation it became all too easy for authorizing and appropriating committees to ignore the fiscal consequences of their actions—getting the money was somebody else's job—and for the revenue committees, in turn, to demand that the other fellow crack down on spending.

During the 1950s and 1960s, when deficits were relatively stable, this state of affairs was tolerable. According to Robert Giaimo, who served in the House from 1958 to 1980 and was the Budget Committee chairman in the late 1970s, "No one, including myself, in Congress in the 1960s ever asked what anything would

cost. All we thought about was, Does this sound like a good program? Can we get it through?"

The budget process was intended to bring together the questions of how much to spend, how to spend it, and where the funds would come from with a single resolution that would both guide Congress and impose a series of spending ceilings to control the deficit. Congress would have, say, a certain ceiling for transporation, and if it wanted to add funds to subway construction, it would have to remove a like amount from highways.

Ideally this would have been accomplished through some merging of the authorizing, appropriating, and revenue committees. But merger would have required that at least two powerful chairmen, plus many subcommittee chairmen, surrender their posts. So an entirely new procedural tier, the budget committees, complete with two important new chairmanships, was set on top. The result is what Howard Baker calls "a three-layer cake." In theory, on receiving the President's budget requests, in early winter, the budget committees quickly produce a nonbinding first resolution to set general ceilings. Then the authorizing committees write policy-setting legislation within those ceilings, and the appropriating committees—after learning of the authorizing committees' policy objectives—award the money. Near the end of this cycle the budget committees produce a second resolution to reconcile the inevitable differences between what the budget ceilings allow and what the committees are actually spending. This resolution is binding, and after it is passed, in theory the remaining pieces fall smoothly into place.

In practice the budget process isn't working anything like that. Budget resolutions have become the subjects of such contention that this year the first resolution, due on May 15, wasn't passed until October 1—even though it was nonbinding. Appropriating and authorizing committees work concurrently and nearly year-round, the appropriating committees choosing dollar amounts before, from the standpoint of policy, they know how the money will be used. The Budget Act breaks down spending into functional categories different from those employed by the committee structure, so when a budget resolution is being debated, wrestling goes on over which portion of which ceiling should apply to which committee, a procedure known as "crosswalk." Thus the process leads to a continuous frenzy of activity but few decisions that count.

In order to prepare the fiscal 1984 defense budget, the Senate Appropriations Committee held seventeen days of hearings, producing about 5,300 pages of testimony. The Senate Armed Services Committee held twenty-seven days of hearings on the defense budget and called 192 witnesses, many of whom also appeared before the Appropriations Committee to make the same statements. The Senate Budget Committee held hearings on the subject as well, producing two resolutions that had to be debated and voted on by the full Senate.

Meanwhile, in the House, the Armed Services, Appropriations, and Budget committees were duplicating this work, and the full chamber was voting on a different budget resolution. And none of it was final.

When the defense bill itself came to the Senate floor, it sparked weeks of debate; the (different) House bill caused a similar swirl on the floor. Even after that the defense budget wasn't finished. A House-Senate conference committee had to be created to resolve the discrepancies between the two versions, and then the conference-committee bill had to be debated and voted on by both chambers. Spending levels for the Defense Department weren't finally set until mid-November of 1983, seven weeks after the fiscal year had begun. . . .

MULTIPLE LOBBYING

There are so many lobbyists today largely because there are so many opportunities to lobby. The breakdown of the seniority system and the weakening of congressional leadership has drastically increased the number of people on whom the touch must be put.

A well-informed veteran lobbyist says, "There used to be two to five guys on each side [House and Senate] who had absolute control over any category of bills you might want. All you had to do was get to them. Now getting the top guys is no guarantee. You have to lobby every member on every relevant subcommittee and even [lobby] the membership at large."

Another lobbyist, Eiler Ravnholt, who was for twelve years the administrative assistant to Senator Daniel Inouye, of Hawaii, and who now represents the Hawaiian Sugar Planters Association, adds that it has become necessary to lobby the expanded staff as well. "In the present environment congressmen spend so much time campaigning that they have no choice but to cede much of the legislative authority to their staffs," Ravnholt says. "During the 1960s it was not unusual to walk into the Senate library and see Sam Ervin sitting at a desk, researching a bill. Ervin was an exception, but not that much of an exception;

until fairly recently many congressmen played active roles in the legislative detail work. Now they can't. Nobody can. The staff does the detail work, and so you must lobby the staff." And where before there were a few important individuals on the House and Senate staffs, now there are thousands.

And thousands of lobbyists. There are 6,500 registered lobbyists in Washington (twelve for every congressman), but the figure does not include trade-association officers, lawyers working on retainer to clients, or liaison officials of corporations with Washington offices. The generally accepted total is about 20,000, or thirty-seven lobbyists for every congressman. Determined interest groups often hire several lobbyists, whose contacts grant access to different sectors of Congress. Brewers pressing for a beer-distribution-monopoly bill have, for example, hired the firm of Wagner and Baroody (all-purpose lobbying), Kip O'Neill, son of Tip O'Neill (access to Democrats), the former congressman John Napier, of South Carolina (access to Republicans), and Romano Romani, a former aide to Senator Dennis DeConcini (access to senators). So many lobbyists in Washington now represent so many overlapping interests that a subspecialty has sprung up—lobbying among lobbyists.

The budget process has been a veritable boon to the lobbying profession. With multiple votes, there is a steady progression of brush fires for lobbyists to stamp out—increasing their clients' anxiety and willingness to pay high fees—and also many more opportunities for a lobbyist to make his case. "Now they can wear you down," Senator Patrick Leahy, of Vermont, says. "You might be able to hold out for the public interest on the first, second, third, fourth, fifth votes, but on the sixth vote they're back again, and many give in." . . .

NO FUN ANYMORE

"I often feel that by the time I arrived in Congress, in 1974, the fun was over," Representative Gradison says. "All the landmark legislation, the laws that were exciting and glorious to take part in, had been passed. Now the bills were beginning to fall due, and there would not be glorious work for us, just the struggle to pay those bills."

Through the 1960s and early 1970s Congress made history time and again: the Civil Rights Act; the Voting Rights Act; the Clean Air and Water acts; Medicare and Medicaid; the Resource Conservation and Recovery and Toxic Substances Control acts, which started federal action against toxic wastes; new federal housing programs and aid to education; the successful battles against Nixon and the seniority system; public financing for presidential races; disclosure laws for federal candidates and officials—the list goes on.

Twenty years ago a congressman looking at the nation saw *wrongs*, like legally sanctioned discrimination, that could be righted simply by changing the law. It can be argued that today's political horizon is far different. There are many intractable dilemmas, but few open-and-shut cases such as raw pollution being pumped into a stream. Most current social problems don't have self-evident solutions of the type that Congress could codify in bills and announce tomorrow. Stopping the poll tax against blacks was one thing; moving an entire generation out of the ghetto and into the economic mainstream is quite another, and it's not at all clear how that can be done.

Congressmen face, instead, the tasks of reining in dramatic programs of previous Congresses and cutting the deficit, which are neither politically glamorous nor pleasant tasks. "They build statues and name schools after people who promote great programs," Representative Bill Frenzel, of Minnesota, says. "They never build statues for people who have to say no."

Indeed, what with the fragmentation of Congress, the inherent unpleasantness of cutbacks, and the eye-glazing vista of deficits of $172 billion, it becomes difficult for congressmen to take seriously the idea that any one particular cut matters. Everybody's taking what they can get—why should my program be the one to suffer when the deficit is so vast? What difference could another few hundred million possibly make?

Traditionally, congressmen find it easiest to advocate a bold new spirit of austerity in someone else's state or district. But there is a sense in which congressmen do not even mind excessive spending in other districts: it creates an atmosphere in which overspending is the norm and money for pet programs is less likely to be challenged.

In June, when the $18 billion water-projects authorization bill was about to go to the House floor, James Howard, of New Jersey, the chairman of the Public Works Committee, circulated a roster of the House with black spots next to the names of members in whose districts were programs he planned to attack if they voted against the water bill. Included in the Public Works Committee's bill was $189 million for a dam in the district of the committee's ranking Republican, Representative Gene Snyder, of Kentucky. Representative Harold Wolpe, of Michigan, who got a black dot,

told T. R. Reid, of *The Washington Post*, "You always hear rumors in the cloakroom that they'll kill your project if you dare to oppose anybody's else's, but this is the first time I've ever seen them put it on paper. . . . It's extraordinarily blatant." The more spending in general, the more for my district: everybody does it. Any congressman who goes after another congressman's program knows his will be attacked in turn, both by the congressman and by the program's PACs and lobbyists. Even a congressman who might be willing to accept a cut in his own district knows that in the present undisciplined environment he would be played for a sucker; no other congressman would join in the sacrifice.

This attitude helps explain why, for example, nearly every congressman favors cutting the defense budget in the abstract but votes to preserve the individual programs that make up that budget. In 1983 Congress *added* $4.6 billion to the Pentagon appropriations that President Reagan had asked for. Defense lobbyists in particular are adept, when budget showdowns approach, at avoiding any discussion of whether their projects are the efficient or otherwise proper choice, and at framing the issues strictly in terms of jobs: Congressman, this vote represents 2,000 jobs for your district. Any government expenditure creates jobs—the question is what jobs are best for the nation when national needs, finances, and policies are weighed. But this question is seldom posed to an individual congressman. The question posed is, Do you want these jobs in your district today or not? Do you want your name on them or not? . . . Here are some possibilities congressional leaders might consider:

Committee structures should be combined and simplified; particularly, the quadruple budget/appropriations/authorization/revenue sequence should be reduced by at least one phase. The most logical and least turf-destructive reductions would be to combine the budget committees with the revenue committees, putting the combined groups in control of overall revenue-versus-appropriations ratios, and to eliminate the appropriations committees. Money and policy amount to the same thing. Why must Congress pretend otherwise?

Seniority-system reforms should be reeled back somewhat—not to return to the stagnant old days but to stop the tail from wagging the dog.

Congressmen should receive a substantial raise and in return be required to forsake all forms of outside income. They are supposed to function as judges of society's needs; they should be as far above reproach (and influence) as judges.

There should be an absolute freeze on present federal-spending levels, extending to all entitlement programs and defense. If Congress wanted to allocate more money to one program, it would have to take some away from somewhere else. Congressmen cannot hope to reverse the "everybody does it" mentality of deficit increases without a political tool—a means by which they can argue to constituents (in simple, twenty-second terms) that they would like to give them more but just can't. There is nothing in the original social compacts of Social Security and other entitlement programs that confers a "right" to perpetual increases or to benefits for those who don't need them; those "rights" are political creations of Congress, and can be reversed.

A pay-as-you-go law should be enacted. Advocated by Senator John Glenn and others, pay-as-you-go would be a direct means of accomplishing what the budget process attempts to accomplish indirectly: tying government revenues to spending. Any legislation allocating new funds would at the same time have to provide a source for those funds, in the form of either a tax increase or a deduction from another program. When a person buys something, he considers the purchase not in the abstract but in light of how much he has to spend and what will be left over for other purchases. Businesses act the same way. Only government separates the question of what to spend from what is affordable. Pay-as-you-go would have far more teeth than the strictly symbolic balanced-budget amendment, which would require Congress to balance the budget unless, on an annual basis, it voted otherwise. The balanced-budget amendment would add another showy "process" but no actual discipline.

Budgets should be drawn up on a two-year cycle to reduce duplication. Multiyear procurement cycles should be employed for the development and manufacture of complicated items like weapons. Military contractors may feed at the public trough in a shameless manner, but in their behalf it should be said that changing their instructions regularly, as Congress is prone to do, does not make for efficient business. To help longer-cycle budgets work, Congress should devise a "this time we really mean it" clause that could prevent budget decisions from being constantly reopened for tinkering.

Lobbyists should be denied access to the Capitol. Of course lobbyists are not all sinister; most are simply doing their job. But the number of supplicants gathered round to demand handouts makes it difficult for congressmen to think clearly. Imagine lobbyists for parties in a lawsuit allowed in to see the judge—how credible would his decision be? And having lobbyists crowd outside the chambers of the House and Senate, flashing thumb signs to congressmen like coaches issuing orders to Little Leaguers, is a national disgrace.

There should be a cap on total campaign expenditures for each candidate. The existence of PACs and interest groups is far less corrupting than the need to raise great and ever-greater sums. If House races were limited to, say, $100,000 and Senate races to $500,000, the temptation to pander would be greatly reduced. Also, all campaign funds unspent after a given election should either be returned to donors or be contributed toward retiring the federal debt. If there were a cap on what congressmen could spend and no way for them to hoard what they didn't spend, fund-raising would be far less addictive than it is today. Restraining nonconnected and soft-money groups would not be as easy as restraining congressmen. But at least this proposal would get the congressmen out of fund-raising and back to their responsibilities.

What can be done to restrain indirect spending on campaigns when the Constitution guarantees freedom of speech? Preserve that freedom by limiting all advertising *to speech*. Whether by candidates or by representatives of soft-money or ideological groups, only *speech*, in which an actual, real, named, identifiable person stands and talks, would be permitted. No electronic graphics; no talking cows; no actors pretending to be men in the street; no sunset walks along the beach. Banning Madison Avenue-style advertising from politics has been advocated by Curtis Gans, the director of the Committee for the Study of the American Elec-

torate. The Supreme Court ruled in 1976 that money used to buy time on or space in communication media equates to the freedom of speech. This ruling has caused many people to think that the Gans approach would be held unconstitutional. But what do special effects, actors, and graphics have to do with any freedom we hold dear? Their purpose is to evade political debate, not advance it. Let money be used to buy TV spots, but only ones that hold to a standardized format, in which real candidates or real spokesmen for groups stand before the same solid-color background and state their ideas—whatever those ideas might be—with absolute privilege. This would surely satisfy the Founding Fathers, reduce the cost of campaigning, and by the way return the focus of politics to the issues.

The congressional calendar should be fixed, making it harder to put off decisions over and over again. A quarter system might be appropriate. During three quarters of the year congressmen would not be permitted to shuttle home to campaign but would be required to stay in Washington and attend to their work. During the fourth quarter Congress would shut down, and congressmen could return to their districts to find out for themselves what is happening there. During this time they could also hold away-from-Washington hearings—an art that died with television and instant access to publicity—in order to hear testimony from average Americans, not members of the Washington expert set.

None of these reforms would be easy to implement, especially those that involve intrusions upon existing turf and perquisites. But if congressmen cannot govern Congress, how can they hope to govern the country?

NO

Gary Orfield

CONGRESSIONAL POWER

POPULAR STEREOTYPES OF CONGRESS

Americans continually proclaim their pragmatic flexibility and realism. Yet they maintain the oldest set of stable political institutions in the world and repeatedly describe the operations of that structure in terms of seldom challenged myths. These myths include a view of Congress as a declining and hopelessly fragmented body trying with little success to cope with the expansive and even dangerous power of a stronger institution, the Presidency.

Even in early 1974, when, with the deepening of the Watergate crisis, respect for Presidential authority approached its modern low point Congress was seen in even more intensely unfavorable light. While the polls showed that only a fourth of the public approved of the job President Nixon was doing, they also showed that Congress had the respect and approval of only one American in five. Even Congress's impressive performance in the impeachment proceedings, which forced President Nixon's resignation, has produced little confidence that Congress can play a major positive role in the formation of national policy.

The assumptions about the sorry state of Congress have often been so pervasive that observers don't even bother to look at the evidence. This book will argue that the popular stereotype is fundamentally wrong. Congress is alive and well, at least in the field of domestic policy. If it is not progressive, it is usually reasonably representative and responsive. As public opinion changes, as Presidents define their constituency in different ways, and political circumstances gradually alter the membership of the House and Senate, Congress has been moving away from its traditional conservative or passive role in the development of national policy. This change became quite apparent with the beginning of the Nixon Administration. As the President moved sharply to the right on social policy, and the Supreme Court was largely neutralized by a series of four conservative appointments, Congress often remained the most progressive of the three branches in dealing with social policy issues.

The early 1970s did not see Congress become a seedbed for liberal activism. Although the legislative branch was now often more responsive to new social needs than the other principal institutions of government, there were still very broad and important areas of inaction and stalemate in domestic policy. This analysis will show that there is nothing in the institutional structure of Congress which renders the legislative branch either weak or conservative. In fact, Congress regularly exercises more power than it is credited with, and the ideological impact of its participation shifts from issue to issue and from political circumstance to political circumstance.

Our political system's lack of responsiveness to some of the very real social crises that preoccupy many intellectuals is not inherent in the Congressional process. Congressional reformers are simply wrong when they claim that institutional changes will produce "good" responses to the environmental problem, to inequitable taxation, irrational urban policies, and other major difficulties. The basic problem is more fundamental, and arises from the fact that the major progressive political force in this society, the activist liberal wing of the Democratic Party, is almost always a minority. Reformers spread the illusion that different procedures within Congress would produce answers to problems most Americans simply didn't want to face. So long as Congress is a representative body, it is highly unlikely to produce decisive answers to controversial questions before public opinion accepts the necessity of action. . . .

THE CHANGING PRESIDENCY

The Presidency, political scientists have often said, is inherently progressive because the Presidential election system has a built-in liberal bias, while Congressional power grows out of an electoral structure that magnifies local concerns. A number of Presidential campaigns during the past several decades have been organized around competition for the big blocks of electoral votes in the large urbanized states. At the same time Congressional malapportionment overrepresented rural areas in the House, while the lightly populated nonindustrial states have always been greatly overrepresented in the Senate.

Most political scientists have argued that the great importance of the big, closely divided states in Presidential elections has magnified the political influence of the urban minorities concentrated in these states. The political situation, analysts argued, made the President the natural spokesman for minority and urban needs. This very argument was used by some Congressional liberals in 1969 against adoption of a Constitutional amendment for direct election of the President.

Whatever the historical validity of these assertions, they no longer hold. In the 1964, 1968, and 1972 Presidential campaigns the GOP candidates wrote off the black vote and operated on the assumption that the real swing vote was in the suburbs. The Republican nominees saw the black vote, not as a swing vote, but as an integral locked-in element of the Democratic Party base. Turning their backs on the declining central-city electorate, they looked to the suburbs. In dramatic contrast to previous elections, the GOP adamantly refused to concede the South to the Democrats. By following a strategy that ignored the urban ghettos and put primary importance on the Southern and Border states, the Republicans were altering the Presidential political base from a source of liberal leverage to a collection of forces desiring to slow and reverse social changes already underway. . . .

THE DECLINE OF CONSERVATIVE POWER IN CONGRESS

While a new interpretation of the Presidential constituency was taking hold in the minds of many, something quite the opposite was beginning to become evident in Congress. As the 1970s began, the big cities enjoyed reasonable representation and growing seniority power within Congress. As political competition in the South spread and produced real challenges in former one-party districts, a growing proportion of the safe, stable, one-party districts that remained were located in the central cities, where Democratic voters frequently constitute overwhelming majorities. Given the continuing decline in central city population and the ten-year time lag before a new reapportionment, the relatively liberal central-city constituencies were destined to have increasing overrepresentation in the House as the 1970s advanced. . . .

The Senate was now seldom in the control of the old, rigidly conservative coalition of Southern Democrats and Republicans. On a number of issues it was now possible to form a moderate-liberal majority in support of social policy proposals.

THE UNCHANGING CRITICISM OF CONGRESS

Congress was changing, but perceptions of Congress remained largely fixed. Denunciations of Congressional ineptitude and legislative stalemate continues to proliferate. Inside and outside of Congress, critics said that only basic reforms could preserve Congress's intended role as a major force in American government. Even while they were sending their local incumbents back to Washington in great numbers, the American people expressed extremely low regard for Congress as an institution.

Characteristically, both the criticisms of Congress and the proposed cures are usually stated in institutional terms. We are told that the Congressional structure is inefficient or unresponsive, or that the rules screen out the competent and stifle innovation. Implicitly, however, the criticisms are political. When a critic says that Congress is not responsive, he obviously has in mind some set of national needs he believes Congress should respond to. Often these are the needs of an oppressed social group or of important decaying public institutions like the central cities and their school systems. The reform proposals often implicitly assume that procedural changes would release a suppressed progressive majority, likely to take a far more activist role in the provision of governmental services. This assumption may well be incorrect.

While the claim that certain major institutional features of Congress imposed a conservative bias on the legislative process has considerable historic validity, the recent picture is unclear. With a few notable exceptions, which run in both liberal and conservative directions, recent Congresses have rather accurately reflected the values and the confusion of the public in dealing with major issues of social change.

If the interpretation offered here is correct, liberals are unlikely to accomplish much by reforming Congressional procedures. The sobering reality is that the real obstacles are not so much on Capitol Hill as in the society as a whole. While tinkering with legislative arrangements may permit some minor improvements, basic social reforms probably require a political movement able to change public values.

Most of the time, we have the Congress we really want and the Congress we deserve. We send the same members back to Washington time after time. Congress is inherently neither liberal nor conservative. Its political tendencies change with the times, with political circumstances, with the delayed responses of the seniority system, and with tides of public opinion. In social policy battles of the early 1970s, Congress became relatively more progressive and activist than the Presidency. . . .

THE NEED FOR
REASSESSMENT OF CONGRESS

We must stop thinking in terms of institutional stereotypes and unexamined assumptions. Both scholars and activists need to devote more attention to reassessing the contemporary reality and future possibilities of Congressional policy initiatives. They need to think less in terms of a handful of visible bills, and more in terms of the whole array of Congressional influences that help shape policy in a given area. It is time for critics to rethink their wildly overoptimistic promises about Congressional reform, and to recognize that Congress often

only reflects the indecision or contradictory desires of the local publics and the local political structures.

It is a delusion for liberals to think that there is a hidden majority for basic social reform somewhere inside Congress that could be liberated by a few institutional reforms. Activist liberals must begin with the realization that they have only a minority in Congress, particularly in the House. On some issues, in fact, a more Democratic House might be an even less progressive House. If strong progressive programs are to prevail in Congress, their supporters must first prevail in elections.

CONGRESS AND SOCIAL POLICY:
A SUMMARY

The United States has been passing through a period of massive social and economic change during the past decade. Congress has played an extremely important role in shaping the uneven governmental responses to those changes. Contrary to popular cliches, the nation has not entered a period of an imperial Presidency and a passive Congress, nor has deadlock totally paralyzed action in most areas of policy.

The past decade has brought profound changes in the position of blacks, women, and young people in the social and political system. The major civil rights laws were a powerful response to the central shame of American democracy, governmental enforcement of the racial caste system of the South. After decades of resistance, Congress not only passed these laws, but strengthened them and then protected them from a hostile President. Congressional action has been crucial to the women's movement's attack on concepts of female status ingrained in Western culture. Congressional action making eighteen-year-olds full citizens has had little visible immediate impact, but will surely make the political system more open and responsive to young people.

After Congress approved the vast expansion of the federal role in domestic programs in the 1960s, the determined efforts of a conservative President to reverse the trend tested the real dispositions of the Democratic Congress. The period found even the more conservative elements of the legislative branch operating more progressively than the President. This was very apparent, for example, in the massive Social Security boosts approved by the Ways and Means and the Senate Finance committees, and in the continual rejection of the President's meager education and health budgets by both Appropriations committees. In most cases Congress led the executive branch in responding to new ecological issues and in creating new tools for control of the economy.

The period of the late 1960s and early 1970s witnessed simultaneously the advance of sweeping claims of Presidential powers, and the decline of the real strength of the Presidency. During the period between the end of the Second World War and the late 1960s, Presidents enjoyed great latitude in the conduct of foreign policy and military affairs. This freedom of action, and the bipartisan Congressional support that sustained it, began to erode when rising opposition to the Vietnam War destroyed the Johnson Presidency. At first it affected the margins of international power, such as foreign military assistance, but by the early 1970s it had produced serious Congressional pressures to restrain the military apparatus and to subject Presidential action to legislative control. War powers legislation—passed over a Presidential veto—and some reductions in the defense and foreign aid budgets began to cut into the muscle of executive leadership; 1973 saw the extraordinary spectacle of Congress forcing the end of military action in Cambodia by cutting off funds, and Congress rejecting trade legislation central to the policy of detente with the U.S.S.R.

The Nixon period witnessed the resurgence of some long neglected legislative powers in domestic affairs and the most striking Congressional rejection of a President's domestic program in decades. In the major Supreme Court nomination fights, Congress resumed an active role in the constitution of the highest Court, a power that had lain dormant for most of the twentieth century. When the early phases of the Watergate scandal indicated grave improprieties in the executive branch, Congress acted both through a massive investigation and through insistence on an independent special prosecutor to force revelation of the most serious corruption in American history. When the investigation came under Administration attack, very heavy Congressional pressure persuaded the President to retreat. Eventually he was forced to leave office. . . .

The period of Presidential reaction on social policy under President Nixon showed that the close tie between Congress and various organized constituencies could have liberal as well as conservative consequences. Coming to office with the belief that he had a mandate to reverse many of the domestic innovations of the Great Society, the President encountered determined resistance from Congress. Congress responded by rejecting a higher portion of

Nixon legislative proposals than those of any recent President, even though Nixon presented a relatively slim set of innovations. Only by stretching executive powers and spending his political authority in bitter confrontations with Congress over vetoes and impoundments was the President able to slow the momentum of those programs. Eventually, the price to be paid was strong Congressional attempts to cut back on the powers of the executive branch.

In arguing that Congress possesses a substantial capacity to initiate new national policies, and that those policies may well be more "progressive" or "responsive" than positions taken by a President, this book certainly does not mean to support another false view of Congress. While Congress may be *relatively* more activist than a conservative President, it can hardly be described as a liberal institution. The major liberal force in American politics is the Northern and Western wing of the Democratic Party. Only when political circumstances give that wing of the party an operating majority in Congress (a rare circumstance) or predominant influence in the executive branch (a more common occurrence) does that institution become the primary focus for policy innovation.

During the Nixon Administration Congress succeeded in putting a few major new social issues on the national agenda, and in protecting much of the Great Society framework. On many other issues, however, its record was far more mixed. Design of new housing policies, for example, was long stalled by a stalemate within Congress, as well as by one between Congress and the White House. Congress delegated vast powers over the economy to the executive branch without making basic policy decisions. Con-

gress preserved existing civil rights laws, aimed primarily at the classic Southern forms of discrimination, but proved incapable of developing policies to cope with the intensifying racial separation of the urban North. There were few significant new ideas in education policy in the legislation of the early 1970s, and the intense national discussion of health care needs yielded little on Capitol Hill. Efforts to reform the tax structure or to alter the basic assumptions of welfare policy were largely barren. The list goes on and on.

Judged against the national goals of activist liberal groups, or even against the Democratic Party platform, the record of Congress was fundamentally inadequate. Congress has not responded forcefully to a number of evident social needs. The obstacle has been sometimes the President, and sometimes Congress itself.

The important thing to remember is that the failings criticized by activists are usually not failings produced by the structure or procedures of Congress, but by the vision of its members. The shortcomings—and many of the achievements—result from reasonably effective Congressional representation of widely held and often contradictory values of the public and of the members' active and important constituents. The unwillingness to move forward in some significant areas of social policy reflects far less the inadequacies of Congress as an organization than the failure of middle-class Americans to recognize that any social crisis exists. The basic reason why neither Congress nor the President is truly liberal is that liberalism normally represents a minority position in the United States—a fact often obscured by the assumption that the Democratic

Party is a liberal party, rather than an exceedingly broad coalition.

Much of the national movement for extensive Congressional reform is based on false assumptions. Reform and rationalization of committee jurisdiction, chairmen's powers, the budget process, Congressional staff capacity, etc., may produce a more efficient legislative body, more equitable to individual members, and perhaps better able to compete with the executive branch. These are worthwhile goals, but they are not likely to transform the substance of Congressional decisions. Reformers who promise an institutional answer to a political question are likely to be disappointed. There are no shortcuts. Probably the only way to build a new Congress is to undertake the hard political work necessary to send new men and women to Capitol Hill. . . .

It is vital to realize that the making of national domestic policy takes place in a context of genuinely divided power, and that the Congress as well as the President possesses both the ability to initiate and the power to veto major policy changes. The system works well when there is a clear consensus in the country, or clear control of both branches by the dominant wing of either party. Usually these conditions are not present and the system is biased either toward compromise and incremental change, or toward confrontation and inaction. The Nixon period clearly shows that the modern Presidency can be quite as efficient an engine of negative social policy as was Congress during certain earlier progressive Administrations.

It is only fair to recognize that much of the criticism that has been aimed at Congress has been misdirected. It is really criticism of the inefficiencies and delays built into the American Constitutional system, and of the nebulous and often contradictory ideological bases of the alliances that constitute the national political parties. Failure to correctly identify these underlying causes leads one to misjudge the solutions.

The people of the United States generally have the kind of legislative body they want and deserve. It is a Congress that has the power to take decisive action, but most of whose members rarely believe the public demands such change. It is an evolving institution and an increasingly representative one. It has great power but rarely selects leaders who use that power with energy, skill, and imagination. With a few significant exceptions, the altering of its internal rules will not change its decisions much. Congress is likely to be a moderately progressive institution in the next years. If it is to be much more than that—or less—its membership must be significantly changed.

POSTSCRIPT

Is Congress Too Weak?

Very few commentators, including some members of Congress, appear to have unqualified praise for how Congress works. Nor does anyone have a constitutional alternative to Congress. The practical question, then, is: What does it take to make Congress work well?

Nothing less than a fundamental constitutional change could lead to a more effective exercise of congressional power, according to James Mac-Gregor Burns. He has argued this thesis most recently in *The Power to Lead: The Crisis of the American Presidency* (Simon & Schuster, 1984). Philip Stern is unremitting in his criticism of Congress's dependency on PACs and private financing, and the ways in which this influences legislative behavior, in his book *The Best Congress Money Can Buy* (Pantheon Books, 1988).

Arthur Maass dissents from the critics in *Congress and the Common Good* (Basic Books, 1984). He describes, analyzes, and defends the role of Congress in the democratic political process.

An illuminating study of how members of Congress actually function can be found in Burdett Loomis's *The New American Politician: Ambition, Entrepreneurship, and the Changing Face of Political Life* (Basic Books, 1988). Loomis takes an inside look at members of Congress who were elected in 1974 and follows their legislative careers over the next decade, providing insights into where Congress has succeeded and where it has failed.

A classic study of the legislative process is being revised for publication. Bertram M. Gross and Edward V. Schneier's book, *The Legislative Struggle: A Study in Social Combat* (St. Martin's Press), will be published in 1992. Students seeking up-to-date information on Congress and legislative issues will find no more reliable source of information than the *Congress Quarterly Weekly Report* and the annual *Congressional Quarterly Almanac*.

Perhaps before asking what is wrong with Congress, we should ask what is wrong with *us*. Far fewer than half of all American adults actually vote to elect Congress and more than 95 percent of all members of the House of Representatives get reelected every two years. If the caliber of Congress depends in large part on the concern of voters, we must consider how to motivate the American people to desire and to elect a better Congress.

ISSUE 6

Has the Power of the Presidency Been Eroded?

YES: Theodore B. Olson, from "The Impetuous Vortex: Congressional Erosion of Presidential Authority," in Crovitz and Rabkin, eds., *The Fettered Presidency: Congressional Erosion of Presidential Authority* (AEI, 1989)

NO: Robert Nisbet, from *The Present Age: Progress and Anarchy in Modern America* (Harper & Row, 1988)

ISSUE SUMMARY

YES: Lawyer Theodore B. Olson worries that Congress is restricting and impinging on powers that should be wielded by the president.
NO: Historian Robert Nisbet feels that the growth of presidential power has been largely unchecked and that it poses a serious threat to American democracy.

"Energy in the Executive," wrote Alexander Hamilton in 1787, "is a leading character in the definition of good government." Hamilton dreamed of a vast American empire whose lynchpin was to be a powerful managerial president. A single executive would have the necessary "decision, activity, secrecy, and dispatch" to handle all the crises that were certain to menace the new nation. The president was to be "the bulwark of national security."

By the second half of the twentieth century, Hamilton's vision seemed more than fulfilled. As chief executive and commander in chief, the president headed an executive establishment of nearly three million civilian employees and another three million men and women in uniform. He could, by himself, initiate nuclear war. He was also chief of state, chief diplomat, party leader, and manager of the nation's prosperity. Indeed, his power had expanded by means of which Hamilton would hardly have approved, for the growth of democracy—a form of government which Hamilton distrusted—turned the president into a "steward of the people." Theodore Roosevelt also applied that term to himself, and a later promoter of the presidency admiringly referred to the office as a "republican king." During the 1950s and early 1960s, academic liberals like Arthur M. Schlesinger, Jr., and James M. Burns promoted the idea of a strong, "activist" presidency. Their model was Franklin D. Roosevelt, whose buoyant leadership and reformist policies inspired the younger, post-war generation of American historians and political scientists. For them, the presidency was, or at any rate could be, an instrument of progressive change. Congress, on the other hand, seemed to be little more than a patchwork of reactionary interests.

Later in the 1960s, events caused liberals to reconsider their views. Lyndon Johnson, who became president after the assassination of John F. Kennedy, was highly energetic, but his energies were soon directed toward escalating America's involvement in Vietnam. After Johnson came Richard Nixon, another activist president, who escalated the air war in Vietnam, invaded Cambodia, and, shortly into his second term, got entangled in the Watergate scandal. By the early 1970s, Schlesinger had come out with a book entitled *The Imperial Presidency,* and other prominent liberals were no less critical of the "republican king." After Watergate led to Nixon's forced resignation, the next two presidents, Gerald Ford and Jimmy Carter, tried hard to divest the presidency of its kingly aura—Ford by his relaxed and easy-going manner, Carter by his down-home populism. Still, the critics were not disarmed. Regardless of who occupied the White House, the pendulum of academic opinion had decisively swung against the office of the presidency. Proposals were made for establishing a plural presidency, for making the president submit to questioning by Congress, for forcing the president to put opposition members in his cabinet, and so on. None of these came to anything, but they were indications not only of liberal disenchantment with presidential power but of a renewed interest in Congress as an institution for checking that power. During the eight years of Ronald Reagan's presidency, Congress assumed an even greater role as a challenger of and counter to the conservative policies of the White House. The fights between president and Congress on a number of fronts—from the arming of Contras in Nicaragua to the confirmation of Reagan's judicial nominees—were often bitter. President Bush's relationship to Congress is less confrontational than was Reagan's, but tensions and frictions are still evident as the two branches pursue their different approaches to public policy.

What has been the effect of these rivalries? Has there been much effect? Has Congress succeeded in checking the growth of presidential power, or does the history of the presidency remain, as a famous commentator once wrote, "a history of aggrandizement"? Or could the opposite be happening—could it be that the Congress has succeeded all too well in checking presidential power, that it has, in fact, destroyed necessary powers that rightly belong in the White House? These questions are debated in the following selections. Theodore Olson, former assistant U.S. attorney general, worries that Congress is restricting and impinging on powers that should be wielded by the president. But historian Robert Nisbet thinks that the growth of presidential power has been largely unchecked and that it poses a serious threat to American democracy.

YES

Theodore B. Olson

THE IMPETUOUS VORTEX: CONGRESSIONAL EROSION OF PRESIDENTIAL AUTHORITY

The single most important characteristic of the U.S. Constitution, responsible for the preservation of individual freedom and liberty for 200 years, is its carefully balanced structure of divided yet interdependent powers. One principle with which most Americans found themselves in agreement in 1787 was that "no political truth is . . . of greater intrinsic value, or is stamped with the authority of more enlightened patrons of liberty, than that . . . [t]he accumulation of all powers, legislative, executive, and judiciary, in the same hands, whether of one, a few, or many . . . may justly be pronounced the very definition of tyranny."[1]

To avoid the accumulation of power, the first three articles of the Constitution allocated legislative, executive, and judicial power to three separate, coordinate branches of government. The legislative department, created by Article I, vested with the authority to make all laws and appropriate all funds to be drawn from the Treasury, was the most feared of the three branches:

> [W]here the legislative power is exercised by an assembly, which is inspired, by a supposed influence over the people, with an intrepid confidence in its own strength; which is sufficiently numerous to feel all the passions which actuate a multitude, yet not so numerous as to be incapable of pursuing the objects of its passions, by means which reason prescribes; it is against the enterprising ambition of this department that the people ought to indulge all their jealousy and exhaust all their precautions.[2]

Because the legislature's powers are "at once more extensive, and less susceptible of precise limits [than the other branches], it can, with the greater facility, mask, under complicated and indirect measures, the encroachments which it makes on the coordinate departments."[3]

In short, while governmental power was carefully divided among three branches, the framers nonetheless forewarned that the "legislative depart-

From Theodore B. Olson, "The Impetuous Vortex: Congressional Erosion of Presidential Authority," in L. Gordon Crovitz and Jeremy A. Rabkin, eds., *The Fettered Presidency: Congressional Erosion of Presidential Authority* (American Enterprise Institute, 1989). Copyright © 1989 by the American Enterprise Institute for Public Policy Research. Reprinted by permission. Some notes omitted.

ment [would be] everywhere extending the sphere of its activity, and drawing all power into its impetuous vortex."[4] The framers also appreciated that "parchment barriers" would be insufficient protection from the legislature's "encroaching spirit of power." Therefore, along with the judicial and executive powers allocated to the president and the courts, respectively, each of those branches was given authority and protections presumed to be sufficient to resist encroachments by the legislature. The judiciary, for example, was given life tenure. The executive power was vested by Article II in a president who, among other things, was given the exclusive authority to "take care that the Laws be faithfully executed." Thus, the "entire legislature . . . can exercise no executive prerogative."[5] . . .

CONGRESSIONAL EROSIONS AND USURPATIONS OF PRESIDENTIAL POWER

The thoughtful, considered decision of 1787 to vest executive authority in a single individual has been under siege almost from the moment it was made. Congress began almost immediately to involve itself in executive decisions and to erode presidential power. After two centuries of unrelenting encroachments by Congress, concerns that are occasionally expressed concerning an "imperial presidency" are simply misplaced. Today's executive has been diluted, divided, fragmented, and parceled out to literally scores of agencies, commissions, "independent" officials, boards, and corporations. Those powers that have not been taken from the president altogether have been so encrusted with congressional or congressional committee involve-

ment or tangled with procedural impediments to vigorous decision making that the president can exercise little real authority. President Kennedy, speaking nearly thirty years ago, captured what the presidency had become then when he said, "Well, I agree with you, but I'm not sure the government will."

Congress has so adeptly and persistently eroded and disassembled executive power that a comprehensive chronicle of legislative encroachments on executive power with corresponding examples would be a book in itself. The following, however, touches some highlights.

Undermining Presidential Law Enforcement Authority

Congress has created an array of techniques designed to diminish the president's ability to enforce the law. It has set up numerous "independent" regulatory agencies, for example, with the express purpose of removing from the president the power to enforce legislation in various fields. Generally, the president's control is stripped from him by the device of restricting his ability to remove those with law enforcement power: "Once an officer is appointed, it is only the authority that appointed him that he must fear and, in the performance of his functions, obey." If the president must prove incompetence or some other specified cause to a court to justify removing an official who will not comply with his policies, the president has lost all effective control of that official. The clearly stated congressional purpose behind creating agencies whose heads cannot be removed at the president's will is to "require them to act in discharg[ing] their duties independent of executive control."

Agencies that have been given substantial independence from the president include the Federal Trade Commission, the Securities and Exchange Commission, the Federal Election Commission, the Federal Reserve System, the National Labor Relations Board, the Tennessee Valley Authority, the Federal Communications Commission, and the Federal Maritime Commission. Thus, the power given to the president by Article II to "take care" that the laws of the United States are faithfully executed no longer extends to vast areas of federally regulated conduct and behavior. While arguments continue to be made that withdrawing the president, and therefore "politics," from law enforcement is a beneficial system, it is most decidedly not the system created in Philadelphia in 1787.

These erosions of presidential power mean that it is virtually impossible for the president to have an impact upon vast areas of American life. Two agencies, for example, one controlled by the president (the Antitrust Division of the Justice Department), another not controlled by the president (the Federal Trade Commission), enforce the antitrust laws. The president cannot, therefore, implement a uniform antitrust policy. The same is true for communications, energy, and many other areas.

Another result of fractioning the presidency is that it has become exceedingly difficult to effect policies through elections. Indeed, it is often impossible for the public even to know who is responsible for many of our most vital national policies. . . .

Interference with the President's Appointment Power

Congress has devised a number of ways to hinder presidential appointments; among them are the appointments, incompatibility, and ineligibility clauses. The appointments clause of the Constitution, Article II, section 2, provides that "Officers of the United States" must be appointed by the president by and with the advice and consent of the Senate or, where authorized by Congress, by the president alone, the courts, or subordinates of the president. The methods of appointment set forth in the appointments clause are exclusive; officers of the United States therefore cannot be appointed by Congress or by congressional officers. Persons who "exercise significant authority pursuant to the laws of the United States" or who perform "a significant governmental duty . . . pursuant to the laws of the United States" must be officers of the United States and therefore must be appointed in accord with the appointments clause. In *Buckley v. Valeo*, the Supreme Court struck down as unconstitutional attempted appointments by Congress of its own members to the Federal Elections Commission.

Congress, nevertheless, frequently establishes commissions, agencies, advisory boards, or other entities, the functions of which include advisory as well as operational responsibilities, and provides for the appointment of officers of such entities in a manner inconsistent with the appointments clause. When signing such legislation, presidents have often responded by taking the position that bodies of this nature may perform only advisory, investigative, informative, or ceremonial functions and may not perform regulatory, enforcement, or other executive responsibilities. Nonetheless, even advisory councils imposed upon the presidency are appendages that were rejected by the Constitutional Convention, and they are an awkward embarrassment to the president. . . .

Other Methods of Eroding Presidential Power

With ever-increasing frequency, Congress provides for commissions composed of members or appointees of the legislative and executive branches. These commissions are not clearly a part of either branch. The president's statement, upon the signing of the U.S. commission on the Civil Rights Act of 1983, objected to the creation of "agencies which are inconsistent with the tripartite system of government established by the Framers of our Constitution" and stated that the "Civil Rights Commission is . . . unique in form and function [and] should therefore not become a precedent for the creation of similar agencies in the future." Unfortunately, the reconstituted Civil Rights Commission has become such a precedent. Similar provisions were included in an amendment to a House bill to change the tariff treatment with respect to certain articles, which would have established an International Trade and Export Policy Commission; the Patent Law Amendment Act of 1984; the Health Promotion and Disease Prevention Amendments of 1984; the Older Americans Act Amendments of 1984; and the Public Works Improvement Act of 1984.

In many instances, the problems created by a hybrid commission are aggravated because the representatives of the legislative branch on the commission typically far outnumber those of the executive branch. An example is the recently created federal commission to find ways to reduce the federal deficit. The panel was created to have fourteen members, only two of whom are selected by the president. Four are selected by congressional Republicans, six by congressional Democrats, and two by the person

elected president in November. The new president will have to deal with this strange hybrid body's report in March 1989. As William Safire expressed it, "Thus, the next Presidency [will] be emasculated at birth." He adds, "If we are about to fix responsibility for the budgetary mess the Congress has placed us in, let's do it at the polls—and not rig the next economic policy with some stultifying consensus beforehand." . . .

As noted earlier, Congress restrains the president's power to control an official by restricting the circumstances when the official may be removed. There are literally hundreds of manifestations of this form of restriction on presidential power. Significantly, it is precisely this issue that led to major confrontations between President Washington and the First Congress, President Jackson and Congress, President Andrew Johnson and Congress (leading to impeachment), President Roosevelt and Congress, and other serious controversies throughout our history. . . .

Congress consistently attempts to obtain access to the most sensitive executive branch information and opposes with every resource at its disposal arguments that the executive branch, like Congress and the judiciary, must enjoy some measure of protection for confidential exchanges of information if it is to function effectively.

Among the many examples of congressional overreaching in this area are the relatively continuous demands by one committee or another to require the Department of Justice to produce documents from its files relative to current criminal investigations. These demands extend to cases under active investigation before sitting grand juries. Premature release of the material from investigative files may severely damage the confidence and cooperativeness of witnesses, the integrity of the case development, the independence of prosecutorial decisions, and the strategy of future prosecution. . . .

Since the 1970s, Congress has increasingly attempted to assert itself in the president's foreign affairs powers at the expense of the authority traditionally exercised by the president. The history of recent congressional action in this area has been succinctly summarized in the following excerpt from an article by Senator John G. Tower, former chairman of the Senate Armed Services Committee:

> The 1970's were marked by a rash of Congressionally initiated foreign policy legislation that limited the President's range of options on a number of foreign policy issues. The thrust of the legislation was to restrict the President's ability to dispatch troops abroad in a crisis, and to proscribe his authority in arms sales, trade, human rights, foreign assistance and intelligence operations. During this period, over 150 separate prohibitions and restrictions were enacted in Executive Branch authority to formulate and implement foreign policy. Not only was much of this legislation ill conceived, if not actually unconstitutional, it has served in a number of instances to be detrimental to the national security and foreign policy interests of the United States.

One ongoing problem is the War Powers Resolution, enacted in 1973, which provides for congressional oversight "in any case in which United States Armed Forces are introduced into hostilities or into situations where imminent involvement in hostilities is clearly indicated by the circumstances." The president is required to submit a written report to Congress detailing the circumstances of U.S. involvement, and Congress is authorized to order U.S. troops removed by concurrent resolution. After sixty days, the War Powers Resolution provides that the president must automatically terminate the use of U.S. armed forces except in very narrow circumstances.

Other examples of congressional interference in the president's foreign affairs power have involved attempts to restrict his power to negotiate with or recognize foreign governments or governmental entities. A recently passed continuing resolution, for example, contains a provision arguably preventing the president from negotiating with or recognizing the Palestine Liberation Organization (PLO) until the PLO recognizes Israel and complies with other requirements set forth in the provision. Another recent law much in the news lately required the president to close the PLO's mission to the United Nations. The prospect of the enforcement of this law drew near unanimous disapproval in the United Nations because it was said to have violated the treaty obligations of the United States. A 1983 bill would have precluded the president from establishing diplomatic relations with the Vatican. Yet another proposed law would have forced the president to move the American Embassy in Israel from Tel Aviv to Jerusalem.

Congress may interfere with existing investigations, foreign policy, domestic policy, or all three by conducting parallel, intrusive, or clumsy investigations. An example was reported in the *Washington Post*:

> While pursuing their own probe into Wall Street insider trading, four of Rep. John Dingell's investigators cut short a trip to Switzerland last week after being

reprimanded by Swiss officials over their attempts to obtain information from a Geneva bank.

The incident briefly threatened the cooperation the Swiss are providing to U.S. agencies investigating insider trading, according to a Washington lawyer who represents Swiss banks.

Moreover, whatever the merits of the Iran-contra congressional investigation, it exposed and therefore affected a wide range of government policies. The defenders of this investigation undoubtedly believe that it was a proper use of congressional investigative powers, and the merits of that proposition can be debated. It is certainly true, however, that the process illustrated by this investigation is an unusual, embarrassing, and awkward way to conduct or alter foreign policies.

The congressional oversight mechanism provides Congress with an opportunity to interdict executive policy making in the formative process, precludes confidential and candid predeliberative discussions in many cases, occupies inordinate time of policy makers, and otherwise involves Congress and its sizable staff in the minutiae of executive decision making. The result is a tendency toward paralysis of both branches.

Congress has the power to force congressional—and now, through the Independent Counsel law, criminal—investigations of those whose conduct displeases its members. Congress can intimidate, punish, and wreak retribution against those who assist the president in resisting legislative encroachments. Especially when there is political capital to be gained, this phenomenon is becoming an increasingly fashionable way to drive executive policies through threat and intimidation. . . .

CONCLUSION

This review shows how Congress has given life to the fears of the framers by attempting to absorb and weaken presidential power through innumerable complicated and indirect measures. It has vested executive authority in individuals not subject to the president's supervision and more subject to the will of Congress. It has eroded the president's relationships with those who do serve the president by making it impossible for them to report in confidence to the president and making them report instead or simultaneously to Congress. Congress restricts or impinges on the president's power to appoint his subordinates and penalizes those subordinates who serve the president too faithfully.

Those who examine the presidency today will see an institution that is becoming increasingly ineffective and inefficient and less responsible for the management of government, the antithesis of the model created in Philadelphia in 1787.

NOTES

1. *Federalist* No. 47.
2. *Federalist* No. 48.
3. Ibid.
4. Ibid.
5. *Federalist* No. 47.

NO

Robert Nisbet

THE NEW ABSOLUTISM

Any returned Framers of the Constitution would be quite as shocked by the extent and depth of the power of the national state in Americans lives today as they would be by war and the gargantuan military. The most cursory reading of the Constitution itself tells us that behind the labors which produced this document lay an abiding fear, distrust, hatred of the kinds of political power identified with the government of George III and with the centralized despotisms, such as France, Prussia, and Russia, on the Continent. Add to reading of the Constitution even a scanning of the Federalist Papers followed perhaps by a brief dipping into the annals of the Convention, and there can be no doubt of what the Framers most definitely did not want: a highly centralized, unitary political Leviathan.

That, however, is what their work of art has become in two centuries. And with this has come, has had to come, a political absolutism over Americans that would not be lessened or mitigated for the Framers by its manifestly, unchallengeably democratic foundations. There is not the slightest question but that ours is still what Lincoln called it, government of the people, by the people, for the people. But it is still absolutist.

The fact is, democracy can yield a higher degree of absolutism in its relation to the individual than is found in any of the so-called absolute, divine-right monarchies of the early modern era in European history. Louis XIV's *L'état, c'est moi*, notorious for its purported absolutism, was actually a confession of weakness whether the king knew it or not. In between divine-right monarchs and any possible absoluteness of rule lay a thick stratum of intermediate authorities, starting with church and aristocracy, that made farce of any claim to personal authority. The absolute state of the sixteenth century is in fact as much a sham as was the Holy Roman Empire before it. What Walter Lippmann wrote a half-century ago in his *A Preface to Morals* remains apposite:

> A state is absolute in the sense which I have in mind when it claims the right to a monopoly of all the force within the community, to make war, to make peace, to conscript life, to tax, to establish and disestablish property, to define crime,

From Robert Nisbet, *The Present Age: Progress and Anarchy in Modern America* (Harper & Row, 1988). Copyright © 1988 by Robert Nisbet. Reprinted by permission of HarperCollins Publishers.

to punish disobedience, to control education, to supervise the family, to regulate personal habits, and to censor opinions.

The modern state claims all of these powers, and in the matter of theory, there is no real difference in the size of the claim between communists, fascists, and democrats. There are lingering traces in the American constitutional system of the older theory that there are inalienable rights which the government may not absorb. But these rights are not really inalienable for they can be taken away by constitutional amendment. There is no theoretical limit upon the power of ultimate majorities which create the civil government. There are only practical limits. They are restrained by inertia, by prudence, even good will. But ultimately and theoretically they claim absolute authority against all churches, associations, and persons within their jurisdictions.[1]

Much of the energy of political intellectuals, of what I shall call in this chapter the political clerisy, has gone since the New Deal into the demonstration that although state authority has grown constantly heavier, reaching more and more recesses of life, there has not been any real compromise of liberty, inasmuch as the authority has the sanction of the people, and the theory of democracy (the theory at any rate of Jean-Jacques Rousseau) holds that no people can by its volition tyrannize itself. I shall come back to this later.

In our politics as well as in our military, the present age begins with the Great War and with Woodrow Wilson's powerful effect upon America.

"All men of military genius," wrote Tocqueville, "are fond of centralization and all men of centralizing genius are fond of war." The history of the United States is ample illustration of the general soundness of Tocqueville's principle. If we look at the presidents, starting with Andrew Jackson, who if they have not actually relished and sought out war have nevertheless taken to it and to the use of war powers rather more easily than others have, we must include some of our greatest presidents. There was Jackson and Lincoln (who was exceeded by no one in the American presidency in alacrity in precipitating a war and in the free use of war powers during it); there was Theodore Roosevelt, Wilson, Franklin Roosevelt, Kennedy, Johnson, Nixon, and, very much in the procession, Ronald Reagan.

In each of these presidents there is a conspicuous readiness to turn to political centralization, bureaucracy, and the heaping up of powers, so far as possible, in the central government even at the expense of a strictly read Constitution. Woodrow Wilson is the master of them all, in respect to his union of strong instincts toward centralization and use of war powers. His political, economic, social, and even intellectual reorganization of America in the short period 1917-1919 is one of the most extraordinary feats in the long history of war and polity. Through artfully created board, commission, and agency he and his worshipful lieutenants, drawn from all areas—business, academia, law, even entertainment—revolutionized America to a degree never reached in such a short period of time by either the French or the Russian revolution. And Wilson, let it be remembered, in diametrical opposition to the Robespierres and Lenins, demobilized completely the militarized society he had built only a couple of year earlier.

But it was by no means the war imperative alone that spurred Wilson to his work of political power in the Great War. He was an ardent prophet of the state, the state indeed as it was known to European scholars and statesmen. He had written a book on it. He preached it, especially in its American revelation, as no one before had. From him supremely comes the politicization, the centralization, and the commitment to bureaucracy of American society during the past seventy-five years. He only began this evolution, and what he did was chiefly apparent during the two years we were at war with Germany. But the wartime powers assumed by the national government proved to be durable seeds, and by 1939, only twenty years from the time when they had been nominally jettisoned for good, Wilsonian centralization and collectivization were, under FDR, as pervasive as they had been during the Great War. Ever since there has been a unitary, unilinear pattern of development to be seen, only rarely punctuated by sign of reversal, that has centralization of government its embedded goal, with all forms of decentralization and pluralism declared by political elites to be mere eruptions of the dead hand of the past. From Wilson through FDR, Truman, Kennedy, Johnson, Nixon, and Reagan we have seen America develop from its state of innocence in 1914 down to the highly sophisticated power complex that marks American democracy today.

Wilson began it chiefly within the context provided by the Great War. Within a few months he had transformed traditional, decentralized, regional, and localist America into a war state that at its height permeated every aspect of life in America. I shall describe some of the political changes he effected, in a moment. But I think the following passage

from the English historian A. J. P. Taylor is an important prefatory note. It is directed to English experience but it is highly relevant to America:

> Until August 1914 a sensible, law-abiding Englishman could pass through life and hardly notice the existence of the state beyond the post office and the policeman. . . . He could travel abroad or leave his country forever without a passport or any sort of official permission. He could exchange his money without restriction or limit. He could buy goods from any country in the world on the same terms as he bought goods at home. For that matter a foreigner could spend his life in the country without permit and without informing the police. . . .
>
> All this was changed by the impact of the Great War. . . . The state established a hold over its citizens which though relaxed in peace time, was never to be removed and which the Second World War was again to increase. The history of the English people and the English State merged for the first time."[2]

Much the same merging of people and state took place under Wilson after Congress declared war on Germany in April 1917. Congress not only obeyed Wilson's request for a state of war—made with the same prophet's intensity that had, until a few months before, supported his insistence upon neutrality—it also showered war powers on him beyond the dream of an early Caesar. Wilson accepted them as if he had created them himself. "It is not an army we must shape and train for war," he said, "it is a nation." His words came from the mind and heart alike. . . .

The Great Depression hit the United States at the end of the 1920s, to be met within a couple of years by the New Deal under Franklin Roosevelt. He had served Wilson as assistant secretary of the navy in World War I, and had been one of those thrilled by Wilson personally and by certain aspects of the War State. It is interesting to speculate on what form American response to the depression of the 1930s would or might have taken had it not been for the legacy of government planning and regimentation left by the First World War. It is at least possible that some kind of response by government and business beginning in 1933 would have been a great deal less centralized and bureaucratized than what actually came into being.

In striking measure the response made by FDR and his chief aides, men like Raymond Moley and Rexford Tugwell, Henry Wallace and Harold Ickes, one and all political intellectuals rather than businessmen, was simply a revival of structures and relationships which had characterized the Wilson War State. With altered names, many of the same production, labor, banking, and agricultural boards of World War I were simply dusted off, as it were, and with new polish set once again before the American people. This time the enemy was not Germany or any other foreign power but the Depression; this did not, however, prevent Roosevelt from literally declaring war on it and likening himself and his associates to a "trained and loyal army willing to sacrifice for the good of a common discipline." In his inaugural address in 1933 the President pledged to "assume unhesitatingly the leadership of this great army of our people dedicated to a disciplined attack upon our common problems." He perceived America, he said, as a vast army needing only to be mobilized for the war against depression to begin.

The New Deal is a great watershed not only in twentieth-century American history but in our entire national history. In it the mesmerizing idea of a *national community*—an idea that had been in the air since the Progressive era, featured in books by Herbert Croly, Walter Lippmann, John Dewey, and others, and had come into full but brief existence in 1917 under the stimulus of war—was now at long last to be initiated in peacetime, as a measure to combat the evils of capitalism and its "economic royalists."

"At the heart of the New Deal," William Schambra has perceptively written, "was the resurrection of the national idea, the renewal of the vision of national community. Roosevelt sought to pull America together in the face of its divisions by an appeal to national duty, discipline, and brotherhood; he aimed to restore the sense of local community, at the national level. He once explained the New Deal's 'drastic changes in the methods and forms of the functions of government' by noting that 'we have been extending to our national life the old principle of the local community.' " Schambra continues:

The New Deal public philosophy, then, may be understood as a resurrection of the progressive vision of national community: a powerful central government in the service of the national idea, a president articulating that idea and drawing Americans together as neighbors, or as soldiers facing a common enemy. This vision of the national community, this public philosophy, would continue to dominate American politics for three decades, and to this day it strikes a responsive chord in the hearts of millions of Americans. As Irving Howe wrote recently, the "lasting contribution of the Roosevelt era" was the "socialization of concern, the vision of society as community."[3]

The New Deal did not, alas, have any discernible impact on the economic problems of deflation, unemployment, reduced profits, and the virtual disappearance of growth. In this respect we were somewhat behind not only England but Hitler's Germany as late as 1938, which was well before either power commenced rearmament on a significant scale. Neither country suffered the deep recession of 1937, a recession within a depression, that America did.

It was therefore a matter of supreme luck for the New Deal and the national community dream that World War II broke out in September 1939. For the war not only brought the Depression at last to an end in America—once war orders from Europe assumed massive enough force to break all vicious circles in the plight of the American economy—but there was, once again, war to serve the drive toward national community, the while it deluged and intoxicated many millions of long-unemployed, dispirited American workers with high wages, ample jobs, and a very cascade of long-sought economic and social reforms. American soldiers seemed less inspired by war, more prone to seek draft deferment at almost any cost, but from early on, they were promised educational, home-buying, and business benefits after the war that would make it all worthwhile.

Without doubt the idea of national community burns brightly in the American consciousness at the present time. Initiated by President Roosevelt, the idea has been nourished, watered, and tended in one degree or other by each succeeding president. When Governor Mario Cuomo of New York delivered his now historic speech in San Francisco in 1984 before the Democratic Convention, he made the national community his central, spellbinding theme. Over and over he referred to "family" and "community," and once or twice to "wagon train," meaning in each use, not the actual family or local community or wagon train crossing the prairies of earlier America, but rather the national state, the centralized, collectivized, and bureaucratized national state of this late part of the century. . . .

Accompanying the rage to political power in our age is the relentless march of royalism in the federal government. We see this in the presidency perhaps foremost, and I shall restrict myself for the most part to this office. But it would be negligent to overlook the trail of royalism in other departments of government also: in the Supreme Court where, as I have just emphasized, the temptation to make law instead of merely interpreting becomes ever stronger; in the Congress, especially the Senate, where more and more recourse is had to televised performances of Senate committees sitting inquisitorially over individuals, hailed commandingly by subpoena to come in front of it and be interrogated, often sharply, before the many millions of the television audience—descendants perhaps of those who used to enjoy public hangings. Everywhere, in the federal courts, in the halls and offices of Congress, in the White House, the mantle of luxury shines—a luxury of appointments, architecture, and style that one cannot often find in Europe anymore.

This is particularly noticeable in the presidency, in the present-day, post-Kennedy White House, never as resplendent before as under the Reagans; in the luxuriousness that pervades every corner and crevice of the presidential life; in the incessant imaging of the president for public purposes; and in the palace intrigues by now rife in every White House. Capture of the White House has appealed to utopians, reformers, and plain movers and shakers since the beginning of the century. From the time Wilson assumed the absolutism of his war powers in 1917 and commenced the radical transformation of America implicit in the War State, there has been a kind of dream of the strong, active, robust, commanding president that included more than a mere touch of plebiscitary democracy in it.

Basic to the clerisy strategy of magnifying the presidency in the eyes of the people is the parallel work of denigrating Congress and the departments. It is usually a toss-up between Congress and the Department of State as to which will be made, in any given year, the chief donkey of government. It is nearly instinctual in the political clerisy—and this holds true whether the administration is Republican or Democratic—to portray the president as the elected representative of the entire people, "The People," as it is commonly put, with congressmen portrayed as like mayors and city councilmen, mere representatives of wards, sections, and districts, thus a cracked mirror of the People.

This is not, of course, the way the Framers of the Constitution saw the ideal of American government. Ben Franklin is said to have replied, when an outsider asked him which was being effected by the Constitutional Convention, a republic or a monarchy: "A republic, if you can keep it." Franklin's answer would no doubt be the same today were he on the scene, but the words might be uttered with somewhat less confidence or optimism. During the past half-century we have seen the spirit of royalism rise considerably. Wilson is prototypical; not since have direct, personal powers been showered on a president by Congress, and with the approval of the Supreme Court, as they were on Wilson. But his presidency was one of austerity, and when the armistice came, demobilization of forces and return to constitutionality were immediate.

Present-day royalism in the federal government began with FDR. Few then present are likely to forget the excitement generated by his seeming assumption during the Hundred Days of just about all the powers of government. Congress was for the time relegated to the shades; the air was filled with alphabetical symbols of the agencies, bureaus, strategies he was pursuing on his own. He found it possible to receive credit even for entities like the Tennessee Valley Authority and the Reconstruction Finance Agency in which his role was slim at best. He did create on his own the ill-fated National Recovery Administration, a fusion of government and business that suggested Italian Fascism and was rather quickly ruled unconstitutional by the Supreme Court. With undiminished effort at autocracy, FDR sought to get a bill through Congress that would have—on the pretext of enhancing the Court's efficiency—increased significantly the size of the Court, thus making it possible for him to add justices of his own predilection. He was defeated on that by Congress.

Royalism is the essence of Roosevelt's wartime stance. Churchill, true architect of the salvation of the West from both Nazism and Soviet Communism and resplendent leader in action, was obliged, as noted above, to report regularly to

Parliament and almost daily to the powerful War Cabinet. In no way was his leadership diminished; he thought, indeed, that Roosevelt would have been aided by a similar regimen. Roosevelt would have had none of it under any circumstances. His consultation of Congress, once the war was entered, was infrequent and minimal. So was his consultation of the Cabinet. So was his consultation of any high official of government, including the Secretary of State, Cordell Hull. Churchill became the war's most illustrious leader without departing from constitutionalism. Roosevelt came very close to flouting constitutionalism, electing to confide in and listen to Harry Hopkins and, to somewhat less degree, General Marshall.

Under the Kennedy administration royalism was reinvigorated. From the beginning the theme, broadcast widely through a compliant press, was the "power of the president." To this end courtiers—there is no other appropriate word—appeared named Rostow, Schlesinger, Bundy, McNamara, Rusk, Hillsman, and Goodwin. This is the group given journalistic immortality by David Halberstam in his *The Best and the Brightest*. Although they all held regular governmental positions, including high Cabinet secretaryships, the real influence of the group came from their direct, *personal* fealty to the young and histrionic president.

Under President Kennedy's authority alone the number of military advisers to Diem in South Vietnam was increased from a few hundred to more than fifteen thousand, commanded by a four-star general. Under the same authority came the tragic and fateful decision to depose President Diem, thus leading to Diem's murder and also to our eight-year nightmare of war in Asia, eight thousand miles away. Precisely the same kind of exercise of presidential authority, nourished only by courtiers, not genuinely constitutional bodies of advisers like congressional committees and full departments like State and Defense, led at the very beginning of the Kennedy administration to the Bay of Pigs fiasco.

Royalism has not disappeared since Kennedy's assassination, only subsided slightly from time to time. Lyndon Johnson's Tonkin Gulf ruse gave him individual war powers suggestive of Roosevelt's and Wilson's. So did his reshaping of domestic bureaucracy through the Great Society program. Intrigue in the palace was constant; so was public discontent over his war in Vietnam. The President was in effect deposed, saved from that actuality only by grace of the election of 1968.

Since then in the reigns of Nixon and Reagan there have been analogous, even worse, incidents of extreme hypertrophy of White House power. National security, that ancient refuge of despotic monarchs, has become the portmanteau for at least two clutchings for personal power by the president: Watergate and, most recently, Irangate. National security as shield takes on some of the odor of *raison d'état* in Renaissance Europe, the plea of "reason of state" to conceal crime, heresy, or treason, or all three, in a given kingly court. The National Security Adviser—who has his own special power undergirded by a large and growing staff and which is composed for the most part of individuals sworn in fact to the personal being of the president rather than to the seals of government—would make the Framers rub their eyes. For in it, as it has been interpreted almost continuously since the Kennedy administration, lies, by implication at least, almost everything the Fathers of the Constitution loathed and abominated in the Old World.

National security is, like *raison d'état*, a wonderful umbrella for extensions of the presidential-royal power. Whether the president personally, consciously, participates in these extensions in domestic and foreign matters is just as hard to discover as ever it was when a Henry VIII or Louis XIV was involved. For the vast White House power is wielded today by a score of loyal, faithful personal retainers dedicated to protection of the royal presence and largely out of reach of legislative bodies. Government of laws and of offices threatens thus to be supplanted by government of personal retainers, of courtiers—hit men, jesters, confidential clerks, envoys of the most personal and secret responsibility, one and all thrilled at the work of guarding, when necessary, the government and the people from their duly elected, constitutionally vested representatives.

Perhaps the ultimate thus far in *raison d'état* in the name of the higher patriotism and morality that is above the law is the recent Poindexter-North intrigue, possibly even a small coup d'état, as it all unrolled. Here, an admiral and a marine lieutenant-colonel between them, serving as members of the National Security Council staff, took upon themselves the engineering of foreign policy to a degree that strains the vocabulary of the comic as well as the ominous. The height of the dark comedy was reached when the admiral relieved the President of the-buck-stops-here responsibility for the execution of a major, if ultimately farcical, coup in foreign policy.

Inevitably, given the temper of the times and the ubiquity of the political clerisy, the blame for White House coups and secret governments and grossly illegal operations abroad falls on Congress, sometimes the Court but never the royal presence of the president. For the clerisy that would amount to *lèse-majesté*. To shield, protect, conceal, dissemble for the president is now high among the responsibilities of the several hundred *politiques* who fill the White House and adjoining buildings as "staff." This began in the Kennedy administration; there the gravest offense any one of the protecting aides could be found guilty of was failing to absorb the possible blame to the President created by his own action or words. The president is never wrong! If he appears to be wrong in the eyes of press and people, someone in the White House curia, or janissariat, has failed in his job by not instantly absorbing full responsibility. Repeatedly during the Iran-*contra* hearing, Admiral Poindexter and also Colonel North made evident their devotion to the principle that the President must be protected even from his own judgment. This was the ground on which the admiral justified not only his withholding of vital information from the President but his actual destruction of documents signed by the President. Such treatment may be proper occasionally for traditional heads of state, whether kings, emperors, or presidents, who by office and tradition must be above the fray at all times. But it is hardly a fit role for the executive of the government.

NOTES

1. *A Preface to Morals.* New York, 1929. p. 80.
2. *English History: 1914–45.* Oxford University Press, 1965. p. 1.
3. *The Quest for a New Public Philosophy.* American Enterprise Institute. Washington, D.C., 1983.

POSTSCRIPT

Has the Power of the Presidency Been Eroded?

Once again it is the task of Americans to weigh the considerations on both sides of this issue. Do we Americans need further checks on the executive branch, or is there too great a risk that such checks will weaken not only the presidency but the nation itself? As president Abraham Lincoln framed the question: "Must a government of necessity be too strong for the liberties of its own people, or too weak to maintain its own existence?"

As mentioned in the introduction to this issue, the historian Arthur Schlesinger, Jr., who was once an uncritical promoter of the activist presidency, later recanted his position in *The Imperial Presidency* (Houghton Mifflin, 1973), a critical study of presidential power. George Reedy, former press secretary to Lyndon Johnson, offered his own critical perspective on the "monarchical" presidency in 1970; a second edition of this classic work was published in 1987. See Reedy's *The Twilight of the Presidency: From Johnson to Reagan* (New American Library, 1987). An equally classic defense of the presidency written during the Eisenhower administration has also been reissued. The late Clinton Rossiter's *The American Presidency* (Johns Hopkins, 1987) argues that the presidency is adequately checked but hardly needs to be, since only decent men are elected to the office. That last contention may raise eyebrows today, but Rossiter's basic theme—in his words, "Leave your presidency alone!"—is still arguable. James David Barber, in *The Presidential Character* (Prentice Hall, 1985), takes a somewhat different approach. Barber favors presidential activism, but only of a certain kind. "Active-positive" presidents (he puts Franklin Roosevelt and John F. Kennedy in that category) are good for the country, whereas "active-negative" types like Nixon and Johnson are dangerous.

It is important to remember that the presidency and its power are subject to changing fortunes. In 1885 Woodrow Wilson wrote: "The presidential office . . . has fallen from its first estate of dignity because its power has waned; and its power has waned because the power of Congress has become predominant." But in 1908 Wilson reached a radically different conclusion: "If he [the president] rightly interprets the national thought boldly and insists upon it, he is irresistible. . . . His office is anything he has the sagacity and force to make it."

ISSUE 7

Does the Government Regulate Too Much?

YES: **Barry Crickmer,** from "Regulation: How Much Is Enough?" *Nation's Business* (March 1980)

NO: **Susan and Martin Tolchin,** from *Dismantling America* (Houghton Mifflin, 1983)

ISSUE SUMMARY

YES: Editor Barry Crickmer argues that the interests of citizens and consumers could be better served by the forces of the profit motive than by government intervention.

NO: Professor Susan Tolchin and journalist Martin Tolchin contend that without vigorous regulation businesses will destroy the environment and endanger lives in their single-minded pursuit of profit.

Government regulation of economic decision making is as old as the Interstate Commerce Commission, which was established in 1887 to regulate railroad rates. The Sherman and Clayton Antitrust Acts of 1890 and 1914 respectively, as well as the law establishing the Federal Trade Commission in 1914, were also designed to outlaw unfair methods of business competition.

Congress later established regulatory agencies to set standards for natural (or socially useful) monopolies, such as electric power companies and radio and television stations. Between 1920 and 1940, Congress set up the Federal Power Commission, the Federal Communications Commission, and the Civil Aeronautics Board. The national government also created the Federal Reserve System in 1913 and the Securities and Exchange Commission in 1934 (after the stock market crash) to regulate the investment of capital in industry and general banking practices.

Although governmental regulation of commerce on behalf of the public interest was introduced as early as the Pure Food and Drug Act of 1906 (now administered by the Department of Health and Human Services), most activity within this area is relatively recent. The Equal Employment Opportunity Commission was established in 1965. The Environmental Protection Agency, the Occupational Safety and Health Administration, and the National Highway Traffic Safety Administration were all created in 1970. The

Consumer Product Safety Commission was set up in 1973, and the Office of Surface Mining Reclamation and Enforcement (within the Department of the Interior) came into being in 1977. With these and other newly established agencies, the federal government assumed wide-ranging responsibility to protect all persons against certain hazards that unrestrained private economic enterprise might otherwise create.

The rules written by these regulatory bodies have changed our lives in many ways, altering the food we eat, the cars we drive, and the air we breathe. Their defenders have applauded the protection that has been provided against profit-motivated predators who would otherwise adulterate our food, endanger our safety, and pollute the environment in order to maximize profits.

On the other hand, many investigators have joined businessmen in condemning government's movement into these areas. Critics make the following arguments: (1) Regulation inhibits production by suppressing innovation and discouraging risk taking, which results in declining employment. (2) Regulation invariably overregulates by setting standards for every aspect of manufacturing when it could set overall objectives that businesses could meet in whatever ways they devise. Some economists maintain that government would accomplish more by assessing fees or taxes to discourage certain activities rather than fixing rigid standards. (3) Regulation costs to businesses are passed on to the consumer, and increase government payrolls. If government regulation drives a company out of business, the standard of living for those affected will go down. That is to say, the costs outweigh the benefits.

These indictments of the regulatory process were voiced by President Reagan in his 1980 campaign for the presidency. Not surprisingly, when he entered office in 1981 he sought to restrain what he considered to be excessive regulation. His proposed restraints on regulatory agencies called for periodic reviews of agency activities, House and Senate reviews (and vetoes) of proposed new regulations, and economic impact analyses before new rules go into effect.

The lines of this argument are clearly drawn in the following essays. Barry Crickmer argues that the objectives of safety and health, as well as productivity, will be better achieved in the absence of government regulation. Susan and Martin Tolchin are deeply concerned that the thrust toward deregulation will reverse all the progress that has been made in protecting workers, consumers, and the environment.

YES

Barry Crickmer

REGULATION: HOW MUCH IS ENOUGH?

Federal regulation is often called inflationary, irritating, costly, and even farcical. But that's not the worst that can be said of it. The worst is that it isn't working.

The development, methodology, philosophy, and results of federal intervention in the marketplace fit Sir Ernest Benn's definition of politics as "the art of looking for trouble, finding it everywhere, diagnosing it wrongly, and applying unsuitable remedies."

For all the billion of dollars the regulatory agencies have spent and the billions more they have caused to be spent, there is surprisingly little evidence that the world is any better off than it would have been without federal tinkering.

NEEDLESS EXPENSE

Economist Murray Weidenbaum observes that "virtually every study of regulatory experience from trucking to pharmaceuticals to pensions indicates both needless expense and ineffective operations or, worst yet, counterproductive results."

For the old-line, economic regulatory agencies, the evidence of ineffectiveness has convinced even liberals to favor trimming or abolishing their powers. Presidential candidate Edward M. Kennedy (D-Mass.) points proudly to his role in deregulating the airlines. Even Federal Trade Commission Chairman Michael Pertschuk has been extolling the virtues of free market incentives.

But the newer, health-safety-social-environmental regulators still have vigorous defenders, although the defense is of necessity based more on what it is hoped they will do than on what they done so far.

TYPICAL PROBLEMS

The first to document the failure of health and safety regulation may have been University of Chicago economist Sam Peltzman. He is certainly one of the pioneers in the field.

Dr. Peltzman did a cost-benefit analysis of the more stringent drug relations that followed the thalidomide tragedy in Europe.

The Food and Drug Administration was an appropriate target for this seminal work published in 1973-74. Historically, the FDA belongs with the older single-industry regulators; by mission, it resembles the newer health and safety agencies. Further, some of its key problems are typical of most health and safety regulation.

Dr. Peltzman found that the new drug rules were costing American consumers three or four times as much as the economic benefits they produced. He also suggested that a too-cautious approach to approval of new drugs might foreclose or delay lifesaving advances in pharmaceutical technology.

Following Dr. Peltzman's work came a study by William M. Wardell, professor of pharmacology, toxicology, and medicine at the University of Rochester.

Dr. Wardell compared post-thalidomide drug development in the United States and Great Britain, which has fewer restrictions on new drugs. He demonstrated that lives were being saved in Britain and lost in the United States because of the more conservative U.S. policy toward new drugs. The British benefit not only from the more rapid introduction of valuable new drugs, he found, but also from the development of safer substitutes for potentially hazardous drugs in use.

It is easy to understand the FDA's caution. The damage done by a drug that should have been banned is visible and dramatic. The suffering and death that could have been prevented by a drug that was never developed are invisible and conjectural. Bureaucrats can hardly be blamed for trying to minimize known risk at the expense of unknown benefit. This dilemma is endemic to public-sector health safety regulation.

AUTO SAFETY

After making his point about drug regulation, Dr. Peltzman turned to auto safety. In a study published in 1975, he found that "essentially nothing in the post-1965 behavior of the total death rate can corroborate the idea that safety devices provide the kind of lifesaving suggested in safety literature."

A year later, the General Accounting Office reported that auto safety equipment mandated between 1966 and 1970 seemed to have reduced the risk of death and injury significantly, while that required after 1970 has produced no further improvement.

Other critics charge that federal auto safety regulations raise repair costs and waste gasoline.

It appears that the National Highway Traffic Safety Administration didn't know when to stop, stopped to soon, or should never have started.

In its seven years of existence, the Consumer Product Safety Commission has produced a handful of standards dealing with such threats as matchbook covers and swimming pool slides, inadvertently put a company out of business because of a typographical error in a list of hazardous toys, and arrested nine allegedly unsafe trash bins at a shopping center outside Washington, D.C.—in a daring daylight raid, as crime reporters say.

The trash cans went peacefully, if not quietly.

The incident prompted commission officials to search for a less cumbersome way to enforce their safety standards.

The Occupational Safety and Health Administration, like the traffic safety agency, is a very active agency with little to show for its activity. At least four major studies—including one by the Chamber of Commerce of the United States—failed to find any significant OSHA impact on the existing trend of industrial fatalities. Unlike the traffic safety agency, however, OSHA does not even try to subject its rules to cost-benefit analysis.

Similar evidence could be cited concerning the failures of the Environmental Protection Agency, the Energy Department, and other major and minor federal regulators. "The history of regulation is a history of disappointment," Harvard professors Albert Nichols and Richard Zeckhauser observe in a *Public Interest* article.

WHY DOES REGULATION FAIL?

The question is, why? Why has the direct and indirect expenditure of more than $100 billion a year on federal regulation failed to produce results commensurate with the effort? Or in some cases, any positive results at all?

Is the federal government trying to do the impossible? Or is it trying to do the possible in an impossible way? The answer is probably a little of both.

Many of the newer regulatory programs were ill-conceived and ill-considered. Typically, each got started after a single-interest pressure group succeeded in creating a wave of hysteria over an alleged crisis.

When this happens, most members of Congress quickly jump on the reform bandwagon. Those who don't may get crushed under its wheels. Says Rep. George Hansen (R-Idaho): "It's very hard in Congress to vote against mother and home. And how do you vote against something labeled clean meat, safety, and health?"

The news media—especially television—build pressure for quick fixes because they tend to focus on problems that can be presented dramatically, rather than on the comparatively dry analyses of possible solutions. Also, representatives of single-interest groups always have something quotable to say, so they get lots of publicity. Through such exposure, special-issue crusaders develop what Mr. Weidenbaum calls the power of arrogance. Soon, as authors Nichols and Zeckhauser put it, "the appetite for favorable results is . . . so enormous that the probability of success seems almost irrelevant," and the most far-reaching laws are passed with little thought to the consequences.

When OSHA was formed, they point out, no evidence was presented that even relatively modest gains could be achieved.

A similar pattern prevailed during adoption of the tough auto emissions standards of 1970. Congress passed that bill with little debate. And yet, "few people seem to have had any idea of what was in the legislation," said Howard Margolis, a research fellow at the Massachusetts Institute of Technology, writing in *Public Interest*.

"Even a superficial examination of available information" would have shown that the costly new standards could make very little difference in air pollution levels.

The same phenomenon is discussed by economists Dorothy Tella and Paul

MacAvoy in an analysis written for the U.S. Chamber's Council on Trends and Perspective:

"The rapid growth of health, safety, and environmental regulation in the late 1960s and early 1970s is not easy to explain. The market failures cited to justify new regulation did not show up then for the first time, and at least some of the indicators . . . that prompted Congress to regulate . . . were explained almost wholly by demographic factors beyond the reach of the regulatory process. . . .

"In every case where Congress chose to regulate, there were alternatives—court penalties for polluters, tax penalties for employers with poor safety records, government-funded information programs. In general, better arguments could have been made for the alternatives than for agency controls."

If the health and safety regulators were created in response to nonexistent crises, it is surprising they have made little impact on mortality rates.

SAFER AND HEALTHIER

Certainly, health and safety problems do exist and will continue as long as human beings remain fallible. Even so, statistics confirm that the American public is far safer and healthier today than in past years.

Moreover, the same statistics show that most of the progress occurred well before the advent of the health and safety agencies. The general accident rate, for example, peaked at 94.1 fatalities per 100,000 people in 1907, then began a long, steady decline until leveling off at about 20 per 100,000 after 1957.

This long-term improvement in safety suggests another hypothesis to explain the poor record of federal regulators. The private sector is motivated by profits to seek safer working conditions and products. That profit incentive will reduce the accident and disease rate to the lowest level consistent with an efficient allocation of resources.

The federal government is then left with trying to achieve dramatic safety gains when fine-tuning is all that can reasonably be expected.

The theory is difficult to prove because, as long as any hazards remain, they can always be attributed to business misfeasance. But it is not hard to demonstrate the strong profit incentive in improving safety.

Unsafe working conditions can deprive an employer of trained workers, increase insurance costs, and raise wages for dangerous work. Unsafe products expose the manufacturer to civil suit, higher insurance costs, and loss of patronage to competitors.

However, there is no free market incentive for pollution control. Control costs raise prices without increasing the value of a product to the consumer, and a manufacturer who bears the costs of pollution control voluntarily suffers a competitive disadvantage. Consequently, there is agreement on the need for government action to limit pollution. The disagreement comes over the means.

In passing, though, government itself does not show in its own activities a concern for the public interest superior to that of the private sector. Federal facilities are among the worst polluters, from the Tennessee Valley Authority to the Capitol Power Plant. OSHA's offices have violated OSHA's standards. The Equal Employment Opportunity Commission has been found guilty of racial discrimination. Government and private employees alike were exposed to asbestos dust before its harmful effects were known.

People will make mistakes, whether they are in public or private enterprise. But neither pleas of human fallibility nor complaints about cost deter some health and safety regulators from demanding perfection.

"Every worker has a fundamental human right to a safe and healthful workplace," asserted Labor Secretary Ray Marshall in a speech (in 1979). Absolutely safe? Perfectly healthful? On the previous page of his text, the Labor Secretary sagaciously observed that "it is much easier, when dealing with environmental and occupational health, to fall back upon demagoguery. . . ."

Joan Claybrook, administrator of the traffic safety agency, shows a similar lack of perspective.

Accused of requiring more safety than the consumer wants to buy, she replied in *Regulation* magazine that "producers who know how to make a product safer have an obligation to do so, and if they do not fulfill that obligation, then government must take it on . . . the sanctity of life has the highest value in our society."

That statement, praiseworthy on its surface, is the kind of mother-and-home phrase that troubles many legislators. There are many ways to save lives and improve health, but, unfortunately, the government has no rational, established method for choosing among them.

"Why should the government spend almost $30,000 per year to keep a kidney patient alive," University of Virginia professor Steven E. Rhoads asked in *Public Interest*, "and yet not pay for mobile cardiac units that can provide an additional life-year for as little as $1,765?"

At the other end of the scale, the chemical industry has calculated that OSHA's proposed limits on worker exposure to benzene would eliminate one case of leukemia every six years at a cost of $300 million each.

CURIOUS INCONSISTENCIES

A society never has enough resources to do everything that everyone would like to do. But OSHA and its brethren are not responsible for weighing their own plans against alternative uses of resources outside their spheres of influence. Thus, OSHA's efforts to save lives, like the FDA's, may result in a net loss of lives. This lack of a guiding philosphy and a coordinating authority also results in some curious inconsistencies.

Consider the CAT scanner, a very effective and expensive type of X-ray machine.

Federal health planners say physicians and hospitals are acquiring more of these devices than are needed, thereby wasting money. So the government wants to limit their number. In this case, cost-effectiveness is considered more important than the comfort, convenience, and perhaps even safety of the patients affected.

Contrast that policy with OSHA's proposed factory noise controls. OSHA wants employers to silence noisy machinery at great cost, rather than require workers to wear protective earplugs at modest cost.

The protective ear gear is uncomfortable, and workers might not wear it, says OSHA.

So in the case of noise standards, comfort and convenience are more important than cost-effectiveness.

PHILOSOPHICAL CHOICE

Beyond the economic trade-offs, there is a difficult philosophical choice between freedom and safety. Is an adult citizen a peer of the realm or its ward?

Sometimes society permits informed adults to participate in hazardous activities, vocational and avocational. And sometimes the law is used to limit or forbid such decisions.

"Why . . . do we find ourselves serenely contemplating a person's plan to climb a dangerous Himalayan peak at the same time that we propose making it illegal for her to buy a can of Tab?" asked University of California geneticist William R. Havender in a *Regulation* article.

There is little government objection to test pilots, firefighters, police, military personnel, and athletes accepting the risks of their trades.

Yet, industrial workers must apparently be protected from all risk, regardless of cost and their willingness to accept those risks in return for high pay and other benefits. In personal behavior, the government has attempted to force motorcycle riders to wear protective helmets on the ground that deaths and injuries impose costs on society. But if medical authorities are correct, far higher costs are imposed on society by those who smoke, eat, and drink to excess.

PERSONAL COMPULSION

Why do the regulators pick on the motorcycle riders? Perhaps because the motorcycle vote is relatively small.

"The resort to personal compulsion is a last resort when politicians fear that the public will not pay the cost of programs pushed on behalf of abstract principles," said Harvard Law School professor Charles Fried in *Regulation*. And he deplores "the moral obtuseness that treats people as public utilities."

Prof. Fried is not alone in his concern that freedom is endangered by well meaning regulators. That point is often made.

But the regulators also raise some troubling questions. Are citizens always aware of the risk inherent in product or occupation? If not, how can they make rational decisions? Dare we take chances with potentially hazardous environmental contaminants that may cause irreversible damage that does not show up for decades? And where environmental or genetic risk is involved, who represents the interests of future generations?

Americans need to make some painful choices about the priority of first principles. Until there is an agreed-upon basis for making trade-off decisions, it will remain impossible to know how much or how best to regulate.

In the words of Washington Gov. Dixie Lee Ray, a former federal regulator herself: "The reality is that zero defects in products plus zero pollution plus zero risk on the job is equivalent to maximum growth of government plus zero economic growth plus runaway inflation. That's what we have."

NO

Susan and Martin Tolchin

SILENT PARTNER:
THE POLITICS OF DEREGULATION

I don't know anybody who believes in dirty air or dirty water.
                                        —Irving Shapiro, former chairman
                                        of the board of the Du Pont Company

Regulation is the key to civilized society.
                    —The late Jerry Wurf, president of the American Federation
                                        of State, County, and Municipal Employees

Century-old Anaconda, Montana, in the foothills of the well-named Bitter-root Range of the Rocky Mountains, became an instant ghost town on a crisp September morning in 1980. With little warning to its fifteen hundred employees, some of whose fathers and grandfathers had worked for the company, the Anaconda Copper Company closed the smelter that was as old as the town itself, and its reason for existence. The smelter had processed the copper ore mined in Butte, twenty-eight miles southeast, and the smelted copper was then sent by rail to a refinery in nearby Great Falls. The refinery was also closed soon afterward.

The company announced that because of the high cost of complying with government regulations, it would henceforth ship its copper to Japan, where it would be refined and smelted before being returned to the United States, a round trip of about fourteen thousand miles. Anaconda had recently been acquired by the ARCO Oil Company, which claimed that compliance with federal and state standards would cost between $300 and $400 million. At a press conference called to announce the closing, the president of the company explained that the decision was reached after "exhausting every option available" to bring the smelter into compliance with environmental, health, and work place regulations, but the costs of compliance were "prohibitive."

It was part of a pattern in which overregulation was blamed for reducing the United States to an underdeveloped nation, whose minerals were taken by industrialized nations that in turn sent back finished products. This was a reversal of the industrial imperialism that had sent America and other industrial powers roaming the world for natural resources, exploiting their less-developed neighbors and intervening in their internal political and fiscal affairs. The emergence of a potent Japanese lobbying effort in the nation's capital, and its influence on legislation and regulation, is testimony that the United States is considered by some ripe for the picking, and on the verge of joining the industrial have-nots. Like the closing of the steel mills in Youngstown, Ohio, Anaconda highlighted a new trend that has disturbing implications for the national defense, as well as an estimated total nationwide cost of $125 billion in lost production and more than two million jobs.

Skeptics, and there were many, contended that the closing was really triggered by a costly labor dispute preceded by decades of poor management, when technological improvements were shunned in favor of the pursuit of profits. These skeptics cited a short-term approach, in which managers were encouraged to regard their positions as stepping stones to more prestigious and lucrative appointments, rather than developing long-term loyalties to institutions and rejecting immediate profits in favor of capital investments and long-term growth. As early as 1972, *Forbes* magazine observed that "Anaconda's problems seem to have stemmed directly from its corporate style of life; its patrician stance, its attitude of affluence." A major corporate blunder had been the company's failure to foresee the nationalization of its extensive copper mines in Chile by the government of Salvador Allende, which marked the beginning of a steady decline in Anaconda's fiscal fortunes. "The company was making so much money in Chile

that they let their domestic operations go a little flat," said L. R. Mecham, vice president of Anaconda.

Mecham added that labor troubles were a major factor in the closings. The plant had been idle since July, due to a nationwide strike against the copper industry. "Montana was notorious for having some of the worst labor practices in the country," he said.

The ranks of the skeptics also included government regulators, who argued not only that the costs of complying with regulations were far lower than the company's figures, but that they were willing to negotiate flexible timetables for meeting those standards. Challenging Anaconda's figures, the federal Environmental Protection Agency (EPA) put the price tag at about $140 million; the Occupational Safety and Health Administration (OSHA) added another $3 million to the estimate. Roger Williams, a regional administrator of EPA, said the finality of the decision came as a "complete surprise" to him because of Anaconda's earlier commitment to retrofit its existing facilities to meet air pollution requirements. "The company's past failure to investigate options with EPA," he wrote, "coupled with the company's ability to quickly secure profitable contracts with foreign industry piques my interest, and I'm sure the public's, in knowing the reasons behind the company's decision."

The real reasons, that is. For regulation had become the national whipping boy, and it was easier to lay the blame at the feet of faceless bureaucrats in Washington than on mismanagement, the greed of organized labor, the worldwide decline of the copper industry, or the fact that copper smelting's most valuable by-product—sulfuric acid—had become virtually unmarketable in the United States.

"They have used the closing as a political tool, to send a message to Congress about the Clean Air Act," said Steve Rovig, an aide to Senator Max Baucus, Democrat of Montana. . . .

Similarly, the American automobile industry blamed its precipitous decline, not on its high prices, oversized cars, or shoddy products, but on the raft of government regulations intended to improve the safety and fuel efficiency of the vehicles and perhaps make them more marketable. No matter that Japan overcame its long standing reputation for shoddy production by applying rigorous standards of quality control, standards that were abandoned during the same period by Detroit. And how do the steel, copper, and auto industries reconcile their tendency to make regulations the scapegoat with the cold fact that their foreign competitors, most notably Japan, also live with stiff regulations, particularly in the environmental field?

By the late 1970s, complaints of excessive regulation had become management's all-purpose cop-out. Were profits too low? Blame regulation. Were prices too high? Blame regulation. Were inadequate funds and manpower earmarked for research and development? Blame regulation for sapping both funds and manpower. Was American industry unable to compete with foreign competitors? Blame regulation.

In a highly technological society such as ours, the need for increased regulation is manifest. It is inconceivable to think of "lessening the regulatory burden," as some put it, at a time when private industry has the power to alter our genes, invade our privacy, and destroy our environment. A single industrial accident in the 1980s is capable of taking a huge toll in human life and suffering. Only the government has the power to create and enforce the social regulations that protect citizens from the awesome consequences of technology run amuck. Only the government has the ability to raise the national debate above the "balance sheet" perspective of American industry. This is not to dismiss the many socially conscious businessmen who are concerned with the public interest, but, unfortunately, they do not represent the political leadership of the business community. After all, the "bottom line" for business is making a profit, not improving the quality of the environment or the work place. Its primary obligation is to its shareholders, not to the community at large.

Complaints against regulation have become a standard lament of American business, not without some justification. Horror stories abound. Federal bureaucrats were designing everything from toilet seats to university buildings. Small companies complained that they were drowning in paperwork and were being "regulated out of business." Douglas Costle, a former administrator of the Environmental Protection Agency in the Carter administration, estimated that his agency's regulations alone increased the Consumer Price Index by four-tenths of one percent each year, while estimates of the total cost of regulation exceeded $100 billion a year.

The complaints focused on what are known as social regulations, regulations not geared to a specific industry but to the general public. Regulations falling into this category included those whose benefits were designed to provide clean air and water, safety in the work place, product safety, pure food and drugs, and protection for the consumer in the marketplace. Their goals were ambitious, but expensive to implement. . . .

TAKING CHARGE OF REGULATION

The long simmering battle against regulation finally found a champion during the 1980 presidential campaign. Ronald Reagan, en route to the White House, needed little prodding. Once a television host and lecturer for the General Electric Company, he had made a political career of championing the virtues of free enterprise, and had vowed during the campaign to "get the government off the backs of the people." Responding to this deeply bipartisan antiregulatory mandate, the new President initiated a crusade against government regulation and quickly laid the groundwork for the direction of regulation in the 1980s. To Reagan and his allies, the future lay in deregulation, or the removal of regulations from the books whenever possible in order to allow market forces to operate in their stead. Barely a week after his election, Ronald Reagan promised to dismantle existing regulations, and to freeze all new rules for at least a year after his inauguration. In living up to the spirit of his campaign promises, Reagan gave the American people a chance to see for themselves what life would be like without the onerous hand of big government.

The President's appointment of Murray Weidenbaum to chair the Council of Economic Advisers was an important choice, both substantively and symbolically, in the President's war against the regulators. A well-known economics professor at Washington University in St. Louis, Weidenbaum's major distinction was his philosophic opposition to the excesses of regulation. "The encroaching of government power in the private sector in recent years has been massive [and] self-defeating," he wrote prior to his appointment. Afterward, he frequently exhorted federal regulators: "When you have nothing to do, undo."

There is no question, of course, that a President and a Congress can change regulatory priorities. The question is whether such changes are in the interests of a highly technological society, in which private industry has the power to inflict widespread damage to life and health. Additional questions of particular relevance to President Reagan concern administrative procedures. While a President is empowered to change these procedures, with the help of Congress, questions have been raised about whether President Reagan adhered to traditional procedure governing the regulatory process, and the extent to which "undoing regulation" through procedural change has acted to the detriment of society.

The new President was so successful in capitalizing on his public relations victory over regulation that the system virtually reeled from its impact. Environmental protection became a thing of the past, as the EPA studiously ignored the laws and regulations dealing with clean air and water, as well as hazardous waste. Mine deaths shot up as regulations governing the safety of the mines were slowly dismantled through budget cuts and lack of enforcement. Through a program of consistent neglect, worker safety followed a similar path, victim of a more relaxed OSHA. No area of social protection was left untouched by White House efforts to unravel the regulations, the agencies, and the process. Even the nuclear regulators were encouraged to speed up the permit-granting process for nuclear plants by "streamlining" safety regulations.

What had taken years to build was dismantled in the first twelve months of the Reagan administration. Following the dictum that the marketplace could better evaluate the public's needs than government, Reagan trusted his friends in the business community to determine air quality, public safety, and a variety of other social questions far outside their realm of expertise. But the nation had become too complex for a return to this version of nineteenth-century laissez-faire capitalism, as became all too apparent early in the deregulation program. Nobody said anything about dead miners when discussing the burdens of regulation; no one reminded the public that not all industrialists would voluntarily clean up the local waterways and air without big government's interference. More than likely, the midnight dumpers were too busy finding new landfills for their illegal toxic wastes to make speeches about overregulation; now, with lax enforcement, they could probably operate in broad daylight.

It soon became apparent that in dismantling regulation, the President was dismantling America. Regulation is the connective tissue, the price we pay for an industrialized society. It is our major protection against the excesses of technology, whose rapid advances threaten man's genes, privacy, air, water, bloodstream, lifestyle, and virtual existence. It is a guard against the callous entrepreneur, who would have his workers breathe coal dust and cotton dust, who would send children into the mines and factories, who would offer jobs in exchange for health and safety, and leave the victims as public charges in hospitals and on welfare lines. "The child labor laws or the abolition of slavery would never have passed a cost-benefit test," said Mark Green, a public interest advocate, referring to the theory that now dominates regulatory decision making.

Regulations provide protection against the avarice of the marketplace, against shoddy products and unscrupulous marketing practices from Wall Street to Main Street. They protect legitimate businessmen from being driven out of business by unscrupulous competitors, and consumers from being victimized by unscrupulous businessmen. "Regulation is the key to civilized society," said the late Jerry Wurf, president of the American Federation of State, County, and Municipal Employees. The extent to which we take regulations for granted in our daily lives is reflected by the confidence with which we drink our water, eat our food, take our medication, drive our cars, and perform hundreds of other tasks without thought of peril. This provides a striking contrast to the situation in many Third World nations, devoid of regulations, where those tasks can be performed only with extreme care. (Indeed, there is evidence that some of those countries adhere to United States regulations in the absence of their own government protections. The Squibb representative in Egypt, for example, said in 1979 that he could not market his company's drugs in that country unless they had been cleared by the United States Food and Drug Administration.)

In responding so agreeably to the critics of regulation, the politicians so quick to deregulate forgot that it was the very same process that prevented thalidomide—a tranquilizer prescribed to pregnant women that caused birth defects—from reaching the United States marketplace. A conscientious FDA medical officer, Frances Kelsey, spotted the drug and held it up, unimpressed with the fact that it had already been approved by the West German regulators. Critics also forgot that regulations have

helped to restore the Great Lakes, which ten years ago were on their way to a polluted oblivion, and have brought the nation more breathable air by reducing sulfur emmissions by 17 percent since 1972. And although the Anaconda Copper Company complained bitterly about EPA regulations, lung disease in Western Montana declined significantly after the copper company took its first steps toward compliance with air quality standards.

When social regulation works, its benefits are invisible. It is hardly newsworthy, or even noticeable, that the nation's air and water have become considerably cleaner over the last decade, a regulatory development that could be viewed as a stunning success. So could the Consumer Product Safety Commission's regulations that changed the design of cribs and significantly reduced the number of crib deaths by strangulation.

The problem is that those who breathe and those whose lives were saved by a safer crib have no trade association to applaud the unseen and unheralded benefits of the regulatory process—when it is working well. They have no Political Action Committee to reward politicians who support the regulatory system, or to punish those who attack it. Indeed, most people are unaware that regulations play any role in their well-being. No constituency with significant power has developed over the years to bolster, promote, reinforce, and expand these "public goods." Yet this is another reason the regulatory process was created in the first place: to protect those public goods and those who benefit from them. Indeed, ever since the first United States Congress gave the President the power to make rules for trading with the Indians, regulation has grown geometrically, often with the enthusiastic support of Congress and the President, because it represented a system that held the promise of protecting the public against the incursions of more narrowly focused interests. "We created the regulatory agencies to do what we don't have time to do," said the late Sam Rayburn, when he was Speaker of the House. . . .

The social regulatory agencies have become the government's orphans, attacked by both management and labor. Management contends that the cost of compliance will erode profits, while labor fears that it could cost jobs and lead to the destruction of entire industries. In an increasing number of cases, management and labor have joined forces to fight the regulatory agencies, producing formidable alliances. In one successful effort, the grain millers union fought side by side with management against the FTC's antitrust efforts to break up the giant cereal companies. In cases like this, who is left to provide the support network and the constituency so necessary to an agency's effective survival?

In this harsh political climate, it is no wonder that leadership on all fronts is in short supply. When President Carter claimed credit for returning salmon to the Columbia River, few applauded his efforts in cleaning up that once polluted waterway. When he attempted to intervene to cut the cost of environmental regulation, he was quickly branded an "enemy of the environment" by an army of critics. Nor did he find many friends among members of the business community, who faulted him for not moving fast enough to dismantle the regulatory process.

Both Congress and President Reagan learned the political lessons of the past, finding it was much easier to correct regulatory "excesses" by dismantling an

agency, by reducing its budget to a point that renders it virtually ineffective, than to address the issue at hand.

Throwing the baby out with the bath water became a familiar pattern. It was guaranteed to stop an agency that had failed to work efficiently, that was perhaps working too efficiently, or that was working against the interests of a powerful industry. When certain members of Congress began receiving complaints against the FTC, they mounted such a successful campaign to hold up its appropriations that the agency was forced to close down for a few days in the spring of 1980. By 1981, another consumer agency, the Consumer Product Safety Commission, less vigorous than the FTC but equally offensive to business interests, fought valiantly to stay alive, even on its paltry budget of $40 million a year.

Congress regards its interventions as part of its legitimate oversight function to monitor the regulatory agencies. This has more than a grain of truth to it. A closer look reveals, however, that Congress bears considerable responsibility for the current state of siege that confronts the agencies, as well as for the volatility of regulatory politics in general. With its ambiguous mandates, increasingly detailed legislation, vulnerability to special interests, and increased involvement in the budget process, Congress has reinforced the uncertainty surrounding regulation and done little to improve its troubled future.

What few citizens realize is that all regulation stems from a statutory base. Agencies do not regulate on the basis of whim. OSHA did not initiate the guarantee of a safe work place for every worker; Congress wrote the enabling legislation that created the agency and gave it that far-reaching mandate. It was also Congress that set the goals for air quality standards, not the EPA, although both Reagan and Congress eleven years later threatened to reduce the EPA's power during the renewal of the Clean Air Act—essentially penalizing the agency for doing its job.

Under the guise of responding to pressures, Congress is acting out a charade. The members bask in the applause when they are credited with giving the nation clean air and a safe work place, but recoil from the anger of those who must bear the brunt of the high cost of regulation. . . .

WHO BENEFITS AND WHO LOSES?

The most serious consequence of the trend to deregulate is the dismantling of the social regulations, which provide a connective tissue between the needs of the public and private sectors. Private industry is entitled to make a profit, but its employees are entitled to their health and safety, their consumers are entitled to safe and well-made products, and the public is entitled to have its air, water, and quality of life safeguarded.

The rapid pace of technological advances has given industry awesome tools with which to alter our genes, invade our privacy, and even destroy our lives. It is difficult, therefore, to regard the current dismantling of regulation as anything but an aberration, a trend that will soon be reversed. One can thus expect increased pressures on government for protection against forces over which individuals have less and less control. And one would certainly expect those forces to be resisted by the affected industries. That conflict will be resolved in the political arena, which will be the ultimate arbiter in the current attempt at dismantling America.

POSTSCRIPT

Does the Government Regulate Too Much?

Any consideration of social regulation by government must assess both costs and benefits. Society must ask how much it is willing to pay to avoid a given risk, just as workers will demand increased wages for taking greater risks. Most people are likely to agree that there are some benefits that merit the cost, and some costs that outweigh the benefits. Crickmer does not make many concessions, but he does acknowledge that pollution controls are necessary and that the early automobile safety requirements did make a difference in reducing deaths and injuries. On the other side, Susan and Martin Tolchin concede that before Reagan came into office "federal bureaucrats were designing everything from toilet seats to university buildings." Although both essays acknowledge that the other side may have a point or two in its favor, the two remain sharply opposed to one another. This is true even when they quote the same economist: Murray L. Weidenbaum.

Weidenbaum has written a comprehensive account of government regulation: *Business, Government, and the Public* (Prentice-Hall, 1977). His survey and case studies cover consumer products, the environment, and job and automobile safety. Harold Seidman, in *Politics, Position and Power*, 2nd ed. (Oxford, 1975), maintains that conflicts between the regulatory agencies and the elected branches rarely turn on questions of substantive reform or administrative efficiency but are essentially political conflicts between opposing interests. Herbert Kaufman's *Red Tape: Its Origins, Uses, and Abuses* (Brookings, 1977) clearly and briefly explains why bureaucratic institutions, including regulatory agencies, create so many obstacles to compliance.

The world is a dangerous place. The supporters of governmental regulation believe that in the absence of such controls we will face greater hazards and that more dangers will be loosed upon us by unscrupulous entrepreneurs. The opponents hold that we will more surely be strangled by red tape and impoverished by the regulatory costs that make prices higher when they do not actually make production unprofitable. It is tempting to counsel moderation between the extreme principles, but it is difficult to apply moderation in practice. Take, as an example, the debate on the development of nuclear energy for non-military uses. Neither side will be happy with a compromise that means limited utilization of atomic power. Such a policy will not fulfill the hopes of those who see nuclear energy as a solution for the energy crisis, and it will not allay the fears of those who see it as a threat to the lives of millions of people living near nuclear plants. Yet it is possible that, in this area as in others, the give and take of politics will dictate solutions that are unsatisfactory to all concerned and thus keep the issue of regulation alive.

ISSUE 8

Should the Federal Courts Be Bound by the "Original Intent" of the Framers?

YES: Robert H. Bork, from "The Case Against Political Judging," *National Review* (December 8, 1989)

NO: Leonard W. Levy, from *Original Intent and the Framers' Constitution* (Macmillan, 1988)

ISSUE SUMMARY

YES: Educator and former judge Robert H. Bork argues that the "original intent" of the framers of the Constitution can and should be upheld by the federal courts, because not to do so is to have judges perform a political role they were not given.
NO: Professor Leonard W. Levy believes that the "original intent" of the framers cannot be found, and, given these changing times, it could not be applied in dealing with contemporary constitutional issues.

Although the Supreme Court has declared fewer than one hundred acts of Congress unconstitutional, judicial review (the power to exercise this judgment) is a critical feature of American government. It extends to all law—not simply federal law—and includes not only statutes but the actions of all agents of governmental power.

The power of judicial review consists not only of a negative power to invalidate acts contrary to the Constitution but also (and far more frequently) of a positive power to give meaning and substance to constitutional clauses and the laws enacted in accordance with constitutional power. Finally, individual cases have impact and reverberation, which may profoundly influence the future direction of law and behavior. To take a prominent example, when the Supreme Court reinterpreted the equal protection clause of the Constitution's Fourteenth Amendment in 1954, it changed forever the legal and social patterns of race relations in the United States.

Some limitations on judicial review are self-imposed, such as the Court's refusal to consider "political questions"—that is, questions better decided by the elective branches rather than the courts. But it is the Supreme Court that decides which questions are political. The Supreme Court has been notably reluctant to curb a president's extraordinary use of emergency power in wartime and has done so rarely.

Still other limitations on judicial review derive from the judicial process, such as the requirement that the party bringing a case to court (any court) must have sufficient "standing" as an aggrieved party to be heard. Some laws do not appear to give any contesting party the basis for bringing a suit. Other laws rarely present themselves in an appropriate form for judicial decision, such as the ordinary exercise of presidential power in foreign relations. These exceptions qualify, yet do not really negate, the spirit of Alexis de Tocqueville's observation of nearly a century and a half ago that "scarcely any political question arises in the United States that is not resolved, sooner or later, into a judicial question."

Judicial review is exercised by state courts and lower federal courts as well as by the United States Supreme Court, but the last word is reserved to the latter. Because its power is so vast and is exercised in controversial areas, the judiciary is subject to considerable criticism. Critics have argued that the framers of the Constitution did not intend for so great a power to be possessed by so unrepresentative (unelected) an organ of government. The Court has been chided for going too far, too fast (for example, law enforcement agencies protest measures dealing with the rights of accused persons) and for not going far enough, fast enough (for example, by civil rights activists working for racial equality). In the 1930s, liberals castigated the "nine old men" for retarding social progress by invalidating New Deal measures. In the 1950s, conservatives pasted "Impeach Earl Warren" (then chief justice) stickers on their car bumpers, and they bemoaned the Court's so-called coddling of communists and criminals. More recently, liberal critics have viewed the Supreme Court headed by chief justices Warren Burger and William Rehnquist as being less sympathetic to enforced integration, women's rights, the defense of accused persons, and the protection of socially disapproved expression.

The Supreme Court professes to decide these issues on the basis of constitutional principles. One view, argued by former judge Robert Bork, is that the Court should uphold the "original intent" of the framers as it is found in the Constitution and its amendments. To do otherwise is to engage in political decision-making, which is not the Court's business.

The other view, upheld by professor Leonard Levy, is that we cannot find the "original intent" of the framers because the framers (and ratifiers) differed among themselves, and, if we could find it, we could not be bound by it in finding new solutions to new problems.

YES

Robert H. Bork

THE CASE AGAINST POLITICAL JUDGING

What was once the dominant view of constitutional law—that a judge is to apply the Constitution according to the principles intended by those who ratified the document—is now very much out of favor among the theorists of the field. In the legal academies in particular, the philosophy of original understanding is usually viewed as thoroughly passé, probably reactionary, and certainly—the most dreaded indictment of all—"outside the mainstream." That fact says more about the lamentable state of the intellectual life of the law, however, than it does about the merits of the theory.

In truth, only the approach of original understanding meets the criteria that any theory of constitutional adjudication must meet in order to possess democratic legitimacy. Only that approach is consonant with the design of the American Republic.

When we speak of "law," we ordinarily refer to a rule that we have no right to change except through prescribed procedures. That statement assumes that the rule has a meaning independent of our own desires. Otherwise there would be no need to agree on procedures for changing the rule. Statutes, we agree, may be changed by amendment or repeal. The Constitution may be changed by amendment pursuant to the procedures set out in Article V. It is a necessary implication of the prescribed procedures that neither statute nor Constitution should be changed by judges. Though that has been done often enough, it is in no sense proper.

What is the "meaning" of a law, that essence that judges should not change? It is the meaning understood at the time of the law's enactment. What the Constitution's ratifiers understood themselves to be enacting must be taken to be what the public of that time would have understood the words to mean. It is important to be clear about this, because the search is not for a subjective intention. If, for instance, Congress enacted a statute outlawing the sale of automatic rifles and did so in the Senate by a vote of 51 to 49, no court would overturn a conviction under the law because two senators in the majority later testified that they had really intended only to prohibit the *use*

of such rifles. They said "sale" and "sale" it is. Thus, the common objection to the philosophy of original understanding—that Madison kept his notes of the convention at Philadelphia secret for many years—is off the mark. He knew that what mattered was public understanding, not subjective intentions.

Law is a public act. Secret reservations or intentions count for nothing. The original understanding is thus manifested in the words used and in secondary materials, such as debates at the conventions, public discussion, newspaper articles, dictionaries in use at the time, and the like.

THE SEARCH FOR THE INTENT OF THE LAW-maker is the everyday procedure of lawyers and judges when they apply a statute, a contract, a will, or the opinion of a court. To be sure, there are differences in the way we deal with different legal materials, which was the point of John Marshall's observation in *McCulloch v. Maryland* that "we must never forget, that it is a *constitution* we are expounding." By that he meant narrow, legalistic reasoning was not to be applied to the document's broad provisions, a document that could not, but its nature and uses, "partake of the prolixity of a legal code." But in that same opinion he also wrote that a provision must receive a "far and just interpretation," which means that the judge is to interpret what is in the text and not something else. And, it will be recalled, in *Marbury v. Madison* Marshall based the judicial power to invalidate a legislative act upon the fact that a judge was applying the words of a written document. Thus, questions of breadth of approach or of room for play in the joints aside, lawyers and judges should seek in the Constitution what they seek in other legal texts: the original meaning of the words.

We would at once criticize a judge who undertook to rewrite a statute or the opinion of a superior court; and yet such judicial rewriting is often correctable by legislatures or superior courts, whereas the Supreme Court's rewriting of the Constitution is not correctable. At first glance, it seems distinctly peculiar that there should be a great many academic theorists who explicitly defend departures from the understanding of those who ratified the Constitution while agreeing, at least in principle, that there should be no departure from the understanding of those who enacted a statute or joined a majority opinion. A moment's reflection suggests, however, that Supreme Court departures from the original meaning of the Constitution are advocated *precisely because* those departures are not correctable democratically. The point of the academic exercise is to be free of democracy in order to impose the values of an elite upon the rest of us.

It is here that the concept of neutral principles, which Herbert Wechsler has said are essential if the Supreme Court is not to be a naked power organ, comes into play. Wechsler, in expressing his difficulties with the decision in *Brown v. Board of Education*, said the courts must choose principles which they are willing to apply neutrally; to apply, that is, to all cases that may fairly be said to fall within them. This is a safeguard against political judging. No judge will say openly that any particular group or political position is always entitled to win. He will announce a principle that decides the case at hand, and Wechsler has no difficulty with that if the judge is willing to apply the same principle in the next case, even when it means a group favored by the first decision is disfavored by the second.

When a judge finds his principle in the Constitution as originally understood, the problem of the neutral derivation of principle is solved. The judge accepts the ratifiers' definition of the appropriate ranges of majority and minority freedom. The "Madisonian dilemma" (essentially, the conflict of majority rule with minority rights) is resolved in the way that the Founders resolved it, and the judge accepts the fact that he is bound by that resolution as law. He need not, and must not, make unguided value judgments of his own.

This means, of course, that a judge, no matter on what court he sits, may never create new constitutional rights or destroy old ones. Any time he does so, he violates the limits of his own authority and, for that reason, also violates the rights of the legislature and the people. When a judge is given a set of constitutional provisions, then, as to anything not covered by those provisions, he is, quite properly, powerless. In the absence of law, a judge is a functionary without a function.

This is not to say, of course, that majorities may not add to minority freedoms by statute, and indeed a great deal of the legislation that comes out of Congress and the state legislatures does just that. The only thing majorities may not do is invade the liberties the Constitution specifies. In this sense, the concept of original understanding builds in a bias toward individual freedom. Thus, the Supreme Court properly decided in *Brown* that the equal protection clause of the Fourteenth Amendment forbids racial segregation or discrimination by any arm of government, but, because the Constitution addressed only governmental action, the Court could not address the question of private discrimination. Congress did address it in the Civil Rights Act of 1964 and in subsequent legislation, enlarging minority freedoms beyond those mandated by the Constitution.

THE NEUTRAL DEFINITION OF THE PRINCIPLE derived from the historic Constitution is also crucial. The Constitution states its principles in majestic generalities that we know cannot be taken as sweepingly as the words alone might suggest. The First Amendment states that "Congress shall make no law . . . abridging the freedom of speech," but no one has ever supposed that Congress could not make some speech unlawful or that it could not make all speech illegal in certain places, at certain times, and under certain circumstances. Justices Hugo Black and William O. Douglas often claimed to be First Amendment absolutists, but even they would permit the punishment of speech if they thought it too closely "brigaded" with illegal action. From the beginning of the Republic to this day, no one has ever thought Congress could not forbid the preaching of mutiny at sea or disruptive proclamations in a courtroom. One may not cry "Fire!" in a crowded theater.

But the question of neutral definition remains and is obviously closely related to neutral application. Neutral application can be gained by defining a principle so narrowly that it will fit only a few cases. Thus, once a principle is derived from the Constitution, its breadth or the level of generality at which it is stated becomes of crucial importance. The judge must not state the principle with so much generality that he transforms it. The difficulty in finding the proper level of generality has led some critics to claim that the application of the original under-standing is actually impossible. That sounds fairly abstract, but an example will make clear both the point and the answer to it.

In speaking of my view that the Four-teenth Amendment's equal protection clause requires black equality, Dean Paul Brest said:

> The very adoption of such a principle, however, demands an arbitrary choice among levels of abstraction. Just what *is* "the general principle of equality that applies to all cases"? Is it the "core idea of *black* equality" that Bork finds in the original understanding (in which case Allan Bakke [a white who sued because a state medical school gave preference in admissions to other races] did not state a constitutionally cognizable claim), or a broader principle of "*racial* equal-ity" (so that, depending on the precise content of the principle, Bakke might have a case after all), or is it a still broader principle of equality that en-compasses discrimination on the basis of gender (or sexual orientation) as well?
>
> . . . The fact is that all adjudication requires making choices among the levels of generality on which to articulate principles, and all such choices are in-herently non-neutral. No form of con-stitutional decision-making can be salvaged if its legitimacy depends on satisfying Bork's requirements that principles be "neutrally derived, de-fined, and applied."

If Brest's point about the impossibility of choosing the level of generality upon neutral criteria is correct, we must either resign ourselves to a Court that *is* a "naked power organ" or require the Court to stop making "constitutional" decisions. But Brest's argument seem to me wrong, and I think a judge commit-

ted to original understanding can do what Brest says he cannot. We may use Brest's example to demonstrate the point.

The role of a judge committed to the philosophy of original understanding is not to "*choose* a level of abstraction." Rather, it is to find the meaning of a text—a process which includes finding its degree of generality, which is part of its meaning—and to apply that text to a particular situation, which may be diffi-cult if its meaning is unclear. With many if not most textual provisions, the level of generality which is part of their meaning is readily apparent. The problem is most difficult when dealing with the broadly stated provisions of the Bill of Rights. It is to the latter that we confine discussion here. In dealing with such provisions, a judge should state the principle at the level of generality that the text and his-torical evidence warrant. The equal-pro-tection clause was adopted in order to protect freed slaves, but its language, being general, applies to all persons. As we might expect, the evidence of what the drafters, the Congress that proposed the clause, and the ratifiers understood themselves to be requiring is clearest in the case of race relations. It is there that we may begin in looking for evidence of the level of generality intended. Without meaning to suggest what the historical evidence in fact shows, let us assume we find that the ratifiers intended to guaran-tee that blacks should be treated by law no worse than whites, but that it is un-clear whether whites were intended to be protected from discrimination. On such evidence, the judge should protect only blacks from discrimination, and Allan Bakke would not have had a case. The reason is that the next higher level of generality above black equality, which is racial equality, is not shown to be a constitutional principle, and, therefore, there is nothing to be set against a current legislative majority's decision to favor blacks. Democratic choice must be accepted by the judge where the Constitution is silent. The test is the reasonableness of the distinction, and the level of generality chosen by the ratifiers determines that. If the evidence shows the ratifiers understood racial equality to have been the principle they were enacting, then Bakke *would* have a case.

To define a legal proposition or principle involves simultaneously stating its contents and its limits. When, for instance, you state what *is* contained within the clause of the First Amendment guarantee of the free exercise of religion, you necessarily state what is *not* contained within that clause. Because the First Amendment guarantees freedom of speech, judges are required reasonably to define what is speech and what is its freedom. Where the law stops, the legislator may move on to create more; but where the law stops, the judge must stop.

The neutral or nonpolitical application of principle has been discussed in connection with Wechsler's discussion of *Brown*. It is a requirement, like the others, addressed to the judge's integrity. Having derived and defined the principle to be applied, he must apply it consistently and without regard to his sympathy or lack of sympathy with the parties before him. This does not mean that the judge will never change the principle he has derived and defined. Anybody who has dealt extensively with law knows that a new case may seem to fall within a principle as stated and yet not fall within the rationale underlying it. As new cases present new patterns, the principle will often be restated and redefined. There is nothing wrong with that; it is, in fact,

highly desirable. But the judge must be clarifying his own reasoning and verbal formulations and not trimming to arrive at results desired on grounds extraneous to the Constitution. This requires a fair degree of sophistication and self-consciousness on the part of the judge. The only external discipline to which the judge is subject is the scrutiny of professional observers who will be able to tell over a period of time whether or not he is displaying intellectual integrity.

THE STRUCTURE OF GOVERNMENT THE Founders of this nation intended most certainly did not give courts a political role. The debates surrounding the Constitution focused much more upon theories of representation than upon the judiciary, which was thought to be a comparatively insignificant branch. There were, however, repeated attempts at the Constitutional Convention in Philadelphia to give judges a policy-making role. The plan of the Virginia delegation, which, amended and expanded, ultimately became the Constitution of the United States, included a proposal that the new national legislature be controlled by placing a veto power in a Council of Revision consisting of the executive and "a convenient number of the National Judiciary." That proposal was raised four times and defeated each time. Among the reasons, as reported in James Madison's notes, was the objection raised by Elbridge Gerry of Massachusetts that it "was quite foreign from the nature of ye. office to make them judges of policy of public measures." Rufus King, also of Massachusetts, added that judges should "expound the law as it should come before them, free from the bias of having participated in its formation." Judges who create new constitutional rights are judges of the policy of public measures and are biased by having participated in the policy's formation.

The intention of the Convention was accurately described by Alexander Hamilton in *The Federalist* No. 78: "[T]he judiciary, from the nature of its functions, will always be the least dangerous to the political rights of the Constitution; because it will be least in a capacity to annoy or injure them." The political rights of the Constitution are, of course, the rights that make up democratic self-government. Hamilton obviously did not anticipate a judiciary that would injure those rights by adding to the list of subjects that were removed from democratic control. Thus, he could say that the courts were "beyond comparison the weakest of the three departments of power," and he appended a quotation from the "celebrated Montesquieu": "Of the three powers above mentioned [the others being the legislative and the executive], the JUDICIARY is next to nothing." This was true because judges were, as Rufus King said, merely to "expound" the law.

Even if evidence of what the Founders thought about the judicial role were unavailable, we would have to adopt the rule that judges must stick to the original meaning of the Constitution's words. If that method of interpretation were not common in the law, if James Madison and Justice Joseph Story had never endorsed it, if Chief Justice John Marshall had rejected it, we would have to invent the approach of original understanding in order to save the constitutional design. No other method of constitutional adjudication can confine courts to a defined sphere of authority and thus prevent them from assuming powers whose exercise alters, perhaps radically, the design of the American Republic. The philosophy of original understanding is thus a necessary inference from the structure of government apparent on the face of the U.S. Constitution.

WE COME NOW TO THE QUESTION OF PRECEdent. It is particularly important because, as Professor Henry Monaghan of Columbia University Law School notes, "much of the existing constitutional order is at variance with what we know of the original understanding." Some commentators have argued from this obvious truth that the approach of original understanding is impossible or fatally compromised, since they suppose it would require the Court to declare paper money unconstitutional and overturn the centralization accomplished by abandoning restrictions on congressional powers during the New Deal. But to say that prior courts have allowed, or initiated, deformations of the Constitution is not enough to create a warrant for present and future courts to do the same thing.

All serious constitutional theory centers upon the duties of judges, and that comes down to the question: What should the judge decide in the case now before him? Obviously, an originalist judge should not deform the Constitution further. Just as obviously, he should not attempt to undo all mistakes made in the past. At the center of the philosophy of original understanding, therefore, must stand some idea of when the judge is bound by prior decisions and when he is not.

Is judicial precedent an ironclad rule? It is not, and never has been. As Felix Frankfurter once explained, "*stare decisis* is a principle of policy and not a mechanical formula of adherence to the latest decision, however recent and questionable, when such adherence involves collision with a prior doctrine more embracing in its scope, intrinsically sounder, and verified by experience." Thus, in Justice Powell's words, "[i]t is . . . not only [the Court's] prerogative but also [its] duty to re-examine a precedent where its reasoning or understanding of the Constitution is fairly called into question." The Supreme Court frequently overrules its own precedents. *Plessy v. Ferguson*, and the rule of separate-but-equal in racial matters, lasted 58 years before it was dispatched in *Brown v. Board of Education*. In a period of 16 years the Court took three different positions with respect to the constitutionality of federal power to impose wage and price regulations on states and localities as employers. Indeed, Justice Blackmun explained in the last of these decisions that prior cases, even of fairly recent vintage, should be reconsidered if they "disserve principles of democratic self-governance." Every year the Court overrules a number of its own precedents.

The practice of overruling precedent is particularly common in constitutional law, the rationale being that it is extremely difficult for an incorrect constitutional ruling to be corrected through the amendment process. Almost all Justices have agreed with Felix Frankfurter's observation that "the ultimate touchstone of constitutionality is the Constitution itself and not what we have said about it." But that, of course, is only a partial truth. It is clear, first, that Frankfurter was talking about the Supreme Court's obligations with respect to its own prior decisions. Lower courts are not free to ignore what the Supreme Court has said about the Constitution, for that would introduce chaos into the legal system as courts of appeal refused to follow Supreme Court rulings and district courts disobeyed their appellate courts' orders. Second, what "the Constitution itself" says may, as in the case of paper money, be irretrievable, not simply because of "what [the Justices] have said about it," but because of what the nation has done or become on the strength of what the Court said.

To say that a decision is so thoroughly embedded in our national life that it should not be overruled, even though clearly wrong, is not necessarily to say that its principle should be followed in the future. Thus, the expansion of Congress's commerce, taxing, and spending powers has reached a point where it is not possible to state that, as a matter of articulated doctrine, there are any limits left. That does not mean, however, that the Court must necessarily repeat its mistake as congressional legislation attempts to reach new subject areas. Cases now on the books would seem to mean that Congress could, for example, displace state law on such subjects as marriage and divorce, thus ending such federalism as remains. But the Court could refuse to extend the commerce power so far, without overruling its prior decisions, thus leaving existing legislation in place but not giving generative power to the faulty principle by which that legislation was originally upheld. It will be said that this is a lawless approach, but that is not at all clear. The past decisions are beyond reach, but there remains a constitutional principle of federalism that should be regarded as law more profound than the implications of the past decisions. They cannot be overruled, but they can be confined to the subject areas they concern. When we cannot recover the transgressions of the past, then the best we can do is say to the Court, "Go and sin no more."

Finally, it should be said that those who adhere to a philosophy of original understanding are more likely to respect precedent than those who do not. As Justice Scalia has said, if revisionists can ignore "the most solemnly and democratically adopted text of the Constitution and its Amendments . . . on the basis of current values, what possible basis could there be for enforced adherence to a legal decision of the Supreme Court?" If you do not care about stability, if today's result is all-important, there is no occasion to respect either the constitutional text or the decisions of your predecessors.

NO

Leonard W. Levy

THE FRAMERS AND ORIGINAL INTENT

James Madison, Father of the Constitution and of the Bill of Rights, rejected the doctrine that the original intent of those who framed the Constitution should be accepted as an authoritative guide to its meaning. "As a guide in expounding and applying the provisions of the Constitution," he wrote in a well-considered and consistent judgment, "the debates and incidental decisions of the Convention can have no authoritative character." The fact that Madison, the quintessential Founder, discredited original intent is probably the main reason that he refused throughout his life to publish his "Notes of Debates in the Federal Convention," incomparably our foremost source for the secret discussions of that hot summer in Philadelphia in 1787.

We tend to forget the astounding fact that Madison's Notes were first published in 1840, fifty-three years after the Constitutional Convention had met. That period included the beginnings of the Supreme Court plus five years beyond the entire tenure of John Marshall as Chief Justice. Thus, throughout the formative period of our national history, the High Court, presidents, and Congress construed the Constitution without benefit of a record of the Convention's deliberations. Indeed, even the skeletal Journal of the Convention was not published until 1819. Congress could have authorized its publication anytime after President George Washington, who had presided at the 1787 Convention, deposited it at the State Department in 1796. Although the Journal merely revealed motions and votes, it would have assisted public understanding of the secret proceedings of the Convention, no records of which existed, other than the few spotty and jaundiced accounts by Convention members who opposed ratification. The Convention had, after all, been an assembly in which "America," as George Mason of Virginia said, had "drawn forth her first characters," and even Patrick Henry conceded that the Convention consisted of "the greatest, the best, and most enlightened of our citizens." Thomas Jefferson, in Paris, referred to the "assembly of demigods." The failure of the Framers to have officially preserved and published their proceedings seems inexplicable, especially in a nation that promptly turned matters of state into questions of constitutional law; but then, the Framers seem to have thought that "the original understanding at Philadelphia," which Chief Justice William H. Rehnquist has alleged to be of prime importance, did not greatly matter. What mattered to them was the text of the Constitution, construed in light of conventional rules of interpretation, the ratification debates, and other contemporary expositions.

If the Framers, who met in executive sessions every day of their nearly four months of work, had wanted their country and posterity to construe the Constitution in the light of their deliberations, they would have had a stenographer present to keep an official record, and they would have published it. They would not have left the task of preserving their debates to the initiative of one of their members who retained control of his work and a proprietary interest in it. "Nearly a half century" after the convention, Madison wrote a preface to his Notes in which he explained why he had made the record. He had determined to preserve to the best of his ability "an exact account of what might pass in the Convention," because the record would be of value "for the History of a Constitution on which would be staked the happiness of a young people great even in its infancy, and possibly the cause of Liberty throughout the world." That seems to have been a compelling reason for publication as soon as possible, not posthumously—and Madison outlived all the members of the Convention. . . .

A constitutional jurisprudence of original intent is insupportable for reasons other than the fact that the records of the framing and ratification of both the Constitution and the Bill of Rights are inadequate because they are incomplete and inaccurate. Original intent also fails as a

concept that can decide real cases. Original intent is an unreliable concept because it assumes the existence of one intent on a particular issue such as the meaning of executive powers or of the necessary and proper clause, the scope of the commerce clause, or the definition of the obligation of contracts. The entity we call "the Framers" did not have a collective mind, think in one groove, or possess the same convictions.

In fact, they disagreed on many crucial matters, such as the question whether they meant Congress to have the power to charter a bank. In 1789 Hamilton and Washington thought Congress had that power, but Madison and Randolph believed that it did not. Although the Journal of the Convention, except as read by Hamilton, supports Madison's view, all senators who had been at the Convention upheld the power, and Madison later changed his mind about the constitutionality of a bank. Clearly the Convention's "intent" on this matter lacks clarity; revelation is hard to come by when the Framers squabbled about what they meant. They often did, as political controversies during the first score of years under the Constitution revealed.

Sometimes Framers who voted the same way held contradictory opinions on the meaning of a particular clause. Each believed that his understanding constituted the truth of the matter. James Wilson, for example, believed that the ex post facto clause extended to civil matters, while John Dickinson held the view that it applied only to criminal cases, and both voted for the clause. George Mason opposed the same clause because he wanted the states to be free to enact ex post facto laws in civil cases, and he believed that the clause was not clearly confined to criminal cases; but Elbridge

Gerry, who wanted to impose on the states a prohibition against retroactive civil legislation, opposed the clause because he thought it seemed limited to criminal cases. William Paterson changed his mind about the scope of the ex post facto clause. Seeking original intent in the opinions of the Framers is seeking a unanimity that did not exist on complex and divisive issues contested by strong-minded men. Madison was right when he spoke of the difficulty of verifying the intention of the Convention.

A serious problem even exists as to the identity of the Framers and as to the question whether the opinions of all are of equal importance in the determination of original intent. Who, indeed, were the Framers? Were they the fifty-five who were delegates at Philadelphia or only the thirty-nine who signed? If fathoming original intent is the objective, should we not also be concerned about the opinions of those who ratified the Constitution, giving it legitimacy? About 1,600 men attended the various state ratifying conventions, for which the surviving records are so inadequate. No way exists to determine their intent as a guide for judicial decisions; we surely cannot fathom the intent of the members of eight states for which no state convention records exist. The deficiencies of the records of the other five permit few confident conclusions and no basis for believing that a group mind can be located. Understanding ratifier intent is impossible except on the broadest kind of question: Did the people of the states favor scrapping the Articles of Confederation and favor, instead, the stronger Union proposed by the Constitution? Even as to that question, the evidence, which does not exist for a majority of the states, is unsatisfactorily incomplete, and it allows only rough estimates of the answers to questions concerning popular understanding of the meaning of specific clauses of the Constitution. . . .

A CONSTITUTIONAL JURISPRUDENCE OF ORIGINAL INTENT?

A constitutional jurisprudence of original intent would be as viable and sound as Mr. Dooley's understanding of it. Mr. Dooley, Finley Peter Dunne's philosophical Irish bartender, believed that original intent was "what some dead Englishman thought Thomas Jefferson was goin' to mean whin he wrote th' Constitution." Acceptance of original intent as the foundation of constitutional interpretation is unrealistic beyond belief. It obligates us, even if we could grasp that intent, to interpret the Constitution in the way the Framers did in the context of conditions that existed in their time. Those conditions for the most part no longer exist and cannot be recalled with the historical arts and limited time available to the Supreme Court. Anyway, the Court resorts to history for a quick fix, a substantiation, a confirmation, an illustration, or a grace note; it does not really look for the historical conditions and meanings of a time long gone in order to determine the evidence that will persuade it to decide a case in one way rather than another. The Court, moreover, cannot engage in the sort of sustained historical analysis that takes professional historians some years to accomplish. In any case, for many reasons already described, concerning the inadequacies of the historical record and the fact that we cannot in most instances find a collective mind of the Framers, original intent analysis is not really possible, however desirable.

We must keep reminding ourselves that the most outspoken Framers disagreed with each other and did not necessarily reflect the opinions of the many who did not enter the debates. A point that Justice Rufus Peckham made for the Court in an 1897 case about legislative intent carries force with respect to the original intent of the Constitutional Convention. In reference to the difficulty of understanding an act by analyzing the speeches of the members of the body that passed it, Peckham remarked: "Those who did not speak may not have agreed with those who did; and those who spoke might differ from each other; the result being that the only proper way to construe a legislative act is from the language used in the act, and, upon occasion, by a resort to the history of the times when it was passed." We must keep reminding ourselves, too, that the country was deeply divided during the ratification controversy. And we must keep reminding ourselves that the Framers who remained active in national politics divided intensely on one constitutional issue after another—the removal power, the power to charter a corporation, the power to declare neutrality, the executive power, the power to enact excise and use taxes without apportioning them on population, the power of a treaty to obligate the House of Representatives, the power of judicial review, the power to deport aliens, the power to pass an act against seditious libel, the power of the federal courts to decide on federal common law grounds, the power to abolish judicial offices of life tenure, and the jurisdiction of the Supreme Court to decide suits against states without their consent or to issue writs of mandamus

against executive officers. This list is not exhaustive; it is a point of departure. The Framers, who did not agree on their own constitutional issues, would not likely speak to us about ours with a single loud, clear voice. . . .

CONCLUSIONS

Fifty years ago, in his fine study of how the Supreme Court used original intent (not what the Framers and ratifiers believed), Jacobus tenBroek asserted, rightly, that "the intent theory," as he called it, "inverts the judicial process." It described decisions of the Court as having been reached as a result of a judicial search for Framers' intent, "whereas, in fact, the intent discovered by the Court is most likely to be determined by the conclusion that the Court wishes to reach." Original intent analysis involves what tenBroek called "fundamental misconceptions of the nature of the judicial process." It makes the judge "a mindless robot whose task is the utterly mechanical function" of using original intent as a measure of constitutionality. In the entire history of the Supreme Court, as tenBroek should have added, no Justice employing the intent theory has ever written a convincing and reliable study. Lawyers making a historical point will cite a Court opinion as proof, but no competent historian would do that. He knows that judges cannot do their own research or do the right kind of research and that they turn to history to prove some point they have in mind. To paraphrase tenBroek, Justices mistakenly use original intent theory to depict a nearly fixed Constitution, to give the misleading impression that they have decided an issue of constitutionality by finding original intent, and to make a constitutional issue merely a historical question. The entire theory, tenBroek asserted, "falsely describes what the Court actually does," and it "hypothesizes a mathematically exact technique of discovery and a practically inescapable conclusion." That all added up, said tenBroek, to "judicial hokum."

If we could ascertain original intent, one may add, cases would not arise concerning that intent. They arise because the intent is and likely will remain uncertain; they arise because the Framers either had no discernible intent to govern the issue or their intent cannot control it because the problem before the Court would have been so alien to the Framers that only the spirit of some principle implied by them can be of assistance. The Framers were certainly vaguer on powers than on structure and vaguer still on rights.

If, as Robert H. Bork noticed, people rarely raise questions about original intent on issues involving powers or structure, the reason is likely that the Constitution provides the answer, or it has been settled conclusively by the Court, making inquiry futile or unnecessary. For example, the question of constitutional powers to regulate the economy has overwhelmingly been put beyond question by the 1937 "constitutional revolution, limited," in Edward S. Corwin's phrase. Not even the most conservative Justices on today's Court question the constitutionality of government controls. Congress has the constitutional authority under Court decisions to initiate a socialist economy; political restraints, not constitutional ones, prevent that. There are no longer any serious limits on the commerce powers of Congress. The government can take apart the greatest corporations, like Ma Bell; if it does not

proceed against them, the reason is to be found in national defense needs and in politics, not in the Constitution.

The states are supplicants before the United States government, beneficiaries of its largesse like so many welfare recipients, unable to control their own policies, serving instead as administrative agencies of federal policies. Those federal policies extend to realms not remotely within the federal power to govern under the Constitution, except for the fact that the spending power, so called, the power to spend for national defense and general welfare can be exercised through programs of grants-in-aid to states and to over 75,000 substate governmental entities; they take federal tax money and obediently enforce the conditions laid down by Congress and by federal agencies for control of the expenditures. Federalism as we knew it has been replaced by a new federalism that even conservative Republican administrations enforce. The government today makes the New Deal look like a backer of Adam Smith's legendary free enterprise and a respecter of John C. Calhoun's state sovereignty.

Even conservative Justices on the Supreme Court accept the new order of things. William H. Rehnquist spoke for the Court in *PruneYard*, Sandra Day O'Connor in *Hawaii Housing Authority*, and the Court was unanimous in both. In the first of these cases, decided in 1980, the Court held that a state does not violate the property rights of a shopping center owner by authorizing the solicitation of petitions in places of business open to the public. Rehnquist, finding a reasonable police power regulation of private property, asserted that the public right to regulate the use of property is as fundamental as the right to property itself. One might have thought that as a matter of constitutional theory and of original intent, the property right was fundamental and the regulatory power was an exception to it that had to be justified. Rehnquist did not explain why the regulation was justifiable or reasonable; under its rational basis test the Court has no obligation to explain anything. It need merely believe that the legislature had some rational basis for its regulation. . . .

The Constitution of the United States is our national covenant, and the Supreme Court is its special keeper. The Constitution's power of survival derives in part from the fact that it incorporates and symbolizes the political values of a free people. It creates a representative, responsible government empowered to serve the great objectives specified in the Preamble, while at the same time it keeps government bitted and bridled. Through the Bill of Rights and the great Reconstruction amendments, the Constitution requires that the government respect the freedom of its citizens, whom it must treat fairly. Courts supervise the process, and the Supreme Court is the final tribunal. "The great ideals of liberty and equality," wrote Justice Benjamin N. Cardozo, "are preserved against the assaults of opportunism, the expediency of the passing hour, the scorn and derision of those who have no patience with general principles, by enshrining them in constitutions, and consecrating to the task of their protection a body of defenders." Similarly, Justice Hugo L. Black once wrote for the Court, "Under our constitutional system, courts stand against any winds that blow, as havens of refuge for those who might otherwise suffer because they are helpless, weak, outnumbered, or because they are nonconforming victims of prejudice and public excitement."

The Court should have no choice but to err on the side of the constitutional liberty and equality of the individual, whenever doubt exists as to which side requires endorsement. Ours is so secure a system, precisely because it is free and dedicated to principles of justice, that it can afford to prefer the individual over the state. To interpose original intent against an individual's claim defeats the purpose of having systematic and regularized restraints on power; limitations exist for the minority against the majority, as Madison said. Original intent analysis becomes a treacherous pursuit when it turns the Constitution and the Court away from assisting the development of a still freer and more just society.

The history of Magna Carta throws dazzling light on a jurisprudence of original intent. Magna Carta approaches its 800th anniversary. It was originally "reactionary as hell," to quote the chief justice of West Virginia. But the feudal barons who framed it could not control its evolution. It eventually came to signify many things that are not in it and were not intended. Magna Carta is not remotely important for what it intended but for what it has become. It stands now for government by contract of the people, for fundamental law, for the rule of law, for no taxation without representation, for due process of law, for habeaus corpus, for equality before the law, for representative government, and for a cluster of the rights of the criminally accused. No one cares, or should, that the original document signifies none of this. The Constitution is comparably dynamic.

The Court has the responsibility of helping regenerate and fulfill the noblest aspirations for which this nation stands. It must keep constitutional law constantly rooted in the great ideals of the past yet in a state of evolution in order to realize them. Something should happen to a person who dons the black robe of a Justice of the Supreme Court of the United States. He or she comes under an obligation to strive for as much objectivity as is humanly attainable by putting aside personal opinions and preferences. Yet even the best and most impartial of Justices, those in whom the judicial temperament is most finely cultivated, cannot escape the influences that have tugged at them all their lives and inescapably color their judgment. Personality, the beliefs that make the person, has always made a difference in the Court's constitutional adjudication. There never has been a constitutional case before the Court in which there was no room for personal discretion to express itself.

We may not want judges who start with the answer rather than the problem, but so long as mere mortals sit on the Court and construe its majestic but murky words, we will not likely get any other kind. Not that the Justices knowingly or deliberately read their presuppositions into law. There probably has never been a member of the Court who consciously decided against the Constitution or was unable in his own mind to square his opinions with it. Most judges convince themselves that they respond to the words on parchment, illuminated, of course, by historical and social imperatives. The illusion may be good for their psyches or the public's need to know that the nine who sit on the nation's highest tribunal really become Olympians, untainted by considerations that move lesser beings into political office.

Even those Justices who start with the problem rather than the result cannot transcend themselves or transmogrify the obscure or inexact into impersonal truth. At bottom, constitutional law reflects great public policies enshrined in the form of supreme and fundamental commands. It is truer of constitutional law than of any other branch that "what the courts declare to have always been the law," as Holmes put it, "is in fact new. It is legislative in its grounds. The very considerations which judges most rarely mention, and always with an apology, are the secret root from which the law draws all the juices of life. I mean, of course, consideration of what is expedient for the community concerned." Result-oriented jurisprudence or, at the least, judicial activism is nearly inevitable—not praiseworthy, or desirable, but inescapable when the Constitution must be construed. Robert H. Bork correctly said that the best way to cope with the problem "is the selection of intellectually honest judges." One dimension of such honesty is capacity to recognize at the propitious moment a need for constitutional evolution, rather than keep the Constitution in a deepfreeze.

POSTSCRIPT

Should the Federal Courts Be Bound by the "Original Intent" of the Framers?

Robert Bork's view of the limits of judicial power is often characterized as judicial self-restraint. It tends to be conservative and opposed to policies that alter the historical boundaries of the separation of powers, the federal division of power between the nation and the states, or long-observed standards regarding the extent of constitutional liberties and rights. A fuller statement of his position can be found in his book *The Tempting of America: The Political Seduction of the Law* (Free Press, 1990).

By contrast, Leonard Levy's position is usually defined as judicial activism, because it permits elected officials to undertake, and judges to endorse, policies that extend the powers of government and the rights of persons beyond those contemplated by the authors of the Constitution and its amendments.

An interesting and intimate account of how the Supreme Court works can be found in William H. Rehnquist's book, *The Supreme Court: How It Is* (Morrow, 1987), the first interpretation of the highest court by a sitting chief justice. A short history and defense of judicial review, *The Court and the Constitution* (Houghton Mifflin, 1987), has been written by Alexander Cox, law professor, solicitor general, and original Watergate prosecutor. Cox is unsympathetic to the doctrine of original intent as embodying a too narrow interpretation of judicial power.

Several essays on opposing sides of original intent can be found in Steven Anzovin and Janet Podell's book, *The United States Constitution and the Supreme Court* (H. W. Wilson, 1988).

In recent years, the Supreme Court has been narrowly divided in choosing between opposed standards in the controversial issues that come before it, including cases involving affirmative action, flag-burning, abortion rights, and school prayer (see related issues in this volume). Over one hundred and fifty years ago, the French observer Alexis de Tocqueville observed that "scarcely any political question arises in the United States today that is not resolved, sooner or later, into a judicial question." It does not seem like an overstatement today. However, a Supreme Court that applies controversial constitutional standards to bitterly divisive issues cannot escape becoming the subject of political controversy itself.

PART 3

Social Change and Public Policy

It is difficult to imagine any topic more emotional and divisive than one that involves social morality. Whatever consensus once existed on such issues as public school prayer, abortion, equality of opportunity, etc., that consensus has been shattered in recent years as Americans have lined up very clearly on opposing sides—and what is more important, taken those competing views into Congress, state legislatures, and the courts.

The issues in this section generate intense emotions because they ask us to clarify our values on a number of very personal concerns.

Will Tougher Sentencing Reduce Crime?
_____

Is Capital Punishment Justified?
_____

Is Affirmative Action Reverse Discrimination?
_____

Do People Have a Right to Burn the American Flag?
_____

Should Pornography Be Protected as Free Speech?
_____

Should Drugs Be Legalized?
_____

Does Our Welfare System Hurt the Poor?
_____

Should Abortion Be Considered a Basic Right?
_____

Should We Have a "Wall of Separation" Between Church and State?

ISSUE 9

Will Tougher Sentencing Reduce Crime?

YES: James Q. Wilson, from *Thinking About Crime* (Basic Books, 1983)

NO: Linda Rocawich, from "Lock 'Em Up: America's All-Purpose Cure for Crime," *The Progressive* (August 1987)

ISSUE SUMMARY

YES: Political scientist James Q. Wilson says that the prospect of swift and certain punishment is more likely to reduce violent crime than are social programs aimed at relieving poverty.
NO: Editor Linda Rocawich contends that locking people up is inhumane, is often applied in a racially discriminatory manner, and does not deter crime.

Crime is a major social problem in America, and most Americans suspect that it is growing worse. Everyone, except perhaps criminals themselves, wants to eliminate crime. The question is: how?

The problem is serious and complex. In fact, even the federal crime index does not give a precise idea of the incidence of major crime. (Major crimes are identified by the Federal Bureau of Investigation as criminal homicide, rape, robbery, aggravated assault, burglary, larceny over $50, and auto theft.) It is even uncertain whether the incidence of major crimes has increased strikingly in recent decades or whether it is because more crimes are being reported by victims (perhaps because of the increase in personal, automobile, and home insurance) and more accurately recorded by police.

However, some aspects of crime in the United States are indisputable. Crime is widespread, but is more concentrated in urban areas. It is disproportionately committed by the young, the poor, and members of minority groups. The commission of some crimes (those that require public knowledge of the activity, such as prostitution, drug selling, and gambling) involve the corruption of law-enforcement officials. The rates for some crimes, particularly violent crimes, are much higher in the United States than in many other countries. For example, there are more criminal homicides in New York City (where the rate of homicide is lower than that of a number of other American cities) than in all of Great Britain or Japan, which have, respectively, nine and fifteen times the population of New York.

There is little dispute about the increased public awareness of the problem, and the widespread fear that people—particularly parents and older people—feel in high-crime areas. Something needs to be done; but what? Reform society? Reform criminals? Some would deal with crime's "root causes," but as yet we do not know what those root causes are. Others think the solution lies in the severity of punishment, as in the slogan, "Lock them up and throw away the keys!"

Practical, moral, and constitutional questions have been raised about imprisonment. Who should be imprisoned? Only seven percent of new prisoners in federal prisons in 1987 were convicted of violent crimes. More than forty percent were convicted of drug-related crimes, but prisons do not offer drug abuse programs. For how long should criminals be sentenced? Harsher sentencing has contributed to a prison population that doubled between 1980 and 1990. Only the Soviet Union and South Africa have higher incarceration rates.

How much are we willing to pay? A thirty-year sentence is equivalent to a $1 million investment. The cost of prisons at all levels amounted to $20 billion in 1988. The federal system alone is expected to spend more than $70 billion to build new prisons between 1990 and 1995.

Should white-collar offenders be treated differently from street criminals? Does punishment deter people from breaking the law? If it does, is it the severity of the punishment, or its swiftness, or its certainty—or some combination of these— that deters? Are there better, perhaps more enlightened, ways of reducing crime in America? Among the alternatives that are proposed are community service, restitution or compensation to the victim, supervised probation, and psychological and physical treatment. When would any of these work better to reduce crime?

These are some of the questions touched upon by political scientist James Q. Wilson and editor Linda Rocawich in the selections that follow. Like so many thoughtful observers of crime in America, they have come to opposed conclusions.

YES

James Q. Wilson

THINKING ABOUT CRIME

The average citizen hardly needs to be persuaded that crimes will be committed more frequently if, other things being equal, crime becomes more profitable than other ways of spending one's time. Accordingly, the average citizen thinks it obvious that one major reason why crime has increased is that people have discovered they can get away with it. By the same token, a good way to reduce crime is to make its consequences to the would-be offender more costly (by making penalties swifter, more certain, or more severe), or to make alternatives to crime more attractive (by increasing the availability and pay of legitimate jobs), or both.

These citizens may be surprised to learn that social scientists who study crime are deeply divided over the correctness of such views. While some scholars, especially economists, believe that the decision to become a criminal can be explained in much the same way as we explain the decision to become a carpenter or to buy a car, other scholars, especially sociologists, contend that the popular view is wrong—crime rates do not go up because would-be criminals have little fear of arrest, and will not come down just because society decides to get tough on criminals.

This debate over the way the costs and benefits of crime affect crime rates is usually called a debate over deterrence—a debate, that is, over the efficacy (and perhaps even the propriety) of trying to prevent crime by making would-be offenders fearful of punishment. But the theory of human nature that supports the idea of deterrence—the theory that people respond to the penalties associated with crime—also assumes that people will take jobs in preference to crime if the jobs are more attractive. In both cases, we are saying that would-be offenders are rational and that they respond to their perception of the costs and benefits attached to alternative courses of action. When we use the word "deterrence," we are calling attention to only the cost side of the equation. No word in common scientific usage calls attention to the benefit side of the equation, though perhaps "inducement" might serve.

The reason scholars disagree about deterrence is that the consequences of committing a crime, unlike the consequences of shopping around for the best

From James Q. Wilson, *Thinking About Crime*, Revised Edition (Basic Books, 1975). Copyright © 1975 by Basic Books, Inc. Second revised edition copyright © 1983 by Basic Books, Inc. Reprinted by permission of Basic Books, Inc., Publishers.

146

price on a given automobile, are complicated by delay, uncertainty, and ignorance. In addition, some scholars contend that many crimes are committed by persons who are so impulsive, irrational, or abnormal that even if delay, uncertainty, or ignorance were not attached to the consequences of criminality, we would still have a lot of crime.

Imagine a young man walking down the street at night with nothing on his mind but a desire for good times and high living. Suddenly he sees a little old lady standing alone on a dark street corner, stuffing the proceeds of her recently cashed Social Security check into her purse. Nobody else is in view. If the young man steals the purse, he gets the money immediately. The costs of taking it are uncertain—the odds are at least ten to one that the police will not catch a robber, and even if he is caught, the odds are very good that he will not go to prison, unless he has a long record. On the average, no more than three felonies out of a hundred result in the imprisonment of the offender. In addition, whatever penalty may come his way will come only after a long delay—in some jurisdictions, a year or more might be needed to complete the court disposition of the offender, assuming he is caught in the first place. Moreover, this young man might, in his ignorance of how the world works, think the odds against being caught are even greater than they are, or that delays in the court proceedings might result in a reduction or avoidance of punishment.

Compounding the problem of delay and uncertainty is the fact that society cannot feasibly increase by more than a modest amount the likelihood of arrest, and though it can to some degree increase the probability and severity of prison sentences for those who are caught, it cannot do so drastically, by, for example, summarily executing all convicted robbers, or even by sentencing all robbers to twenty-year prison terms. Some scholars note a further complication: the young man may be incapable of assessing the risks of crime. How, they ask, is he to know his chances of being caught and punished? And even if he does know, perhaps he is driven by uncontrollable impulses to snatch purses whatever the risks.

As if all this were not bad enough, the principal method by which scholars have attempted to measure the effect of deterrence on crime has involved using data about aggregates of people (entire cities, counties, states, and even nations) rather than about individuals. In a typical study, the rate at which, say, robbery is committed in each state is "explained" by means of a statistical procedure in which the analyst takes into account both the socioeconomic features of each state that might affect the supply of robbers (for example, the percentage of persons with low incomes, the unemployment rate, the population density of the big cities, the proportion of the population made up of young males) and the operation of the criminal-justice system of each state as it attempts to cope with robbery (for example, the probability of being caught and imprisoned for a given robbery, and the length of the average prison term for robbery). . . .

The best analysis of [problems] in statistical studies of deterrence is to be found in a 1978 report of the Panel on Research on Deterrent and Incapacitative Effects, which was set up by the National Research Council (an arm of the National Academy of Sciences). That panel, chaired by Alfred Blumstein, of Carnegie-Mellon University, concluded that the available statistical evidence (as of 1978) did not warrant any strong conclusions about the extent to which differences among states or cities in the probability of punishment might alter deterrent effect. The panel (of which I was a member) noted that "the evidence certainly favors a proposition supporting deterrence more than it favors one asserting that deterrence is absent," but urged "scientific caution" in interpreting this evidence.

Other criticisms of deterrence research, generally along the same lines as those of the panel, have led some commentators to declare that "deterrence doesn't work," and that we may now get on with the task of investing in those programs, such as job-creation and income maintenance, that *will* have an effect on crime. Such a conclusion is, to put it mildly, premature.

One way to compensate for errors in official statistics relating to crime rates is to consider other measures of crime, in particular reports gathered by Bureau of the Census interviewers from citizens who have been victims of crime. While these victim surveys have problems of their own (such as the forgetfulness of citizens), they are not the same problems as those that affect police reports of crime. Thus, if we obtain essentially the same findings about the effect of sanctions on crime from studies that use victim data as we do from studies that use police data, our confidence in these findings is strengthened. Studies of this sort have been done by Itzhak Goldberg, at Stanford, and by Barbara Boland and myself, and the results are quite consistent with those from research based on police reports. As sanctions become more likely, both sets of data suggest, crimes become less common.

It is possible, as some critics of deterrence say, that rising crime rates swamp the criminal-justice system, so that a negative statistical association between, say, rates of theft and the chances of going to prison for theft may mean not that a decline in imprisonment is causing theft to increase but rather that a rise in theft is causing imprisonment to become less likely. This might occur particularly with respect to less serious crimes, such as shoplifting or petty larceny; indeed, the proportion of prisoners who are shoplifters or petty thieves has gone down over the past two decades. But it is hard to imagine that the criminal-justice system would respond to an increase in murder or armed robbery by letting some murderers or armed robbers off with no punishment. Convicted murderers are as likely to go to prison today as they were twenty years ago. Moreover, the deterrent effect of prison on serious crimes like murder and robbery was apparently as great in 1940 or 1950, when these crimes were much less common, as it is today, suggesting that swamping has not occurred.

Still more support for the proposition that variations in sanctions affect crime can be found in the very best studies of deterrence—those that manage to avoid the statistical errors described above. In 1977, Alfred Blumstein and Daniel Nagin published a study of the relationship between draft evasion and the penalties imposed for draft evasion in each of the states. After controlling for the socio-economic characteristics of the states, they found that the higher the probability of conviction for draft evasion, the lower the evasion rates. This is an especially strong finding, because the study is largely immune to the problems associated with other analyses of deterrence.

Draft evasion is more accurately measured than street crimes, and draft evasion cases could not have swamped the federal courts in which they were tried, in part because such cases made up only a small fraction (about 7 percent) of the workload of these courts, and in part because federal authorities had instructed the prosecutors to give high priority to these cases. For all these reasons, Blumstein and Nagin felt they could safely conclude that draft evasion is deterrable.

White-collar crime can also be deterred. In the late 1970s, Michael Block, Fred Nold, and J.G. Sidak, then at Stanford, investigated the effect of enforcing the antitrust laws on the price of bread in the bakery business. When the government filed a price-fixing complaint against colluding bakery firms, and when those firms also faced the possibility of private suits claiming treble damages for this price-fixing, the collusion ended and the price of bread fell.

Another way of testing whether deterrence works is to look not at differences among states or firms at one point in time but at changes in the nation as a whole over a long period of time. Historical data on the criminal-justice system in America are so spotty that such research is difficult to do here, but it is not at all difficult in England, where the data are excellent. Kenneth I. Wolpin, of Yale, analyzed changes in crime rates and in various parts of the criminal justice system (the chances of being arrested, convicted and punished) for the period 1894 to 1967, and concluded that changes in the probability of being punished seemed to cause changes in the crime rate. He offered reasons for believing that this causal connection could not be explained away by the argument that

the criminal-justice system was being swamped.

Given what we are trying to measure—changes in the behavior of a small number of hard-to-observe persons who are responding to delayed and uncertain penalties—we will never be entirely sure that our statistical manipulations have proved that deterrence works. What is impressive is that so many (but not all) studies using such different methods come to similar conclusions. More such evidence can be found in studies of the death penalty. Though the evidence as to whether capital punishment deters crime is quite ambiguous, most of the studies find that the chances of being imprisoned for murder do seem to affect the murder rate. Even after wading through all this, the skeptical reader may remain unconvinced. Considering the difficulties of any aggregate statistical analysis, that is understandable. But, as we shall shortly see, the evidence from certain social experiments reinforces the statistical studies. . . .

Two well-known changes in sentencing practices are the so-called Rockefeller drug laws in New York and the Bartley-Fox gun law in Massachusetts. In 1973, New York State revised its criminal statutes relating to drug trafficking in an attempt to make more severe and more certain the penalties for the sale and possession of heroin (the law affecting other drugs was changed as well, but the focus of the effort—and the most severe penalties—were reserved for heroin). The major pushers—those who sold an ounce or more of heroin—would be liable for a minimum prison term of fifteen years and the possibility of life imprisonment. But the law had some loopholes. Someone who had sold an ounce could plea bargain the charges against him down, but no lower than to a charge that would entail a mandatory one-year minimum prison sentence. Police informants could get probation instead of prison, and persons under the age of sixteen were exempt from the mandatory sentences. A provision that was made part of some amendments passed in 1975 exempted from the law persons aged sixteen to eighteen. A group was formed to evaluate the effect of this law. The authors of its report, issued in 1977, found no evidence that the law had reduced the availability of heroin on the streets of New York city or reduced the kinds of property crime often committed by drug users. Of course, it is almost impossible to measure directly the amount of an illegal drug in circulation, or to observe the illicit transactions between dealers and users, but a good deal of circumstantial evidence, gathered by the study group, suggests that no large changes occurred. The number of deaths from narcotics overdoses did not change markedly, nor did admissions to drug-treatment programs or the price and purity of heroin available for sale on the street (as inferred from buys of heroin made by undercover narcotics agents).

The explanation for this disappointing experience, in the opinion of the study group, was that difficulties in administering the law weakened its deterrent power, with the result that most offenders and would-be offenders did not experience any significantly higher risk of apprehension and punishment. There was no increase in the number of arrests, and a slight decline in the proportion of indictments resulting in conviction. Offsetting this was a higher probability that a person convicted would go to prison. The net effect was that the probability of imprisonment for arrested drug dealers did not change as a result of the law—it was about one imprisonment per nine arrests both before and after passage of the law. On the other hand, the sentences received by those who did go to prison were more severe. Before the law was passed, only 3 percent of persons imprisoned for selling an ounce or more of heroin received a sentence of three years or more. After the law went into effect, 22 percent received such sentences. Perhaps because sentences became more severe, more accused persons demanded trials instead of pleading guilty; as a result, the time needed to dispose of the average drug case nearly doubled.

Does the experience under the Rockefeller law disprove the claim that deterrence works? The answer is no, but that is chiefly because deterrence theory wasn't satisfactorily tested. If "deterrence" means changing behavior by increasing either the certainty or the swiftness of punishment, then the Rockefeller law, as it was administered, could not have deterred behavior, because it made no change in the certainty of punishment and actually reduced its swiftness. If, on the other hand, "deterrence" means changing behavior by increasing the severity of punishment, then deterrence did not work in this case. What we mainly want to know, however, is whether heroin trafficking could have been reduced if the penalties associated with it had been imposed more quickly and in a higher proportion of cases.

Severity may prove to be the enemy of certainty and speed. As penalties get tougher, defendants and their lawyers have a greater incentive to slow down the process, and those judges who, for private reasons, resist heavy sentences for drug dealing may use their discretionary powers to decline indictment, accept plea bargains, grant continuances, and modify penalties in ways that reduce the certainty and the severity of punishment. The group that evaluated the Rockefeller law suggested that reducing severity in favor of certainty might create the only real possibility for testing the deterrent effect of changes in sentences.

The Bartley-Fox gun law in Massachusetts was administered and evaluated in ways that avoided some of the problems of the Rockefeller drug laws. In 1974, the Massachusetts legislature amended the law that had long required a license for a person carrying a handgun, by stipulating that a violation of this law would entail a mandatory penalty of one year in prison, which sentence would not be reduced by probation or parole or by judicial finagling. When the law went into effect, in April of 1975, various efforts were made to evaluate both the compliance of the criminal-justice system with it and the law's impact on the crimes involving handguns. James A. Beha, II, then at the Harvard Law School, traced the application of the law for eighteen months, and concluded that, despite widespread predictions to the contrary, the police, prosecutors, and judges were not evading the law. As in New York, more persons asked for trials, and delays in disposition apparently increased, but in Massachusetts, by contrast with the experience in New York, the probability of punishment increased for those arrested. Beha estimated in 1977 (at a time when not all the early arrests had yet worked their way through the system) that prison sentences were being imposed five times more frequently on persons arrested for illegally carrying firearms than had been true before the law was passed. Owing to some combination of the heavy public-

ity given to the Bartley-Fox law and the real increase in the risk of imprisonment facing persons arrested while carrying a firearm without a license, the casual carrying of firearms seems to have decreased. This was the view expressed to interviewers by participants in the system, including persons being held in jail, and it was buttressed by a sharp drop in the proportion of drug dealers arrested by the Boston police who, at the time of their arrest, were found to be carrying firearms. . . .

Deterrence and job-creation are not different anti-crime strategies; they are two sides of the same strategy. The former increases the costs of crime; the latter enhances the benefits of alternatives to criminal behavior. The usefulness of each depends on the assumption that we are dealing with a reasonably rational potential offender.

Let us return to our original example. The young man is still yearning for the money necessary to enjoy some high living. Let us assume that he considers finding a job. He knows he will have to look for one; this will take time. Assuming he gets one, he will have to wait even longer to obtain his first paycheck. But he knows that young men have difficulty finding their first jobs, especially in inner-city neighborhoods such as his. Moreover, he cannot be certain that the job he might get would provide benefits that exceed the costs. Working forty hours a week as a messenger, a dishwasher, or a busboy might not seem worth the sacrifice in time, effort, and reputation on the street corner that it entails. The young man may be wrong about all this, but if he is ignorant of the true risks of crime, he is probably just as ignorant of the true benefits of alternatives to crime.

Compounding the problems of delay, uncertainty, and ignorance is the fact that society cannot feasibly make more than modest changes in the employment prospects of young men. Job-creation takes a long time, when it can be done at all, and many of the jobs created will go to the "wrong" (i.e., not criminally inclined) persons; thus, unemployment rates among the young will not vary greatly among states and will change only slowly over time. And if we wish to see differences in unemployment rates (or income levels) affect crime, we must estimate those effects by exactly the same statistical techniques we use to estimate the effect of criminal-justice sanctions.

The problem of measurement error arises because we do not know with much accuracy the unemployment rate among youths by city or state. Much depends on who is looking for work and how hard, how we count students who are looking only for part-time jobs, and whether we can distinguish between people out of work for a long period and those who happen to be between jobs at the moment. Again, since inaccuracies in these data vary from place to place, we will obtain biased results.

The problem of omitted factors is also real, as is evident in a frequently cited study done in 1976 by Harvey Brenner, of Johns Hopkins University. He suggested that between 1940 and 1973, increases in the unemployment rate led to increases in the homicide rate. But he omitted from his analysis any measure of changes in the certainty or the severity of sentences for murder, factors that other scholars have found to have a strong effect on homicide.

Finally, the relationship between crime and unemployment (or poverty) is probably complex, not simple. For example, in a statistical study that manages to overcome the problems already mentioned, we might discover that as unemployment rates go up, crime rates go up. One's natural instinct would be to interpret this as meaning that rising unemployment causes rising crime. But rising crime might as easily cause rising unemployment. If young men examining the world about them conclude that crime pays more than work—that, for instance, stealing cars is more profitable than washing them—they may then leave their jobs in favor of crime. Some young men find dealing in drugs more attractive than nine-to-five jobs, but, technically, they are "unemployed."

Perhaps both crime and unemployment are the results of some common underlying cause. In 1964, the unemployment rate for black men aged twenty to twenty-four was 12.6 percent; by 1978, it was 20 percent. During the same period, crime rates, in particular those involving young black men, went up. Among the several possible explanations are the changes that have occurred where so many young blacks live, in the inner parts of large cities. One such change is the movement out of the inner cities of both jobs and the social infrastructure that is manned by adult members of the middle class. The departure of jobs led to increased unemployment; the departure of the middle class led to lessened social control and hence to more crime. If we knew more than we now know, we would probably discover that all three relationships are working simultaneously: for some persons, unemployment leads to crime; for others, crime leads to unemployment; and for still others, social disintegration or personal inadequacy leads to both crime and unemployment. . . .

The hope, widespread in the 1960s, that job-creation and job-training programs would solve many social problems, including crime, led to countless efforts both to prevent crime by supplying jobs to crime-prone youths and to reduce crime among convicted offenders by supplying them with better job opportunities after their release from prison. One preventive program was the Neighborhood Youth Corps, which gave to poor young persons jobs during the afternoons and evenings and all day during the summer. An evaluation of the results of such programs among poor blacks in Cincinnati and Detroit found no evidence that participation in the Youth Corps had any effect on the proportion of enrollees who came into contact with the police. Essentially the same gloomy conclusion was reached by the authors of a survey of a large number of delinquency-prevention programs, though they reported a few glimmers of hope that certain programs might provide some benefits to some persons. For example, persons who had gone through a Job Corps program that featured intensive remedial education and job training in a residential camp were apparently less likely to be arrested six months after finishing their training than a control group. . . .

The best and most recent effort to identify the link between employment and crime was the "supported-work" program of the Manpower Demonstration Research Corporation (MDRC). In ten locations around the country, MDRC randomly assigned four kinds of people with employment problems to special workshops or to control groups. The four categories were long-term welfare (Aid to Families with Dependent Children) recipients, school dropouts, former drug addicts, and ex-convicts. The workshops provided employment in unskilled jobs supplemented by training in job-related personal skills. The unique feature of the program was that all the participants in a given work setting were people with problems; thus the difficulties experienced by persons with chronic unemployment problems when they find themselves competing with persons who are successful job-seekers and job-holders were minimized. Moreover, the workshops were led by sympathetic supervisors (often themselves ex-addicts or ex-convicts), who gradually increased the level of expected performance until, after a year or so, the trainees were able to go out into the regular job market on their own. This government-subsidized work in a supportive environment, coupled with training in personal skills, was the most ambitious effort of all we have examined to get persons with chronic problems into the labor force. Unlike vocational training in prison, supported work provided real jobs in the civilian world, and training directly related to what one was paid to do. Unlike work-release programs, supported work did not immediately place the ex-convict in the civilian job market to sink or swim on his own.

Welfare recipients and ex-addicts benefited from supported work, but ex-convicts and youthful school dropouts did not. Over a twenty-seven-month observation period, the school dropouts in the project were arrested as frequently as the school dropouts in the control group, and the ex-offenders in the project were arrested *more* frequently (seventeen more arrests per 100 persons) than ex-offenders in the control group.

The clear implication, I think, of the supported-work project—and of all the studies to which I have referred—is that unemployment and other economic factors may well be connected with criminality, but the connection is not a simple one. If, as some people assume, "unemployment causes crime," then simply providing jobs to would-be criminals or to convicted criminals would reduce their propensity to commit crimes. We have very little evidence that this is true, at least for the kinds of persons helped by MDRC. Whether crime rates would go down if dropouts and ex-convicts held on to their jobs we cannot say, because, as the supported-work project clearly showed, within a year and a half after entering the program, the dropouts and ex-convicts were no more likely to be employed than those who had never entered the program at all—despite the great and compassionate efforts made on their behalf. Help, training, and jobs may make a difference for some persons—the young and criminally inexperienced dropout; the older, "burned-out" ex-addict; the more mature (over age thirty-five) ex-convict. But ex-addicts, middle-aged ex-cons, and inexperienced youths do not commit most of the crimes that worry us. These are committed by the young chronic offender. . . .

Some may agree with me but still feel that we should spend more heavily on one side or the other of the cost-benefit equation. At countless scholarly gatherings, I have heard learned persons examine closely any evidence purporting to show the deterrent effect of sanctions, but accept with scarcely a blink the theory that crime is caused by a "lack of opportunities." Perhaps they feel that since the evidence on both propositions is equivocal, it does less harm to believe in—and invest in—the "benign" (i.e., job-creation) program. That is surely wrong. If we try to make the penalties for crime swifter and more certain, and it should turn out that deterrence does not work, then we have merely increased the risks facing persons who are guilty of crimes in any event. If we fail to increase the certainty and swiftness of penalties, and it should turn out that deterrence *does* work, then we have needlessly increased the risk of being victimized for many innocent persons. . . .

But we cannot achieve large reductions in crime rates by making sanctions very swift or very certain or by making jobs very abundant, because things other than the fear of punishment or the desire for jobs affect the minds of offenders, and because while we say we want a speedy, fair, and efficient criminal-justice system, we want other things more.

The behavior of most of us is affected by even small (and possibly illusory) changes in the costs attached to it. We are easily deterred by a crackdown on drunk driving, especially if it is highly publicized, and our willingness to take chances when filling out our tax returns is influenced by how likely we think an audit may be. Why, then, should we not see big changes in the crime rates when we make our laws tougher?

The answer is not that, unlike the rest of us, burglars, muggers, and assaulters are irrational. I am struck by the account given in Sally Engle Merry's book, *Urban Danger,* of her extended interviews with youthful offenders in a big-city neighborhood she observed for a year and a half. She found that these young men had a sophisticated, pragmatic view of their criminal enterprises, even though they were neither "white-collar" criminals nor highly professional burglars. They distinguished carefully between affluent and less-affluent targets, spoke knowledgeably about the chances of being caught in one part of the district as opposed to another, understood that some citizens were less likely to call the police than others, knew which offenses were most and which were least likely to lead to arrest and prosecution, and had formed a judgment about what kinds of stories the judges would or would not believe. Though many committed crimes opportunistically, or in retaliation for what they took to be the hostile attitudes of certain neighbors, they were neither so impulsive nor so emotional as to be unaware of, or indifferent to, the consequences of their actions. . . .

Chronic offenders may attach little or no importance to the loss of reputation that comes from being arrested; in certain circles, they may feel that an arrest has enhanced their reputation. They may attach a low value to the alleged benefits of a legitimate job, because it requires punctuality, deferential behavior, and a forty-hour week, all in exchange for no more money than they can earn in three or four burglaries carried out at their leisure. These values are not acquired merely by trying crime and comparing its benefits with those of non-criminal behavior; if that were all that was involved, far more of us would be criminals. These preferences are shaped by personal temperament, early familial experiences, and contacts with street-corner peers—by character-forming processes that occur in intimate settings, produce lasting effects, and are hard to change.

Whereas the drinking driver, the casual tax cheat, or the would-be draft evader, having conventional preferences, responds quickly to small changes in socially determined risks, the chronic offender seems to respond only to changes in risks that are sufficiently great to offset the large benefits he associates with crime and the low value he assigns to having a decent reputation. Changing risks to that degree is not impossible, but changing those risks permanently and for large numbers of persons is neither easy nor inexpensive, especially since (as we saw in Wayne County, with the felony firearm statute, and in New York, with the Rockefeller drug law) some members of the criminal-justice system resist programs of this kind.

One third of all robberies committed in the United States are committed in the six largest cities, even though they contain only 8 per cent of the nation's population. The conditions of the criminal-justice system in those cities range from poor to disastrous. *The New York Times* recently described one day in New York City's criminal courts. Nearly 4,000 cases came up on that day; each received, on the average, a three-minute hearing from one of seventy overworked judges. Fewer than one case in two hundred resulted in a trial. Three quarters of the summonses issued in the city are ignored; 3.7 million unanswered summonses now fill the courts' files. It is possible that some measure of rough justice results from all this—that the most serious offenders are dealt with adequately, and that the trivial or nonexistent penalties (other than inconvenience) imposed upon minor offenders do not contribute to the production of more chronic offenders. In short, these chaotic courts may not, as the *Times* described them, constitute a "system in collapse." But could such a system reduce the production of chronic offenders by increasing the swiftness, certainty, or severity of penalties for minor offenders? Could it take more seriously spouse assaults where the victim is reluctant to testify? Or monitor more closely the behavior of persons placed on probation on the condition that they perform community service or make restitution to their victims? Or weigh more carefully the sentences given to serious offenders, so as to maximize the crime-reduction potential of those sentences? It seems most unlikely. And yet, doing some or all of these things is exactly what is required by any plan to reduce crime by improving deterrence. For reasons best known to state legislators who talk tough about crime but appropriate too little money for a big-city court system to cope properly with lawbreakers, the struggle against street crime that has supposedly been going on for the last decade or so is in large measure a symbolic crusade.

I had written at length elsewhere about the obstacles that prevent more than small, planned changes in the criminal-justice system. Given the modest effect that changes will have on the observable behavior of chronic offenders, we may want to supplement improvements in the criminal-justice system with programs that would reduce the causes of crime. When I published the first edition of *Thinking About Crime*, in 1975, I argued that a free society lacked the capacity to alter the root causes of crime, since they were almost surely to be found in the character-forming processes that go on in the family. The principal rejoinder to that argument was that these root causes could be found instead in the objective economic conditions confronting the offender. Labor-market or community conditions may indeed have some effect on the crime rate, but since I first wrote, the evidence has mounted

that this effect is modest and hard to measure and that devising programs— even such extraordinary programs as supported work—that will have much impact on repeat offenders or school dropouts is exceptionally difficult.

By contrast, a steadily growing body of evidence suggests that the family affects criminality and that its effect, at least for serious offenders, is lasting. Beginning with the research of Sheldon and Eleanor Glueck in Boston during the 1930s and 1940s, and continuing with the work of Lee Robins, William and Joan McCord, and Travis Hirschi in this country, Donald West and David Farrington in England, Lea Pulkinnen in Finland, Dan Olweus in Norway, and many others, we now have available an impressive number of studies that, taken together, support the following view: Some combination of constitutional traits and early family experiences accounts for more of the variation among young persons in their serious criminality than any other factors, and serious misconduct that appears relatively early in life tends to persist into adulthood. What happens on the street corner, in the school, or in the job market can still make a difference, but it will not be as influential as what has gone before.

If criminals are rational persons with values different from those of the rest of us, then it stands to reason that temperament and family experiences, which most shape values, will have the greatest effect on crime, and that perceived costs and benefits will have a lesser impact. For example, in a society where people cannot be under continuous official surveillance, the pleasure I take in hitting people is likely to have a greater effect on my behavior than the occasional intervention of some person in a blue uniform who objects to my hitting others and sets in motion a lengthy and uncertain process that may or may not result in my being punished for doing the hitting.

In a sense, the radical critics of America are correct. If you wish to make a big difference in crime rates, you must make a fundamental change in society. But what they propose to put in place of existing institutions, to the extent that they propose anything at all except angry rhetoric, would leave us yearning for the good old days when our crime rate may have been higher but our freedom was intact.

There are, of course, ways of reorganizing a society other than along the authoritarian lines of radical Marxism. One can imagine living in a society in which the shared values of the people, reinforced by the operation of religious, educational, and communal organizations concerned with character formation, would produce a citizenry less criminal than ours is now without diminishing to any significant degree the political liberties we cherish. Indeed, we can do more than imagine it; we can recall it. During the latter half of the nineteenth century, we managed in this country to keep our crime rate lower than it might have been in the face of extensive urbanization, rapid industrialization, large-scale immigration, and the widening of class differences. We did this, as I have argued elsewhere ("Crime and American Culture," *The Public Interest*, Winter, 1982), by investing heavily in various systems of impulse control through revival movements, temperance societies, uplift organizations, and moral education—investments that were based on and gave effect to a widespread view that self-restraint was a fundamental element of character.

These efforts were designed to protect (and, where necessary, to replace) the family, by institutionalizing familial virtues in society at large. The efforts weakened as the moral consensus on which they were based decayed: self-expression began to rival self-control as a core human value, at first among young, well-educated persons, and eventually among persons of every station. Child-rearing methods, school curricula, social fashions, and intellectual tendencies began to exalt rights over duties, spontaneity over loyalty, tolerance over conformity, and authenticity over convention.

The criminal-justice system of the nineteenth century was probably no swifter or more certain in its operations than the system of today, at least in the large cities, and the economy was even more subject to booms and busts than anything we have known since the 1930s. The police were primitively organized and slow to respond, plea bargaining was then, as now, rife in the criminal courts, prisons were overcrowded and nontherapeutic, and protection against the vicissitudes of the labor market was haphazard or nonexistent. Yet these larger social processes may have had a greater effect on crime rates then than they do today, because then, unlike now, they were working in concert with social sentiments: society condemned those whom the police arrested, the judge convicted, or the labor market ignored. Shame magnified the effect of punishment, and perhaps was its most important part.

Today, we are forced to act as if the degree of crime control that was once obtained by the joint effect of intimate social processes and larger social institutions can be achieved by the latter alone. It is as if we hope to find in some combination of swift and certain penalties and abundant economic opportunities a substitute for discordant homes, secularized churches, intimidated schools, and an ethos of individual self-expression. We are not likely to succeed.

Nor are we like to reproduce, by plan, an older ethos or its accompanying array of voluntary associations and social movements. And, since we should not abandon essential political liberties, our crime-control efforts for the most part will have to proceed on the assumption—shaky as it is—that the things we can change, at least marginally, will make a significant difference. We must act as if swifter and more certain sanctions and better opportunities will improve matters. Up to a point, I think, they will, but in reaching for that point we must be prepared for modest gains uncertainly measured and expensively priced.

Brighter prospects may lie ahead. By 1990, about half a million fewer eighteen-year-old males will be living in this country than were living here in 1979. As everyone knows, young males commit proportionately more crimes than older ones. Since it is the case in general that about 6 percent of young males become chronic offenders, we will in 1990 have 30,000 fewer eighteen-year-old chronic offenders; if each chronic offender commits ten offenses (a conservative estimate) per year, we will have a third of a million fewer crimes from this age group alone. But other things may happen as well as the change in numbers. A lasting drop in the birthrate will mean that the number of children per family will remain low, easing the parental problem of supervision. A less youthful society may be less likely to celebrate a "youthful culture," with its attendant emphasis on unfettered self-expression. A society less attuned to youth may find it can more easily re-assert traditional values and may be more influenced by the otherwise marginal effects of improvements in the efficiency of the criminal-justice system and the operation of the labor market. Natural and powerful demographic forces, rather than the deliberate re-establishment of an older culture, may increase the values of those few policy tools with which a free society can protect itself. In the meantime, justice requires that we use those tools, because penalizing wrong conduct and rewarding good conduct are right policies in themselves, whatever effect they may have.

NO

Linda Rocawich

LOCK 'EM UP

In 1790, when Philadelphia Quakers opened the Walnut Street Jail, the first prison in the world to use confinement as punishment for crime, they were following the lead of Cesare Beccaria, the Italian criminologist who advocated imprisonment as an alternative to execution. Their experiment, now copied everywhere in the world, will shortly be 200 years old, but don't expect that bicentennial to be commemorated on your cereal boxes.

America's prisons are an overcrowded mess. Our society officially expects these mean, gloomy, brutal places somehow to turn criminals into pillars of the community. They have a better chance of doing the reverse—and probably do, on the rare occasions when they get a shot at a pillar of the community.

But we keep building them, and then we fill them up faster than we can build still more.

Now, in 1987, we lock up so many people every week that, at the end of seven days, our state and Federal prisons hold a thousand more than they did the week before. Fifty thousand *more* prisoners every year.

Fifteen years ago, the population of our prisons was about 200,000. Ten years ago it was near 300,000. On December 31, 1986, the population was 546,659 and growing.

Ten years ago, critics of our criminal-justice system often said that only the Soviet Union and South Africa, among industrialized nations, imprisoned a larger proportion of their people than the United States. This may no longer be true. The U.S. incarceration rate—the number of prisoners per 100,000 in the general population—was seventy-nine in 1925. In 1980, it was 179; in 1985, it was 201. That is about double the incarceration rate in most Western European nations.

White Americans are incarcerated at a rate of 114 per 100,000. But for black Americans, the story is much different: The rate is well over 700. On this front, we definitely are Number One, according to Steven Whitman of Northwestern University's Center for Urban Affairs and Policy Research. "Incredibly," Whitman says, "blacks in the United States go to prison more often than blacks in South Africa. In fact, the United States' black imprisonment rate is the highest in the world."

What is going on here? The crime rate explains nothing, and no one has a tidy answer. But those who study the prison-population explosion blame the extremely conservative ideology that permeates our society, an individualistic, every-man-for-himself ideology. When it comes to crime, this is manifested in a vicious punitive streak—lock 'em up and throw away the key.

Research into the nature of the prison population bears this out. Judges are handing down longer sentences than before because they perceive a public demand for them. For the same reason, they are sending people to prison for crimes that formerly did not merit incarceration.

The strength of the punitive impulse is demonstrated by what it costs. At a time of extreme fiscal conservatism, Americans spend $9 billion a year just to operate the state prisons. Billions more go to the Federal system and to capital outlays and construction costs for new prisons.

As public policy, this is insane.

The libraries are full of exposés of prison conditions, descriptions of what is wrong with them, why they achieve none of their "purposes" but punishment, which many corrections professionals won't even admit is a purpose.

Periodically, the prisons explode with riots and waves of violence. These are often followed by the appointment of Presidential commissions to look into the crisis. The commissions always come to the same conclusion: The prisons are a mess and we should not be using them to warehouse people. The National Advisory Commission on Criminal Justice Standards and Goals advised the nation in 1973, for example, that prisons should be society's *last resort* for dealing with its problems. The Commission said prisons fail to reduce crime, succeed in punishing but not deterring criminals, provide only temporary protection to the community, and change the offender (but mostly for the worse).

Obviously, the nation wasn't listening.

CRIME RATES HAVE NOTHING TO DO WITH incarceration rates. Of the ten states with the highest rates of violent crime, only Nevada, South Carolina, Maryland, and Arizona also rank in the top ten on incarceration. Incarceration rates for other states with the highest crime rates are way down the list—New York is twentieth; California is twenty-first; Illinois is twenty-sixth.

Racism, however, explains a great deal. Nine of the eleven states of the Old Confederacy are in the top sixteen on incarceration rate. The top twenty also include the former slave states of Delaware, Maryland, Oklahoma, and Missouri. Social scientist William Nagel studied the phenomenon in the 1970s and found that states with large nonwhite populations, even those with low crime rates, have large prison populations. "There is no significant correlation between a state's racial composition and its crime rate," he wrote, "but there is a very great positive relationship between its racial composition and its incarceration rate."

Steven Whitman, the researcher who calculated the incarceration rate of blacks at more than 700, recently wrote about "The Crime of Black Imprisonment" for the *Chicago Tribune*. About one of every four black men, he says, will go to prison in his lifetime. A reader later objected to Whitman's conclusion that blacks go to prison because they are black. "The reason more blacks go to prison," said this letter, "is that they commit more crimes."

The letter writer is wrong.

Blacks commit crimes and whites commit crimes. After that, they aren't treated the same. Criminologist Donald Taft studied the subject more than thirty years ago. In a 1956 criminology text, he summarized what he found: "Negroes are more likely to be suspected of crime than are whites. They are also more likely to be arrested. If the perpetrator of a crime is known to be a Negro, the police may arrest all Negroes who were near the scene—a procedure they would rarely dare to follow with whites. After arrest, Negroes are less likely to secure bail, and so are more liable to be counted in jail statistics. They are more liable than whites to be indicted and less likely to have their cases *nol prossed* or otherwise dismissed. If tried, Negroes are more likely to be convicted. If convicted, they are less likely to be given probation. For this reason they are more likely to be included in the count of prisoners. Negroes are also more liable than whites to be kept in prison for the full terms of their commitments and correspondingly less like to be paroled.

No one who has seriously studied the subject since then disputes Taft's findings.

THE STATUS OF WOMEN IN THE PRISON SYSTEM *is* changing, however, and the new punitive streak is at work. For about fifty years after incarceration rates were first computed in 1925, the rate for women varied between six and nine per 100,000. It hit ten in 1977 and has been climbing steadily ever since, to its current rate of seventeen-plus. The female prison population has grown at a faster rate than the male population every year since 1981. About 27,000 women were in Federal or state custody in 1986, an increase of about 15 percent over the year before.

While several recent studies show a jump in the number of violent crimes committed by women since the women's movement came to prominence, what is more noticeable is a tendency to sentence women to prison for crimes for which they used to get probation—thus making them more equal to men.

The fast growth in the female prison population is "the result of harsher sentencing" says Nicole Hahn Rafter, author of a history of the women's prison system called *Partial Justice*. She recently told *The Christian Science Monitor* that the nature of the crimes committed by most women convicts and the backgrounds of the women do not warrant their being in prison. "Most of them don't belong there," she said.

What is "the nature of their crimes"? Typically, according to *The Monitor's* report, women serve time for relatively minor crimes such as larceny, welfare fraud, prostitution, receiving stolen property, and shoplifting. Drug or alcohol abuse is often a complicating factor. The violent crimes for which women most often go to prison are murder or manslaughter of men who have abused them over a period of years, according to the American Correctional Association (ACA).

"Battered Women and Criminal Justice" is the report of New York State researchers who looked into the cases of twelve women whose physical abuse led them to kill their husbands. Three are under life sentence; the others average a maximum term of fifteen years. "The nature of their crimes and the existence of a very low recidivism rate for those who have committed murder and manslaughter provide substantial evidence that these women and others like them are not a danger to society," the study finds. "The wisdom of imprisoning them at all is certainly questionable."

If the wisdom of imprisoning women who have killed is in question, what about the vast majority who haven't lifted a violent finger? The ACA—which, as an association of professionals who work, for the most part, within the system, has never been known as a gang of raving reformers—has just put out a new handbook on public policy for corrections. Attorney Edwin Meese III has even endorsed it.

The ACA handbook, noting that most women in the prison system's net were arrested for property crimes, says that few pose a risk to society. "Community placement," it says, "can provide the level of structure and support needed by many female offenders. At the same time, community placement considerably reduces the cost burden to taxpayers."

To take this story one step further: If the wisdom of imprisoning all these women is in question, what about imprisoning all those men? The people who know them best, the prison administrators, don't believe very many of their boarders belong behind bars.

Arnold Pontesso has been among the more vocal. A retired Federal warden who began his career as a guard almost fifty years ago, Pontesso has also been director of Oklahoma's correctional system, running not only the prisons but also the state's parole and probation department. He has often testified as an expert witness for the inmates in lawsuits complaining of unconstitutional or unlawful prison conditions, and he is always careful to insist that there are some offenders whom society must lock up. When pressed for a number—how many ought to be in prison, how many would we do better to handle some other way—Pontesso usually says no more than about 5 per cent of prisoners belong inside. Certainly, he adds, no one whose offense was nonviolent should be imprisoned.

As much as Pontesso's former colleagues hate to see him take the stand when the inmates are suing them, his opinion is not much different from theirs. When Jessica Mitford was writing *Kind and Usual Punishment*, her book on the prison business, she discovered, "Even the toughest wardens of the roughest prisons will quote some such figure off the record. Somewhere between 10 per cent and 25 per cent of 'hard-core' criminals are 'too dangerous' to be loosed on society." Ronald Goldfarb and Linda Singer reached a similar conclusion in their study *After Conviction*. "We have asked every experienced, practicing prison official we know," they said, "how many of the inmates currently held in confinement really need to be incarcerated in order to protect the public from personal injury. All agree that only a small minority of all the present inmates in American prisons—most estimated between 10 and 15 per cent—could be considered to be so dangerous."

Why are the prisons bursting at their seams if the professionals believe what they say they believe?

Their stock answer is that they don't control the number of prisoners. An official of the Texas Department of Corrections once patiently explained to me that not he but judges and juries sentence convicted offenders to serve time in his prisons, and then they stay there until they're paroled or their sentences are up or they die.

That's true as far as it goes. But prison officials could exercise their credibility as law-and-order types by telling legislatures and judges and every public forum they can find what they seem to tell only inquiring journalists and social scientists.

Moreover, correctional policies do affect the size of the population. The administration of discipline and the classification of inmates affect both the amount of "good time" prisoners earn (extra credit toward time served) and their parole eligibility. And, in the case of the Texas system, officials (including the one who lectured me) often used to testify in favor of legislation, such as bills affecting parole policy, which had the direct effect of increasing the number of inmates.

WHAT TO DO WITH CRIMINAL OFFENDERS, IF not lock them up? This has been a major preoccupation of reformers. A task force of the American Friends Service Committee charged with studying crime and punishment in America pointed out with some exasperation in 1971 that ever since Alexis de Tocqueville and Charles Dickens separately expressed their condemnations of America's prisons, the experts' prescriptions for change had made no significant progress. "The apparent novelty," the group said, "is merely a manifestation of the public's ignorance of the history of penal and legal reform."

Aside from more extensive use of probation and parole, "community-based corrections" have been the reform of choice for the past twenty years. These are billed as "alternatives to incarceration" because they are supposed to be sentences meted out to people who oth-

erwise would be sent to prison. The President's Crime Commission in 1967 and the National Advisory Commission in 1973 both advocated sentencing based on the principle of the "least restrictive alternative" appropriate to the individual offender.

There are new wrinkles, of course. A popular experiment is intensive-supervision probation—a program in which probation officers have small caseloads and a probationer has a team of supervisors instead of just one. In the age of Reagan, it was inevitable that economic programs would also enter the field; in one such, the states offer local jurisdictions financial incentives not to sentence offenders to the state prison but, instead, to figure out something to do with them at home.

Both these ideas show some promise. But so did many of the old kinds of "alternatives to incarceration."

The difficulty arises as the new programs become institutionalized. Instead of being a less restrictive alternative to prison, as intended, they become ways to "help" those offenders the system had no way to "help" in the past.

Say a man commits a minor crime, a nonviolent misdemeanor, his first offense. He has a stable home and job. Say the judge and court workers who make pre-sentence recommendations must choose between sending him to jail and a fine or restitution. So the judge lectures him, fines him, and sends him on his way. If the court has a probation department, however, the judge chooses probation—the *more* restrictive alternative.

Halfway houses for parolees, designed to let people out of prison sooner than parole boards would have released them to society at large, became halfway houses for troublesome probationers: halfway in instead of halfway out.

When a program is new, it often operates as intended: to keep some offenders out of prison. But when the judges and prosecutors and pre-sentence investigators get used to having the program around, they start using it to slap more restrictions on the people who clearly shouldn't be jailed.

This pattern has been repeated time and again, with program after program. And it will happen again with the new "alternatives to incarceration."

The surprise would be if this system functioned other than it does. Most judges are people who enjoy exercising power and authority over other people—it's why they wanted to be judges. And most criminal-court personnel—the probation department caseworkers who do the pre-sentence investigations and supervise probationers—are social workers who think the "clients" are better off not left alone.

The proof is in the prison-population explosion. Almost twenty years ago, Congress passed the Omnibus Crime Control and Safe Streets Act, in the wake of the reformist prescriptions of the President's Crime Commission. Among many other things, the Safe Streets Act created the Law Enforcement Assistance Administration. Best known for its aid to police departments across the land—gifts of helicopter gunships for crowd control and SWAT teams for terrorist control—LEAA also gave the states millions of dollars in the 1970s and early 1980s to experiment with community-based correctional programs: alternatives to incarcertion. Some of the programs died quiet deaths after a few years; others live on as regular components of the system.

And now, after all that, the prison population has tripled. So has the number of people on parole. The number of probationers is eight times what it was twenty years ago. In fact, one in every thirty-five adult males in the United States is under correctional supervision. And *no one* knows how many people regularly get sucked into the informal pretrial programs that "divert" offenders, without benefit of conviction, into "voluntary" supervision and treatment programs.

Meanwhile, nothing much has happened to the crime rate.

IT WAS A PRETTY FALL SUNDAY IN NASHville, but threatening rain. A group of people—twenty, maybe a few more—gathered just outside the walls of the Tennessee State Prison around the perimeter of a grassy circular mound of earth with a flagpole in its middle. It was still too early for flags to be flying.

The people carried pots and pans, spoons and spatulas to bang on the pans, and other improvised tools for raising a racket. They sang hymns, held hands, walked around the circle, listened to a preacher, and prayed, but mostly they made noise. They took their text from Joshua at the Battle of Jericho; they were trying to make the walls come tumbling down.

"Bunch of religious yippies," muttered a man standing near me. He was keeping his distance, just outside the circle, snapping pictures. But the spirit was infectious, and his resistance was breaking down.

Then an inmate, a trustee, walked out the prison door, broke through our circle, and raised the flags. He was trying not to stare but couldn't help himself. He seemed to think we were out of our minds. Soon after going back inside, he reappeared along with a few other men. They watched from a distance. Some of us called to them to join us in the noise-making, but they wouldn't. Who would risk his trustee status to join a bunch of nuts who think they can make prisons disappear?

None of us expected the walls to crumble, of course, but we did really want to make prisons disappear. Some in the crowd, in fact, worked full-time toward that end. Not everyone thought all prisons should be abolished, but many did.

That was 1979. The demonstration was the closing event of an annual meeting of the Southern Coalition on Jails and Prisons. Coalition staff and sympathizers could be found in the forefront of the opposition any time a Southern state announced plans to build a new prison. There were like-minded activists in many other places and an umbrella group—the National Moratorium on Prison Construction, a project since the mid-1970s of the Unitarian Universalist Service Committee.

The people trying to stop prison construction didn't always win the individual battles, but sometimes they did. They also kept the issue alive and in the public eye.

No more. The National Moratorium closed its doors this spring. The Southern Coalition folks—many of them the same people who gathered eight years ago at the Tennessee prison—are still a bright spot of activism and still opposed to prison construction. But most of them have found it necessary to turn their attention to saving the lives of the thousand of Southerners languishing on Death Rows. Other prison deconstructionists burned out or decided other issues were more important.

It's been a long time since I heard about a demonstration like the one in Nashville, or even a concerted effort to stop a new prison.

Yet the problem, of course, is more overwhelming than ever—the states are building spaces to lock up an additional 100,000 people, and the Federal Bureau of Prisons figures it must be able to accommodate about 100,000 inmates by the turn of the century, almost 60,000 more than today.

ARE PRISONS APPROPRIATE PLACES EVEN for that 5 or 10 or 15 per cent of the prison population that the professionals think belong there?

Certainly for as long as our society is as unjust as it is, some people will react in dangerously violent ways to their environment. Probably a few would be that way even in a just society. And the rest of us need protection from them. Prisons as we know them, however, are not the answer, they only brutalize the violent among their inmates. Something different will be needed.

Who should decide, and on what grounds, which individuals should be incarcerated? Our present criminal-justice system certainly inspires little confidence in its ability to handle the task fairly—or even rationally. Can we devise a system that protects the individual "offender" as well as the rest of us?

In a long tradition of abolitionist thinking, no one has satisfactorily answered these questions, but they do not have to be answered before we begin undoing a great deal, if not all, of the evils of the present system. We can, today, start to let go of the first 90 per cent of the prison population, and figure out what to do with the rest when we have freed up all the mental and financial resources now used to lock the first half-million away.

There is something absurd, something not really believable, about a society with our wealth and talent that can find no solution but warehouses to its social problems. We have had 200 years to try to make the prison idea work. It doesn't and it won't. It will never be "reformed" into a system we can point to with pride. The time is long since past when we should abandon the idea and tear down the walls.

POSTSCRIPT

Will Tougher Sentencing Reduce Crime?

It may be said of crime—as Mark Twain said of the weather—that everyone talks about it but nobody does anything about it. Perhaps that is because the easy solutions only sound easy. If we are to "lock 'em all up," where are we going to put them? The public applauds tough talk but seems unwilling to pay for new prison space. On the other hand, getting at the so-called root causes of crime—which supposedly include poverty and discrimination—is no easier. This approach assumes that these phenomena *are* the basic causes of crime. Yet violent crime was much lower during the poverty-ridden, racist decade of the 1930s than it was during the affluent and enlightened 1960s. Unfortunately, crime is a problem that will not yield to slogans, whether those slogans are liberal or conservative in origin.

Dramatic increases in prison population and the rising cost of imprisonment have been accompanied by revelations of appalling conditions that cannot contribute to rehabilitation. Larry E. Sullivan, in *The Prison Reform Movement: Forlorn Hope* (Twayne, 1990), explores the possibilities of reforming prisons.

Much recent writing about crime and punishment examines the possibility of alternatives to prison, particularly for people guilty of so-called victimless crimes, such as marijuana smoking, curfew violations, or public drunkenness. Restitution, community work service, monitored home confinement, and other sanctions are considered in Andrew R. Klein's *Alternative Sentencing: A Practitioner's Guide* (Anderson, 1988).

In addition to sentencing reform, Michael Tonry and Franklin E. Zimring, editors of *Reform and Punishment: Essays on Criminal Sentencing* (U. Chicago, 1983), look at how the criminal justice system deals with the mentally ill, and they examine sentencing in European countries.

In *Criminal Violence, Criminal Justice* (Random House, 1978), Charles Silberman concludes that police action cannot do much to control crime if the community's morale and spirit of self-control have disintegrated.

No matter which solutions are attempted, Rocawich and Wilson have helped to set the terms of the debate. Rocawich considers crime to be largely a reaction of people oppressed by our unjust society. Wilson sees crime as a deliberate and calculated act by rational persons with values different from those of the rest of us. For Rocawich, the solution is to rely less on prison and more on social reform. For Wilson, the solution is to make punishment swifter and more certain, and, if possible, to restore some of the old ethic of self-restraint. Both are adept at finding the weakness in the positions they reject. If together they fail to inspire fresh answers to the crime problem, they at least show us that the old answers, whether grounded upon "toughness" or "compassion," need considerable rethinking.

ISSUE 10

Is Capital Punishment Justified?

YES: Walter Berns, from *For Capital Punishment: Crime and the Morality of the Death Penalty* (Basic Books, 1979)

NO: Donal E. J. MacNamara, from "The Case Against Capital Punishment," *Social Action* (April 1961)

ISSUE SUMMARY

YES: Professor Walter Berns is convinced that the death penalty has a place in modern society and that it serves a need now, as it did when the Constitution was framed.

NO: Criminologist Donal MacNamara presents a ten-point argument against capital punishment, raising ethical and practical questions concerning the death penalty.

Although capital punishment (the death penalty) is ancient, both the definition of a capital crime and the methods used to put convicted persons to death have changed. In eighteenth-century Massachusetts, there were fifteen capital crimes, including blasphemy and the worship of false gods. Slave states often imposed the death sentence upon blacks for crimes that were punished by only two or three years' imprisonment when committed by whites. It has been estimated that in this century approximately ten percent of all legal executions have been for the crime of rape, one percent for all other crimes (robbery, burglary, attempted murder, etc.), and nearly ninety percent for the commission of murder.

Long before the Supreme Court severely limited the use of the death penalty, executions in the United States were becoming increasingly rare. In the decade of the 1930s there were 1,667; the total for the 1950s was 717. In the 1960s, the numbers fell even more dramatically. For example, seven persons were executed in 1965, one in 1966, and two in 1967. Put another way, in the 1930s and 1940s, there was one execution for every sixty or seventy homicides committed in states that had the death penalty; in the first half of the 1960s, there was one execution for every two hundred homicides; and by 1966 and 1967, there were only three executions for approximately twenty thousand homicides.

Then came the case of *Furman v. Georgia* (1972), which many thought—mistakenly—"abolished" capital punishment in America. Actually, only two members of the *Furman* majority thought that capital punishment *per se* violates the Eighth Amendment's injunction against "cruel and unusual punishment." The other three members of the majority took the view that capital punishment is unconstitutional only when applied in an arbitrary or a racially discriminatory manner, as they believed it was in this case. There were four dissenters in the *Furman* case, who were prepared to uphold capital punishment both in general and in this particular instance. Not surprisingly, then, with a slight change of Court personnel—and with a different case before the Court—a few years later, the majority vote went the other way.

In the latter case, *Gregg v. Georgia* (1976), the majority upheld capital punishment under certain circumstances. In his majority opinion in the case, Justice Potter Stewart noted that the law in question (a new Georgia capital punishment statute) went to some lengths to avoid arbitrary procedures in capital cases. For example, Georgia courts were not given complete discretion in handing out death sentences to convicted murderers, but had to consult a series of guidelines spelling out "aggravating circumstances," such as whether the murder had been committed by someone already convicted of murder, whether the murder endangered the lives of bystanders, and whether the murder was committed in the course of a major felony. These guidelines, Stewart said, together with other safeguards against arbitrariness included in the new statute, preserved it against Eighth Amendment challenges.

Although the Court has upheld the constitutionality of the death penalty, it can always be abolished by state legislatures. However, that seems unlikely to happen in many states. If anything, the opposite is occurring. Almost immediately after the *Furman* decision of 1972, state legislatures began enacting new death penalty statutes designed to meet the objections raised in the case. By the time of the *Gregg* decision, thirty-five new death penalty statutes had been enacted.

In the readings that follow, Donal E. J. MacNamara sums up virtually every widely used argument against the death penalty, while Walter Berns focuses his defense upon the moral right of retribution and its compatibility with the American Constitution.

YES

Walter Berns

CRIME AND THE MORALITY
OF THE DEATH PENALTY

It must be one of the oldest jokes in circulation. In the dark of a wild night a ship strikes a rock and sinks, but one of its sailors clings desperately to a piece of wreckage and is eventually cast up exhausted on an unknown and deserted beach. In the morning, he struggles to his feet and, rubbing his salt-encrusted eyes, looks around to learn where he is. The only human thing he sees is a gallows. "Thank God," he exclaims, "civilization." There cannot be many of us who have not heard this story or, when we first heard it, laughed at it. The sailor's reaction was, we think, absurd. Yet, however old the story, the fact is that the gallows has not been abolished in the United States even yet, and we count ourselves among the civilized peoples of the world. Moreover, the attempt to have it abolished by the U.S. Supreme Court may only have succeeded in strengthening its structure. . . .

Perhaps the Court began to doubt its premise that a "maturing society" is an ever more gentle society; the evidence on this is surely not reassuring. The steady moderating of the criminal law has not been accompanied by a parallel moderating of the ways of criminals or by a steadily evolving decency in the conditions under which men around the world must live their lives. . . .

An institution that lacks strength or purpose will readily be what its most committed constituents want it to be. Those who maintain our criminal justice institutions do not speak of deferring to public opinion but of the need to "rehabilitate criminals"—another pious sentiment. The effect, however, is the same. They impose punishments only as a last resort and with the greatest reluctance, as if they were embarrassed or ashamed, and they avoid executing even our Charles Mansons. It would appear that Albert Camus was right when he said that "our civilization has lost the only values that, in a certain way, can justify [the death] penalty." It is beyond doubt that our intellectuals are of this opinion. The idea that the presence of a gallows could indicate the presence of a civilized people is, as I indicated at the outset, a joke. I certainly thought so the first time I heard the story; it was only a few years ago that I began to suspect that that sailor may have been right. What led me to change my mind was the phenomenon of Simon Wiesenthal.

Like most Americans, my business did not require me to think about criminals or, more precisely, the punishment of criminals. In a vague way, I was aware that there was some disagreement concerning the purpose of punishment—deterrence, rehabilitation, or retribution—but I had no reason then to decide which was right or to what extent they may all have been right. I did know that retribution was held in ill repute among criminologists. Then I began to reflect on the work of Simon Wiesenthal, who, from a tiny, one-man office in Vienna, has devoted himself since 1945 exclusively to the task of hunting down the Nazis who survived the war and escaped into the world. Why did he hunt them, and what did he hope to accomplish by finding them? And why did I respect him for devoting his life to this singular task? He says that his conscience forces him "to bring the guilty ones to trial." And if they are convicted, then what? Punish them, of course. But why? To rehabilitate them? The very idea is absurd. To incapacitate them? But they represent no present danger. To deter others from doing what they did? That is a hope too extravagant to be indulged. The answer—to me and, I suspect, everyone else who agrees that they should be punished—was clear: *to pay them back.* And how do you pay back SS Obersturmführer Franz Stangl, SS Untersturmführer Wilhelm Rosenbaum, SS Obersturmbannführer Adolf Eichmann, or someday—who knows?—Reichsleiter Martin Bormann? As the world knows, Eichmann was executed, and I suspect

that most of the decent, *civilized* world agrees that this was the only way he could be paid back. . . .

The argument . . . does not turn on the answer to the utilitarian question of whether the death penalty is a deterrent . . . The evidence on this is unclear and, besides, as it is usually understood, deterrence is irrelevant. The real issue is whether justice permits or even requires the death penalty. I am aware that it is a terrible punishment, but there are terrible crimes and terrible criminals. . . .

Anger is expressed or manifested on those occasions when someone has acted in a manner that is thought to be unjust, and one of its bases is the opinion that men are responsible, and should be held responsible, for what they do. Thus, anger is accompanied not only by the pain caused by him who is the object of anger, but by the pleasure arising from the expectation of exacting revenge on someone who is thought to deserve it. We can become very angry with an inanimate object (the door we run into and then kick in return) only foolishly attributing responsibility to it, and we cannot do that for long, which is why we do not think of returning later to revenge ourselves on the door. For the same reason, we cannot be more than momentarily angry with an animate creature other than man: only a fool or worse would dream of taking revenge on a dog. And, finally, we tend to pity rather than to be angry with men who—because they are insane, for example—are not responsible for their acts. Anger, then, is a very human passion not only because only a human being can be angry, but also because it acknowledges the humanity of its objects: it holds them accountable for what they do. It is an expression of that element of the soul that is connected with the view that there is responsibility in the world; and in holding particular men responsible, it pays them that respect which is due them as men. Anger recognizes that only men have the capacity to be moral beings and, in so doing, acknowledges the dignity of human beings. Anger is somehow connected with justice, and it is this that modern penology has not understood; it tends, on the whole, to regard anger as merely a selfish passion. . . .

Criminals are properly the objects of anger, and the perpetrators of terrible crimes—for example, Lee Harvey Oswald and James Earl Ray—are properly the objects of great anger. They have done more than inflict an injury on an isolated individual; they have violated the foundations of trust and friendship, the necessary elements of a moral community, the only community worth living in. A moral community, unlike a hive of bees or a hill of ants, is one whose members are expected freely to obey the laws and, unlike a tyranny, are trusted to obey the laws. The criminal has violated that trust, and in so doing has injured not merely his immediate victim but the community as such. He has called into question the very possibility of that community by suggesting that men cannot be trusted freely to respect the property, the person, and the dignity of those with whom they are associated. If, then, men are not angry when someone else is robbed, raped, or murdered, the implication is that there is no moral community because those men do not care for anyone other than themselves. Anger is an expression of that caring, and society needs men who care for each other, who share their pleasures and their pains, and do so for the sake of the others. It is the passion that can cause us to act for rea-

sons having nothing to do with selfish or mean calculation; indeed, when educated, it can become a generous passion, the passion that protects the community or country by demanding punishment for its enemies. It is the stuff from which heroes are made. . . .

THE CONSTITUTIONAL ARGUMENT

We Americans have debated the morality and necessity of the death penalty throughout almost the entire period of our experience as a nation, and, until 1976 when the Supreme Court ruled in favor of its constitutionality, it had been debated among us in constitutional terms, which is not true elsewhere. The Eighth Amendment clearly and expressly forbids the imposition of "cruel and unusual punishments," a prohibition that applies now to the states as well as to the national government; it was argued that the death penalty was such a punishment.

It is, of course, incontestable that the death penalty was not regarded as cruel and unusual by the men who wrote and ratified the amendment. They may have forbidden cruel and unusual punishments but they acknowledged the legitimacy of capital punishment when, in the Fifth Amendment, they provided that no person "shall be held to answer for a capital . . . crime, unless on a presentment or indictment of a Grand Jury," and when in the same amendment they provided that no one shall, for the same offense, "be twice put in jeopardy of life or limb," and when, in the Fifth as well as in the Fourteenth Amendment, they forbade, not the taking of life, but the taking of life "without due process of law." We also know that the same Congress which proposed the Eighth Amendment also provided for the death penalty for murder and treason, and George Washington, despite powerful entreaties, could not be persuaded to commute the death sentence imposed on Major John Andre, the British officer and spy involved in Benedict Arnold's treachery. So the death penalty can be held to be cruel and unusual in the constitutional sense only if it has somehow become so in the passage of time. . . .

In 1958 the Supreme Court . . . said that the meaning of cruel and unusual depends on "the evolving standards of decency that mark the progress of a maturing society." Surely, it is argued, hanging or electrocution or gassing is, in our day, regarded as equally cruel as expatriation, if not more cruel. Is it not relevant that the American people have insisted that executions be carried out by more humane methods, that they not be carried out in public, and that the penalty be imposed for fewer and fewer crimes; and is it not significant that juries have shown a tendency to refuse to convict for capital crimes? In these ways the people are merely demonstrating what has been true for centuries, namely, that when given the opportunity to act, the average man (as opposed to judges and vindictive politicians) will refuse to be a party to legal murder. . . . The fact of the matter, or so it is alleged, is that American juries have shown an increasing tendency to avoid imposing the death penalty except on certain offenders who are distinguished not by their criminality but by their race or class. Justice Douglas emphasized this in his opinion in the 1972 capital punishment cases. "One searches our chronicles in vain for the execution of any members of the affluent strata of this society," he said. "The

Leopolds and Loebs are given prison terms, not sentenced to death." . . . Death sentences are imposed not out of a hatred of the crimes committed, it is said, but out of a hatred of blacks. Of the 3,859 persons executed in the United States in the period 1930–1967, 2,066 or 54 percent, were black. More than half of the prisoners now under sentence of death are black. In short, the death penalty, we have been told, "may have served" to keep blacks, especially southern blacks, "in a position of subjugation and subservience." That in itself is unconstitutional.

In the 1972 cases only two of the nine justices of the Supreme Court argued that the death penalty as such is a violation of the Eighth Amendment, regardless of the manner of its imposition. Justice Brennan was persuaded by what he saw as the public's growing reluctance to impose it that the rejection of the death penalty "could hardly be more complete without becoming absolute." Yet, on the basis of his own evidence it is clear that the American people have not been persuaded by the arguments against the death penalty and that they continue to support it for *some* criminals—so long as it is carried out privately and as painlessly as possible. At the very time he was writing there were more than 600 persons on whom Americans had imposed the sentence of death. He drew the conclusion that the American people had decided that capital punishment does not comport with human dignity, and is therefore unconstitutional, but the facts do not support this conclusion. This may explain why his colleague, Justice Marshall, felt obliged to take up the argument.

Marshall acknowledged that the public opinion polls show that, on the whole, capital punishment is supported by a majority of the American people, but he denied the validity—or the "utililty"—of ascertaining opinion on this subject by simply polling the people. The polls ask the wrong question. It is not a question of whether the public accepts the death penalty, but whether the public when "fully informed as to the purposes of the penalty and its liabilities would find [it] shocking, unjust, and unacceptable."

In other words, the question with which we must deal is not whether a substantial proportion of American citizens would today, if polled, opine that capital punishment is barbarously cruel, but whether they would find it to be so in the light of all information presently available.

This information, he said, "would almost surely convince the average citizen that the death penalty was unwise." He conceded that this citizen might nevertheless support it as a way of exacting retribution, but, in his view, the Eighth Amendment forbids "punishment for the sake of retribution"; besides, he said, no one has ever seriously defended capital punishment on retributive grounds. It has been defended only with "deterrent or similar theories." From here he reached his conclusion that "the great mass of citizens" would decide that the death penalty is not merely unwise but also "immoral and therefore unconstitutional." They would do so if they knew what he knew, and what he knew was that retribution is illegitimate and unconstitutional and that the death penalty is excessive and unnecessary, being no more capable than life imprisonment of deterring the crimes for which it is imposed. He conceded that the evidence on the deterrence issue is not "convincing beyond all doubt, but it is persuasive."

Thus, the death penalty *is* cruel and unusual punishment because the American people *ought* to think so. Shortly after this decision thirty-five states enacted new statutes authorizing the death penalty for certain crimes.

This public support for capital punishment is a puzzling fact, especially in our time. It is a policy that has almost no articulate supporters in the intellectual community. The subject has been vigorously debated and intensively investigated by state after state and country after country—California and Connecticut, Texas and Wisconsin; Britain and Canada, Ceylon and "Europe"; even the United Nations; and, of course, various committees of the U.S. Congress. Among those willing to testify and publish their views, the abolitionists outweigh the "retentionists" both in number and, with significant exceptions, in the kind of authority that is recognized in the worlds of science and letters. Yet the Harris poll reports 59 percent of the general population to be in favor of capital punishment, and that proportion is increasing—at this time, at least. . . .

It is sometimes argued that the opinion polls are deceptive insofar as the question is posed abstractly—and can only be posed abstractly—and that the responses of these publics would be different if they had to decide whether particular persons should be executed. This is entirely possible, or even probable; nevertheless, there is no gainsaying the fact that juries, for whom the issue is very concrete indeed, continue to impose death sentences on a significant number of criminals. Ordinary men and women seem to be unpersuaded by the social science argument against deterrence, or they regard it as irrelevant: they seem to be oblivious to the possibility that innocent people might be executed; they know nothing about the natural public law disagreement between Beccaria and Kant; they surely do not share the opinion that executions are contrary to God's commands; indeed, they seem to display the passions of many a biblical character in their insistence that, quite apart from all these considerations, murderers should be paid back. In fact, the essential difference between the public and the abolitionists is almost never discussed in our time; it has to do with retribution: the public insists on it without using the word and the abolitionists condemn it whenever they mention it.

The abolitionists condemn it because it springs from revenge, they say, and revenge is the ugliest passion in the human soul. They condemn it because it justifies punishment for the sake of punishment alone, and they are opposed to punishment that serves no purpose beyond inflicting pain on its victims. Strictly speaking, they are opposed to punishment. They may, like Beccaria, sometimes speak of life imprisonment as the alternative to executions, but they are not in fact advocates of life imprisonment and will not accept it. . . .

They condemn retribution because they see it, rightly or wrongly, as the only basis on which the death penalty can be supported. To kill an offender is not only unnecessary but precludes the possibility of reforming him, and reformation, they say, is the only civilized response to the criminal. Even murderers—indeed, especially murderers—are capable of being redeemed or of repenting their crimes. . . .

The goal of the abolitionists is not merely the elimination of capital punishment but the reform or rehabilitation of the criminal, *even,* if he is a murderer.

The public that favors capital punishment is of the opinion that the murderer deserves to be punished, and does not deserve to be treated, even if by treatment he *could* be rehabilitated. . . .

When abolitionists speak of the barbarity of capital punishment and when Supreme Court justices denounce expatriation in almost identical language, they ought to be reminded that men whose moral sensitivity they would not question have supported both punishments. Lincoln, for example, albeit with a befitting reluctance, authorized the execution of 267 persons during his presidency, and ordered the "Copperhead" Clement L. Vallandigham banished; and it was Shakespeare's sensitivity to the moral issue that required him to have Macbeth killed. They should also be given some pause by the knowledge that the man who originated the opposition to both capital and exilic punishment, Cesare Beccaria, was a man who argued that there is no morality outside the positive law and that it is reasonable to love one's property more than one's country. There is nothing exalted in these opinions, and there is nothing exalted in the versions of them that appear in today's judicial opinions. Capital punishment was said by Justice Brennan to be a denial of human dignity, but in order to reach this conclusion he had to reduce human dignity to the point where it became something possessed by "the vilest criminal." Expatriation is said by the Court to be unconstitutional because it deprives a man of his right to have rights, which *is* his citizenship, and no one, no matter what he does, can be dispossessed of the right to have rights. (Why not a right to the right to have rights?) Any notion of what Justice Frankfurter in dissent referred to as "the communion of our citizens," of a community that can be violated by murderers or traitors, is wholly absent from these opinions; so too is any notion that it is one function of the law to protect that community.

But, contrary to abolitionist hopes and expectations, the Court did not invalidate the death penalty. It upheld it. It upheld it on retributive grounds. In doing so, it recognized, at least implicitly, that the American people are entitled *as a people* to demand that criminals be paid back, and that the worst of them be made to pay back with their lives. In doing this, it gave them the means by which they might strengthen the law that makes them a people, and not a mere aggregation of selfish individuals.

NO

Donal E. J. MacNamara

THE CASE AGAINST
CAPITAL PUNISHMENT

The infliction of the death penalty is becoming less frequent and the actual execution of the sentence of death even more rare, both in the United States and in foreign countries. Not only is this trend apparent in those nations and states which have formally repudiated the *lex talionis* and have eliminated capital punishment from their penal codes but it is almost equally clear in many of the jurisdictions which still retain the ultimate sanction for from one to fourteen crimes. The diminished frequency is a reflection of the popular distaste for executions and of the recognition by many criminologically and psychiatrically oriented judges, juries, prosecutors, and commuting and pardoning authorities that capital punishment is as ineffective as a special capital crimes deterrent as it is ethically and morally undesirable.

The case against the death penalty is supported by many arguments—with the order of their importance or precedence dependent upon the orientation of the proponent or the composition of the audience to whom the argument is being addressed. The late Harold Laski, in opening his series of lectures to one of my graduate seminars in political theory, suggested that a lecturer or writer was under obligation to his audience to define both the articulate and inarticulate basic premises upon which his theoretical structure, and its practical application to the matters under discussion, rested. This writer, then, is a practicing criminologist with both administrative and operational experience in police and prison work over a period of more than two decades; he was brought up in a Catholic household, went to parochial schools for twelve years, and then took degrees from two non-sectarian institutions. He is a "convert" to abolition, for during his active police and prison career he not only accepted the death penalty pragmatically as existent, necessary, and therefore desirable but participated in one or another formal capacity in a number of executions.

The case against capital punishment is ten-fold:

1. *Capital punishment is criminologically unsound.* The death penalty is the antithesis of the rehabilitative, non-punitive, non-vindictive orientation of

twentieth century penology. It brutalizes the entire administration of criminal justice. No criminologist of stature in America or abroad gives it support. And those "arm-chair" and so-called "utilitarian" criminologists who plead its necessity (never its desirability or morality) do so in terms of Darwinian natural selection and/or as a eugenics-oriented, castration-sterilization race purification technique, an economical and efficient method of disposing of society's jetsam. Those who advance these arguments are probably not aware that they are rationalizing a residual lust for punishment or propagating an immoral, virtually paganistic, philosophy.

2. *Capital punishment is morally and ethically unacceptable.* The law of God is "Thou shall not kill," and every system of ethics and code of morals echoes this injunction. It is well recognized that this Commandment (and the laws of man based upon it) permit the killing of another human being "in the lawful defense of the slayer, or of his or her husband, wife, parent, child, brother, sister, master or servant, or of any other person in his presence or company" when there is "imminent danger" and in "actual resistance" to an assault or other criminal act. It is equally well recognized that society, organized as a sovereign state, has the right to take human life in defending itself in a just war against either internal or external unjust aggression. But the individual citizen has no right in law or morals to slay as punishment for an act, no matter how vile, already committed; nor has he legal or moral justification to kill when—his resistance to an attempted criminal act having proved successful short of fatal force—the imminent danger is eliminated and the criminal attack or attempt discontinued.

Individuals in groups or societies are subject to the same moral and ethical codes which govern their conduct as individuals. The state, through its police agents, may take human life when such ultimate measure of force is necessary to protect its citizenry from the imminent danger of criminal action and in actual resistance to felonious attempts (including attempts forcibly to avoid arrest or escape custody). Once, however, the prisoner has been apprehended and either voluntarily submits to custody, or is effectively safeguarded against escape (maximum security confinement), the right of the state to take his life as punishment, retribution, revenge, or retaliation for previously committed offenses (no matter how numerous or heinous) or as an "example" to deter others, or as an economical expedient, does not exist in moral law.

I argue this despite the fact that it is a position which is contrary to that expounded by a number of eminent theologians, notably Thomas Aquinas. Writing in times long past and quite different, and expressing themselves in terms of conditions, logic and experiences of those times, such theologians have defended the right of the state to take human life as a punishment "when the common good requires it." Moreover, they have held that, under certain conditions, the state is morally bound to take human life and that not to take it would be sinful. Although I am philosophically opposed to war whether as an extension of diplomacy or an instrument of national policy, I recognize the right of a nation, through its armed forces and in accord with the rules of civilized warfare, to take human life in defense of its sovereignty, its national territory, and its citizens. Such recognition is in no way inconsistent with my views [against] the death penalty, for the Geneva Convention makes it clear that the killing of one's enemy (no matter how many of one's troops he has slaughtered in battle) after he has laid down his arms, surrendered, or been taken prisoner, will not be countenanced by civilized nations.

3. *Capital punishment has demonstrably failed to accomplish its stated objectives.* The proponents of the death penalty base their support largely on two basic propositions: (1) that the death penalty has a uniquely deterrent effect on those who contemplate committing capital crimes; and (2) that the provision of the death penalty as the mandatory or alternative penalty for stated offenses in the statute books removes for all time the danger of future similar offenses by those whose criminal acts have made them subject to its rigors.

Neither of these propositions will stand logical or statistical analysis. Proposition 1 is dependent upon acceptance of the repudiated "pleasure-pain" principle of past-century penology. This theory presupposes a "rational man" weighing the prospective profit or pleasure to be derived from the commission of some future crime against the almost certain pain or loss he will suffer in retribution should he be apprehended and convicted. That many persons who commit crimes are not "rational" at the time the crime is committed is beyond dispute. Avoiding the area of psychiatric controversy for the moment, let it be sufficient to report that Dr. Shaw Grigsby of the University of Florida in his recent studies at the Raiford (Florida) State Penitentiary

found that more than seventy-five percent of the males and more than ninety percent of the females then in confinement were under the influence of alcohol at the time they committed the offenses for which they were serving sentence; and that Dr. Marvin Wolfgang's studies of the patterns in criminal homicide in Philadelphia in large measure lend support to Dr. Grigsby's findings.

While perhaps the theological doctrine of "sufficient reflection and full consent of the will" as necessary prerequisites to mortal sin is somewhat mitigated by the mandate to "avoid the occasions of sin" in the determination of moral responsibility, we are here discussing rationality in terms of weighing alternatives of possible prospective deterrence rather than adjudicated post-mortem responsibility. Proposition 1 further presupposes knowledge by the prospective offender of the penalty provided in the penal code for the offense he is about to commit—a knowledge not always found even among lawyers. It further assumes a non-self-destructive orientation of the offender and, most importantly, a certainty in his mind that he will be identified, apprehended, indicted, convicted, sentenced to the maximum penalty, and that the ultimate sanction will indeed be executed. When one notes that of 125 persons indicted for first degree murder in the District of Columbia during the period 1953–1959, only one (a Negro) was executed despite the mandatory provision of the law; and further that, despite the fact that more than three million major felonies were known to the police in 1960, the total prison population (federal and state) at the 1961 prison census (including substantially all the convicted felons of 1960 and many from prior years) stood at a minuscule 190,000, the rational criminal might very well elect to "play the odds."

The second part of the proposition assumes that all or a high proportion of those who commit crimes for which the death penalty is prescribed will in fact be executed—an assumption, rebutted above, which was false even in the heyday of capital punishment when more than two hundred offenses were punishable on the gallows. It shows no awareness that the mere existence of the death penalty may in itself contribute to the commission of the very crimes it is designed to deter, or to the difficulty of securing convictions in capital cases. The murderer who has killed once (or committed one of the more than thirty other capital crimes) and whose life is already forfeit if he is caught would find little deterrent weight in the prospect of execution for a second or third capital crime—particularly if his victim were to be a police officer attempting to take him into custody for the original capital offense. The suicidal, guilt-haunted psychotic might well kill (or confess falsely to a killing) to provoke the state into imposing upon him the punishment which in his tortured mind he merits but is unable to inflict upon himself.

Prosecutors and criminal trial lawyers have frequently testified as to the difficulty of impanelling juries in capital cases and the even greater difficulty of securing convictions on evidence which in non-capital cases would leave little room for reasonable doubt. Appeals courts scan with more analytical eye the transcripts in capital cases, and error is located and deemed prejudicial which in non-capital cases would be overlooked. The Chessman case is, from this viewpoint, a monument to the determination on the part of American justice that no man shall be executed while there is the slightest doubt either as to his guilt or as to the legality of the process by which his guilt was determined. Criminologists have pointed out repeatedly that the execution of the small number of convicts (fewer than fifty each year in the United States) has a disproportionately brutalizing effect on those of us who survive. Respect for the sanctity and inviolability of human life decreases each time human life is taken. When taken formally in the circus-like atmosphere which unfortunately characterizes twentieth century trials and executions (both here and abroad), emotions, passions, impulses and hostilities are activated which may lead to the threshold of murder many who might never have incurred the mark of Cain.

4. *Capital punishment in the United States has been and is prejudicially and inconsistently applied.* The logic of the retentionist position would be strengthened if the proponents of capital punishment could demonstrate that an "even-handed justice" exacted the supreme penalty without regard to race or nationality, age or sex, social or economic condition; that all or nearly all who committed capital crimes were indeed executed; or, at least, that those pitiful few upon whom the sentence of death is carried out each year are in fact the most dangerous, the most vicious, the most incorrigible of all who could have been executed. But the record shows otherwise.

Accurate death penalty statistics for the United States are available for the thirty-year period, 1930–1959. Analysis of the more than three thousand cases in which the death penalty was exacted discloses that more than half were Negroes, that a very significant proportion were defended by court-appointed lawyers, and that few of them were professional killers. Whether a man died for his offense depended, not on the gravity of his crime, not on the number of such crimes or the number of his victims, not on his present or prospective danger to society, but on such adventitious factors as the jurisdiction in which the crime was committed, the color of his skin, his financial position, whether he was male or female (we seldom execute females), and indeed oftentimes on what were the character and characteristics of his victim (apart from the justifiability of the instant homicidal act).

It may be exceedingly difficult for a rich man to enter the Kingdom of Heaven but case after case bears witness that it is virtually impossible for him to enter the execution chamber. And it is equally impossible in several states to execute a white man for a capital crime against a Negro. Professional murderers (and the directors of the criminal syndicates which employ them) are seldom caught. When they are arrested either they are defended successfully by eminent and expensive trial counsel; or they eliminate or intimidate witnesses against them. Failing such advantages, they wisely bargain for a plea of guilty to some lesser degree of homicide and escape the death chamber. The homicidal maniac, who has massacred perhaps a dozen, even under our archaic M'Naghten Rule, is safely outside the pale of criminal responsibility and escapes not only the death penalty but often even its alternatives.

5. *The innocent have been executed.* There is no system of criminal jurisprudence which has on the whole provided as many safeguards against the conviction and possible execution of an innocent man as the Anglo-American. Those of us who oppose the death penalty do not raise this argument to condemn our courts or our judiciary, but only to underline the fallibility of human judgment and human procedures. We oppose capital punishment for the guilty; no one save a monster or deluded rationalist (e.g., the Captain in Herman Melville's *Billy Budd*) would justify the execution of the innocent. We cannot however close our minds or our hearts to the greater tragedy, the more monstrous injustice, the ineradicable shame involved when the legal processes of the state, knowingly or unknowingly, have been used to take the life of an innocent man.

The American Bar Foundation, or some similar research-oriented legal society, might well address itself to an objective analysis of the factors which led to the convictions of the many men whose sentences for capital crimes have in the past few decades been set aside by the appellate courts (or by the executive authority after the courts had exhausted their processes), and who later were exonerated either by trial courts or by the consensus of informed opinion. Especial attention should be directed to the fortunately much smaller number of cases (e.g., the Evans-Christie case in England and the Brandon case in New Jersey) in which innocent men were actually executed. Perhaps, too, a reanalysis would be profitable of the sixty-five cases cited by Professor Edwin Borchard in his *Convicting the Innocent*, the thirty-six cases mentioned by U.S. Circuit Court of Appeals Judge Jerome Frank in *Courts on Trial*, and the smaller number of miscarriages of justice outlined by Erle Stanley Gardner in *Court of Last Resort*.

6. *There are effective alternative penalties.* One gets the impression all too frequently,

both from retentionist spokesmen and, occasionally, from the statements of enthusiastic but ill-informed abolitionists, that the only alternative to capital punishment is no punishment; that, if the death penalty does not deter, then surely no lesser societal response to the violation of its laws and injury to its citizens will prove effective.

The record in abolition jurisdictions, some without the death penalty, both in the United States and abroad, in which imprisonment for indeterminate or stated terms has been substituted for the penalty of death, is a clear demonstration that alternative penalties are of equal or greater protective value to society than is capital punishment.

In every instance in which a valid statistical comparison is possible between jurisdictions scientifically equated as to population and economic and social conditions, the nations and states that have abolished capital crimes have a smaller capital crimes rate than the comparable jurisdictions that have retained the death penalty. Further, the capital crimes rate in those jurisdictions which, while retaining the death penalty, use it seldom or not at all is in most instances lower than the capital crimes rates in the retentionist jurisdictions which execute most frequently.

And finally, comparing the before, during, and after capital crimes rates in those jurisdictions (nine in the United States) which abolished capital punishment and then restored it to their penal codes, we find a consistently downward trend in capital crimes unaffected by either abolition or restoration. Startling comparisons are available. The United State Navy has executed no one in more than 120 years; yet it has maintained a level of discipline, effectiveness, and mo-rale certainly in no sense inferior to that of the United States Army which has inflicted the death penalty on more than 150 soldiers in just the last three decades.

Delaware, the most recent state to abolish the death penalty, experienced a remarkable drop in its capital crimes rate during the first full year of abolition. No criminologist would argue that abolition would necessarily reduce capital crimes; nor will he attempt to demonstrate a causal connection between absence of the death penalty and low capital crime rates. In point of fact, homicide is the one major felony which shows a consistent downward trend in both capital punishment and abolition jurisdictions—indicating to the student of human behavior that the crime of murder, particularly, is largely an irrational reaction to a concrescence of circumstances, adventitiously related, wholly independent of and neither positively nor negatively correlatable with the legal sanction provided in the jurisdiction in which the crime actually took place. Dr. Marvin Wolfgang has pointed out with some logic that our decreasing murder rate is probably in no small part due to improved communications (ambulance gets to the scene faster), improved first aid to the victim, and the antibiotics, blood banks, and similar advances in medicine which save many an assault victim from becoming a corpse—and of course his assailant from being tagged a murderer. The consistent upward trend in assaultive crimes gives support to Dr. Wolfgang's thesis.

7. *Police and prison officers are safer in non-death penalty states.* The studies of Donald Campion, S.J., associate editor of *America,* and others indicate (albeit with restricted samplings) that the life of a police officer or a prison guard is slightly safer in the non-death penalty states,

although the difference is so slight as to be statistically insignificant. Prison wardens overwhelmingly support abolition but large segments of the police profession support the retention of the death penalty both as a general crime deterrent (which it demonstrably is not) and as a specific safeguard to members of their own profession. Significantly, few of the police officers who serve in non-death penalty states are active in the fight to restore capital punishment and most of those who oppose abolition in their own jurisdictions have never performed police duties in an abolition state. It is a criminological axiom that it is the certainty, not the severity, of punishment that deters. Improvements in the selection, training, discipline, supervision, and operating techniques of our police will insure a higher percentage of apprehensions and convictions of criminals and, even without the death penalty, will provide a greater general crime deterrent and far more safety both for the general public and for police officers than either enjoys at present.

8. *Paroled and pardoned murderers are no threat to the public.* Studies in New Jersey and California, and less extensive studies of paroled and pardoned murderers in other jurisdictions, indicate that those whose death sentences have been commuted, or who have been paroled from life or long-term sentences, or who have received executive pardons after conviction of capital crimes are by far the least likely to recidivate. Not only do they not again commit homicide, but they commit other crimes or violate their parole contracts to a much lesser extent than do paroled burglars, robbers, and the generality of the non-capital crimes convicts on parole. My own study of nearly 150 murderers showed that not a single one had killed again and only two had committed any other crime subsequent to release. Ohio's Governor Michael DiSalle has pointed out (as Warden Lewis Lawes and other penologists have in the past) that murderers are by and large the best and safest prisoners; and he has demonstrated his confidence by employing eight convicted murderers from the Ohio State Penitentiary in and about the Executive Mansion in Columbus in daily contact with members of his family.

9. *The death penalty is more costly than its alternatives.* It seems somewhat immoral to discuss the taking of even a murderer's life in terms of dollars and cents; but often the argument is raised that capital punishment is the cheapest way of "handling" society's outcasts and that the "good" members of the community should not be taxed to support killers for life (often coupled with the euthanasian argument that "they are better off dead"). The application of elementary cost accounting procedures to the determination of the differential in costs peculiar to capital cases will effectively demonstrate that not only is it not "cheaper to hang them"; but that, on the contrary, it would be cheaper for the taxpayers to maintain our prospective executees in the comparative luxury of first-rate hotels, with all the perquisites of non-criminal guests, than to pay for having them executed. The tangible costs of the death penalty in terms of long-drawn-out jury selection, extended trials and retrials, appeals, extra security, maintenance of expensive, seldom-used death-houses, support of the felon's family, etc., are heavy.

10. *Capital punishment stands in the way of penal reform.* Man has used the death penalty and other forms of retributive

punishment throughout the centuries to control and govern the conduct of his fellows and to force conformity and compliance to laws and codes, taboos and customs. The record of every civilization makes abundantly clear that punishment, no matter how severe or sadistic, has had little effect on crime rates. No new approach to the criminal is possible so long as the death penalty, and the discredited penology it represents, pervades our criminal justice system. Until it is stricken from the statute books, a truly rehabilitative approach to the small percentage of our fellowmen who cannot or will not adjust to society's dictates is impossible of attainment. That there is a strong positive correlation between advocacy of the death penalty and a generally punitive orientation cannot be gainsaid. Analysis of the votes for corporal punishment bills, votes against substitution of alternatives for mandatory features in the new mandatory death penalty jurisdictions, votes against study commissions and against limited period moratoria, and comparison with votes for bills increasing the penalties for rape, narcotics offenses, and other felonies discloses a pattern of simple retributive punitiveness, characterizing many of our legislators and the retentionist witnesses before legislative committees.

Many church assemblies of America and individual churchmen of every denomination have underscored the moral and ethical nonacceptability of capital punishment. Church members have the responsibility to support the campaign to erase this stain on American society. Capital punishment is brutal, sordid, and savage. It violates the law of God and is contrary to the humane and liberal respect for human life characteristic of modern democratic states. It is unsound criminologically and unnecessary for the protection of the state or its citizens. It makes miscarriages of justice irredeemable; it makes the barbaric *lex talionis* the watchword and inhibits the reform of our prison systems. It encourages disrespect for our laws, our courts, our institutions; and, in the words of Sheldon Glueck, "bedevils the administration of justice and is the stumbling block in the path of general reform in the treatment of crime and criminals."

POSTSCRIPT
Is Capital Punishment Justified?

Opinion on the death penalty has always been sharply divided in the United States. While Massachusetts in 1785 defined nine capital crimes (that is, crimes punishable by death) and North Carolina as late as 1837 had more than twenty, other states rejected the death sentence entirely at an early date. American sentiment has been so divided that at least eleven states have abolished the death penalty only to restore it some years later.

In the readings in this issue, MacNamara catalogues the most popular arguments for the removal of the death penalty, then rebuts each in turn. Berns uses a different tactic. He narrows in on one of the more controversial justifications for punishment—retribution, "paying back" the criminal—and tries to show that it speaks to something decent and humane in our nature. Neither of these closely reasoned arguments is likely to be upset by further statistical or historical data. Facts, even inconvenient ones, can usually be incorporated into a wide variety of viewpoints. Nevertheless, the debate can only be enriched by empirical study, and the student will find a trove of it in William J. Bowers's *Executions in America* (Lexington Books, 1974). The movement that led to the abolition of the death penalty in Great Britain prompted the publication of several books, the most stimulating of which is Arthur Koestler and C. H. Rolph's *Hanged by the Neck* (Penguin, 1961). Probably the most reflective, and almost certainly the most engrossing, literature on the subject is to be found in the many books dealing with the executions of Sacco and Vanzetti (plays and films have also dealt with their case), the Rosenbergs, and Caryl Chessman. In each of these cases, deep feelings favoring and opposing their execution were aroused by political issues and questions regarding their guilt, as well as by divided sentiments on the exercise of capital punishment.

Apart from the constitutional issues, the debate is more narrowly drawn than in earlier times. Although the death penalty is sometimes urged as punishment for such acts as treason or skyjacking, it is principally considered in connection with the crime of murder. There is little dispute over the proposition that the manner of execution should be as painless as possible (no one is drawn and quartered in civilized society), although there is no unanimity of opinion about whether death by electrocution, gas, or hanging best meets that test. Some states, such as Texas and New Jersey, have adopted the method of fatal injections, though the experience with its use in Texas has raised doubts about its painlessness. It may well be that the firing squad, perhaps the most violent means of execution permitted in the United States, could also be the quickest and most painless. However, how or how often to impose capital punishment is not the question society must examine, but whether we should take a life for a life.

ISSUE 11

Is Affirmative Action Reverse Discrimination?

YES: Glenn C. Loury, from "Beyond Civil Rights," *The New Republic* (October 7, 1985)

NO: Herbert Hill, from "Race, Affirmative Action and the Constitution," *Rosenberg/Humphrey Lecture at City College of New York* (April 27, 1988)

ISSUE SUMMARY

YES: Harvard professor Glenn Loury contends that insistence on "ill-suited" civil rights strategies makes it impossible for blacks to achieve full equality in American society.
NO: Professor Herbert Hill argues that affirmative action is necessary to reverse America's long history of racist practices.

"We didn't land on Plymouth Rock, my brothers and sisters—Plymouth Rock landed on *us!*" Malcolm X's observation is borne out by the facts of American history. Snatched from their native land, transported thousands of miles—in a nightmare of disease and death—and sold into slavery, blacks were reduced to the legal status of farm animals. Even after emancipation, blacks were segregated from whites—in some states by law, and by social practice almost everywhere. American *apartheid* continued for another century.

In 1954 the Supreme Court declared state-compelled segregation in schools unconstitutional, and it followed up that decision with others that struck down many forms of official segregation. Still, discrimination survived, and in most southern states blacks were either discouraged or prohibited from exercising their right to vote. Not until the 1960s was compulsory segregation finally and effectively challenged. Between 1964 and 1968 Congress passed the most sweeping civil rights legislation since the end of the Civil War. It banned discrimination in employment, public accommodations (hotels, motels, restaurants, etc.), and housing; it also guaranteed voting rights for blacks, and even authorized federal officials to take over the job of voter registration in areas suspected of disenfranchising blacks. Today, several agencies in the federal government exercise sweeping powers to enforce these civil rights measures.

But is that enough? Equality of condition between blacks and whites seems as elusive as ever. The black unemployment rate is double that of whites, and the percentage of black families living in poverty is nearly four times that of whites. Only a small percentage of blacks ever make it into medical school or law school.

Advocates of affirmative action have focused upon these *de facto* differences to bolster their argument that it is no longer enough just to stop discrimination. The damage done by three centuries of racism now has to be remedied, they argue, and effective remediation requires a policy of "affirmative action." At the heart of affirmative action is the use of "numerical goals." Opponents call them "racial quotas." Whatever the name, what they imply is the setting aside of a certain number of jobs or positions for blacks or other historically oppressed groups. Opponents charge that affirmative action really amounts to reverse discrimination, that it penalizes innocent people simply because they are white, that it often results in unqualified appointments, and that it ends up harming blacks instead of helping them.

Affirmative action has had an uneven history in our federal courts. In *Regents of the University of California v. Bakke* (1978), which marked the first time the Supreme Court directly dealt with the merits of affirmative action, a 5–4 majority ruled that a white applicant to a medical school had been wrongly excluded due to the school's affirmative action policy; yet the majority also agreed that "race-conscious" policies may be used in admitting candidates—as long as they do not amount to fixed quotas. The ambivalence of *Bakke* has run through the Court's treatment of the issue since 1978. Decisions have gone one way or the other depending on the precise circumstances of the case (such as whether it was a federal or state policy, whether it was mandated by a congressional statute, and whether quotas were required or simply permitted). Decisions may also be affected by the changing personnel on the Supreme Court, so that an increasingly conservative Court could finally strike down affirmative action of any kind.

In the following selections, professors Glenn C. Loury and Herbert Hill debate the merits of affirmative action. Loury, who rose from a Chicago ghetto to Harvard's prestigious Kennedy School, argues that affirmative action demoralizes blacks. Hill, the former labor director of the National Association for the Advancement of Colored People, maintains that it is an essential tool for undoing the effects of racism.

YES

Glenn C. Loury

BEYOND CIVIL RIGHTS

There is today a great deal of serious discussion among black Americans concerning the problems confronting them. Many, if not most, people now concede that not all problems of blacks are due to discrimination, and that they cannot be remedied through civil rights strategies or racial politics. I would go even further: using civil rights strategies to address problems to which they are ill-suited thwarts more direct and effective action. Indeed, the broad application of these strategies to every case of differential achievement between blacks and whites threatens to make it impossible for blacks to achieve full equality in American society.

The civil rights approach has two essential aspects: first, the cause of a particular socioeconomic disparity is identified as a racial discrimination; and second, advocates seek such remedies for the disparity as the courts and administrative agencies provide under the law.

There are fundamental limitations on this approach deriving from our liberal political heritage. What can this strategy do about those important contractual relationships that profoundly affect one's social and economic status but in which racial discrimination is routinely practiced? Choice of marital partner is an obvious example. People discriminate here by race with a vengeance. A black woman does not have an opportunity equal to that of a white woman to become the wife of a given white man. Since white men are on the whole better off financially than black men, this racial inequality of opportunity has substantial monetary costs to black women. Yet surely it is to be hoped that the choice of husband or wife will always be beyond the reach of the law.

The example is not facetious. All sorts of voluntary associations—neighborhoods, friends, business partnerships—are the result of choices often influenced by racial criteria, but which lie beyond the reach of civil rights laws. A fair housing law cannot prevent a disgruntled white resident from moving away if his neighborhood becomes predominantly or even partly black. Busing for desegregation cannot prevent unhappy parents from sending their children to private schools. Withdrawal of university support for student clubs with discriminatory selection rules cannot prevent student cliques from forming along racial lines. And a vast majority of Americans would have it no other way.

As a result, the nondiscrimination mandate has not been allowed to interfere much with personal, private, and intimately social intercourse. Yet such exclusive social connections along group lines have important economic consequences. An extensive literature in economics and sociology documents the crucial importance of family and community background in determining a child's later success in life. Lacking the right "networks," blacks with the same innate abilities as whites wind up less successful. And the elimination of racial discrimination in the economic sphere—but not in patterns of social attachment—will probably not be enough to make up the difference. There are thus elemental limits on what one can hope to achieve through the application of civil rights strategies to what must of necessity be a restricted domain of personal interactions.

The civil rights strategy has generally been restricted to the domain of impersonal, public, and economic transactions such as jobs, credit, and housing. Even in these areas, the efficacy of this strategy can be questioned. The lagging economic condition of blacks is due in significant part to the nature of social life *within* poor black communities. After two decades of civil rights efforts, more than three-fourths of children in some inner-city ghettos are born out of wedlock; black high school dropout rates hover near 50 percent in Chicago and Detroit; two-fifths of murder victims in the country are blacks killed by other blacks; fewer black women graduate from col-

lege than give birth while in high school; more than two in five black children are dependent on public assistance. White America's lack of respect for blacks' civil rights cannot be blamed for all these sorry facts. This is not to deny that, in some basic sense, most of these difficulties are related to our history of racial oppression, but only to say that these problems have taken on a life of their own, and cannot be effectively reversed by civil rights policies.

Higher education is a case in point. In the not too distant past, blacks, Asians, and women faced severe obstacles to attending or teaching at American colleges and universities, especially at the most prestigious institutions. Even after black scholars studied at the great institutions, their only possibilities for employment were at the historically black colleges, where they faced large teaching loads and burdensome administrative duties. Their accomplishments were often acknowledged by their white peers only grudgingly, if at all.

Today opportunities for advanced education and academic careers for blacks abound. Major universities throughout the country are constantly searching for qualified black candidates to hire as professors, or to admit to study. Most state colleges and universities near black population centers have made a concerted effort to reach those in the inner city. Almost all institutions of higher learning admit blacks with lower grades or test scores than white students. There are special programs funded by private foundations to help blacks prepare for advanced study in medicine, economics, engineering, public policy, law, and other fields.

Yet, with all these opportunities (and despite improvement in some areas), the number of blacks advancing in the academic world is distressingly low. The percentage of college students who are black, after rising throughout the 1970s, has actually begun to decline. And though the proportion of doctorates granted to blacks has risen slightly over the last decade, a majority of black doctorates are still earned in the field of education. Despite constant pressure to hire black professors and strenuous efforts to recruit them, the percentage of blacks on elite university faculties has remained constant or fallen in the past decade.

Meanwhile, other groups traditionally excluded are making impressive gains. Asian-Americans, though less than two percent of the population, make up 6.6 percent of U.S. scientists with doctorates; they constitute 7.5 percent of the students at Yale, and nine percent at Stanford. The proportion of doctorates going to women has risen from less than one-seventh to nearly one-third in the last decade. Less than two percent of Harvard professors at all ranks are black, but more than 25 percent are women.

Now, it is entirely possible that blacks experience discrimination at these institutions. But as anyone who has spent time in an elite university community knows, these institutions are not racist in character, nor do they deny opportunities to blacks with outstanding qualifications. The case can be made that just the opposite is true—that these institutions are so anxious to raise the numbers of blacks in their ranks that they overlook deficiencies when making admissions or appointment decisions involving blacks.

One obvious reason for skepticism about discrimination as the cause of the problem here is the relatively poor academic performance of black high school and college students. Black performance on standardized college admissions tests, though improving, still lags far behind whites. In 1982 there were only 205 blacks in the entire country who scored above 700 on the math component of the SAT. And, as Robert Klitgaard shows convincingly in his book *Choosing Elites*, post-admissions college performance by black students is less than that of whites, even when controlling for differences in high school grades and SAT scores. These differences in academic performance are not just limited to poor blacks, or to high school students. On the SAT exam, blacks from families with incomes in excess of $50,000 per year still scored 60 to 80 points below comparable whites. On the 1982 Graduate Record Exam, the gap between black and white students' average scores on the mathematics component of this test was 171 points. According to Klitgaard, black students entering law school in the late 1970s had median scores on the LSAT at the eighth percentile of all students' scores.

Such substantial differences in educational results are clearly a matter of great concern. Arguably, the government should be actively seeking to attenuate them. But it seems equally clear that this is not a civil rights matter that can be reversed by seeking out and changing someone's discriminatory behavior. Moreover, it is possible that great harm will be done if the problem is defined and pursued in those terms.

Take the controversy over the racial quotas at the Boston Latin School, the pride and joy of the city's public school system. It was founded before Harvard, in 1635, and it has been recognized ever since as a center of academic excellence. Boston Latin maintains its very high standards through a grueling program of study, including Latin, Greek, calculus, history, science, and the arts. Three hours of homework per night are typical. College admissions personnel acknowledge the excellence of this program; 95 percent of the class of 1985 will go to college.

The institution admits its students on the basis of their marks in primary school and performance on the Secondary School Admissions Test. In 1974, when Boston's public schools became subject to court-ordered desegregation, Judge Arthur Garrity considered closing Boston Latin, because the student population at the time was more than 90 percent white. In the end, a racial admissions quota was employed, requiring that 35 percent of the entering classes be black and Hispanic. Of the 2,245 students last year, over half were female, 57 percent white, 23 percent black, 14 percent Asian, and six percent Hispanic.

Historically the school has maintained standards through a policy of academic "survival of the fittest." Those who were unable to make it through the academic rigors simply transferred to another school. Thus, there has always been a high rate of attrition; it is now the range of 30 percent to 40 percent. But today, unlike the pre-desegregation era, most of those who do not succeed at Boston Latin are minority students. Indeed, though approximately 35 percent of each entering class is black and Hispanic, only 16 percent of last year's senior class was. That is, for each non-Asian minority student who graduates from Latin, there is one who did not. The failure rate for whites is about half that. Some advocates of minority student interest have complained of discrimination, saying in effect that the school is not doing enough to assist those in academic difficulty. Yet surely one reason for the poor performance of the black and Hispanic students

is Judge Garrity's admissions quota. To be considered for admission, whites must score at the 70th percentile or higher on the admissions exam, while blacks and Hispanics need only score above the 50th percentile.

Recently Thomas Atkins, former general counsel of the NAACP, who has been representing the black plaintiffs in the Boston school desegregation lawsuit, which has been going on for ten years, proposed that the quota at Boston Latin be raised to roughly 50 percent black, 20 percent Hispanic and Asian, and 30 percent white—a reflection of the racial composition of the rest of Boston's public schools. Unless there were a significant increase in the size of the school, this could only be accomplished by doubling the number of blacks admitted while cutting white enrollment in half. This in turn, under plausible distributional assumptions, would require that the current difference of 20 points in the minimum test scores required of black and white students accepted be approximately doubled. Since the additional black students admitted would be less prepared than those admitted under the current quota, one could expect an even higher failure rate among minorities were this plan to be accepted. The likely consequence would be that more than three-fourths of those leaving Boston Latin without a degree would be blacks and Hispanics. It is also plausible to infer that such an action would profoundly alter, if not destroy, the academic climate in the school.

This is not simply an inappropriate use of civil rights methods, though it is surely that. It is an almost wanton moral surrender. By what logic of pedagogy can these students' difficulties be attributed to racism, in view of the fact that the school system has been run by court order for over a decade? By what calculus of fairness can those claiming to be fighting for justice argue that outstanding white students, many from poor homes themselves (80 percent of Latin graduates require financial aid in college), should be denied the opportunity for this special education so that minority students who are not prepared for it may nonetheless enroll? Is there so little faith in the aptitude of the minority young people that the highest standards should not be held out for them? It would seem that the real problem here—a dearth of academically outstanding black high school students in Boston—is not amendable to rectification by court order.

Another example from the field of education illustrates the "opportunity costs" of the civil rights strategy. In 1977 the Ann Arbor public school system was sued by public interest lawyers on behalf of a group of black parents with children in the primary grades. The school system was accused of denying equal educational opportunity to these children. The problem was that the black students were not learning how to read at an acceptable rate, though the white youngsters were. The suit alleged that by failing to take into account in the teaching of reading to these children the fact that they spoke an identifiable, distinct dialect of the English language—Black English—the black students were denied equal educational opportunity. The lawsuit was successful.

As a result, in 1979 the court ordered that reading teachers in Ann Arbor be given special "sensitivity" training so that, while teaching standard English to these children, they might take into account the youngsters' culturally distinct patterns of speech. Ann Arbor's public school system has dutifully complied. A recent discussion of this case with local educators revealed that, as of six years after the initial court order, the disparity in reading achievement between blacks and whites in Ann Arbor persists at a level comparable to the one before the lawsuit was brought. It was their opinion that, though of enormous symbolic importance, the entire process had produced little in the way of positive educational impact on the students.

This is not intended as a condemnation of those who brought the suit, nor do I offer here any opinion on whether promotion of Black English is a good idea. What is of interest is the process by which the problem was defined, and out of which a remedy was sought. In effect, the parents of these children were approached by lawyers and educators active in civil rights, and urged to help their children learn to read by bringing this action. Literally thousands of hours went into conceiving and trying this case. Yet, in the end only a hollow, symbolic victory was won.

But it is quite possible that this line of attack on the problem caused other more viable strategies not to be pursued. For example, a campaign to tutor the first and second graders might have made an impact, giving them special attention and extra hours of study through the voluntary participation of those in Ann Arbor possessing the relevant skills. With roughly 35,000 students at the University of Michigan's Ann Arbor campus (a fair number of whom are black), it would have required that only a fraction of one percent of them spare an afternoon or evening once a week for there to be sufficient numbers to provide the needed services. There were at most only a few hundred poor black students in the primary grades experiencing reading difficulties. And, more than providing this needed aid for specific kids, such an undertaking would have helped to cultivate a more healthy relationship between the university and the town. It could have contributed to building a tradition of direct services that would be of more general value. But none of this happened, in part because the civil rights approach was almost reflexively embraced by the advocating parties concerned.

The danger to blacks of too broad a reliance on civil rights strategies can be subtle. It has become quite clear that affirmative action creates uncertain perceptions about the qualifications of those minorities who benefit from it. In an employment situation, for example, if it is known that different selection criteria are used for different races, and that the quality of performance on the job depends on how one did on the criteria of selection, then in the absence of other information, it is rational to expect lower performance from persons of the race that were preferentially favored in selection. Using race as a criterion of selection in employment, in other words, creates objective incentives for customers, co-workers, and others to take race into account after the employment decision has been made.

The broad use of race preference to treat all instances of "underrepresentation" also introduces uncertainty among the beneficiaries themselves. It undermines the ability of people confidently to assert, if only to themselves, that they are as good as their achievements would seem to suggest. It therefore undermines the extent to which the personal success of any one black can become the basis of guiding the behavior of other blacks.

Fewer individuals in a group subject to such preferences return to their communities of origin to say, "I made it on my own, through hard work, self-application, and native ability, and so can you!" Moreover, it puts even the "best and brightest" of the favored group in the position of being supplicants of benevolent whites.

And this is not the end of the story. In order to defend such programs in the political arena—especially at the elite institutions—it becomes necessary to argue that almost no blacks could reach these heights without special favors. When there is internal disagreement among black intellectuals, for example, about the merits of affirmative action, critics of the policy are often attacked as being disingenuous, since (it is said) they clearly owe their own prominence to the very policy they criticize. The specific circumstances of the individual do not matter in this, for it is presumed that *all* blacks, whether directly or indirectly, are indebted to civil rights activity for their achievements. The consequence is a kind of "socialization" of the individual's success. The individual's effort to claim achievement for himself (and thus to secure the autonomy and legitimacy needed to deviate from group consensus, should that seem appropriate) is perceived as a kind of betrayal. There is nothing wrong, of course, with acknowledging the debt all blacks owe to those who fought and beat Jim Crow. There is everything wrong with a group's most accomplished persons feeling that the celebration of their personal attainment represents betrayal of their fellows.

In his recent, highly esteemed comparative history of slavery, *Slavery and Social Death*, sociologist Orlando Patterson defines slavery as the "permanent, violent domination of natally alienated and generally dishonored persons." Today's policy debates frequently focus on (or perhaps more accurately, appropriate) the American slave experience, especially the violent character of the institution, its brutalization of the Africans, and its destructive effects on social life among the slaves. Less attention is paid nowadays to the *dishonored* condition of the slave, and by extension, of the freedman. For Patterson this dishonoring was crucial. He sees as a common feature of slavery wherever it has occurred the parasitic phenomenon whereby masters derive honor and standing from their power over slaves, and the slaves suffer an extreme marginality by virtue of having no social existence except that mediated by their masters. Patterson rejects the "property in people" definition of slavery, arguing that relations of respect and standing among persons are also crucial. But if this is so, it follows that emancipation—the ending of the master's property claim—is not of itself sufficient to convert a slave (or his descendant) into a genuinely equal citizen. There remains the intractable problem of overcoming the historically generated "lack of honor" of the freedman.

This problem, in my judgment, remains with us. Its eventual resolution is made less likely by blacks' broad, permanent reliance on racial preferences as remedies for academic or occupational under-performance. A central theme in Afro-African political and intellectual history is the demand for respect—the struggle to gain inclusion within the civic community, to become coequal participants in the national enterprise. This is, of course, a problem that all immigrant groups also faced, and that most have overcome. But here, unlike some other areas of social life, it seems that the black population's slave origins, subsequent racist exclusion, and continued dependence on special favors from the majority uniquely exacerbates the problem.

Blacks continue to seek the respect of their fellow Americans. And yet it becomes increasingly clear that, to do so, black Americans cannot substitute judicial and legislative decree for what is to be won through the outstanding achievements of individual black persons. That is, neither the pity, nor the guilt, nor the coerced acquiescence in one's demands—all of which have been amply available to blacks over the last two decades—is sufficient. *For what ultimately is being sought is the freely conveyed respect of one's peers.* Assigning prestigious positions so as to secure a proper racial balance—this as a permanent, broadly practiced policy—seems fundamentally inconsistent with the attainment of this goal. It is a truth worth noting that not everything of value can be redistributed.

If in the psychological calculus by which people determine their satisfaction such status considerations of honor, dignity, and respect are important, then this observation places basic limits on the extent to which public policy can bring about genuine equality. This is especially so with respect to the policy of racially preferential treatment, because its use to "equalize" can actually destroy the good that is being sought on behalf of those initially unequal. It would seem that, where the high regard of others is being sought, there is no substitute for what is to be won through the unaided accomplishments of individual persons.

NO

Herbert Hill

RACE, AFFIRMATIVE ACTION AND THE CONSTITUTION

1988 begins the third century of the United States Constitution and having survived the ritual celebration of the 1987 bicentennial, it is appropriate that we take a fresh critical look at that document and its legacy. As we examine the historical circumstances in which the Constitution emerged, we must acknowledge the continuing centrality of race in the evolution of the Constitution and of this nation.

Under the original Constitution, a system of slavery based on race existed for many generations, a system that legally defined black people as property and declared them to be less than human. Under its authority an extensive web of racist statutes and judicial decisions emerged over a long period. The Naturalization Law of 1790 explicitly limited citizenship to "white persons," the Fugitive Slave Acts of 1793 and 1850, made a travesty of law and dehumanized the nation, and the Dred Scott Decision of 1857, where Chief Justice Taney declared that blacks were not people but "articles of merchandise," are but a few of the legal monuments grounded on the assumption that this was meant to be a white man's country and that all others had no rights in the law.

With the ratification of the 13th, 14th, and 15th Amendments in 1865, 1868 and 1870 respectively and the adoption of the Civil Rights Acts of 1866, 1870 and 1875, a profoundly different set of values was asserted. This new body of law affirmed that justice and equal treatment were not for white persons exclusively, and that black people, now citizens of the nation, also were entitled to "the equal protection of the laws."

The Civil Rights Amendments and the three related Acts proclaim a very different concept of the social order than that implicit in the "three-fifths" clause contained in Section 2 of Article 1 of the Constitution. A concept that required the reconstruction of American society so that it could be free of slavery, free of a racism that was to have such terrible long-term consequences for the entire society.

The struggle to realize the great potential of the Reconstruction amendments to the Constitution, the struggle to create a just, decent and compassionate society free of racist oppression, is a continuing struggle that has taken many different forms in each era since the Reconstruction Period and one that continues today. In our own time the old conflict between those interests intent on perpetuating racist patterns rooted in the past and the forces that struggle for a society free of racism and its legacy continues in the raging battle for and against affirmative action.

During the late 1950's and early 1960's, as a result of direct confrontation with the system of state imposed segregation, together with the emergence of a new body of constitutional law on race, a hope was born that the legacy of centuries of slavery and racism would finally come to an end. But that hope was not yet to be realized. The high moral indignation of the 1960's was evidently but a passing spasm which was quickly forgotten.

A major manifestation of the sharp turning away from the goals of justice and equality is to be found in the shrill and paranoid attacks against affirmative action. The effort to eliminate the present effects of past discrimination, to correct the wrongs of many generations was barely underway when it came under powerful attack. And now, even the very modest gains made by racial minorities through affirmative action are being erased, as powerful institutions try to turn the clock of history back to the dark and dismal days of a separate and unequal status for black Americans.

Judging by the vast outcry, it might be assumed that the remedy of affirmative action to eliminate racist and sexist patterns has become as widespread and destructive as discrimination itself. And once again, the defenders of the racial *status quo* have succeeded in confusing the remedy with the original evil. The term "reverse discrimination," for example, has become another code word for resisting the elimination of prevailing patterns of discrimination.

The historic dissent of Justice John Marshall Harlan in the 1883 decision of the Supreme Court in the Civil Rights Cases defines the constitutional principle requiring the obligation of the government to remove all the "badges and incidents" of slavery. Although initially rejected, the rationale of Harlan's position was of course vindicated in later Supreme Court decisions, as in *Brown v. Board of Education* in 1954 and *Jones v. Mayer* in 1968, among others.

The adoption by Congress of the Civil Rights Act of 1964 further confirmed this constitutional perception of the equal protection clause of the 14th Amendment and reinforced the legal principle that for every right there is a remedy. I believe that what Justice Harlan called the "badges and incidents" of slavery include every manifestation of racial discrimination, not against black people alone, but also against other people of color who were engulfed by the heritage of racism that developed out of slavery.

In this respect, I believe that an interpretation of the law consistent with the meaning of the 13th and 14th Amendments to the Constitution holds that affirmative action programs carry forth the contemporary legal obligation to eradicate the consequences of slavery and racism. In order to do that, it is necessary to confront the present effects of past discrimination and the most effective remedy to achieve that goal is affirmative action. Mr. Justice Blackmun in his opinion in *Bakke* wrote, " . . . in order to get beyond racism, we must first take account of race. There is no other way."

By now it should be very clear, that the opposition to affirmative action is based on perceived group interest rather than on abstract philosophical differences about "quotas," "reverse discrimination," "preferential treatment" and the other catch-phrases commonly raised in public debate. After all the pious rhetoric equating affirmative action with "reverse discrimination" is stripped away, it is evident that the opposition to affirmative action is in fact the effort to perpetuate the privileged position of white males in American society.

In his dissent in *Bakke*, Justice Thurgood Marshall wrote, "The experience of Negroes in America has been different in kind, not just in degree, from that of other ethnic groups. It is not merely the history of slavery alone but also that a whole people were marked as inferior by the law. And that mark has endured. The dream of America as the great melting pot has not been realized for the Negro; because of his skin color he never even made it into the pot."

I propose to examine some important aspects of the historical process so aptly described by Mr. Justice Marshall. A major recomposition of the labor force occurred in the decades after the Civil War. By the end of the 19th century the American working class was an immigrant working class and European immigrants held power and exercised great influence within organized labor. For example, in 1900, Irish immigrants or their descendants held the presidencies of over fifty of the 110 national unions in the American Federation of Labor. Many of the other unions were also led by immigrants or their sons, with Germans following the Irish in number and prominence, while the president of the AFL was a Jewish immigrant. Records of labor organizations confirm the dominant role of immigrants and their descendants in many individual unions and city and state labor bodies throughout the country at the turn of the century and for decades later.

For the immigrant worker loyalty was to the ethnic collective, and it was understood that advancement of the individual was dependent upon communal advancement. Participation in organized labor was a significant part of that process, and many of the dramatic labor conflicts of the 19th and 20th centuries were in fact ethnic group struggles. For blacks, both before and after emancipation, the historical experience was completely different. For them, systematic racial oppression was the basic and inescapable characteristic of the society, north and south, and it was the decisive fact of their lives. The problems of the white immigrant did not compare with the oppression of racism, an oppression that was of a different magnitude, of a different order.

Initially isolated from the social and economic mainstream, white immigrants rapidly came to understand that race and ethnic identity was decisive in providing access to employment and in the eventual establishment of stable communities. For white immigrant workers assimilation was achieved through group mobility and collective ethnic advancement that was directly linked to the work place. The occupational frame of reference was decisive.

Wages, and the status derived from steady work could only be obtained by entering the permanent labor force and labor unions were most important in providing access to the job market for many groups of immigrant workers. In contrast to the white ethnics, generations of black workers were systematically barred from employment in the primary sectors of the labor market, thereby denied the economic base that made possible the celebrated achievements and social mobility of white immigrant communities.

An examination of briefs *amicus curiae* filed in the Supreme Court cases involving affirmative action reveal the active role these two historically interrelated groups, white ethnics and labor unions have played in the repeated attacks against affirmative action. With some few exceptions, this has been the pattern from *De Funis* in 1974 and *Bakke* in 1978 to the most recent cases.[1] Given the context in which this issue evolved, the historical sources of the opposition to affirmative action are not surprising.

The nineteenth-century European migrations to the United States took place during the long age of blatant white supremacy, legal and extralegal, formal and informal, and as the patterns of segregation and discrimination emerged north and south, the doors of opportunity were opened to white immigrants but closed to blacks and other non-whites. European immigrants and their descendants explain their success as the result of their devotion to the work ethic, and ignore a variety of other factors such as the systematic exclusion of non-Caucasians from competition for employment. As white immigrants moved up in the social order, black workers and those of other non-white races could fill only the least desirable places in a marginal secondary labor market, the only places open to them.

The elimination of traditional patterns of discrimination required by the Civil Rights Act of 1964 adversely affected the expectations of whites, since it compelled competition with black workers and other minority group members where none previously existed. White worker expectations had become the norm and any alteration of the norm was considered "reverse discrimination." When racial practices that have historically placed blacks at a disadvantage are removed to eliminate the present effects of past discrimination, whites believe that preferential treatment is given to blacks. But it is *the removal of the preferential treatment traditionally enjoyed by white workers at the expense of blacks as a class* that is at issue in the affirmative action controversy.

In many different occupations, including a variety of jobs in the public sector such as in police and fire departments, white workers were able to begin their climb on the seniority ladder precisely because non-whites were systematically excluded from the competition for jobs. Various union seniority systems were established at a time when racial minorities were banned from employment and union membership. Obviously blacks as a group, not just as individuals, constituted a class of victims who could not develop seniority status. A seniority system launched under these conditions inevitably becomes the institutionalized mechanism whereby whites as a group are granted racial privileges.

After long delay and much conflict, a new comprehensive body of law is emerging that has a significant potential and gives hope to women and racial minorities in the labor force.

On March 25, 1987, in *Johnson v. Transportation Agency*, the Supreme Court issued its fifth affirmative action ruling within an eleven month period. In *Johnson*, the Court upheld a voluntary affirmative action plan for hiring and promoting women and minorities adopted by the Transportation Agency of Santa Clara County, California. *Johnson* firmly supports the conclusion that affirmative action is a valid remedy to eliminate discrimination in public sector employment.

In *United States v. Paradise*, the Court upheld a lower court's decision requiring the Alabama Department of Public Safety to promote one black state trooper for each white promoted until either 25 percent of the job category was black or until an acceptable alternative promotion plan was put into place.

Wygant v. Jackson Board of Education, in which the Court struck down a provision in a collective bargaining agreement which provided that, in the event of teacher layoffs, the percentage of minority personnel laid off would be no greater than the percentage of minority personnel employed by the Jackson, Michigan, school system at the time of the layoffs. However, a majority of the Court agreed that voluntary affirmative action plans by public employers are constitutional in some instances.

Local 28 of the Sheet Metal Workers International Association v. EEOC, in which the Court upheld a lower court's order requiring a New York construction union to adopt an affirmative action plan, including a special fund to recruit and train minority workers and a 29 percent minority membership goal. This decision was the culmination of almost forty years of struggle in state and federal courts to end the racist practices of this AFL-CIO affiliate. Other cases involving unions in the building trades have a similar history and after years of litigation are still pending in Federal courts. (See for example, *Commonwealth of Pennsylvania*

and Williams v. Operating Engineers, Local 542, 347 F. Supp. 268, E. D. PA. 1979.)

Local No. 93, International Association of Firefighters v. City of Cleveland, in which the Court upheld a consent decree which contained promotion goals for minorities and other affirmative action provisions in settlement of a job discrimination suit by minority firefighters.

The adverse decision in *Wygant* notwithstanding, these decisions of the Supreme Court in conjunction with the Court's 1979 decision in *Steelworkers v. Weber* make it very clear that the principle of affirmative action applied in several different contexts is well established in the law and recognized as an effective and valid remedy to eliminate traditional discriminatory employment practices. But the opponents of affirmative action continue their attacks. Powerful forces, through a well-orchestrated propaganda campaign, based upon misrepresentation and the manipulation of racial fears among whites continue their efforts to perpetuate discriminatory practices. In this, they have been aided and abetted again and again by the Reagan Administration, the most reactionary administration on civil rights in the 20th century.

In reviewing the attacks upon affirmative action, it is necessary to note the disingenuous argument of those who state that they are not against affirmative action, but only against "quotas." Affirmative action without numbers, whether in the form of quotas, goals, or timetables, is meaningless; there must be some benchmark, some tangible measure of change. Statistical evidence to measure performance is essential. Not to use numbers is to revert to the era of symbolic gesture or, at best, "tokenism."

White ethnic groups and many labor unions frequently argue that affirmative action programs will penalize innocent whites who are not responsible for past discriminatory practices. This argument turns on the notion of individual rights and sounds very moral and highminded. But it ignores social reality. It ignores the fact that white workers benefited from the systematic exclusion of blacks in many trades and industries. As has been repeatedly demonstrated in lawsuits, non-whites and women have been denied jobs, training and advancement not as individuals but as a class, no matter what their personal merit and qualification. Wherever discriminatory employment patterns exist, hiring and promotion without affirmative action perpetuate the old injustice.

Before the emergence of affirmative action remedies, the legal prohibitions against job discrimination were for the most part declarations of abstract morality that rarely resulted in any change. Pronouncements of public policy such as state and municipal fair employment practice laws were mainly symbolic, and the patterns of job discrimination remained intact. Because affirmative action programs go beyond individual relief to attack long-established patterns of discrimination and, if vigorously enforced by government agencies over a sustained period can become a major instrument for social change, they have come under powerful and repeated attack.

As long as Title VII litigation was concerned largely with procedural and conceptual issues, only limited attention was given to the consequences of remedies. However, once affirmative action was widely applied and the focus of litigation shifted to the adoption of affirmative action plans, entrenched interests were threatened. And as the gains of the 1960's are eroded, the nation becomes even more mean-spirited and self-deceiving.

Racism in the history of the United States has not been an aberration. It has been systematized and structured into the functioning of the society's most important institutions. In the present as in the past, it is widely accepted as a basis for promoting the interests of whites. For many generations the assumptions of white supremacy were codified in the law, imposed by custom and often enforced by violence. While the forms have changed, the legacy of white supremacy is expressed in the continuing patterns of racial discrimination, and for the vast majority of black and other non-white people, race and racism remain the decisive factors in their lives.

The current conflict over affirmative action is not simply an argument about abstract rights or ethnic bigotry. In the final analysis it is an argument between those who insist upon the substance of a long-postponed break with the traditions of American racism, and those groups that insist upon maintaining the valuable privileges and benefits they now enjoy as a consequence of that dismal history.

NOTES

1. In *De Funis*, briefs attacking affirmative action came from the Anti-Defamation League of B'nai B'rith, the American Jewish Committee, the American Jewish Congress and the Jewish Rights Council. The National Organization of Jewish Women filed a brief in support of affirmative action which was endorsed by the Commission on Social Action of the Union of American Hebrew Congregations. The AFL-CIO filed a brief against affirmative action, as did the National Association of Manufacturers. The United Auto Workers, United Farm Workers, American Federation of State, County, and Municipal Employees filed briefs in support, as did the United Mine Workers. In *Bakke*, among the groups which filed *amici* briefs against affirmative action were

the American Jewish Committee, American Jewish Congress, Anti-Defamation League of B'nai
B'rith, Jewish Labor Committee, National Jewish
Commission on Law and Public Affairs, UNICO
National (the largest Italian American organization in the U.S.). Italian-American Foundation,
Chicago Division of UNICO, Hellenic Bar Association of Illinois, Ukrainian Congress Committee of America, Polish American Affairs Council,
and Polish American Educators Association. All
seven Jewish organizations filed briefs opposing
affirmative action, the two Jewish groups that
had supported affirmative action in the *De Funis*
case did not file in *Bakke*. The American Federation of Teachers, an affiliate of the AFL-CIO, filed
against affirmative action, while some other
unions submitted a joint brief in support. In
Weber (1979), five *amici* briefs urged the Supreme
Court to decide against affirmative action; these
were from the Anti-Defamation League of B'nai
B'rith, the National Jewish Commission on Law
and Public Affairs, the Ukrainian Congress Committee of America, and UNICO National. Several
unions with large black memberships filed in
support. In *Fullilove* (1980), the Anti-Defamation
League of B'nai B'rith joined with employer
groups and the Pacific League Foundation to
argue against affirmative action. The Anti-Defamation League filed briefs in opposition to affirmative action in several lower court cases and
has been among the most active of all groups in
attacking affirmative action in the Courts. In
1982, the ADL filed a brief against minority interests in the Boston Firefighters case *(Boston Firefighters Union, Local 718 v. Boston Branch, NAACP)*
with the Supreme Court as did the AFL-CIO and
the U.S. Department of Justice. One June 12,
1984, the Supreme Court in the Memphis firefighters case *(Firefighters Local Union No. 1784 v.
Stotts)* held that layoffs must be made on the
basis of applicable union seniority rules even if
advances in minority employment as a result of
court ordered affirmative action are destroyed in
the process. In this case, many labor unions and
ethnic organizations again joined with the Justice Department in urging the Court to rule
against affirmative action.

POSTSCRIPT

Is Affirmative Action Reverse Discrimination?

Much of the argument between Loury and Hill turns on the question of "color blindness." To what extent should our laws be color blind? During the 1950s and early 1960s, civil rights leaders were virtually unanimous on this point. Said Martin Luther King, Jr., "I have a dream my four little children will one day live in a nation where they will not be judged by the color of their skin but by the content of their character." This was the consensus view in 1963, but today Hill seems to be suggesting that the statement needs to be qualified. In order to *bring about* color blindness, it may be necessary to become temporarily color conscious. But for how long? And is there a danger that this temporary color consciousness may become a permanent policy?

Robert M. O'Neil, in *Discriminating Against Discrimination* (Indiana, 1975), studied preferential admissions to universities and supports preferential treatment without racial quotas. Lina A. Graglia's *Disaster by Decree* (Cornell, 1976) is highly critical of busing. The focus of Allan P. Sindler's *Bakke, DeFunis, and Minority Admissions* (Longman, 1978) is on affirmative action in higher education, as is Nicholas Capaldi's *Out of Order: Affirmative Action and the Crisis of Doctrinaire Liberalism* (Prometheus, 1985). A more general discussion is found in Thomas Sowell's *Civil Rights: Rhetoric or Reality* (Morrow, 1984). Chapter 13 of *The Constitution: That Delicate Balance*, by Fred W. Friendly and Martha J. H. Elliott (Random House, 1984), provides an account of the events leading to the landmark *Bakke* case on affirmative action.

Affirmative action is one of those issues, like abortion, in which the opposing sides seem utterly intransigent. It is hard to imagine any compromise acceptable to both sides of the controversy. But there may be a large middle sector of opinion that is simply weary of the whole controversy and may be willing to support any expedient solution worked out by pragmatists in the executive and legislative branches.

ISSUE 12

Do People Have a Right To Burn the American Flag?

YES: William J. Brennan, Jr., from Majority Opinion, *Texas v. Johnson*, U.S. Supreme Court (1989)

NO: William H. Rehnquist, from Opposing Opinion, *Texas v. Johnson*, U.S. Supreme Court (1989)

ISSUE SUMMARY

YES: Retired Supreme Court Justice William Brennan argues that flag-burning deserves First Amendment protection as a speech activity.
NO: Supreme Court Chief Justice William Rehnquist contends that flag-burning is not speech but an inarticulate, vicious act undeserving of constitutional protection.

We live by symbols, and symbols—invisible signs or patterns meant to stand for some larger meaning—are all around us. Some symbols (the stick figures on roadside signs, restroom doors, and parking spaces) are simply meant to be useful. Others are emotionally charged. Religious symbols fall into that category, as do peace symbols and environmental emblems.

Flags are emotionally charged symbols. People salute them, weep over them, and, on occasion, fight battles for their possession. These reactions are not necessarily irrational, for symbols often convey very real meanings. In the 1860s, it made a great deal of difference to black Americans whether the Stars and Stripes or the Stars and Bars prevailed in the Civil War. In World War II, the swastika stood for a much different way of life than that symbolized by the American flag. Emotion occupies a central place in the symbolism of the flag. Nobody would salute or weep if we simply wrote "American flag" on a piece of white cloth and waved it around. The mute symbolism of the flag's colors triggers reactions that words cannot evoke.

If flag-waving gets people emotional, flag-burning gets them enraged. To say, "I hate the American flag" or even, "I hate America" is to make a statement. However inflammatory those statements are, they at least require some translation from words into thoughts and emotions. But burning the flag is an act, and the sight of it touches a raw nerve. The flag-burner is making a speech of sorts, but the speech is an offensive act meant to stir intense emotions.

The First Amendment protects words: Congress may make "no law . . . abridging the freedom of speech, or of the press." Does it also protect acts, such as flag-burning, that are intended to serve the same function as words? In considering this question, we must first keep in mind that words and acts are not always easy to distinguish from one another. For years the Supreme Court has struggled with the distinction. In *Schenck v. United States*, a landmark 1919 case, the Court suggested that words can sometimes become practically indistinguishable from acts. Using the analogy of falsely shouting "fire!" in a crowded theater, the Court said that certain kinds of speech in certain situations may create a "clear and present danger" of an act, which government may rightly punish. The Court ruled that such speech activities are not entitled to First Amendment protection. In a later case, *Chaplinsky v. New Hampshire* (1942), the Court upheld the conviction of a man who had gotten into a fight after calling a city marshal of Rochester, New York, "a god-damned racketeer" and a "damned fascist." Such "fighting words," the Court said, are not protected by the First Amendment.

If speech can be tantamount to actions, can actions serve as speech—and be protected as such? The Court has long recognized the concept of symbolic speech, that is, action intended as a political statement, and has extended First Amendment protection to it. As far back as 1931, the Court upheld the right of a man to display a Communist flag, and, in more recent cases, it upheld the right of a high school student to wear a black armband to school as part of an antiwar protest, and the right of another protestor to display an American flag with a peace symbol taped over part of it. Yet it has also qualified its protection of symbolic speech. In 1968 it upheld the conviction of a protestor of the Vietnam War for burning his draft card, despite his claim that such activity was protected by the First Amendment. Still, the most recent cases make it clear that a narrow 5-to-4 majority on the Court is ready to uphold and even broaden protection for symbolic speech. In 1989 the Court majority reversed the conviction of a Texas man for flag desecration and struck down the Texas law under which he was convicted. Five years earlier, Gregory Lee Johnson had doused the flag in kerosene and set it on fire as fellow demonstrators chanted "America, the red, white and blue, we spit on you!" The ruling in *Texas v. Johnson* (1989) set off a storm of controversy. President Bush denounced it and supported a constitutional amendment to reverse it. Instead of an amendment, Congress passed a federal statute outlawing flag desecration, but in less than a year that was also struck down by the same 5-to-4 majority in the case of *United States v. Eichman* (1990).

Here we present opinions from the 1989 *Johnson* case. William Brennan, speaking for the Court, argues that flag-burning deserves First Amendment protection as a speech activity, whereas William Rehnquist insists that flag-burning is not speech but an inarticulate, vicious act, which is undeserving of constitutional protection.

YES

William J. Brennan, Jr.

MAJORITY OPINION, *TEXAS V. JOHNSON*

I

While the Republican National Convention was taking place in Dallas in 1984, respondent Johnson participated in a political demonstration dubbed the "Republican War Chest Tour." As explained in literature distributed by the demonstrators and in speeches made by them, the purpose of this event was to protest the policies of the Reagan administration and of certain Dallas-based corporations. The demonstrators marched through the Dallas streets, chanting political slogans and stopping at several corporate locations to stage "die-ins" intended to dramatize the consequences of nuclear war. On several occasions they spray-painted the walls of buildings and overturned potted plants, but Johnson himself took no part in such activities. He did, however, accept an American flag handed to him by a fellow protestor who had taken it from a flag pole outside one of the targeted buildings.

The demonstration ended in front of Dallas City Hall, where Johnson unfurled the American flag, doused it with kerosene, and set it on fire. While the flag burned, the protestors chanted, "America, the red, white, and blue, we spit on you." After the demonstrators dispersed, a witness to the flag-burning collected the flag's remains and buried them in his backyard. No one was physically injured or threatened with injury, though several witnesses testified that they had been seriously offended by the flag-burning.

Of the approximately 100 demonstrators, Johnson alone was charged with a crime. The only criminal offense with which he was charged was the desecration of a venerated object. . . . After a trial, he was convicted, sentenced to one year in prison, and fined $2,000. The Court of Appeals for the Fifth District of Texas at Dallas affirmed Johnson's conviction, . . . but the Texas Court of Criminal Appeals reversed, . . . holding that the State could not, consistent with the First Amendment, punish Johnson for burning the flag in these circumstances. . . .

From *Texas v. Johnson* in *Supreme Court Reporter*, vol. 109 (1989), pp. 2536–2548. Some notes omitted.

II

Johnson was convicted of flag desecration for burning the flag rather than for uttering insulting words.[1] This fact somewhat complicates our consideration of his conviction under the First Amendment. We must first determine whether Johnson's burning of the flag constituted expressive conduct, permitting him to invoke the First Amendment in challenging his conviction. . . . If his conduct was expressive, we next decide whether the State's regulation is related to the suppression of free expression. . . .

The First Amendment literally forbids the abridgement only of "speech," but we have long recognized that its protection does not end at the spoken or written word. While we have rejected "the view that an apparently limitless variety of conduct can be labeled 'speech' whenever the person engaging in the conduct intends thereby to express an idea" . . . we have acknowledged that conduct may be "sufficiently imbued with elements of communication to fall within the scope of the First and Fourteenth Amendments." . . . Attaching a peace sign to the flag, . . . saluting the flag, . . . and displaying a red flag, . . . we have held, . . . may find shelter under the First Amendment. . . . That we have had little difficulty identifying an expressive element in conduct relating to flags should not be surprising. The very purpose of a national flag is to serve as a symbol of our country; it is, one might say, "the one visible manifestation of two hundred years of nationhood." . . .

The State of Texas conceded for purposes of its oral argument in this case that Johnson's conduct was expressive conduct, . . . and this concession seems to us as prudent as was Washington's in

Spence. Johnson burned an American flag as part—indeed, as the culmination—of a political demonstration that coincided with the convening of the Republican Party and its renomination of Ronald Reagan for President. The expressive, overtly political nature of this conduct was both intentional and overwhelmingly apparent. At his trial, Johnson explained his reasons for burning the flag as follows: "The American Flag was burned as Ronald Reagan was being renominated as President. And a more powerful statement of symbolic speech, whether you agree with it or not, couldn't have been made at that time. It's quite a just position [juxtaposition]. We had a new patriotism and no patriotism." . . . In these circumstances, Johnson's burning of the flag was conduct "sufficiently imbued with elements of communication," *Spence,* 418 U.S. . . . to implicate the First Amendment. . . .

III

Texas claims that its interest in preventing breaches of the peace justifies Johnson's conviction for flag desecration.[2] However, no disturbance of the peace actually occurred or threatened to occur because of Johnson's burning of the flag. Although the State stresses the disruptive behavior of the protestors during their march toward City Hall, Brief for Petitioner 34–36, it admits that "no actual breach of the peace occurred at the time of the flagburning or in response to the flagburning." The State's emphasis on the protestors' disorderly actions prior to arriving at City Hall is not only somewhat surprising given that no charges were brought on the basis of this conduct, but it also fails to show that a disturbance of the peace was a likely reaction to *Johnson's* conduct. The only evidence offered by the State at trial to show the reaction to Johnson's actions was the testimony of several persons who had been seriously offended by the flag-burning. *Id.,* at 6–7.

The State's position, therefore, amounts to a claim that an audience that takes serious offense at particular expression is necessarily likely to disturb the peace and that the expression may be prohibited on this basis.[3] Our precedents do not countenance such a presumption. On the contrary, they recognize that a principal "function of free speech under our system of government is to invite dispute. It may indeed best serve its high purpose when it induces a condition of unrest, creates dissatisfaction with conditions as they are, or even stirs people to anger." . . .

Nor does Johnson's expressive conduct fall within that small class of "fighting words" that are "likely to provoke the average person to retaliation, and thereby cause a breach of the peace." *Chaplinsky v. New Hampshire*, 315 U.S. 568. . . . No reasonable onlooker would have regarded Johnson's generalized expression of dissatisfaction with the policies of the Federal Government as a direct personal insult or an invitation to exchange fisticuffs. . . .

We thus conclude that the State's interest in maintaining order is not implicated on these facts. The State need not worry that our holding will disable it from preserving the peace. We do not suggest that the First Amendment forbids a State to prevent "imminent lawless action." . . . And, in fact, Texas already has a statute specifically prohibiting breaches of the peace, . . . which tends to confirm that Texas need not punish this flag desecration in order to keep the peace. . . .

IV

It remains to consider whether the State's interest in preserving the flag as a symbol of nationhood and national unity justifies Johnson's conviction.

As in *Spence*, "[w]e are confronted with a case of prosecution for the expression of an idea through activity," and "[a]ccordingly, we must examine with particular care the interests advanced by [petitioner] to support its prosecution." . . . Johnson was not, we add, prosecuted for the expression of just any idea; he was prosecuted for his expression of dissatisfaction with the policies of this country, expression situated at the core of our First Amendment values. . . .

Moreover, Johnson was prosecuted because he knew that his politically charged expression would cause "serious offense." If he had burned the flag as a means of disposing of it because it was dirty or torn, he would not have been convicted of flag desecration under this Texas law: federal law designates burning as the preferred means of disposing of a flag "when it is in such condition that it is no longer a fitting emblem for display," . . . and Texas has no quarrel with this means of disposal. . . . The Texas law is thus not aimed at protecting the physical integrity of the flag in all circumstances, but is designed instead to protect it only against impairments that would cause serious offense to others.[4] . . .

According to Texas, if one physically treats the flag in a way that would tend to cast doubt on either the idea that nationhood and national unity are the flag's referents or that national unity actually exists, the message conveyed thereby is a harmful one and therefore may be prohibited.[5]

If there is a bedrock principle underlying the First Amendment, it is that the

Government may not prohibit the expression of an idea simply because society finds the idea itself offensive or disagreeable. . . .

In holding in *Barnette* that the Constitution did not leave this course open to the Government, Justice Jackson described one of our society's defining principles in words deserving of their frequent repetition: "If there is any fixed star in our constitutional constellation, it is that no official, high or petty, can prescribe what shall be orthodox in politics, nationalism, religion, or other matters of opinion or force citizens to confess by word or act their faith therein." . . .

We never before have held that the Government may ensure that a symbol be used to express only one view of that symbol or its referents. Indeed, in *Schacht v. United States*, we invalidated a federal statute permitting an actor portraying a member of one of our armed forces to " 'wear the uniform of that armed force if the portrayal does not tend to discredit that armed force.' " . . . This proviso, we held, "which leaves Americans free to praise the war in Vietnam but can send persons like Schacht to prison for opposing it, cannot survive in a country which has the First Amendment." . . .

We perceive no basis on which to hold that the principle underlying our decision in *Schacht* does not apply to this case. To conclude that the Government may permit designated symbols to be used to communicate only a limited set of messages would be to enter territory having no discernible or defensible boundaries. Could the Government, on this theory, prohibit the burning of state flags? Of copies of the Presidential seal? Of the Constitution? In evaluating these choices under the First Amendment, how would we decide which symbols were sufficiently special to warrant this unique status? To do so, we would be forced to consult our own political preferences, and impose them on the citizenry, in the very way that the First Amendment forbids us to do. . . .

There is, moreover, no indication—either in the text of the Constitution or in our cases interpreting it—that a separate juridical category exists for the American flag alone. Indeed, we would not be surprised to learn that the persons who framed our Constitution and wrote the Amendment that we now construe were not known for their reverence for the Union Jack. The First Amendment does not guarantee that other concepts virtually sacred to our Nation as a whole—such as the principle that discrimination on the basis of race is odious and destructive—will go unquestioned in the marketplace of ideas. . . .

We are tempted to say, in fact, that the flag's deservedly cherished place in our community will be strengthened, not weakened, by our holding today. Our decision is a reaffirmation of the principles of freedom and inclusiveness that the flag best reflects, and of the conviction that our toleration of criticism such as Johnson's is a sign and source of our strength. Indeed, one of the proudest images of our flag, the one immortalized in our own national anthem, is of the bombardment it survived at Fort McHenry. It is the Nation's resilience, not its rigidity, that Texas sees reflected in the flag—and it is that resilience that we reassert today.

The way to preserve the flag's special role is not to punish those who feel differently about these matters. It is to persuade them that they are wrong. . . .

We can imagine no more appropriate response to burning a flag than waving one's own, no better way to counter a flag-burner's message than by saluting the flag that burns, no surer means of preserving the dignity even of the flag that burned than by—as one witness here did—according its remains a respectful burial. We do not consecrate the flag by punishing its desecration, for in doing so we dilute the freedom that this cherished emblem represents.

NOTES

1. Because the prosecutor's closing argument observed that Johnson had led the protestors in chants denouncing the flag while it burned, Johnson suggests that he may have been convicted for uttering critical words rather than for burning the flag. Brief for Respondent 33–34. He relies on *Street v. New York*, 394 U.S. 576, 578, 89 S.CT. 1354, 1358, 22 L.Ed.2d 572 (1969), in which we reversed a conviction obtained under a New York statute that prohibited publicly defying or casting contempt on the flag "either by words or act" because we were persuaded that the defendant may have been convicted for his words alone. Unlike the law we faced in *Street*, however, the Texas flag-desecration statute does not on its face permit conviction for remarks critical of the flag, as Johnson himself admits. See Brief for Respondent 34. Nor was the jury in this case told that it could convict Johnson of flag desecration if it found only that he had uttered words critical of the flag and its referents.

Johnson emphasizes, though, that the jury was instructed—according to Texas' law of parties— that " 'a person is criminally responsible for an offense committed by the conduct of another if acting with intent to promote or assist the commission of the offense, he solicits, encourages, directs, aids, or attempts to aid the other person to commit the offense.' " Brief for Respondent 2, n. 2, quoting 1 Record 49. The State offered this instruction because Johnson's defense was that he was not the person who had burned the flag. Johnson did not object to this instruction at trial, and although he challenged it on direct appeal, he did so only on the ground that there was insufficient evidence to support it. 706 S.W.2d 120, 124 (Tex.App. 1986). It is only in this Court that Johnson has argued that the law-of-parties instruction might have led the jury to convict him for his words alone. Even if we were to find that this argument is properly raised here, however, we would conclude that it has no merit in these circumstances. The instruction would not

have permitted a conviction merely for the pejorative nature of Johnson's words, and those words themselves did not encourage the burning of the flag as the instruction seems to require. Given the additional fact that "the bulk of the State's argument was premised on Johnson's culpability as a sole actor," *ibid.*, we find it too unlikely that the jury convicted Johnson on the basis of this alternative theory to consider reversing his conviction on this ground.

2. Relying on our decision in *Boos v. Barry*, 485 U.S. 312, 108 S.Ct. 1157, 99 L.Ed.2d 333 (1988), Johnson argues that this state interest is related to the suppression of free expression within the meaning of *United States v. O'Brien*, 391 U.S. 367, 88 S.Ct. 1673, 20 L.Ed.2d 672 (1968). He reasons that the violent reaction to flag-burnings feared by Texas would be the result of the message conveyed by them, and that this fact connects the State's interest to the suppression of expression. Brief for Respondent 12, n. 11. This view has found some favor in the lower courts. See *Monroe v. State Court of Fulton County*, 739 F.2d 568, 574–575 (CA11 1984). Johnson's theory may overread *Boos* insofar as it suggests that a desire to prevent a violent audience reaction is "related to expression" in the same way that a desire to prevent an audience from being offended is "related to expression." Because we find that the State's interest in preventing breaches of the peace is not implicated on these facts, however, we need not venture further into this area.

3. There is, of course, a tension between this argument and the State's claim that one need not actually cause serious offense in order to violate § 42.09. See Brief for Petitioner 44.

4. *Cf. Smith v. Goguen*, 415 U.S., at 590–591, 94 S.Ct., at 1255–1256 (BLACKMUN, J., dissenting) (emphasizing that lower court appeared to have construed state statute so as to protect physical integrity of the flag in all circumstances); *id.*, at 597–598, 94 St.Ct., at 1259 (REHNQUIST, J., dissenting) (same).

5. Texas claims that "Texas is not endorsing, protecting, avowing or prohibiting any particular philosophy." Brief for Petitioner 29. If Texas means to suggest that its asserted interest does not prefer Democrats over Socialists, or Republicans over Democrats, for example, then it is beside the point, for Johnson does not rely on such an argument. He argues instead that the State's desire to maintain the flag as a symbol of nationhood and national unity assumes that there is only one proper view of the flag. Thus, if Texas means to argue that its interest does not prefer *any* viewpoint over another, it is mistaken; surely one's attitude towards the flag and its referents is a viewpoint.

NO

William H. Rehnquist

DISSENTING OPINION,
TEXAS V. JOHNSON

In holding this Texas statute unconstitutional, the Court ignores Justice Holmes' familiar aphorism that "a page of history is worth a volume of logic." . . . For more than 200 years, the American flag has occupied a unique position as the symbol of our Nation, a uniqueness that justifies a governmental prohibition against flag burning in a way respondent Johnson did here.

At the time of the American Revolution, the flag served to unify the Thirteen Colonies at home, while obtaining recognition of national sovereignty abroad. . . .

One immediate result of the flag's adoption was that American vessels harassing British shipping sailed under an authorized national flag. Without such a flag, the British could treat captured seamen as pirates and hang them summarily; with a national flag, such seamen were treated as prisoners of war. . . .

The American flag played a central role in our Nation's most tragic conflict, when the North fought against the South. The lowering of the American flag at Fort Sumter was viewed as the start of the war. G. Preble, History of the Flag of the United States of America 453 (1880). The Southern States, to formalize their separation from the Union, adopted the "Stars and Bars" of the Confederacy. The Union troops marched to the sound of "Yes We'll Rally Round The Flag Boys, We'll Rally Once Again." President Abraham Lincoln refused proposals to remove from the American flag the stars representing the rebel States, because he considered the conflict not a war between two nations but an attack by 11 States against the National Government. . . . By war's end, the American flag again flew over "an indestructible union, composed of indestructible states." . . .

In the First and Second World Wars, thousands of our countrymen died on foreign soil fighting for the American cause. At Iwo Jima in the Second World War, United States Marines fought hand-to-hand against thousands of Japanese. By the time the Marines reached the top of Mount Suribachi, they

From *Texas v. Johnson* in *Supreme Court Reporter,* vol. 109 (1989), pp. 2548–2555.

raised a piece of pipe upright and from one end fluttered a flag. That ascent had cost nearly 6,000 American lives. The Iwo Jima Memorial in Arlington National Cemetery memorializes that event. President Franklin Roosevelt authorized the use of the flag on labels, packages, cartons, and containers intended for export as lend-lease aid, in order to inform people in other countries of the United States' assistance. . . .

The flag symbolizes the Nation in peace as well as in war. It signifies our national presence on battleships, airplanes, military installations, and public buildings from the United States Capitol to the thousands of county courthouses and city halls throughout the country. Two flags are prominently placed in our courtroom. Countless flags are placed by the graves of loved ones each year on what was first called Decoration Day, and is now called Memorial Day. The flag is traditionally placed on the casket of deceased members of the Armed Forces, and it is later given to the deceased's family. . . .

No other American symbol has been as universally honored as the flag. In 1931, Congress declared "The Star Spangled Banner" to be our national anthem. . . . In 1949, Congress declared June 14th to be Flag Day. . . . In 1987, John Philip Sousa's "The Stars and Stripes Forever" was designated as the national march. . . . Congress has also established "The Pledge of Allegiance to the Flag" and the manner of its deliverance. . . . The flag has appeared as the principal symbol on approximately 33 United States postal stamps and in the design of at least 43 more, more times than any other symbol. . . .

The American flag, then, throughout more than 200 years of our history, has come to be the visible symbol embodying our Nation. It does not represent the views of any particular political party, and it does not represent any particular political philosophy. The flag is not simply another "idea" or "point of view" competing for recognition in the marketplace of ideas. Millions and millions of Americans regard it with an almost mystical reverence regardless of what sort of social, political, or philosophical beliefs they may have. I cannot agree that the First Amendment invalidates the Act of Congress, and the laws of 48 of the 50 States, which make criminal the public burning of the flag. . . .

But the Court insists that the Texas statute prohibiting the public burning of the American flag infringes on respondent Johnson's freedom of expression. Such freedom, of course, is not absolute. See *Schenck v. United States*, . . . (1919). In *Chaplinsky v. New Hampshire*, (1942), a unanimous Court said:

"Allowing the broadest scope to the language and purpose of the Fourteenth Amendment, it is well understood that the right of free speech is not absolute at all times and under all circumstances. There are certain well-defined and narrowly limited classes of speech, the prevention and punishment of which have never been thought to raise any Constitutional problem. These include the lewd and obscene, the profane, the libelous, and the insulting or 'fighting' words— those which by their very utterance inflict injury or tend to incite an immediate breach of the peace. It has been well observed that such utterances are no essential part of any exposition of ideas, and are of such slight social value as a step to truth that any benefit that may be derived from them is clearly outweighed by the social interest in order and morality." . . .

Here it may equally be said that the public burning of the American flag by Johnson was no essential part of any exposition of ideas, and at the same time it had a tendency to incite a breach of the peace. Johnson was free to make any verbal denunciation of the flag that he wished; indeed, he was free to burn the flag in private. He could publicly burn other symbols of the Government or effigies of political leaders. He did lead a march through the streets of Dallas, and conducted a rally in front of the Dallas City Hall. He engaged in a "die-in" to protest nuclear weapons. He shouted out various slogans during the march, including: "Reagan, Mondale, which will it be? Either one means World War III"; "Ronald Reagan, killer of the hour, Perfect example of U.S. power"; and "red, white and blue, we spit on you, you stand for plunder, you will go under." . . . For none of these acts was he arrested or prosecuted; it was only when he proceeded to burn publicly an American flag stolen from its rightful owner that he violated the Texas statute.

The Court could not, and did not, say that Chaplinsky's utterances were not expressive phrases—they clearly and succinctly conveyed an extremely low opinion of the addressee. The same may be said of Johnson's public burning of the flag in this case; it obviously did convey Johnson's bitter dislike of his country. But his act, like Chaplinsky's provocative words, conveyed nothing that could not have been conveyed and was not conveyed just as forcefully in a dozen different ways. As with "fighting words," so with flag burning, for purposes of the First Amendment: It is "no essential part of any exposition of ideas, and [is] of such slight social value as a step to truth that any benefit that may be derived

from [it] is clearly outweighed" by the public interest in avoiding a probable breach of the peace. . . .

In *Spence v. Washington*, . . . the Court reversed the conviction of a college student who displayed the flag with a peace symbol affixed to it by means of removable black tape from the window of his apartment. Unlike the instant case, there was no risk of a breach of the peace, no one other than the arresting officers saw the flag, and the defendant owned the flag in question. The Court concluded that the student's conduct was protected under the First Amendment, because "no interest the State may have in preserving the physical integrity of a privately owned flag was significantly impaired on these facts." . . . The Court was careful to note, however, that the defendant "was not charged under the desecration statute, nor did he permanently disfigure the flag or destroy it." . . .

The Court concludes its opinion with a regrettably patronizing civics lecture, presumably addressed to the Members of both Houses of Congress, the members of the 48 state legislatures that enacted prohibitions against flag burning, and the troops fighting under that flag in Vietnam who objected to its being burned: "The way to preserve the flag's special role is not to punish those who feel differently about these matters. It is to persuade them that they are wrong." . . . The Court's role as the final expositor of the Constitution is well established, but its role as a platonic guardian admonishing those responsible to public opinion as if they were truant school children has no similar place in our system of government. The cry of "no taxation without representation" animated those who revolted against the English Crown to found our Nation—the idea that those who submitted to government should have some say as to what kind of laws would be passed. Surely one of the high purposes of a democratic society is to legislate against conduct that is regarded as evil and profoundly offensive to the majority of people—whether it be murder, embezzlement, pollution, or flag burning. . . .

Uncritical extension of the constitutional protection to the burning of the flag risks the frustration of the very purpose for which organized governments are instituted. The Court decides that the American flag is just another symbol, about which not only must opinions pro and con be tolerated, but for which the most minimal public respect may not be enjoined. The government may conscript men into the Armed Forces where they must fight and perhaps die for the flag, but the government may not prohibit the public burning of the banner under which they fight.

POSTSCRIPT

Do People Have a Right to Burn the American Flag?

Rehnquist and Brennan agree that, if Gregory Lee Johnson had confined himself to verbally insulting the flag, that would have been protected by the First Amendment. This disagreement turns on whether or not the act of physically burning the American flag is protected speech. This prompts some questions. Would Rehnquist extend First Amendment protection to someone who burned a photograph or a painting of the flag? As for Brennan, does he think that the Ku Klux Klan has a First Amendment right to burn a cross in front of the Lincoln Memorial? The logic of both justices can be pushed to perplexing lengths.

Nat Henthoff's *The First Freedom: The Tumultuous History of Free Speech in America* (Delacorte, 1980) is a lively study of major free speech battles. Franklyn C. Haiman's *Speech and Law in a Free Society* (University of Chicago, 1981) surveys various meanings given to the clauses in the First Amendment. Richard Polenberg's *Fighting Faiths* (Knopf, 1987) is a study of political dissent and American reactions to it.

United States v. Eichman, the 1990 flag-burning case, was similar to the *Johnson* case except that the statute challenged was federal rather than state and was crafted to avoid the charge that it was a suppression of speech. The Texas statute in the earlier case had punished flag desecration "that the actor notes will seriously offend" onlookers, whereas the new federal statute simply prohibited flag destruction (although it made an exception for disposing of worn-out flags). The Court majority was unimpressed by the distinction. In William Brennan's words, "the Act still suffers from the same fundamental flaw: it suppresses expression out of concern for its likely communicative impact."

ISSUE 13

Should Pornography Be Protected as Free Speech?

YES: Donna A. Demac, from *Liberty Denied: The Current Rise of Censorship in America* (PEN American Center, 1988)

NO: James C. Dobson, from "Enough Is Enough," in Tom Minnery, ed., *Pornography: A Human Tragedy* (Tyndale House, 1986)

ISSUE SUMMARY

YES: Lawyer Donna Demac believes that, with the exception of child pornography, the cure of censorship is worse than the disease of pornography, whose social harm is unproven.
NO: President of Focus on the Family James Dobson argues that pornography is humiliating to women, harmful to children, related to sexual exploitation and crime, and unprotected by the First Amendment.

In 1990 in Cincinnati, a museum director was ordered to stand trial for exhibiting homoerotic photographs. In Florida, a federal judge ruled that a rap music album by 2 Live Crew was sexually explicit and obscene. He noted that the issue was "a case between two ancient enemies: Anything Goes and Enough Already."

Perhaps that poses the choice too broadly. Thoughtful defenders of unrestrained expression do not rejoice that "anything goes." They believe that no one can be trusted to exercise the wisdom to decide what goes and what does not, and they say that censors, in the name of decency, often ban challenging ideas and innovative art. In response, those who would limit or ban pornography argue that some means must be used to protect society from material that graphically displays sick and violent sexual acts, especially since there seems to be no practical way children can be shielded from exposure to it.

Where do we draw the line? The First Amendment to the U.S. Constitution says: "Congress shall make no law . . . abridging the freedom of speech, or of the press." The language is clear—or is it? The Supreme Court has often acknowledged that certain categories of speech or expression simply are not included within that constitutional protection, including lewd and obscene, libelous, or seditious speech, and "fighting words" that incite a breach of the peace.

Remarkably, the Supreme Court did not establish a constitutional rule for obscenity until 1957—although it has never since been entirely free of the issue. The 1957 decision (*Roth v. U.S.*) excluded obscenity from the constitutional protection accorded freedom of expression. Justice William J. Brennan, Jr., author of the *Roth* opinion, carefully distinguished obscenity from sex: "Obscene material is material which deals with sex in a manner appealing to prurient interests." As for "prurient interests," Brennan adopted a dictionary definition: "itching, longing; . . . lewd." For some people, the Bible or Shakespeare might cause itching or longing, so Brennan added that the "dominant theme of the material taken as a whole" must seem prurient to "the average person, applying contemporary community standards."

The Court was seriously divided in deciding *Roth*. Two justices would not accept the argument that obscenity, or for that matter any other type of expression, should be excluded from First Amendment protection. Another justice would have distinguished between the standards applied to the federal government and those applied to the states. (He would have given the states greater latitude to define obscenity according to their standards.) Still another justice held that the crucial element was not the content of the allegedly obscene material but the way it was distributed and advertised—that is, its commercial exploitation.

The four Nixon appointees to the Court reflected or responded to that criticism. In five obscenity cases decided in 1973, a new majority (the Nixon appointees plus Justice Byron White) made successful prosecution of obscenity easier and, therefore, more likely. It is no longer necessary to demonstrate that the allegedly obscene material is "utterly without redeeming social value," only that it lacks "serious value." Furthermore, for the first time the Court made clear that the community standards to be applied were those of the local community. The increase in prosecutions since 1973 has been prompted not only by the change in judicial attitude but also by change in the postal law, which now allows prosecution of those connected with obscene material in the place of delivery or receipt as well as the place of mailing. Therefore, if a prosecution fails in one place, it can still be attempted elsewhere.

Nevertheless, despite occasional successful prosecutions, the bounds of permissible expression have been broadened. The 1990 controversy over whether the National Endowment for the Arts should subsidize artists who create pornographic or obscene works does not address their legality. It is clear that even PG-rated movies, as well as videotapes and cable television, contain obscene language and depict sexual activity that would have been censored severely a generation ago. In the following selections, Donna Demac defends this freedom and James Dobson argues that society pays too high a price and can impose limits.

YES

Donna A. Demac

THE GUARDIANS OF DECENCY
The Pornography Debate in the Print, Broadcast, and Music Industries

My concept? You can't do anything with anybody's body to make it dirty to me. Six people, eight people, one person—you can do only one thing to make it dirty: kill it.
—Lenny Bruce[1]

In 1986 North Carolina enacted a law that makes it a felony for adults to view erotic material—even in their own homes. At about the same time, it was reported that the mayor of Scottsdale, Arizona, had urged local residents to supply police with the license-plate numbers of people seen entering movie theaters showing X-rated films. At the federal level, the FBI, the Postal Service, and the Justice Department have all launched "antiporn" campaigns involving prosecutions, steep fines, and the confiscation of property.

The bluenoses are back, and they are stronger than ever. During the 1980s a great many groups have launched an ambitious assault on what they consider obscenity in books, magazines, films, records, videos, and virtually any other medium found to offend their various standards of decency. From the National Federation for Decency to the Moral Majority, such self-appointed crusaders for propriety have found sympathetic ears in local governments as well as in the Reagan administration. Such groups, which regard organized opposition against obscenity as a component of their conservative social agenda, have also forged an unlikely alliance with some feminists who support the suppression of pornography as a step toward ending the degradation of women.

Smut-busting is not peculiar to our time. For more than a century there have been efforts to rid the nation of sexually explicit images. The difference today is that "antiporn" forces no longer limit their battle to small-time purveyors of dirty pictures plying their trade in back alleys. In an era when erotic products and images are all around us and sex is used to sell everything from motor oil to mouthwash, the crusaders are a growing

From Donna A. Demac, *Liberty Denied: The Current Rise of Censorship in America.* Originally published by PEN American Center. Copyright © 1988 by PEN American Center. Revised edition copyright © 1990 by Donna A. Demac, published by Rutgers University Press. Reprinted by permission of Rutgers University Press. Some notes omitted.

influence throughout society. They are particularly concerned, of course, with explicit sexual messages, and indeed there are plenty of those; "Dial-A-Porn" telephone services alone account for a billion-dollar trade, and even greater profits are derived from "adult" printed matter, films, and videos that are readily available in most parts of the country.

For some the rise in the volume and relative openness of the sex business is a healthy sign of a breakdown in social taboos, an offshoot of the so-called sexual revolution. Others regard it as an indication that growing numbers of people—daunted by confusing sexual mores and the risk of fatal disease—are opting for fantasy rather than the real thing. Still others see it as part of a general decay of moral standards.

Whatever the reason, there is no question that what amounts to a powerful pornography-bashing backlash raises serious threats to individual liberties. Surely some materials might elicit abhorrence from almost everyone—those involving graphic depictions of violence, for example—yet there is no practical way of drawing the line.

What is more troubling is that many of the moral crusaders do not stop at the most offensive cases. Their range of targets is much wider, and their efforts amount to a frightening assault on freedom of expression and individual privacy. The fight against pornography inevitably turns into a campaign for another form of censorship.

FROM HOMER TO COMSTOCK

. . . For centuries, sexuality and nudity were conventional ingredients of great works of art and popular entertainment. The writings of Aristophanes, Boccaccio,

Chaucer, and Rabelais, to name a few, contained healthy doses of bawdiness. The paintings of Raphael, Titian, Rubens, and many other artists openly depicted the undraped human form.

The urge to censor such works emerged in the seventeenth century. In Puritan England, bodily pleasure was branded sinful and immoral. Even then, laws against obscenity evolved slowly in the Anglo-Saxon world. It was only with the spread of printed matter that the guardians of morality became worried about what would happen if material they considered objectionable fell into the hands of the masses. The first anti-obscenity legislation enacted in England was adopted in 1824; it prohibited exposing an obscene book or print in public places. By 1857, in what became known as the Campbell Act, English law prohibited the dissemination of all obscene materials.

In the New World, all thirteen colonies made blasphemy or profanity a criminal offense, yet only Massachusetts had a law, passed in 1712, prohibiting the circulation of sexually explicit material. Linking profane speech to religious heresy, it outlawed the "composing, writing, printing, or publishing of any filthy, obscene, or profane song, pamphlet, libel, or mock sermon in imitation or mimicking of religious services."[2]

During the first half of the nineteenth century, many states adopted laws to deal with obscene works. The first federal anti-obscenity statute, aimed at halting the importation of lurid postcards, was adopted in 1842. In 1865, in response to concerns that soldiers had been corrupted by "dirty" literature during the Civil War, Congress passed the first law prohibiting the sending of obscene materials through the mails.

At about this time, Anthony Comstock,[3] a former grocery clerk, embarked on what would be a forty-year career as the nation's leading crusader against vice. Assisted by the YMCA, he formed the Society for the Suppression of Vice to lobby for stringent state and national anti-obscenity legislation, a campaign that led Congress to pass an omnibus anti-obscenity bill in 1873: the Comstock Law. Comstock himself was made a special agent of the Post Office in charge of enforcing the statute. His less than savory tactics included the use of informers and decoys and the harassment of birth-control reformers.[4]

By 1900 some thirty states had adopted companion anti-obscenity legislation. It is interesting to note that the laissez-faire notions of the age did not extend to this area. Comstock's vice squads, crusading under the banner of "Morals, Not Art or Literature," were supported by wealthy individuals—including financier J. P. Morgan—many of whom had their own private collections of erotica.

Aside from their concern for morality, the crusaders for decency of the era (like those today) expressed concern about those they considered to be harmed by the disputed material. Until the 1950s many books, plays, films, and other works of art were suppressed under the Hicklin doctrine, derived from a nineteenth-century British case that judged obscenity by the "effect of isolated passages upon the most susceptible persons."[5]

By the 1920s the mood of social progress in the country made the actions of antivice groups less popular. On one particular front, the American literary community became impatient at the policy of the U.S. Customs Bureau that barred from United States shores the works of such classic authors as Balzac, Voltaire, and Rousseau and newer writers like D. H. Lawrence and James Joyce.

In 1933, Bennett Cerf of Random House tested an eleven-year ban of Joyce's *Ulysses* by arranging to have a copy sent to him from abroad. The ensuing trial resulted in a landmark decision by Federal Judge John Woolsey that overturned the ban. While he noted that *Ulysses* was a difficult work that might not appeal to all tastes, Woolsey stated, "I have not found anything that I consider to be dirt for dirt's sake."

Shortly after this, the Catholic Church established the National Office for Decent Literature, which circulated monthly lists of books it considered indecent. The authors whom subscribers were warned to avoid included celebrated writers like John Dos Passos and William Faulkner. During the same period the film industry set up the Hays Office to enforce stricter moral standards in movies. Nevertheless, the government generally reduced its activities as the ultimate guardian of decency.[6]

SEXUAL EXPLICITNESS EXPANDS

This is not to say that the obscenity issue was dead. In *Roth v. U.S.* in 1957 the Supreme Court set regulation in this area on a new course with a decision restating the application of the First Amendment to sexually explicit material. Since nudity and other titillating images did not necessarily create a "clear and present danger"—the only exception under which otherwise constitutionally protected expression could be enjoined—the Court needed some other basis, which it found by declaring obscenity totally outside the range of speech encompassed by the First Amendment.

Obscene expression, the Court ruled, was material that had no redeeming social value. However, the Court made it clear that this was to be a very limited category, much narrower than the "weakest person" Hicklin standard. The portrayal of sex and obscenity were not to be considered synonymous; indeed, the Court said, "sex, a great and mysterious motive force in human life, has indisputably been a subject of absorbing interest." Only what it defined as true obscenity—speech that was considered totally worthless—could be suppressed.

After this ruling, judicial tolerance for the censorship of erotic material declined greatly. In 1959, a court lifted the thirty-year ban on D. H. Lawrence's *Lady Chatterley's Lover*. By 1966, when a Massachusetts ban on the erotic novel *Fanny Hill* was reversed, many observers concluded that the 1957 Supreme Court ruling made it all but impossible to prosecute for obscenity, except when material was sold to minors.[7] Nonetheless, some controversial figures suffered harassment. In the early 1960s comedian Lenny Bruce was repeatedly arrested and charged with obscenity by local authorities because of his ribald nightclub acts.

That decade as a whole produced a growing degree of tolerance for—not to mention demand for—greater openness in artistic and personal expression. Freedom from sexual inhibitions was a major theme of the day, one that became inseparable from the alternative political initiatives that were also burgeoning.

Sex and politics were joined in the underground press. Many publications that started out focusing on politics soon found that perhaps the only way to survive was to include sexual content in their editorial material, as well as candid personal ads. Sometimes the sex over-whelmed the politics, as when Jim Buckley, the leftist editor of the *New York Free Press*, joined publisher Al Goldstein to start *Screw* magazine, which he called "the Consumer's Report of Sex."[8] It boosted its circulation to 100,000 by publishing graphic articles about masturbation and homosexuality, interviews with prostitutes, and unrestrained displays of human anatomy. Its taste was often questionable, and *Screw* helped set a new standard of immodesty among openly sold publications.

BACKLASH AND THE 1967 PORNOGRAPHY COMMISSION

Not everyone welcomed the uninhibited new atmosphere. Prodecency forces around the country regrouped and exerted pressure on the federal government to limit what they regarded as a flood of smut circulating in schools, stores, homes, and in the mails. In 1967 Congress responded with legislation that established a National Commission on Pornography. . . .

After two years of research, the Commission arrived at conclusions that came as a major disappointment to the anti-pornography crusaders. First, it found that much of the problem regarding sexual images was not based in the material but rather stemmed "from the inability or reluctance of people in our society to be open and direct in dealing with sexual matters." Moreover, one of the Commission's major public opinion surveys indicated that only two percent of Americans viewed sexually explicit material as a significant social problem. Because of its broadly worded questions, the survey drew considerable criticism. . . .

Most government officials were not pleased with these conclusions. Many members of Congress, along with President Nixon and other conservatives, loudly rejected the Commission's report. As a result, no obscenity statutes were repealed; on the contrary, not long after the report was issued, Congress approved an amendment to the Postal Reorganization Act that prohibited the mailing of sexually oriented commercial advertising to persons who indicated they did not want it.

The next important development in the field occurred in 1973, when the Supreme Court made yet another attempt to define obscenity as a form of speech that feel outside the province of constitutional protection. In a case that remains the standard, Marvin Miller, a major publisher of pornography, was convicted of violating California law by distributing unsolicited obscene materials through the mail. He appealed to the Supreme Court, arguing that the law was unconstitutional.

In a 5 to 4 decision, the Court refused to hold that all state obscenity laws violated the First Amendment. Instead, it established a new three-part test based on community standards for states and localities to use in determining whether material is obscene.

Since 1973, innumerable attempts have been made by local authorities to exercise the new authority granted under the *Miller* standard. But many of them came up against a 1974 Supreme Court ruling in a case that involved an attempt to suppress the film *Carnal Knowledge*: Local juries did not have "unbridled discretion" in deciding what was obscene and such a determination could be applied only to material depicting "patently offensive hard-core sexual conduct."

Obviously, the standard remained somewhat unclear, and so the battles continued to rage. They also spread to different arenas as erotic material found its way into new communications media. With satellite-transmitted television, sex flies through space; with Dial-A-Porn services it comes through the phone lines; and with erotic computer games like Leather Goddesses of Phobos it pops up in the home PC.

TIPPER GORE VERSUS JELLO BIAFRA

The self-appointed forces of decency also have to contend with the fact that sexual content is on the rise even in mainstream channels of communication like network television. Prime-time programs such as *Dallas, Dynasty,* and *Miami Vice,* as well as daytime soap operas, are filled with verbal and visual sexual innuendos. In other programs, such as *Cagney and Lacey,* the plots are deliberately constructed to raise such social issues as infidelity and contraception; this approach has gained credibility and popularity as a result of public concern about AIDS and teenage pregnancy. In an effort to educate viewers, public service ads have sometimes been even more sexually explicit. The trend toward "permissiveness" has also been seen in rock music, films, and most other dimensions of cultural life.

Once again the slide toward openness has been accompanied by a resurgence of antipornography activism. One of the most successful crusaders of recent vintage is Tipper Gore, the founder of the Parents Music Resource Center. Gore has effectively used her position as the wife of a U.S. senator in her campaign against what she regards as socially harmful lyrics in rock music. Acting on her homespun analysis, she is seeking to shield children from what she and her supporters believe is a major cause of teenage suicide, the breakup of families, and a litany of other social problems.

Largely because Gore solicited the participation of fifteen other congressional spouses, she was able to arrange a special congressional hearing on rock lyrics and to pressure the music industry into agreeing to place warning labels on records with explicit sexual lyrics. After this success Gore expanded the scope of her campaign to include music videos, television programs, and videocassettes.

Gore argues that her efforts do not amount to censorship, that her aim is simply a rating system like the one that is in effect in the motion picture industry. (That system has not been flawless: Numerous filmmakers have been forced to tone down or delete footage in order to avoid X or R ratings, since theater owners in some parts of the country refuse to display movies with those designations.)

The introduction of warning labels for music already has had repercussions for performers, some of whom have been forced to modify lyrics and album art. Gore has also helped create a climate in which musicians can be prosecuted. In 1986 Jello Biafra, lead singer of the Dead Kennedys, a politically oriented punk band, was charged with violating a California law prohibiting the distribution of materials harmful to minors. The alleged offense was the enclosure, in the album *Frankenchrist*, of a poster showing the disembodied genitalia of men and women. The album cover featured a sticker warning that there was an enclosure "that some people may find shocking, repulsive, or offensive. Life can sometimes be that way." Although Biafra was acquitted, the suit led to the disbanding of the group and, according to Biafra, kept him from performing for more than a year.

There is no doubt that groups like the Dead Kennedys are deliberately provocative in their lyrics and their performances, but outrageous behavior has been a hallmark of rock music from its very beginning. The attempts of adults to eliminate the raunchier aspects of the music are as foolish today as they were when cameramen were told to crop out the pulsating lower half of Elvis Presley's body when he appeared on *The Ed Sullivan Show*.

Tipper Gore and others claim that today's music is sometimes unacceptably offensive. By her standards Gore may be right, but no individual or group should be able to take the position of arbiter of what is available to others with less "refined" tastes. Our human tendency to attribute to the potential actions of "lesser" others what we fear in our own imaginations needs to be recognized and curtailed.

MEESE AND HIS MISSION

With the rise of the New Right and the election of Ronald Reagan, the anti-obscenity forces looked forward to a new era of success. The administration did indeed develop strong links to the Moral Majority, the National Federation for Decency, and other organizations whose agenda included stamping out what they regard as smut. The antipornography issue seemed a natural ingredient for the federal government's efforts to restore "traditional values," which included shoring up the nuclear family. To this intent, people who were active in right-wing circles, including moral crusader Alfred Regnery, were appointed to key positions that enabled them to use taxpayer money to fund research and otherwise allocate funds for their own objectives.

Acting under pressure from "pro-decency" organizations, the administration in 1985 created a commission on pornography under the authority of Attorney General Edwin Meese. From the start, it was clear that the goal of the Meese Commission was to rebut the findings of the earlier National Commission on Pornography and its controversial 1970 report. The body was also expected to provide justification for expanded law enforcement and private campaigns against sexually explicit material. The bias of the Meese Commission was apparent in its list of appointees, which included nine known conservatives and several law enforcement officers. The Commission chair, Henry Hudson, was a Virginia district attorney who was well-known for his drives against pornography. . . .

Despite its efforts to do so, the Commission was unable to produce proof of support the contention that pornographic materials inflict harm on society; it could assert only that certain kinds of especially violent material seem to have a pernicious effect. The Commission also allowed that it could not come up with a better definition of obscenity than the one contained in the Supreme Court's *Miller* decision.

This lack of supporting evidence did not stop the Commission from recommending that prosecutors use a number of laws originally enacted for non-speech-related purposes to curtail the activities of persons it deemed to be violating certain standards of decency. Among the actions it proposed were prosecuting pornographers for unfair labor practices, seizing the assets of companies involved in the smut business, and creating a federal database on those persons convicted for or suspected of activity related to obscenity . . .

THE AFTERMATH

The Meese Commission report has given a green light to the efforts of local anti-pornography crusaders. Bills modeled after the Commission's recommendations have been introduced in numerous states. The Kansas legislature passed a law making retailers of pornography responsible for the content of what they sell. In Belgrade, Montana, a town of 3,200 with no "adult" bookstores, a committee was set up to ban such material in the event that it became necessary. Virginia officials are awaiting a decision from the Supreme Court regarding the constitutionality of a state law making it a crime for a bookstore to display materials harmful to minors. The danger of allowing local officials to set standards was made frighteningly clear in 1987 when police in Orlando, Florida, nearly destroyed a Picasso print that was mixed in with confiscated pornographic material being thrown into an incinerator.

At the federal level, Edwin Meese's Justice Department has formed an Obscenity Enforcement Unit and has announced that racketeering charges would be used to prosecute pornographers. The Administration has shrewdly placed its greatest emphasis on the suppression of child pornography—the aspect of the anti-obscenity effort that enjoys the most public support. Action in this area is based on a 1977 federal law as well as a 1982 Supreme Court ruling flatly denying First Amendment protection to portrayals of specifically described sexual acts by children under sixteen years of age.

In September 1987 *New York Newsday* revealed that the U.S. Postal Service was running a "sting" operation to track down buyers as well as distributors of child pornography. The program, code-named Project Looking Glass, angered even some strong supporters of the crackdown on child pornography because of the entrapment involved in having postal inspectors solicit customers through a phony business front. More than one hundred alleged purchasers of child pornography were indicted in the scheme.

The campaign against pornography in the electronic media has escalated as well. One major area of debate has been cable television. For a number of years heated debate has surrounded the ability of government authorities to regulate the erotic programming that became part of the fare as cable systems spread across the country in the 1970s. Cable operators did not like the controversy generated by offerings like the Playboy Channel, but they did covet the revenues such programming brought in, and to stay consistent with their resistance to the government control of rates, they had to come out against government censorship. Nonetheless, a number of states and localities passed restrictive legislation. The most aggressive was Utah, which enacted three laws, including one overruled by the Supreme Court in 1987 on First Amendment grounds.

The Federal Communications Commission has also gotten into the act with a new policy aimed at suppressing "indecent" programming by television and radio broadcasters. Despite the FCC's dogged promotion of the deregulation of other aspects of broadcasting, it decided to take a more interventionist stance in this particular regard, noting that its 1987 decision was made in response to mounting public complaints about allegedly offensive radio talk shows.

The FCC's right to prohibit what it considered indecent (not to mention obscene) broadcasts was affirmed by the Supreme Court in 1978 in a case arising out of the airing of a comedy monologue by George Carlin called "Filthy Words" by listener-sponsored WBAI-FM in New York City. Although it prevailed in the WBAI case, the FCC's tendency in the following decade has been to limit its role to prohibiting the utterance on the air of the seven words it found objectionable and thus relegated as taboo in the Carlin routine.

That changed with the 1987 policy shift. The FCC indicated that it would once again apply a stricter interpretation of indecency during those hours that children were likely to be in the audience; at other times, defined as the period from midnight to six A.M., broadcasters were given more latitude, though even during this liberated time period viewers and listeners have to be warned when material termed offensive is about to be broadcast on their radio or television.

Despite the relatively safe harbor created for late-night programming, the FCC's new approach has sent a chill through the broadcasting world. In light of the uncertain climate, WBAI sought to get clearance from the FCC on the station's plan to air its annual reading of Joyce's *Ulysses*; the FCC declined to give an advance ruling. WBAI's parent organization, the Pacifica Foundation, decided it was too risky to broadcast a program featuring Allen Ginsberg reading his famous poem *Howl*. The Pacifica stations did air an interview with Ginsberg, in which he described the FCC's approach as "a mirror image of the Stalinist mentality."

FEMINISTS AND THE PORNOGRAPHY ISSUE

As the antipornography movement gained new momentum in recent years, it created a great furor in the feminist community. Most feminists agreed that pornography, at least in some forms, contributed to the oppression of women. But the movement became deeply split on whether this fact justified joining with those activists, usually from quarters that were not sympathetic to the feminist cause, who called for restrictions on the production and sale of objectionable material.

Positions tended to be polarized because of the hard line taken in favor of suppressing pornography, by activists like Susan Brownmiller, Andrea Dworkin, and Catharine MacKinnon. . . .

Feminist opposition to the Dworkin/MacKinnon approach has not been limited to the legal issues. In publications such as *Caught Looking*, the anticensorship forces have also resisted what they see as the tendency of the pornography debate to ignore the erotic impulses of women. Moreover, Betty Friedan and other writers have called the pornography issue a red herring that takes attention away from more pressing matters for women, such as domestic violence, child care, and poverty.

SEXUAL McCARTHYISM

The antipornography movement of the 1980s represents yet another attempt by certain groups to impose their morals on the rest of society. What makes these efforts more threatening than those of the past is the extent to which they have been abetted by federal, state, and local authorities. The climate engendered by initiatives such as the Meese Commission has been described with only a bit of hyperbole by Hugh Hefner as "sexual McCarthyism."

Maintaining a strong defense against these drives for censorship is made more difficult by the alarmingly high level of sexual violence and abuse that continues to plague American society. But there is still no definitive evidence that sexually explicit materials contribute to the problem. Focusing on pornography amounts to attacking the symptoms rather than the disease itself, which is the actual subordination of women—a condition that many of the nonfeminist crusaders prefer not to address. In addition, zealous antipornography efforts end up targeting all erotic material, thus contributing to another form of sexual repression. With the exception of child pornography—where the participants in the production of the material are exploited against their will—there is no justification for allowing the state to decide what words and images we may or may not expose ourselves to. The spread of censorship is ultimately more offensive than any pornography.

NOTES

1. John Cohen, ed., *The Essential Lenny Bruce* (New York: Ballantine Books, 1967), p. 288.
2. Brennan dissent, Roth v. U.S., 354 U.S. 476 (1957).
3. For more on Comstock, see Gay Talese, *Thy Neighbor's Wife* (New York: Dell, 1980), p. 65. Talese calls Comstock "the most awesome censor in the history of America."
4. See Barbara Ehrenreich's criticism of the Meese Commission report in Philip Nobile and Eric Nadler, *United States of America vs. SEX* (New York: Minotaur, 1986), p. 334.
5. In the Hicklin case, the Court said that the test of obscenity was "whether the tendency of the matter charged as obscenity is to deprave and corrupt those whose minds are open to such immoral influences, and into whose hands a publication of this sort may fall." This quotation

is from the Brennan dissent in Paris Adult Theatre I. v. Slatoon, 413 U.S. 49 (1973).

6. But once in a while a decision went the other way, as in the case of Edmund Wilson's *Memoirs of Hecate County* (New York: Doubleday, 1946), in which the book was found obscene by the courts of New York. The Supreme Court split 4 to 4, with Judge Frankfurter abstaining because of his friendship with Wilson, thereby sustaining the conviction.

7. One exception to this trend involved the conviction of Ralph Ginzburg in 1966 for mailing erotic advertising. Here, the Court appeared to base its decision not on content but on evidence that Ginzburg was "pandering."

8. For more about the 1960s marriage of the underground press and mass-market erotica, see Laurence Leamer, *The Paper Revolutionaries* (New York: Simon and Schuster, 1972).

NO

James C. Dobson

ENOUGH IS ENOUGH

While we were slumbering these past three decades, an $8 billion pornography industry was assembled by members of organized crime, operating virtually tax free and with governmental acquiescence. This empire now pervades our lives and contributes to the destruction of countless families each year. Something must be done to deal with the plague that infects our beloved land.

It was this moral concern that led President Reagan to authorize a second commission to study the affects of pornography on individuals, on families, and on society at large. I happened to be at the White House that day as he made this proposal, not knowing that I would be asked to participate in the effort. One year later, Attorney General Edwin Meese responded to the president's mandate by appointing an eleven-member commission. My name was on the list . . .

Having been a faculty member at a large medical school and having served on the attending staff at a major children's hospital for seventeen years, I thought I had seen and heard about everything. I have stood in an operating room while a team of surgeons massaged a woman's heart for hours after her husband blasted her at point-blank range with a shotgun. She never regained consciousness. I've seen children with pitiful deformities that tore at my heart. I've witnessed cancer in its final stages and all of the tragedies that arrive in hospital emergency facilities on busy weekends. Even under such circumstances, I have learned to control my emotions and have continued to function. Nevertheless, nothing in my training or experience fully prepared me for the confrontation with pornography that was to come. Purchasers of this material, like vultures, prefer their meat rancid and raw.

FROM BAD TO WORSE

I knew that the world of X-rated movies and obscene magazines had steadily deteriorated since 1970, but I was unaware of the depth of that plunge. Most American citizens are even more uninformed. They think pornography consists largely of airbrushed nudity in *Playboy* magazines. Such images are pornographic, of course, but they are not even in the same league with mainstream hard-core material sold in sex shops today. The world of hard-core obscenity has become unbelievably sordid and perverse. Its dimensions are wretched beyond description.

Let me explain how we got into the mess we face today. One of the characteristics of human nature is the natural progression that occurs in sexual experimentation. For example, a boy and a girl may find it exciting to hold hands on the first date, but more physical contact is likely to occur on the second encounter. Unless they make an early effort to slow that progression, they will move systematically down the road toward sexual intercourse. That is just the way we are made. Now obviously, pornographers understand that principle. They know that their products must constantly change in order to avoid boredom, and that change must always be in the direction of more explicit materials. Thus, the public has been taken from peek-a-boo glimpses of nudity in the mid-fifties to the infinitely more graphic publications offered today.

That progression from soft-core to hard-core pornography got an enormous boost in 1970 when the First Presidential Commission on Pornography issued its report. They said, in effect, that sexually explicit materials were a good thing and should not be inhibited in any way. Not only did they tell us that smut was not harmful; they perceived it to be advantageous to society, reducing sexual tensions and promising to lower the incidences of rape and child abuse. The pornography industry was delighted! Barriers that had stood for 200 years began to tumble as photographs were published of consummate sexual acts between men and women. *Heaven help us,* we thought. *They have shown it all!*

Well, not quite. It seems that this mad dash toward explicitness presented the pornographers with a minor challenge. What could they do for an encore? What could they offer to customers who had become bored with photographs of normal, heterosexual activity? Something new and exciting was needed, and indeed, they found it in the presentation of perversions. Thus, the course was set for a journey into the incredibly debased hard-core pornography available in massive quantities today.

THE SHOCK OF HARD-CORE PORNOGRAPHY

How can I describe that world to my readers without being obscene myself? I don't know. I struggle at this moment as I weigh the terribleness of this subject against the need for Christians to understand their enemy. In order to fight this plague with the passion of a crusader, it is necessary to comprehend the virus that is rotting us from within. Forgive me, then, for the explicitness with which I am about to write. I urge you to skip the next two paragraphs if you really don't want to know. But someone must have the courage to describe the pornographic scene in sufficient detail to stir us into action, and someone else must have the courage to read it.

X-rated movies and magazines today feature oral, anal, and genital sex between women and donkeys, pigs, horses, dogs, and dozens of other animals. In a single sex shop in New York City, there were forty-six films and videos available which featured bestiality of every type.

Other offerings focused on so-called "bathroom sports" including urination (golden showers), defecation, eating feces and spreading them on the face and body, mutilation of every type (including voluntary amputation, fishhooks through genitalia, fists in rectums, mousetraps on breasts), oral and anal sex between groups of men and women, and (forgive me) the drinking of ejaculate in champagne glasses. Simulated child pornography depicts females who are actually eighteen years of age or older but appear to be fourteen or fifteen. They are shown with shaved genitalia, with ribbons in their hair and surrounded by teddy bears. Their "fathers" are often pictured with them in consummate incestuous settings. The magazines in sex shops are organized on shelves according to topic, such as Gay Violence, Vomiting, Rape, Enemas, and topics that I cannot describe even in a frank discussion of this nature.

THE ACLU AND CHILD PORN

By far the most distressing experience for me personally during the twelve-month assignment was the child pornography to which we were exposed. Though categorically illegal since 1983, a thriving cottage industry still exists in this country. Fathers, stepfathers, uncles, teachers, and neighbors find ways to secure photographs of children in their care. Then they sell or trade the pictures to fellow pedophiles. I will never forget a particular set of photographs shown to us at our first hearings in Washington, D.C. It focused on a cute, nine-year-old boy who had fallen into the hands of a molester. In the first picture, the blond-haired lad was fully clothed and smiling at the camera. But in the second, he was nude, dead, and had a butcher knife protruding from his chest. My knees buckled and tears came to my eyes as hundreds of other photographs of children were presented showing pitiful boys and girls with their rectums enlarged to accommodate adult males and their vaginas penetrated with pencils, toothbrushes, and guns. Perhaps the reader can understand my anger and disbelief when a representative for the American Civil Liberties Union testified a few minutes later. He advocated the free exchange of pornography, all pornography, in the marketplace. He was promptly asked about material depicting children such as those we had seen. This man said, with a straight face, that it is the ACLU's position that child pornography should not be produced, but once it is in existence, there should be no restriction on its sale or distribution. In other words, the photographic record of a child's molestation and abuse should be legal source of profit for those who wish to reproduce, sell, print, and distribute it for the world to see. As the child grows up and becomes an adult, this visualization of his rape and molestation could continue to face him in the marketplace for the profit of pornographers. The victim would have no legal recourse against them. Likewise, the photographs of a woman's rape could be legally reproduced and sold despite her objections. And that, the ACLU representative said, was the intent of the First Amendment of the Constitution. . . .

The final report of our commission does no violence to the First Amendment to the Constitution. The *Miller* standard, by which the Supreme Court clearly reaffirmed the illegality of obscene matter in 1973, was not assaulted during any of our deliberations. No suggestion was made that the Court had been too lenient, or that a Constitutional Amendment should lower the threshold of obscenity, or that the Justices should reconsider their position. No, the *Miller* standard was accepted and even defended as the law of the land. What *was* recommended, to the consternation of pornographers, was that government should begin enforcing the obscenity laws that are already on the books, criminal laws that have stood constitutional muster! Considering the unwillingness of our elected representatives to deal with this issue, that would be novel, indeed.

THE HARM OF PORNOGRAPHY

But why *should* these laws be enforced? Why is it the business of government to object if some people want to amuse themselves with explicit materials? Is obscenity really a threat to society and to the individuals within it? The answers to those questions are linked to the findings that emerged from commission hearings. Many specific sources of harm associated with pornography became evident from professional testimony and from the wrenching stories told by victims of pornography. A few of those harms are described as follows:

1. *Depictions of violence against women are related to violence against women in real life.* Our commission was unanimous in recognizing that fact. Among the totality of evidence that supported this linkage was a study by Malamuth and Feshback[1] at the University of California at Los Angeles, who found that 51 percent of male students exposed to violent pornography indicated a likelihood of raping a woman if they could get away with it. Violent pornography also contributes to the so-called "rape myth," leading men to believe that women really want to be abused even when they vigorously deny it. Thus, it was the conclusion of the commission that there is no place in this culture for material deemed legally obscene by the courts which depicts the dismemberment, burning, whipping, hanging, torturing or raping of women. The time has come to eradicate such materials and prosecute those who produce it. There was no disagreement on that point.

2. *Pornography is degrading and humiliating to women.* They are shown nude, bound, and hanging from trees, being penetrated by broom handles, covered with blood, and kneeling submissively in the act of fellatio. These depictions assault female modesty and represent an affront to an entire gender. I would take that case to any jury in the land. Remember that *men* are the purchasers of pornography. Many witnesses testified that women are typically repulsed by visual depictions of the type herein described. It is provided primarily for the lustful pleasure of men and boys who use it to gratify themselves. And it is my belief, as stated above, that a small but dangerous minority will then choose to act aggressively against the nearest available females. Pornography is the theory; rape is the practice.

3. *For a certain percentage of men, the use of pornography is progressive and addictive in nature.* Like the addiction to drugs, alcohol, or food, those who get hooked on sexually explicit materials become obsessed by their need. In time it encompasses their entire world. These images can also interfere with normal sexual relationships between husbands and wives, since nothing in reality can possibly compete with airbrushed fantasies.

Thus, even the casual use of pornography in a marital context carries some risk.

For vulnerable men, such exposure will set off a lifelong passion for explicit materials, leading inexorably toward marital disinterest and conflict. Many victims of this process testified before our commission.

4. *Organized crime controls more than 85 percent of all commercially produced pornography in America.* The sale and distribution of these materials produces huge profits for the crime lords who also sell illegal drugs to our kids and engage in murder, fraud, bribery, and every vice known to man. Are we to conclude, as the libertarians would have us believe, that the industry that produces millions of tax-free dollars for the Mafia each year is not harmful to society? Is malignant melanoma destructive to the human body?

(Incidentally, the Mafia tolerates no competition in the production and distribution of pornography. Those who attempt to grab a piece of the action are usually mutilated or killed. One ambitious man who insisted on barging into this business was tied against a brick wall and a truck was driven into his knees. He got the message.)

5. *Pedophiles, who abuse an average of 366 boys and girls in a lifetime, typically use pornography to soften children's defenses against sexual exploitation.* They show them nude pictures of adults, for example, and say, "See. This is what mommies and daddies do." They are then stripped of innocence and subjected to brutalities that will be remembered for a lifetime. And incredibly, this horror often leads to the sexually transmitted diseases (STD's) that are rampant among children today. More boys and girls are infected by STD's

per year than were stricken with polio during the entire epidemic of 1942–1953.

6. *Outlets for obscenity are magnets for sex-related crimes.* When a thriving adult bookstore moves into a neighborhood, an array of "support-services" typically develops around it. Prostitution, narcotics, and street crime proliferate. From this perspective, it is interesting that law enforcement officials often claim they do not investigate or attempt to control the flow of obscenity because they lack the resources to combat it. In reality, their resources will extend farther if they first enforce the laws relating to pornography. The consequent reduction in crime makes this a cost-effective use of taxpayer's funds. In Cincinnati, Ohio, for example, the city demonstrated how a community can rid itself of obscenity without inordinate expenditures of personnel and money.

7. *So-called adult bookstores are often centers of disease and homosexual activity.* Again, the average citizen is not aware that the primary source of revenue in adult bookstores is derived from video and film booths. Patrons enter these three-by-three-foot cubicles and deposit a coin in the slot. They are then treated to about ninety seconds of a pornographic movie. If they want to see more, they must continue to pump coins (usually quarters) into the machine. The booths I witnessed on New York's Times Square were even more graphic. Upon depositing the coin, a screen was raised, revealing two or more women and men who performed live sex acts upon one another on a small stage. Everything that is possible for heterosexuals, homosexuals, or lesbians to do was demonstrated a few feet from the viewers. The booths from which these videos or live performers are viewed become filthy be-

yond description as the day progresses. The stench is unbearable and the floor becomes sticky with semen, urine, and saliva.

Holes in the walls between the booths are often provided to permit anonymous sexual encounters between adult males, etc. Given the current concern over sexually transmitted diseases and especially Acquired Immune Deficiency Syndrome (AIDS), it is incredible that local health departments have not attempted to regulate such businesses. State that will not allow restaurant owners, hairdressers, counselors, or acupuncturists to operate without licenses have permitted these wretched cesspools to escape governmental scrutiny. To every public health officer in this country I would ask: "Why?"

8. *I want to give special emphasis to the harm associated with pornography that falls into the hands of children and adolescents.* It would be extremely naive for us to assume that the river of obscenity that has inundated the American landscape has not invaded the world of children. There are more stores selling pornographic videos than there are McDonald hamburger restaurants. Latchkey kids by the millions are watching porn on cable and reading their parents' adult magazines. For fifty cents, they can purchase their own pornographic newspapers from vending machines on the street. At an age when elementary children should be reading *Tom Sawyer* and viewing traditional entertainment in the spirit of Walt Disney, they are learning perverted facts which neither their minds nor bodies are equipped to handle.

Adolescents are even more commonly exposed to explicit pornography. The Canadian study by Check,[2] reviewed by our commission, indicated that children between twelve and seventeen had the greatest interest in pornographic matter and were prime purchasers of it. Also, a study by Zillman and Bryant[3] surveyed 100 males and 100 females from each of three age categories: junior high, high school, and adult 19-30.

They found:

1. 91 percent of males and 82 percent of females had seen a magazine which depicted couples or groups in explicit sexual acts.

2. The average age of first exposure was 13.5 years.

3. A larger percentage of high school students had seen X-rated films than any other age group, including adults.

4. 84 percent reported exposure to such films.

5. 46 percent of junior high school students had seen one or more X-rated movies, and the average age of first exposure for these students was 14 years, 8 months.

SELLING OBSCENITY TO KIDS

What a tragedy! If the explicit descriptions I've offered in this chapter have been disturbing to you, the mature reader, imagine how much more destructive the actual visualizations are to children and adolescents. Teenagers especially are prone to imitate what they see and hear. One year ago, the American Broadcasting Company featured a prime-time television program on teen suicide. In a drama, two attractive adolescents took their lives by piping carbon monoxide from their automobile exhaust to the passenger compartment. Immediately after the program aired, teenagers began imitating what they had seen on the screen. In the days that followed, reports of similar tragedies came from despairing parents around the country. Everyone who works with teenagers is familiar with this "herd" behavior. Modeling, good and bad, directly shapes the thoughts and actions of the next generation. It is a measurable phenomenon.

Why would it not be true, then, that the behavior of an entire generation of teenagers is adversely affected by the current emphasis on premarital sexuality and eroticism seen in adult materials and even in the movies? It is not surprising that the incidence of unwed pregnancy and abortions has skyrocketed since 1970. Teens are merely doing what they've been taught—that they should get into bed together, early and often.

Even more disturbing to me is the current effort by pornographers to market their product directly to our children and teenagers. Two examples of this outrage are worthy of specific concern. The first focuses on pornography in rock music. I invite you to turn to the appendix of this book and read excerpts from a verbal report submitted to the commission by Kandy Stroud on June 19, 1985. [Appendix not included in this excerpt.—Ed.] Of course, by the time this chapter is printed and distributed, the songs and even the musicians cited by Mrs. Stroud may have passed from the scene. But one thing is certain: if something is not done to police the rock music industry, these examples will be succeeded by even more wretched songs and singers.

DIAL-A-PORN

The second example of pornography that is being peddled directly to our children often involves even younger boys and girls.

It has been difficult enough to shield our sons and daughters from explicit adult sexuality on television, rock videos, and immoral movies. But now, a new plague has appeared on the horizon, this one invading our homes via the telephone. It's known as "dial-a-porn," and it delivers the most obscene and profane messages imaginable to anyone choosing to call—anyone. Predictably, the word has spread rapidly among school-aged children, and thousands of boys and girls now tune in to the pornographic recordings (or live conversations) every day. Some are younger than eight years of age. . . .

How did it happen? How did this pipeline to pornography come to exist? It started in 1983 when *High Society* Magazine, Inc., obtained a "dial it" number in a lottery conducted by the New York Telephone System. This service was intended for use by organizations which offered information to the public (sports, weather, finance, etc.). But *High Society* had other intentions. It used the "dial it" number to provide audio messages depicting actual or simulated sexual behavior. State law provided no controls over the content of recordings, and pornographers suddenly discovered a new vehicle for selling their uncensored messages to the public at large. It's a sad commentary on Western civilization that this "service" became an overnight success. Sources estimate that *High Society* now receives up to 500,000 calls every twenty-four hours from people across the country. That's lucrative business for the entrepreneur who reportedly earns $10,000 daily; it's even more profitable for New York Telephone, which collects as much as $35,000 each day. It is not surprising that similar "services" are springing up in other locations across North America. Now is the time, as Judith Trevillian says, to do something about this exploitation of children. Indeed, a few irate mothers and fathers have been protesting to their congressmen and to the Federal Communications Commission in recent months.

Attempting to respond, the FCC adopted regulations in 1985 that required these pornographic services to operate only between 9:00 P.M. and 8:00 A.M. But the U.S. Second Circuit Court of Appeals in New York overturned the ruling, stating that the FCC had violated First Amendment rights and had not demonstrated sufficient research on this issue. Strike another blow against the family!

Since the FCC anticipates that the debate over this issue will undoubtedly be extended, it is eager for public input. You can be assured that the pornographers have mobilized their forces to oppose these proposals. In fact, the FCC has already received scores of letters for dial-a-porn customers who want no limits placed on their assess to the service. In effect, the pornography industry and telephone companies are sitting on a gold mine and they want no restrictions that will limit their profits. If children are among their customers, then so be it. Unfortunately, there has been minimal response from parents or citizens who oppose this assault on our children. I do not understand the deafening silence!

THE RESPONSE FROM WASHINGTON

Raising healthy children is the primary occupation of families, and anything that invades the childhoods and twists the minds of boys and girls must be seen as abhorrent to the mothers and fathers who gave them birth. Furthermore, what is at stake here is the future of the family itself. We are sexual creatures, and the

physical attraction between males and females provides the basis for every dimension of marriage and parenthood. Thus, *anything* that interjects itself into that relationship must be embraced with great caution. Until we *know* that pornography is not addictive and progressive, until we are *certain* that the passion of fantasy does not destroy the passion of reality, until we are *sure* that obsessive use of obscene materials will not lead to perversions and conflict between husbands and wives, then we dare not adorn them with the crown of respectability. Society has an absolute obligation to protect itself from material which crosses the line established objectively by its legislators and court system. That is not sexual repression. That is self-preservation.

Presumably, members of Congress were cognizant of the dangers when they drafted legislation to control sexually explicit material. The president and his predecessors would not have signed those bills into criminal laws if they had not agreed. The Supreme Court must have shared the same concerns when it ruled that obscenity is not protected by the First Amendment.

How can it be, then, that these carefully crafted laws are not being enforced? The refusal of federal and local officials to check the rising tide of obscenity is a disgrace and an outrage! It is said that the production and distribution of pornography is the only unregulated industry remaining in America today. Indeed, the salient finding emerging from twelve months of testimony before our commission reflected this utter paralysis of government in response to the pornographic plague. As citizens of a democratic society, we have surrendered our right to protect ourselves in return for protection by the state. Thus, our governmental representatives have a constitutional mandate to shield us from harm and criminal activity, including that associated with obscenity. It is time our leaders were held accountable for their obvious malfeasance.

Attorney General Edwin Meese, who has courageously supported other unpopular causes, has been reluctant to tackle this one. Now that he has the report of the commission, we will see whether he mobilizes the Department of Justice. But his predecessors have no such excuse for their dismal record. Under Attorney General William French Smith, there was not a single indictment brought against the producers of adult pornography in 1983. There were only six in 1982, but four of those were advanced by one motivated prosecutor. In 1981 there were two. Of the ninety-three U.S. attorneys, only seven have devoted any effort to the prosecution of obscenity. Obviously, the multi-billion-dollar porn industry is under no serious pressure from federal prosecutors.

Considering this apathy, perhaps it is not surprising that the Department of Justice greeted our commission with something less than rampant enthusiasm. For example, the first presidential commission received $2 million (in 1967 money) and was granted two years to complete their assignment. Our commission was allocated only $500,000 (in 1985 money) and was given one year in which to study an industry which had expanded exponentially.

Repeated requests for adequate time and funding were summarily denied. Considering the presidential mandate to establish the commission, the Department of Justice had no choice but to execute the order. But it did very little to guarantee its success or assist with the enormous workload. Quite frankly, failure would have been inevitable were it not for the dedication of eleven determined commissioners who worked under extreme pressure and without compensation to finish the task. We were also blessed with a marvelous staff and executive director who were committed to the challenge.

WHO'S AT FAULT?

Other branches of government must also be held accountable for their unwillingness to enforce the criminal laws. The U.S. Post Office Department makes virtually no effort to prosecute those who send obscene material through the mail. Attorney Paul McGeady testified that there are conservatively 100,000 violations of postal regulations every day of the year. Likewise, the Federal Trade Commission and Interstate Commerce Commission do not attempt to regulate the interstate transportation of obscene material. Eighty percent of all pornography is produced in Los Angeles County and then shipped to the rest of the country. It would not be difficult to identify and prosecute those who transport it across state lines.

The Federal Communications Commission does not regulate obscenity on cable or satellite television. The Customs Service makes no effort to prevent adult pornography from entering this country, and catches only 5 percent of child porn sent from abroad. The Internal Revenue Service permits organized crime to avoid taxes on the majority of its retail sales, especially the video booth market. The Federal Bureau of Investigation assigns only 2 of 8,700 special agents to ob-

NO James C. Dobson / 237

scenity investigation, even though organized crime controls the industry. And on and on it goes.

Local law enforcement agencies are equally unconcerned about obscenity. The city of Miami has assigned only 2 of 1,500 policemen to this area, neither of whom is given a car. Chicago allocates 2 for 12,000 officers to obscenity control. Los Angeles assigns 8 out of 6,700, even though L.A. is the porn capital of the country. Not one indictment has been brought against a pornographer in Los Angeles County in more than ten years, despite the glut of materials produced there.

Another serious concern is also directed at the court system and the judges who have winked at pornography. Even when rare convictions have been obtained, the penalties assessed have been pitiful. Producers of illegal materials may earn millions in profit each year, and yet it convicted, serve no time in prison and pay fines of perhaps $100. One powerful entrepreneur in Miami was found guilty on obscenity charges for the sixty-first time, yet received a fine of only $1,600. The judge in another case refused to even look at child pornography which the defendant had supposedly produced. He said it would prejudice him to examine the material. That judge had never sentenced a single pornographer to a day in prison.

In another striking example, the producer of the movie *Deep Throat* invested $25,000 and earned more than $50 million in profits. He was subsequently charged with obscenity, requiring three years of litigation to obtain a conviction. He was finally sentenced to two years in prison, but was permitted instead to work nights in the Salvation Army headquarters. Is there any wonder why

America is inundated with sexually explicit material today?

CONCLUSION

So we come to the bottom line. We've looked at the conditions that have led to the present situation. Now we must consider the mid-course maneuvers that will correct it. I believe that the recommendations offered in the commission's final report will provide an effective guide toward that end. We not only attempted to assess the problem; we have offered a proposed resolution. The testimonies on which it is based make it clear that we are engaged in a winnable war! According to a recent Gallop Poll, 73 percent of the American people are opposed to hardcore pornography; with this support, we can rid ourselves of obscenity in eighteen months if the recommendations offered in the report are implemented. We have provided a roadmap for fine-tuning federal and state legislation and for the mobilization of law enforcement efforts around the country.

Unfortunately, I can tell you with certainty that aggressive action against pornography *will not occur* unless our citizens demand the response of government. Our leaders have ignored the violations in the past, and they will continue their malfeasance unless we besiege them from every corner of the land. Our commission report will either become another expensive dust collector on bureaucratic shelves, or it will serve as the basis for a new public policy. The difference will be determined by the outcry that accompanies its release or the deafening silence of an unconcerned populous. . . .

During the hearings in Chicago, we met on the twenty-fourth floor of a government building which overshadowed a smaller structure in the process of demolition. I stood at the window and watched the wrecking ball do its destructive work. I thought to myself as it crashed into the remaining walls on the roof, *That is what the pornographers are doing to my country. They are hammering down the supporting columns and blasting away the foundations. We must stop the devastation before the entire superstructure crashes to the earth!* With the diligent prayers and personal involvement of God-fearing people, we can save the great edifice called America. But there is not a minute to lose. "But each one is tempted when he is carried away and enticed by his own lust. Then when lust has conceived, it gives birth to sin; and when sin is accomplished, it brings forth death" (James 1:14–16, NASB).

NOTES

1. N. M. Malamuth, M. Heim and S. Feshback, "Sexual Responsiveness of College Students to Rape Depictions: Inhibitory and Disinhibitory Effects," *Journal of Personality and Social Psychology* 84, 1980. See also N. M. Malamuth, F. Haber, and S. Feshback, "Testing Hypotheses Regarding Rape: Exposure to Sexual Violence, Sex Differences and the 'Normality' of Rapists," *Journal of Research on Personality* 14, 1980.

2. J. V. P. Check, "A Survey of Canadian Attitudes Regarding Sexual Content in the Media," *Report to the Lamarsh Research Program on Violence and Conflict Resolution and the Canadian Broadcasting Corporation* in Toronto, Canada, 1985.

3. Unpublished testimony of D. Zillman and J. Bryant before the U.S. Attorney General's Commission on Pornography in Houston, Texas, on 13 September 1985.

POSTSCRIPT

Should Pornography Be Protected as Free Speech?

In modern America, a distinction between obscene speech and hate speech may be disappearing. Some feminists claim that pornography is a hateful and menacing depiction of women. In 1978 the Supreme Court upheld the right of a group of American Nazis to march in the Chicago suburb of Skokie, where many Holocaust survivers lived. By 1990 some civil libertarians were having second thoughts. In 1990 Stanford University adopted a code punishing verbal, written, or symbolic attacks against individuals "on the basis of their sex, race, color, handicap, religion, sexual orientation or national or ethnic origin."

Perhaps the danger to civil society lies not in obscenity *per se* but in the verbal and visual portrayal of racist, bigoted, antifeminist, and other gratuitously violent depictions of hateful beliefs and behavior. Edward Donnerstein, Daniel Linz, and Steven Penrop, in *The Question of Pornography* (Free Press, 1987), examined social science studies of violence against women, and reached the striking conclusion that "the violence against women in some types of R-rated films shown in neighborhood theaters and on cable television far exceeds that portrayed in even the most graphic pornography."

Dr. Thomas Radecki, research director for the National Coalition on Television Violence, estimates that one out of eight Hollywood movies has a rape theme, and, by age 18, the average American will have seen 250,000 acts of violence and 40,000 attempted murders on television. The experience may not make us rapists, but it is likely to make us insensitive to sexual violence. Should we then go beyond obscenity and pornography to restrict any expression which can be considered demeaning or threatening to any significant group in society?

The context changes, but the basic questions obstinately remain the same. Where do we draw the line? Who draws it? How? And, if we opt not to draw it, how do we cope with the cultural and social consequences that are likely to occur in a society that has no standards?

ISSUE 14

Should Drugs Be Legalized?

YES: Ethan A. Nadelmann, from "The Case for Legalization," *The Public Interest* (Summer 1988)

NO: James Q. Wilson, from "Against the Legalization of Drugs," *Commentary* (February 1990)

ISSUE SUMMARY

YES: Educator Ethan Nadelmann contends that drug legalization would help put the criminal drug dealers out of business while protecting the rights of adults to make their own choices, free of criminal sanctions.

NO: Political scientist James Q. Wilson argues that drug legalization would vastly increase dangerous drug use and the social ills created by such usage.

A century ago, drugs of every kind were freely available to Americans. Laudanum, a mixture of opium and alcohol, was popularly used as a painkiller. One drug company even claimed that it was a very useful substance for calming hyperactive children, and they called it Mother's Helper. Morphine came into common use during the Civil War. Heroin, developed as a supposedly less addictive substitute for morphine, began to be marketed at the end of the nineteenth century. By that time, drug paraphernalia could be ordered through Sears and Roebuck catalogues, and Coca-Cola, which contained small quantities of cocaine, had become a popular drink.

Public concerns about addiction and dangerous patent medicines, and an active campaign for drug laws waged by Dr. Harvey Wiley, a chemist in the U.S. Department of Agriculture, led Congress to pass the first national drug regulation act in 1906. The Pure Food and Drug Act required that medicines containing certain drugs, such as opium, must say so on their labels. Later amendments to the Act required that the labels must also state the quantity of each drug and affirm that the drug met official standards of purity. The Harrison Narcotic Act of 1914 went much further and cut off completely the supply of legal opiates to addicts. Since then, ever stricter drug laws have been passed by Congress and by state legislatures.

Drug abuse in America again came to the forefront of public discourse during the 1960s, when heroin addiction started growing rapidly in inner-city neighborhoods. Also, by the end of the decade, drug experimentation had spread to the middle-class, affluent Baby Boomers who were then attending college. (The name "Baby Boom" generation has been given to Americans born during the late 1940s through 1960, whose cohort history has been widely analyzed and widely publicized because they are far more numerous than were older generations.) Indeed, certain types of drugs began to be celebrated by some of the leaders of the counterculture. Heroin was still taboo, but other drugs, notably marijuana and LSD (a psychedelic drug), were regarded as harmless and even spiritually transforming. At music festivals like Woodstock in 1969, marijuana and LSD were used openly and associated with love, peace, and heightened sensitivity. Much of this enthusiasm cooled over the next twenty years as Baby Boomers entered the work force full-time and began their careers. But even among the careerists, certain types of drugs enjoyed high status. Cocaine, noted for its highly stimulating effects, became the drug of choice for many hard-driving young lawyers, TV writers, and Wall Street bond traders.

The high price of cocaine put it out of reach for many people, but by the early 1980s, cheap substitutes began to appear on the streets and to overtake poor urban communities. Crack cocaine, a potent, highly addictive, smokable form of cocaine, came into widespread use. More recent reports indicate that "ice," or as it is called on the West Coast, "L.A. glass," a smokable form of amphetamine, is the newest drug to hit the streets. These stimulants tend to produce very violent, disorderly behavior. Moreover, the street gangs who sell it are frequently at war with one another and are well-armed. Not only gang members but also many innocent people have become victims of contract killings, street battles, and drive-by shootings.

This new drug epidemic has prompted President Bush to declare a "war on drugs." He appointed former Education Secretary William Bennett to the Cabinet-level post of "drug czar," and he has asked Congress to appropriate $10.6 billion for the fight. Reaction has been mixed. Some support it in its entirety; others think that more money is needed, or that spending priorities should be shifted more toward treatment than law enforcement. Still, the vast majority of Americans seem ready to support some version of a major national campaign to fight drugs. Others, however, see the whole effort as doomed to failure, and they argue that the best solution to the drug problem would be to legalize, tax, and control drugs, as has been done with alcohol.

These contrasting views are presented in the readings that follow, with Ethan Nadelmann arguing for legalization and political scientist James Q. Wilson arguing against it.

YES

Ethan A. Nadelmann

THE GREAT DRUG DEBATE: I

THE CASE FOR LEGALIZATION

What can be done about the "drug problem"? Despite frequent proclamations of war and dramatic increases in government funding and resources in recent years, there are many indications that the problem is not going away and may even be growing worse. During the past year alone, more than thirty million Americans violated the drug laws on literally billions of occasions. Drug-treatment programs in many cities are turning people away for lack of space and funding. In Washington, D.C., drug-related killings, largely of one drug dealer by another, are held responsible for a doubling in the homicide rate over the past year. In New York and elsewhere, courts and prisons are clogged with a virtually limitless supply of drug-law violators. In large cities and small towns alike, corruption of policemen and other criminal-justice officials by drug traffickers is rampant. . . .

If there were a serious public debate on this issue, far more attention would be given to one policy option that has just begun to be seriously considered, but which may well prove more successful than anything currently being implemented or proposed: legalization. Politicians and public officials remain hesitant even to mention the word, except to dismiss it contemptuously as a capitulation to the drug traffickers. Most Americans perceive drug legalization as an invitation to drug-infested anarchy. Even the civil-liberties groups shy away from this issue, limiting their input primarily to the drug-testing debate. The minority communities in the ghetto, for whom repealing the drug laws would promise the greatest benefits, fail to recognize the costs of our drug-prohibition policies. And the typical middle-class American, who hopes only that his children will not succumb to drug abuse, tends to favor any measures that he believes will make illegal drugs less accessible to them. Yet when one seriously compares the advantages and disadvantages of the legalization strategy with those of current and planned

From Ethan A. Nadelmann, "The Case for Legalization," *The Public Interest*, vol. 92, no. 3 (1988). Copyright © 1988 by Ethan A. Nadelmann. Reprinted by permission of the author. Notes omitted.

policies, abundant evidence suggests that legalization may well be the optimal strategy for tackling the drug problem. . . .

There is, of course, no single legalization strategy. At one extreme is the libertarian vision of virtually no government restraints on the production and sale of drugs or any psychoactive substances, except perhaps around the fringes, such as prohibiting sales to children. At the other extreme is total government control over the production and sale of these goods. In between lies a strategy that may prove more successful than anything yet tried in stemming the problems of drug abuse and drug-related violence, corruption, sickness, and suffering. It is one in which government makes most of the substances that are now banned legally available to competent adults, exercises strong regulatory powers over all large-scale production and sale of drugs, makes drug-treatment programs available to all who need them, and offers honest drug-education programs to children. This strategy, it is worth noting, would also result in a net benefit to public treasuries of at least ten billion dollars a year, and perhaps much more.

There are three reasons why it is important to think about legalization scenarios, even though most Americans remain hostile to the idea. First, current drug-control policies have failed, are failing, and will continue to fail, in good part because they are fundamentally flawed. Second, many drug-control efforts are not only failing, but also proving highly costly and counter-productive; indeed, many of the drug-related evils that Americans identify as part and parcel of the "drug problem" are in fact caused by our drug-prohibition policies. Third, there is good reason to believe that repealing many of the drug laws would not lead, as many people fear, to a dramatic rise in drug abuse. . . .

By most accounts, the dramatic increase in drug-enforcement efforts over the past few years has had little effect on the illicit drug market in the United States. The mere existence of drug-prohibition laws, combined with a minimal level of law-enforcement resources, is sufficient to maintain the price of illicit drugs at a level significantly higher than it would be if there were no such laws. Drug laws and enforcement also reduce the availability of illicit drugs, most notably in parts of the United States where demand is relatively limited to begin with. Theoretically, increases in drug-enforcement efforts should result in reduced availability, higher prices, and lower purity of illegal drugs. That is, in fact, what has happened to the domestic marijuana market (in at least the first two respects). But in general the illegal drug market has not responded as intended to the substantial increases in federal, state, and local drug-enforcement efforts.

Cocaine has sold for about a hundred dollars a gram at the retail level since the beginning of the 1980s. The average purity of that gram, however, has increased from 12 to 60 percent. Moreover, a growing number of users are turning to "crack," a potent derivative of cocaine that can be smoked; it is widely sold in ghetto neighborhoods now for five to ten dollars per vial. Needless to say, both crack and the 60 percent pure cocaine pose much greater threats to users than did the relatively benign powder available eight years ago. Similarly, the retail price of heroin has remained relatively constant even as the average purity has risen from 3.9 percent in 1983 to 6.1 percent in 1986. Throughout the southwestern part of the United States, a particularly potent form of heroin known as "black tar" has become increasingly prevalent. And in many cities, a powerful synthetic opiate, Dilaudid, is beginning to compete with heroin as the preferred opiate. The growing number of heroin-related hospital emergencies and deaths is directly related to these developments.

All of these trends suggest that drug-enforcement efforts are not succeeding and may even be backfiring. There are numerous indications, for instance, that a growing number of marijuana dealers in both the producer countries and the United States are switching to cocaine dealing, motivated both by the promise of greater profits and by government drug-enforcement efforts that place a premium on minimizing the bulk of the illicit product (in order to avoid detection). It is possible, of course, that some of these trends would be even more severe in the absence of drug laws and enforcement. At the same time, it is worth observing that the increases in the potency of illegal drugs have coincided with decreases in the potency of legal substances. Motivated in good part by health concerns, cigarette smokers are turning increasingly to lower-tar and nicotine tobacco products, alcohol drinkers from hard liquor to wine and beer, and even coffee drinkers from regular to decaffeinated coffee. This trend may well have less to do with the nature of the substances than with their legal status. It is quite possible, for instance, that the subculture of illicit-drug use creates a bias or incentive in favor of riskier behavior and more powerful psychoactive effects. If this is the case, legalization might well succeed in reversing today's trend toward more potent drugs and more dangerous methods of consumption.

The most "successful" drug-enforcement operations are those that succeed in identifying and destroying an entire drug-trafficking organization. Such operations can send dozens of people to jail and earn the government millions of dollars in asset forfeitures. Yet these operations have virtually no effect on the availability or price of illegal drugs throughout much of the United States. During the past few years, some urban police departments have devoted significant manpower and financial resources to intensive crackdowns on street-level drug dealing in particular neighborhoods. Code-named Operation Pressure Point, Operation Clean Sweep, and so on, these massive police efforts have led to hundreds, even thousands, of arrests of low-level drug dealers and drug users, and have helped improve the quality of life in the targeted neighborhoods. In most cases, however, drug dealers have adapted relatively easily by moving their operations to nearby neighborhoods. In the final analysis, the principal accomplishment of most domestic drug-enforcement efforts is not to reduce the supply or availability of illegal drugs, or even to raise their price; it is to punish the drug dealers who are apprehended, and cause minor disruptions in established drug markets. . . .

THE COSTS OF PROHIBITION

The fact that drug-prohibition laws and policies cannot eradicate or even significantly reduce drug abuse is not necessarily a reason to repeal them. They do, after all, succeed in deterring many people from trying drugs, and they clearly reduce the availability and significantly increase the price of illegal drugs. These accomplishments alone might warrant retaining the drug laws, were it not for the fact that these same laws are also responsible for much of what Americans identify as the "drug problem." Here the analogies to alcohol and tobacco are worth noting. There is little question that we could reduce the health costs associated with use and abuse of alcohol and tobacco if we were to criminalize their production, sale, and possession. But no one believes that we could eliminate their use and abuse, that we could create an "alcohol-free" or "tobacco-free" country. Nor do most Americans believe that criminalizing the alcohol and tobacco markets would be a good idea. Their opposition stems largely from two beliefs: that adult Americans have the right to choose what substances they will consume and what risks they will take; and that the costs of trying to coerce so many Americans to abstain from those substances would be enormous. It was the strength of these two beliefs that ultimately led to the repeal of Prohibition, and it is partly due to memories of that experience that criminalizing either alcohol or tobacco has little support today. . . .

COSTS TO THE TAXPAYER

Since 1981, federal expenditures on drug enforcement have more than tripled—from less than one billion dollars a year to about three billion. According to the National Drug Enforcement Policy Board, the annual budgets of the Drug Enforcement Administration (DEA) and the Coast Guard have each risen during the past seven years from about $220 million to roughly $500 million. During the same period, FBI resources devoted to drug enforcement have increased from $8 million a year to over $100 million; U.S. Marshals resources from $26 million to about $80 million; U.S. Attorney resources from $20 million to about $100

million; State Department resources from $35 million to $100 million; U.S. Customs resources from $180 million to over $400 million; and Bureau of Prison resources from $77 million to about $300 million. Expenditures on drug control by the military and the intelligence agencies are more difficult to calculate, although by all accounts they have increased by at least the same magnitude, and now total hundreds of millions of dollars per year. Even greater are the expenditures at lower levels of government. In a 1987 study for the U.S. Customs Service by Wharton Econometrics, state and local police were estimated to have devoted 18 percent of their total investigative resources, or close to five billion dollars, to drug-enforcement activities in 1986. This represented a 19 percent increase over the previous year's expenditures. All told, 1987 expenditures on all aspects of drug enforcement, from drug eradication in foreign countries to imprisonment of drug users and dealers in the United States, totalled at least ten billion dollars.

Of course, even ten billion dollars a year pales in comparison with expenditures on military defense. Of greater concern than the actual expenditures, however, has been the diversion of limited resources—including the time and energy of judges, prosecutors, and law-enforcement agents, as well as scarce prison space—from the prosecution and punishment of criminal activities that harm far more innocent victims than do violations of the drug laws. . . .

DRUGS AND CRIME

The drug/crime connection is one that continues to resist coherent analysis, both because cause and effect are so difficult to distinguish and because the role of the drug-prohibition laws in causing and labelling "drug-related crime" is so often ignored. There are four possible connections between drugs and crime, at least three of which would be much diminished if the drug-prohibition laws were repealed. First, producing, selling, buying, and consuming strictly controlled and banned substances is itself a crime that occurs billions of times each year in the United States alone. In the absence of drug-prohibition laws, these activities would obviously cease to be crimes. Selling drugs to children would, of course, continue to be criminal, and other evasions of government regulation of a legal market would continue to be prosecuted; but by and large the drug/crime connection that now accounts for all of the criminal-justice costs noted above would be severed.

Second, many illicit-drug users commit crimes such as robbery and burglary, as well as drug dealing, prostitution, an numbers running, to earn enough money to purchase the relatively high-priced illicit drugs. Unlike the millions of alcoholics who can support their habits for relatively modest amounts, many cocaine and heroin addicts spend hundreds and even thousands of dollars a week. If the drugs to which they are addicted were significantly cheaper—which would be the case if they were legalized—the number of crimes committed by drug addicts to pay for their habits would, in all likelihood, decline dramatically. Even if a legal-drug policy included the imposition of relatively high consumption taxes in order to discourage consumption, drug prices would probably still be lower than they are today.

The third drug/crime connection is the commission of crimes—violent crimes in particular—by people under the influence of illicit drugs. This connection seems to have the greatest impact upon the popular imagination. Clearly, some drugs do "cause" some people to commit crimes by reducing normal inhibitions, unleashing aggressive and other antisocial tendencies, and lessening the sense of responsibility. Cocaine, particularly in the form of crack, has gained such a reputation in recent years, just as heroin did in the 1960s and 1970s, and marijuana did in the years before that. Crack's reputation for inspiring violent behavior may or may not be more deserved than those of marijuana and heroin; reliable evidence is not yet available. No illicit drug, however, is as widely associated with violent behavior as alcohol. According to Justice Department statistics, 54 percent of all jail inmates convicted of violent crimes in 1983 reported having used alcohol just prior to committing their offense. The impact of drug legalization on this drug/crime connection is the most difficult to predict. Much would depend on overall rates of drug abuse and changes in the nature of consumption, both of which are impossible to predict. It is worth noting, however, that a shift in consumption from alcohol to marijuana would almost certainly contribute to a decline in violent behavior.

The fourth drug/crime link is the violent, intimidating, and corrupting behavior of the drug traffickers. Illegal markets tend to breed violence—not only because they attract criminally-minded individuals, but also because participants in the market have no resort to legal institutions to resolve their disputes. . . .

The conspicuous failure of law-enforcement agencies to deal with this drug/crime connection is probably most responsible for the demoralization of neighborhoods and police departments alike. Intensive police crackdowns in urban neighborhoods do little more than chase the menace a short distance away to infect new areas. By contrast, legalization of the drug market would drive the drug-dealing business off the streets and out of the apartment buildings, and into legal, government-regulated, tax-paying stores. It would also force many of the gun-toting dealers out of business, and would convert others into legitimate businessmen. Some, of course, would turn to other types of criminal activities, just as some of the bootleggers did following Prohibition's repeal. Gone, however, would be the unparalleled financial temptations that lure so many people from all sectors of society into the drug-dealing business.

THE COSTS OF CORRUPTION

All vice-control efforts are particularly susceptible to corruption, but none so much as drug enforcement. When police accept bribes from drug dealers, no victim exists to complain to the authorities. Even when police extort money and drugs from traffickers and dealers, the latter are in no position to report the corrupt officers. What makes drug enforcement especially vulnerable to corruption are the tremendous amounts of money involved in the business. Today, many law-enforcement officials believe that police corruption is more pervasive than at any time since Prohibition. In Miami, dozens of law-enforcement officials have been charged with accepting bribes, stealing from drug dealers, and even dealing drugs themselves. Throughout many small towns and rural communities in Georgia, where drug smugglers en route from Mexico, the Caribbean, and Latin America drop their loads of cocaine and marijuana, dozens of sheriffs have been implicated in drug-related corruption. In New York, drug-related corruption in one Brooklyn police precinct has generated the city's most far-reaching police-corruption scandal since the 1960s. More than a hundred cases of drug-related corruption are now prosecuted each year in state and federal courts. Every one of the federal law-enforcement agencies charged with drug-enforcement responsibilities has seen an agent implicated in drug-related corruption.

It is not difficult to explain the growing pervasiveness of drug-related corruption. The financial temptations are enormous relative to other opportunities, legitimate or illegitimate. Little effort is required. Many police officers are demoralized by the scope of the drug traffic, their sense that many citizens are indifferent, and the fact that many sectors of society do not even appreciate their efforts—as well as the fact that many of the drug dealers who are arrested do not remain in prison. Some police also recognize that enforcing the drug laws does not protect victims from predators so much as it regulates an illicit market that cannot be suppressed, but can be kept underground. In every respect, the analogy to Prohibition is apt. Repealing the drug-prohibition laws would dramatically reduce police corruption. By contrast, the measures currently being proposed to deal with the growing problem, including better funded and more aggressive internal investigations, offer relatively little promise.

Among the most difficult costs to evaluate are those that relate to the widespread defiance of the drug-prohibition laws: the effects of labelling as criminals the tens of millions of people who use drugs illicitly, subjecting them to the risks of criminal sanction, and obliging many of these same people to enter into relationships with drug dealers (who may be criminals in many more senses of the word) in order to purchase their drugs; the cynicism that such laws generate toward other laws and the law in general; and the sense of hostility and suspicion that many otherwise law-abiding individuals feel toward law-enforcement officials. It was costs such as these that strongly influenced many of Prohibition's more conservative opponents.

PHYSICAL AND MORAL COSTS

Perhaps the most paradoxical consequence of the drug laws is the tremendous harm they cause to the millions of drug users who have not been deterred from using illicit drugs in the first place. Nothing resembling an underground Food and Drug Administration has arisen to impose quality control on the illegal-drug market and provide users with accurate information on the drugs they consume. Imagine that Americans could not tell whether a bottle of wine contained 6 percent, 30 percent, or 90 percent alcohol, or whether an aspirin tablet contained 5 or 500 grams of aspirin. Imagine, too, that no controls existed to prevent winemakers from diluting their product with methanol and other dangerous impurities, and that vineyards and tobacco fields were fertilized with harmful substances by ignorant growers and sprayed with poisonous herbicides by government agents. Fewer people would use such substances, but more of those who did would get sick. Some would die.

The above scenario describes, of course, the current state of the illicit drug market. Many marijuana smokers are worse off for having smoked cannabis that was grown with dangerous fertilizers, sprayed with the herbicide paraquat, or mixed with more dangerous substances. Consumers of heroin and the various synthetic substances sold on the street face even severer consequences, including fatal overdoses and poisonings from unexpectedly potent or impure drug supplies. More often than not, the quality of a drug addict's life depends greatly upon his or her access to reliable supplies. Drug-enforcement operations that succeed in temporarily disrupting supply networks are thus a double-edged sword: they encourage some addicts to seek admission into drug-treatment programs, but they oblige others to seek out new and hence less reliable suppliers; the result is that more, not fewer, drug-related emergencies and deaths occur.

Today, over 50 percent of all people with AIDS in New York City, New Jersey, and many other parts of the country, as well as the vast majority of AIDS-infected heterosexuals throughout the country, have contracted the disease directly or indirectly through illegal intravenous drug use. Reports have emerged of drug dealers beginning to provide clean syringes together with their illegal drugs. But even as other governments around the world actively attempt to limit the spread of AIDS by and among drug users by instituting free syringe-exchange programs, state and municipal governments in the United States resist following suit, arguing that to do so would "encourage" or "condone" the use of illegal drugs. Only in January 1988 did New York City approve such a program on a very limited and experimental basis. At the same time, drug-treatment programs remain notoriously underfunded, turning away tens of thousands of addicts seeking help, even as billions of dollars more are spent to arrest, prosecute, and imprison illegal drug sellers and users. In what may represent a sign of shifting priorities, the President's Commission on AIDS, in its March 1988 report, emphasized the importance of making drug-treatment programs available to all in need of them. In all likelihood, however, the criminal-justice agencies will continue to receive the greatest share of drug-control funds.

Most Americans perceive the drug problem as a moral issue and draw a moral distinction between use of the illicit drugs and use of alcohol and tobacco. Yet when one subjects this distinction to reasoned analysis, it quickly disintegrates. The most consistent moral perspective of those who favor drug laws is that of the Mormons and the Puritans, who regard as immoral any intake of substances to alter one's state of consciousness or otherwise cause pleasure: they forbid not only the illicit drugs and alcohol, but also tobacco, caffeine, and even chocolate. The vast majority of Americans are hardly so consistent with respect to the propriety of their pleasures. Yet once one acknowledges that there is nothing immoral about drinking alcohol or smoking tobacco for non-medicinal purposes, it becomes difficult to condemn the consumption of marijuana, cocaine, and other substances on moral grounds. The "moral" condemnation of some substances and not others proves to be little more than a prejudice in favor of some drugs and against others.

The same false distinction is drawn with respect to those who provide the psychoactive substances to users and abusers alike. If degrees of immorality were measured by the levels of harm caused by one's products, the "traffickers" in tobacco and alcohol would be vilified as the most evil of all substance purveyors. That they are perceived instead as respected members of our community, while providers of the no more dangerous illicit substances are punished with long prison sentences, says much about the prejudices of most Americans with respect to psychoactive substances, but little about the morality or immorality of their activities. . . .

THE BENEFITS OF LEGALIZATION

Repealing the drug-prohibition laws promises tremendous advantages. Between reduced government expenditures on enforcing drug laws and new tax revenue from legal drug production and sales, public treasuries would enjoy a net benefit of at least ten billion dollars a year, and possibly much more. The quality of urban life would rise significantly. Homicide rates would decline. So would robbery and burglary rates. Organized criminal groups, particularly the newer ones that have yet to diversify out of drugs, would be dealt a devastating setback. The police, prosecutors, and courts would focus their resources on combatting the types of crimes that people cannot walk away from. More ghetto residents would turn their backs on criminal careers and seek out legitimate opportunities instead. And the health and quality of life of many drug users—and even drug abusers—would improve significantly.

All the benefits of legalization would be for naught, however, if millions more Americans were to become drug abusers. Our experience with alcohol and tobacco provides ample warnings. Today, alcohol is consumed by 140 million Americans and tobacco by 50 million. All of the health costs associated with abuse of the illicit drugs pale in comparison with those resulting from tobacco and alcohol abuse. In 1986, for example, alcohol was identified as a contributing factor in 10 percent of work-related injuries, 40 percent of suicide attempts, and about 40 percent of the approximately 46,000 annual traffic deaths in 1983. An estimated eighteen million Americans are reported to be either alcoholics or alcohol abusers. The total cost of alcohol abuse to American society is estimated at over 100 billion dollars annually. Alcohol has been identified as the direct cause of 80,000 to 100,000 deaths annually, and as a contributing factor in an additional 100,000 deaths. The health costs of tobacco use are of similar magnitude. In the United States alone, an estimated 320,000 people die prematurely each year as a consequence of their consumption of tobacco. By comparison, the National Council on Alcoholism reported that only 3,562 people were known to have died in 1985 from use of all illegal drugs combined. Even if we assume that thousands more deaths were related in one way or another to illicit drug abuse but not reported as such, we are still left with the conclusion that all of the health costs of marijuana, cocaine, and heroin combined amount to only a small fraction of those caused by tobacco and alcohol. . . .

CAN LEGALIZATION WORK?

It is impossible to predict whether legalization would lead to much greater levels of drug abuse, and exact costs comparable to those of alcohol and tobacco abuse. The lessons that can be drawn from other societies are mixed. China's experience with the British opium pushers of the nineteenth century, when millions became addicted to the drug, offers one worst-case scenario. The devastation of many native American tribes by alcohol presents another. On the other hand, the legal availability of opium and cannabis in many Asian societies did not result in large addict populations until recently. Indeed, in many countries U.S.-inspired opium bans imposed during the past few decades have paradoxically contributed to dramatic increases in heroin consumption among Asian youth. Within the United States, the decriminalization of marijuana by about a dozen states during the 1970s did not lead to increases in marijuana consumption. In the Netherlands, which went even further in decriminalizing cannabis during the 1970s, consumption has actually declined significantly. The policy has succeeded, as the government intended, in making drug use boring. Finally, late nineteenth-century America was a society in which there were almost no drug laws or even drug regulations—but levels of drug use then were about what they are today. Drug abuse was considered a serious problem, but the criminal-justice system was not regarded as part of the solution.

There are, however, reasons to believe that none of the currently illicit substances would become as popular as alcohol or tobacco, even if they were legalized. Alcohol has long been the principal intoxicant in most societies, including many in which other substances have been legally available. Presumably, its diverse properties account for its popularity—it quenches thirst, goes well with food, and promotes appetite as well as sociability. The popularity of tobacco probably stems not just from its powerful addictive qualities, but from the fact that its psychoactive effects are sufficiently subtle that cigarettes can be integrated with most other human activities. The illicit substances do not share these qualities to the same extent, nor is it likely that they would acquire them if they were legalized. Moreover, none of the illicit substances can compete with alcohol's special place in American culture and history.

An additional advantage of the illicit drugs is that none of them appears to be as insidious as either alcohol or tobacco. Consumed in their more benign forms, few of the illicit substances are as damaging to the human body over the long term as alcohol and tobacco, and none is as strongly linked with violent behavior as alcohol. On the other hand, much of the damage caused today by illegal drugs stems from their consumption in particularly dangerous ways. There is good reason to doubt that many Americans would inject cocaine or heroin into their veins even if given the chance to do so legally. And just as the dramatic growth in the heroin-consuming population during the 1960s leveled off for reasons apparently having little to do with law enforcement, so we can expect a levelling-off—which may already have begun—in the number of people smoking crack. The logic of legalization thus depends upon two assumptions: that most illegal drugs are not so dangerous as is commonly believed; and that the drugs and methods of consumption that are most risky are unlikely to prove appealing to many people, precisely because they are so obviously dangerous.

Perhaps the most reassuring reason for believing that repeal of the drug-prohibition laws will not lead to tremendous increases in drug-abuse levels is the fact that we have learned something from our past experiences with alcohol and tobacco abuse. We now know, for instance, that consumption taxes are an effective method of limiting consumption rates. We also know that restrictions and bans on advertising, as well as a campaign of negative advertising, can make a difference. The same is true of other government measures, including restrictions on time and place of sale, prohibition of consumption in public places, packaging requirements, mandated adjustments in insurance policies, crackdowns on driving while under the influence, and laws holding bartenders and hosts responsible for the drinking of customers and guests. There is even some evidence that government-sponsored education programs about the dangers of cigarette smoking have deterred many children from beginning to smoke.

Clearly it is possible to avoid repeating the mistakes of the past in designing an effective plan for legalization. We know more about the illegal drugs now than we knew about alcohol when Prohibition was repealed, or about tobacco when the anti-tobacco laws were repealed by many states in the early years of this century. Moreover, we can and must avoid having effective drug-control policies undermined by powerful lobbies like those that now protect the interests of alcohol and tobacco producers. We are also in a far better position than we were sixty years ago to prevent organized criminals from finding and creating new opportunities when their most lucrative source of income dries up.

It is important to stress what legalization is not. It is not a capitulation to the drug dealers—but rather a means to put them out of business. It is not an endorsement of drug use—but rather a recognition of the rights of adult Americans to make their own choices free of the fear of criminal sanctions. It is not a repudiation of the "just say no" approach—but rather an appeal to government to provide assistance and positive inducements, not criminal penalties and more repressive measures, in support of that approach. It is not even a call for the elimination of the criminal-justice system from drug regulation—but rather a proposal for the redirection of its efforts and attention.

There is no question that legalization is a risky policy, since it may lead to an increase in the number of people who abuse drugs. But that is a risk—not a certainty. At the same time, current drug-control policies are failing, and new proposals promise only to be more costly and more repressive. We know that repealing the drug-prohibition laws would eliminate or greatly reduce many of the ills that people commonly identify as part and parcel of the "drug problem." Yet legalization is repeatedly and vociferously dismissed, without any attempt to evaluate it openly and objectively. The past twenty years have demonstrated that a drug policy shaped by exaggerated rhetoric designed to arouse fear has only led to our current disaster. Unless we are willing to honestly evaluate our options, including various legalization strategies, we will run a still greater risk: we may never find the best solution for our drug problems.

NO
James Q. Wilson

AGAINST THE LEGALIZATION OF DRUGS

In 1972, the President appointed me chairman of the National Advisory Council for Drug Abuse Prevention. Created by Congress, the Council was charged with providing guidance on how best to coordinate the national war on drugs. (Yes, we called it a war then, too.) In those days, the drug we were chiefly concerned with was heroin. When I took office, heroin use had been increasing dramatically. Everybody was worried that this increase would continue. Such phrases as "heroin epidemic" were commonplace.

That same year, the eminent economist Milton Friedman published an essay in *Newsweek* in which he called for legalizing heroin. His argument was on two grounds: as a matter of ethics, the government has no right to tell people not to use heroin (or to drink or to commit suicide); as a matter of economics, the prohibition of drug use imposes costs on society that far exceed the benefits. Others, such as the psychoanalyst Thomas Szasz, made the same argument.

We did not take Friedman's advice. (Government commissions rarely do.) I do not recall that we even discussed legalizing heroin, though we did discuss (but did not take action on) legalizing a drug, cocaine, that many people then argued was benign. Our marching orders were to figure out how to win the war on heroin, not to run up the white flag of surrender.

That was 1972. Today, we have the same number of heroin addicts that we had then—half a million, give or take a few thousand. Having that many heroin addicts is no trivial matter; these people deserve our attention. But not having had an increase in that number for over fifteen years is also something that deserves our attention. What happened to the "heroin epidemic" that many people once thought would overwhelm us?

The facts are clear: a more or less stable pool of heroin addicts has been getting older, with relatively few new recruits. In 1976 the average age of heroin users who appeared in hospital emergency rooms was about twenty-seven; ten years later it was thirty-two. More than two-thirds of all heroin users appearing in emergency rooms are now over the age of thirty. Back in the early 1970's, when heroin got onto the national political agenda, the

From James Q. Wilson, "Against the Legalization of Drugs," *Commentary* (February 1990). Reprinted by permission of *Commentary* and the author. All rights reserved.

typical heroin addict was much younger, often a teenager. Household surveys show the same thing—the rate of opiate use (which includes heroin) has been flat for the better part of two decades. More fine-grained studies of inner-city neighborhoods confirm this. John Boyle and Ann Brunswick found that the percentage of young blacks in Harlem who used heroin fell from 8 percent in 1970–71 to about 3 percent in 1975–76.

Why did heroin lose its appeal for young people? When the young blacks in Harlem were asked why they stopped, more than half mentioned "trouble with the law" or "high cost" (and high cost is, of course, directly the result of law enforcement). Two-thirds said that heroin hurt their health; nearly all said they had had a bad experience with it. We need not rely, however, simply on what they said. In New York City in 1973–75, the street price of heroin rose dramatically and its purity sharply declined, probably as a result of the heroin shortage caused by the success of the Turkish government in reducing the supply of opium base and of the French government in closing down heroin-processing laboratories located in and around Marseilles. These were short-lived gains for, just as Friedman predicted, alternative sources of supply—mostly in Mexico—quickly emerged. But the three-year heroin shortage interrupted the easy recruitment of new users.

Health and related problems were no doubt part of the reason for the reduced flow of recruits. Over the preceding years, Harlem youth had watched as more and more heroin users died of overdoses, were poisoned by adulterated doses, or acquired hepatitis from dirty needles. The word got around: heroin can kill you. By 1974 new hepatitis cases and drug-overdose deaths had dropped to a fraction of what they had been in 1970.

Alas, treatment did not seem to explain much of the cessation in drug use. Treatment programs can and do help heroin addicts, but treatment did not explain the drop in the number of *new* users (who by definition had never been in treatment) nor even much of the reduction in the number of experienced users.

No one knows how much of the decline to attribute to personal observation as opposed to high prices or reduced supply. But other evidence suggests strongly that price and supply played a large role. In 1972 the National Advisory Council was especially worried by the prospect that U.S. servicemen returning to this country from Vietnam would bring their heroin habits with them. Fortunately, a brilliant study by Lee Robins of Washington University in St. Louis put that fear to rest. She measured drug use of Vietnam veterans shortly after they had returned home. Though many had used heroin regularly while in Southeast Asia, most gave up the habit when back in the United States. The reason: here, heroin was less available and sanctions on its use were more pronounced. . . .

RELIVING THE PAST

Suppose we had taken Friedman's advice in 1972. What would have happened? We cannot be entirely certain, but at a minimum we would have placed the young heroin addicts (and, above all, the prospective addicts) in a very different position from the one in which they actually found themselves. Heroin would have been legal. Its price would have been reduced by 95 percent (minus whatever we chose to recover in taxes). Now that it could be sold by the same people who make aspirin, its quality would have been assured—no poisons, no adulterants. Sterile hypodermic needles would have been readily available at the neighborhood drugstore, probably at the same counter where the heroin was sold. No need to travel to big cities or unfamiliar neighborhoods—heroin could have been purchased anywhere, perhaps by mail order.

There would no longer have been any financial or medical reason to avoid heroin use. Anybody could have afforded it. We might have tried to prevent children from buying it, but as we have learned from our efforts to prevent minors from buying alcohol and tobacco, young people have a way of penetrating markets theoretically reserved for adults. . . .

Under these circumstances, can we doubt for a moment that heroin use would have grown exponentially? Or that a vastly larger supply of new users would have been recruited? Professor Friedman is a Nobel Prize-winning economist whose understanding of market forces is profound. What did he think would happen to consumption under his legalized regime? Here are his words: "Legalizing drugs might increase the number of addicts, but it is not clear that it would. Forbidden fruit is attractive, particularly to the young."

Really? I suppose that we should expect no increase in Porsche sales if we cut the price by 95 percent, no increase in whiskey sales if we cut the price by a comparable amount—because young people only want fast cars and strong liquor when they are "forbidden." Perhaps Friedman's uncharacteristic lapse from the obvious implications of price theory

can be explained by a misunderstanding of how drug users are recruited. In his 1972 essay he said that "drug addicts are deliberately made by pushers, who give likely prospects their first few doses free." If drugs were legal it would not pay anybody to produce addicts, because everybody would buy from the cheapest source. But as every drug expert knows, pushers do not produce addicts. Friends or acquaintances do. In fact, pushers are usually reluctant to deal with non-users because a non-user could be an undercover cop. Drug use spreads in the same way any fad or fashion spreads: somebody who is already a user urges his friends to try, or simply shows already-eager friends how to do it.

But we need not rely on speculation, however plausible, that lowered prices and more abundant supplies would have increased heroin usage. Great Britain once followed such a policy and with almost exactly those results. Until the mid-1960's, British physicians were allowed to prescribe heroin to certain classes of addicts. (Possessing these drugs without a doctor's prescription remained a criminal offense.) For many years this policy worked well enough because the addict patients were typically middle-class people who had become dependent on opiate painkillers while undergoing hospital treatment. There was no drug culture. The British system worked for many years, not because it prevented drug abuse, but because there was no problem of drug abuse that would test the system.

All that changed in the 1960's. A few unscrupulous doctors began passing out heroin in wholesale amounts. One doctor prescribed almost 600,000 heroin tablets—that is, over thirteen pounds—in just one year. A youthful drug culture emerged with a demand for drugs far different from that of the older addicts. As a result, the British government required doctors to refer users to government-run clinics to receive their heroin.

But the shift to clinics did not curtail the growth in heroin use. Throughout the 1960's the number of addicts increased—the late John Kaplan of Stanford estimated by fivefold—in part as a result of the diversion of heroin from clinic patients to new users on the streets. An addict would bargain with the clinic doctor over how big a dose he would receive. The patient wanted as much as he could get, the doctor wanted to give as little as was needed. The patient had an advantage in this conflict because the doctor could not be certain how much was really needed. Many patients would use some of their "maintenance" dose and sell the remaining part to friends, thereby recruiting new addicts. As the clinics learned of this, they began to shift their treatment away from heroin and toward methadone, an addictive drug that, when taken orally, does not produce a "high" but will block the withdrawal pains associated with heroin abstinence.

Whether what happened in England in the 1960's was a mini-epidemic or an epidemic depends on whether one looks at numbers or at rates of change. Compared to the United States, the numbers were small. In 1960 there were 68 heroin addicts known to the British government; by 1968 there were 2,000 in treatment and many more who refused treatment. (They would refuse in part because they did not want to get methadone at a clinic if they could get heroin on the street.) Richard Hartnoll estimates that the actual number of addicts in England is five times the number officially registered. At a minimum, the number of British addicts increased by thirtyfold in ten years; the actual increase may have been much larger.

In the early 1980's the numbers began to rise again, and this time nobody doubted that a real epidemic was at hand. The increase was estimated to be 40 percent a year. By 1982 there were thought to be 20,000 heroin users in London alone. Geoffrey Pearson reports that many cities—Glasgow, Liverpool, Manchester, and Sheffield among them—were now experiencing a drug problem that once had been largely confined to London. The problem, again, was supply. The country was being flooded with cheap, high-quality heroin, first from Iran and then from Southeast Asia. . . .

BACK TO THE FUTURE

Now cocaine, especially in its potent form, crack, is the focus of attention. Now as in 1972 the government is trying to reduce its use. Now as then some people are advocating legalization. Is there any more reason to yield to those arguments today than there was almost two decades ago?[1]

I think not. If we had yielded in 1972 we almost certainly would have had today a permanent population of several million, not several hundred thousand, heroin addicts. If we yield now we will have a far more serious problem with cocaine.

Crack is worse than heroin by almost any measure. Heroin produces a pleasant drowsiness and, if hygienically administered, has only the physical side effects of constipation and sexual impotence. Regular heroin use incapacitates many users, especially poor ones, for any productive work or social responsibility. They will sit nodding on a street corner, helpless but at least harmless. By contrast, regular cocaine use leaves the user neither helpless nor harmless. When smoked (as with crack) or injected, cocaine produces instant, intense, and short-lived euphoria. The experience generates a powerful desire to repeat it. If the drug is readily available, repeat use will occur. Those people who progress to "bingeing" on cocaine become devoted to the drug and its effects to the exclusion of almost all other considerations— job, family, children, sleep, food, even sex. Dr. Frank Gawin at Yale and Dr. Everett Ellinwood at Duke report that a substantial percentage of all high-dose, binge users become uninhibited, impulsive, hypersexual, compulsive, irritable, and hyperactive. Their moods vacillate dramatically, leading at times to violence and homicide.

Women are much more likely to use crack than heroin, and if they are pregnant, the effects on their babies are tragic. Douglas Besharov, who has been following the effects of drugs on infants for twenty years, writes that nothing he learned about heroin prepared him for the devastation of cocaine. Cocaine harms the fetus and can lead to physical deformities or neurological damage. Some crack babies have for all practical purposes suffered a disabling stroke while still in the womb. The long-term consequences of this brain damage are lowered cognitive ability and the onset of mood disorders. Besharov estimates that about 30,000 to 50,000 such babies are born every year, about 7,000 in New York City alone. There may be ways to treat such infants, but from everything we now know the treatment will be long, difficult, and expensive. Worse, the

mothers who are most likely to produce crack babies are precisely the ones who, because of poverty or temperament, are least able and willing to obtain such treatment. In fact, anecdotal evidence suggests that crack mothers are likely to abuse their infants.

The notion that abusing drugs such as cocaine is a "victimless crime" is not only absurd but dangerous. Even ignoring the fetal drug syndrome, crack-dependent people are, like heroin addicts, individuals who regularly victimize their children by neglect, their spouses by improvidence, their employers by lethargy, and their co-workers by carelessness. Society is not and could never be a collection of autonomous individuals. We all have a stake in ensuring that each of us displays a minimal level of dignity, responsibility, and empathy. We cannot, of course, coerce people into goodness, but we can and should insist that some standards must be met if society itself—on which the very existence of the human personality depends—is to persist. Drawing the line that defines those standards is difficult and contentious, but if crack and heroin use do not fall below it, what does?

The advocates of legalization will respond by suggesting that my picture is overdrawn. Ethan Nadelmann of Princeton argues that the risk of legalization is less than most people suppose. Over 20 million Americans between the ages of eighteen and twenty-five have tried cocaine (according to a government survey), but only a quarter million use it daily. From this Nadelmann concludes that at most 3 percent of all young people who try cocaine develop a problem with it. The implication is clear: make the drug legal and we only have to worry about 3 percent of our youth.

The implication rests on a logical fallacy and a factual error. The fallacy is this: the percentage of occasional cocaine users who become binge users *when the drug is illegal* (and thus expensive and hard to find) tells us nothing about the percentage who will become dependent when the drug is legal (and thus cheap and abundant). Drs. Gawin and Ellinwood report, in common with several other researchers, that controlled or occasional use of cocaine changes to compulsive and frequent use "when access to the drug increases" or when the user switches from snorting to smoking. More cocaine more potently administered alters, perhaps sharply, the proportion of "controlled" users who become heavy users.

The factual error is this: the federal survey Nadelmann quotes was done in 1985, *before* crack had become common. Thus the probability of becoming dependent on cocaine was derived from the responses of users who snorted the drug. The speed and potency of cocaine's action increases dramatically when it is smoked. We do not yet know how greatly the advent of crack increases the risk of dependency, but all the clinical evidence suggests that the increase is likely to be large.

It is possible that some people will not become heavy users even when the drug is readily available in its most potent form. So far there are no scientific grounds for predicting who will and who will not become dependent. Neither socioeconomic background nor personality traits differentiate between casual and intensive users. Thus, the only way to settle the question of who is correct about the effect of easy availability on drug use, Nadelmann or Gawin and Ellinwood, is to try it and see. But that social experiment is so risky as to be no experiment at all, for if cocaine is legalized and if the rate of its abusive use increases dramatically, there is no way to put the genie back in the bottle, and it is not a kindly genie.

HAVE WE LOST?

Many people who agree that there are risks in legalizing cocaine or heroin still favor it because, they think, we have lost the war on drugs. "Nothing we have done has worked" and the current federal policy is just "more of the same." Whatever the costs of greater drug use, surely they would be less than the costs of our present, failed efforts.

That is exactly what I was told in 1972—and heroin is not quite as bad a drug as cocaine. We did not surrender and we did not lose. We did not win, either. What the nation accomplished then was what most efforts to save people from themselves accomplish: the problem was contained and the number of victims minimized, all at a considerable cost in law enforcement and increased crime. Was the cost worth it? I think so, but others may disagree. What are the lives of would-be addicts worth? I recall some people saying to me then, "Let them kill themselves." I was appalled. Happily, such views did not prevail.

Have we lost today? Not at all. High-rate cocaine use is not commonplace. The National Institute of Drug Abuse (NIDA) reports that less than 5 percent of high-school seniors used cocaine within the last thirty days. Of course this survey misses young people who have dropped out of school and miscounts those who lie on the questionnaire, but even if we inflate the NIDA estimate by some plausible percentage, it is still not much above 5 percent. Medical examiners reported in 1987 that about 1,500 died from cocaine use; hospital emergency rooms reported about 30,000 admissions related to cocaine abuse.

These are not small numbers, but neither are they evidence of a nationwide plague that threatens to engulf us all. Moreover, cities vary greatly in the proportion of people who are involved with cocaine. To get city-level data we need to turn to drug tests carried out on arrested persons, who obviously are more likely to be drug users than the average citizen. The National Institute of Justice, through its Drug Use Forecasting (DUF) project, collects urinalysis data on arrestees in 22 cities. As we have already seen, opiate (chiefly heroin) use has been flat or declining in most of these cities over the last decade. Cocaine use has gone up sharply, but with great variation among cities. New York, Philadelphia, and Washington, D.C., all report that two-thirds or more of their arrestees tested positive for cocaine, but in Portland, San Antonio, and Indianapolis the percentage was one-third or less.

In some neighborhoods, of course, matters have reached crisis proportions. Gangs control the streets, shootings terrorize residents, and drug-dealing occurs in plain view. The police seem barely able to contain matters. But in these neighborhoods—unlike at Palo Alto cocktail parties—the people are not calling for legalization, they are calling for help. And often not much help has come. Many cities are willing to do almost anything about the drug problem except spend more money on it. The federal government cannot change that; only local voters and politicians can. It is not clear that they will.

It took about ten years to contain heroin. We have had experience with crack for only about three or four years. Each year we spend perhaps $11 billion on law enforcement (and some of that goes to deal with marijuana) and perhaps $2 billion on treatment. Large sums, but not sums that should lead anyone to say, "We just can't afford this any more."

The illegality of drugs increases crime, partly because some users turn to crime to pay for their habits, partly because some users are stimulated by certain drugs (such as crack or PCP) to act more violently or ruthlessly than they otherwise would, and partly because criminal organizations seeking to control drug supplies use force to manage their markets. These also are serious costs, but no one knows how much they would be reduced if drugs were legalized. Addicts would no longer steal to pay black-market prices for drugs, a real gain. But some, perhaps a great deal, of that gain would be offset by the great increase in the number of addicts. These people, nodding on heroin or living in the delusion-ridden high of cocaine, would hardly be ideal employees. Many would steal simply to support themselves, since snatch-and-grab, opportunistic crime can be managed even by people unable to hold a regular job or plan an elaborate crime. Those British addicts who get their supplies from government clinics are not models of law-abiding decency. Most are in crime, and though their per-capita rate of criminality may be lower thanks to the cheapness of their drugs, the total volume of crime they produce may be quite large. Of course, society could decide to support all unemployable addicts on welfare, but that would mean that gains from lowered rates of crime would have to be offset by large increases in welfare budgets.

Proponents of legalization claim that the costs of having more addicts around would be largely if not entirely offset by having more money available with which to treat and care for them. The money would come from taxes levied on the sale of heroin and cocaine.

To obtain this fiscal dividend, however, legalization's supporters must first solve an economic dilemma. If they want to raise a lot of money to pay for welfare and treatment, the tax rate on the drugs will have to be quite high. Even if they themselves do not want a high rate, the politicians' love of "sin taxes" would probably guarantee that it would be high anyway. But the higher the tax, the higher the price of the drug, and the higher the price the greater the likelihood that addicts will turn to crime to find the money for it and that criminal organizations will be formed to sell tax-free drugs at below-market rates. If we managed to keep taxes (and thus prices) low, we would get much less money to pay for welfare and treatment and more people could afford to become addicts. There may be an optimal tax rate for drugs that maximizes revenue while minimizing crime, bootlegging, and the recruitment of new addicts, but our experience with alcohol does not suggest that we know how to find it.

THE BENEFITS OF ILLEGALITY

The advocates of legalization find nothing to be said in favor of the current system except, possibly, that it keeps the number of addicts smaller than it would otherwise be. In fact, the benefits are more substantial than that.

First, treatment. All the talk about providing "treatment on demand" implies that there is a demand for treatment.

That is not quite right. There are some drug-dependent people who genuinely want treatment and will remain in it if offered; they should receive it. But there are far more who want only short-term help after a bad crash; once stabilized and bathed, they are back on the street again, hustling. And even many of the addicts who enroll in a program honestly wanting help drop out after a short while when they discover that help takes time and commitment. Drug-dependent people have very short time horizons and a weak capacity for commitment. These two groups—those looking for a quick fix and those unable to stick with a long-term fix—are not easily helped. Even if we increase the number of treatment slots—as we should—we would have to do something to make treatment more effective.

One thing that can often make it more effective is compulsion. Douglas Anglin of UCLA, in common with many other researchers, has found that the longer one stays in a treatment program, the better the chances of a reduction in drug dependency. But he, again like most other researchers, has found that dropout rates are high. He has also found, however, that patients who enter treatment under legal compulsion stay in the program longer than those not subject to such pressure. His research on the California civil-commitment program, for example, found that heroin users involved with its required drug-testing program had over the long term a lower rate of heroin use than similar addicts who were free of such constraints. If for many addicts compulsion is a useful component of treatment, it is not clear how compulsion could be achieved in a society in which purchasing, possessing, and using the drug were legal. It could be managed, I suppose, but I would not want to have to answer the challenge from the American Civil Liberties Union that it is wrong to compel a person to undergo treatment for consuming a legal commodity.

Next, education. We are now investing substantially in drug-education programs in the schools. Though we do not yet know for certain what will work, there are some promising leads. But I wonder how credible such programs would be if they were aimed at dissuading children from doing something perfectly legal. We could, of course, treat drug education like smoking education: inhaling crack and inhaling tobacco are both legal, but you should not do it because it is bad for you. That tobacco is bad for you is easily shown; the Surgeon General has seen to that. But what do we say about crack? It is pleasurable, but devoting yourself to so much pleasure is not a good idea (though perfectly legal)? Unlike tobacco, cocaine will not give you cancer or emphysema, but it will lead you to neglect your duties to family, job, and neighborhood? Everybody is doing cocaine, but you should not?

Again, it might be possible under a legalized regime to have effective drug-prevention programs, but their effectiveness would depend heavily, I think, on first having decided that cocaine use, like tobacco use, is purely a matter of practical consequences; no fundamental moral significance attaches to either. But if we believe—as I do—that dependency on certain mind-altering drugs *is* a moral issue and that their illegality rests in part on their immorality, then legalizing them undercuts, if it does not eliminate altogether, the moral message.

That message is at the root of the distinction we now make between nico-

tine and cocaine. Both are highly addictive; both have harmful physical effects. But we treat the two drugs differently, not simply because nicotine is so widely used as to be beyond the reach of effective prohibition, but because its use does not destroy the user's essential humanity. Tobacco shortens one's life, cocaine debases it. Nicotine alters one's habits, cocaine alters one's soul. The heavy use of crack, unlike the heavy use of tobacco, corrodes those natural sentiments of sympathy and duty that constitute our human nature and make possible our social life. To say, as does Nadelmann, that distinguishing morally between tobacco and cocaine is "little more than a transient prejudice" is close to saying that morality itself is but a prejudice.

THE ALCOHOL PROBLEM

Now we have arrived where many arguments about legalizing drugs begin: is there any reason to treat heroin and cocaine differently from the way we treat alcohol?

There is no easy answer to that question because, as with so many human problems, one cannot decide simply on the basis either of moral principles or of individual consequences; one has to temper any policy by a common-sense judgment of what is possible. Alcohol, like heroin, cocaine, PCP, and marijuana, is a drug—that is, a mood-altering substance—and consumed to excess it certainly has harmful consequences: auto accidents, barroom fights, bedroom shootings. It is also, for some people, addictive. We cannot confidently compare the addictive powers of these drugs, but the best evidence suggests that crack and heroin are much more addictive than alcohol.

Many people, Nadelmann included, argue that since the health and financial costs of alcohol abuse are so much higher than those of cocaine or heroin abuse, it is hypocritical folly to devote our efforts to preventing cocaine or drug use. But as Mark Kleiman of Harvard has pointed out, this comparison is quite misleading. What Nadelmann is doing is showing that a *legalized* drug (alcohol) produces greater social harm than *illegal* ones (cocaine and heroin). But of course. Suppose that in the 1920's we had made heroin and cocaine legal and alcohol illegal. Can anyone doubt that Nadelmann would now be writing that it is folly to continue our ban on alcohol because cocaine and heroin are so much more harmful?

And let there be no doubt about it—widespread heroin and cocaine use are associated with all manner of ills. Thomas Bewley found that the mortality rate of British heroin addicts in 1968 was 28 times as high as the death rate of the same age group of non-addicts, even though in England at the time an addict could obtain free or low-cost heroin and clean needles from British clinics. Perform the following mental experiment: suppose we legalized heroin and cocaine in this country. In what proportion of auto fatalities would the state police report that the driver was nodding off on heroin or recklessly driving on a coke high? In what proportion of spouse-assault and child-abuse cases would the local police report that crack was involved? In what proportion of industrial accidents would safety investigators report that the forklift or drill-press operator was in a drug-induced stupor or frenzy? We do not know exactly what the proportion would be, but anyone who asserts that it would not be much higher than it is now would have to believe that these drugs have little appeal except when they are illegal. And that is nonsense. . . .

IF I AM WRONG . . .

No one can know what our society would be like if we changed the law to make access to cocaine, heroin, and PCP easier. I believe, for reasons given, that the result would be a sharp increase in use, a more widespread degradation of the human personality, and a greater rate of accidents and violence.

I may be wrong. If I am, then we will needlessly have incurred heavy costs in law enforcement and some forms of criminality. But if I am right, and the legalizers prevail anyway, then we will have consigned millions of people, hundreds of thousands of infants, and hundreds of neighborhoods to a life of oblivion and disease. To the lives and families destroyed by alcohol we will have added countless more destroyed by cocaine, heroin, PCP, and whatever else a basement scientist can invent.

Human character is formed by society; indeed, human character is inconceivable without society, and good character is less likely in a bad society. Will we, in the name of an abstract doctrine of radical individualism, and with the false comfort of suspect predictions, decide to take the chance that somehow individual decency can survive amid a more general level of degradation?

I think not. The American people are too wise for that, whatever the academic essayists and cocktail-party pundits may say. But if Americans today are less wise than I suppose, then Americans at some future time will look back on us now and wonder, what kind of people were they that they could have done such a thing?

NOTES

1. I do not here take up the question of marijuana. For a variety of reasons—its widespread use and its lesser tendency to addict—it presents a different problem from cocaine or heroin. For a penetrating analysis, see Mark Kleiman, *Marijuana: Costs of Abuse, Costs of Control* (Greenwood Press, 217 pp., $37.95).

POSTSCRIPT

Should Drugs Be Legalized?

The analogy often cited by proponents of drug legalization is the ill-fated attempt to ban the sale of liquor in the United States, which lasted from 1919 to 1933. Prohibition has been called "an experiment noble in purpose," but it was an experiment that greatly contributed to the rise of organized crime. The repeal of Prohibition brought about an increase in liquor consumption and alcoholism, but it also deprived organized crime of an important source of income. Would drug decriminalization similarly strike a blow at the drug dealers? Possibly, and such a prospect is obviously appealing. But would drug decriminalization also exacerbate some of the ills associated with drugs? Would there be more violence, more severe addiction, more crack babies born to addicted mothers?

David F. Musto's *The American Disease* (Yale, 1973) is a classic discussion of the drug problem in America. H. Wayne Morgan's *Drugs in America: A Social History, 1800–1980* (Syracuse University, 1981) is also useful for anyone seeking an historical background on the drug problem. James A. Inciardi's book *The War on Drugs: Heroin, Cocaine, Crime and Public Policy* (Mayfield, 1986) gives a close-up look at the cocaine and crime scene. Numerous periodicals are devoted to discussions of drugs in America. For example, *The Drug Policy Letter*, published every two months by the Drug Policy Foundation in Washington, D.C., considers issues relating to the legal status of drugs. *The Drug Educator*, published quarterly by the American Council for Drug Education of Rockville, Maryland, stresses the health hazards associated even with so-called soft drugs like marijuana.

Erich Goode, *Drugs in American Society* (McGraw-Hill, 1988), provides a sociological perspective on drugs. Larry Sloman's book *Reefer Madness: The History of Marijuana in America* (Grove Press, 1983) describes changing attitudes and laws regarding marijuana, while Lester Brinspoon and James B. Bakalar do the same for cocaine in *Cocaine: A Drug and Its Social Evolution* (Basic Books, 1985). Thomas S. Szasz, *Ceremonial Chemistry: The Ritual Persecution of Drugs, Addicts, and Pushers,* revised ed. (Learning Publications, 1985), criticizes our current antidrug crusades.

Whatever the future of drug abuse in America, the present situation is grim. The use of hard drugs has been linked to the staggering increases in crime, violence, and AIDS over the past decade. All sides agree that something must be done. The question is what: what will work without causing undue restrictions on personal freedoms? The debate, partly pragmatic and partly an argument over the value and place of liberty in America, will continue for as long as drugs continue to plague the nation.

ISSUE 15

Does Our Welfare System Hurt the Poor?

YES: Charles Murray, from *Losing Ground: American Social Policy, 1950–1980* (Basic Books, 1984)

NO: William Julius Wilson, from *The Truly Disadvantaged: The Inner City, the Underclass, and Public Policy* (University of Chicago, 1987)

ISSUE SUMMARY

YES: Political scientist Charles Murray maintains that the best welfare policy, at least for able-bodied working-age people, is no welfare support by the government.

NO: Professor William Julius Wilson argues that welfare policy has *not* contributed to economic decline for the poor; what has had an effect on poverty rates are social changes leading to a sharp rise in black male unemployment.

The Great Depression that began with the stock market crash of 1929 and continued through the 1930s led to the adoption of far-reaching government policies designed to put people to work. These in turn led to the Social Security Act in 1935, to provide some measure of economic protection for retired workers and their survivors, disabled workers, and the unemployed.

Social Security insured only working people, and neither it nor Aid to Families with Dependent Children nor public housing programs met the needs of the poorest people. President Franklin D. Roosevelt called attention in 1937 to the plight of "one-third of a nation, ill-housed, ill-clad, ill-nourished," and, a generation later, President Johnson proposed a War on Poverty "to lift this forgotten fifth of our nation above the poverty line." Almost surely the proportion was less than it had been, but it was clear that poverty remained widespread and deeply rooted in American society.

It was during Johnson's presidency that the federal government initiated food stamps, Medicaid for the poor, Medicare for the elderly, Head Start educational programs for underprivileged children, and the Job Corps. Still later came Supplemental Security Income for the blind, disabled, and low-income aged.

The election of Ronald Reagan in 1980 and his reelection in 1984 brought to the presidency an opponent of welfare policies who succeeded in securing sharp cuts in the growth rate of such welfare programs as food stamps and Aid to Families with Dependent Children. Although he spoke of a "safety net" to ensure that those who genuinely required governmental assistance would be able to secure it, his critics maintained that the so-called net was full of holes. He attacked "welfare chiselers" and non-needy recipients. Many who were receiving government assistance were removed from benefits lists, but some won reinstatement on appeal, and Congress acted to make it more difficult to remove recipients by executive action.

President George Bush, by contrast, frequently speaks of a "kinder, gentler nation," but he nevertheless shares most of Reagan's economic philosophy. Bush advocates more reliance on the stimulation of business activity and less on welfare. For example, he favors a reduction in taxes on investment income as a means of increasing investment, which would result in more job opportunities for the poor. Reagan had said, "A rising tide lifts all boats." The problem, critics argue, is that a rising tide will not raise shipwrecks from the bottom of the sea. People too long unemployed become unemployable because they lack both the skills they would need in the workplace and the will to find employment.

The least controversial American welfare programs have probably been Social Security, Medicare, college grants and loans, and unemployment insurance. These programs are universal or nearly so in bestowing benefits, as distinguished from programs which involve a means test in order to make them available only to the poor.

During the last decade there has been an increasing public perception of the growing number of homeless people. How many people in America are homeless is disputed, with 1990 figures ranging from 300,000 to 3 million. There is even less agreement on the causes of homelessness. Among the most frequently cited reasons are the unprofitability of low-cost housing and the decline of government subsidies, soaring rents, and the fact that many mentally ill people have been released from institutions without being provided shelter and economic support. Here, as with other welfare issues, conservatives are skeptical of the value of throwing money at the problem. George Gilder, an articulate opponent of welfare policies, argues that "hard work, stability, and faith in God are indispensable to upward mobility."

In 1988 Congress adopted "workfare," a system designed to provide work incentives for adults receiving public assistance, and the idea behind it is that work will enable adults receiving public assistance to support themselves and to end the cycle of dependency. Critics charge that this program is unfair to single mothers and their children (an increasing proportion of the poor) because it provides training that can only lead to jobs that pay barely more than welfare and do not offer the benefits of daycare or Medicaid.

Can poverty be eliminated or sharply reduced, or must the poor always be with us? Has government intervention failed because it sought to do too much or because it hasn't done enough? Why does the poverty level remain high in a nation in which so many enjoy a high standard of living? Why is the disparity between poor and rich Americans wider than in other prosperous industrial nations?

YES

Charles Murray

THE WELFARE SYSTEM DOESN'T WORK

If social policy may be construed, as I suggest . . . , as transfers from the haves to the have-nots, the proper first question is, "What is the justification for any transfers at all?" Why should one person give *anything* to a stranger whose only claim to his help is a common citizenship?

Suppose that I am not opposed to the notion of government transfers, but neither do I think that equality of outcome is always a good in itself. I attach considerable value to the principle that people get what they deserve. In other words, "I" am a fairly typical citizen with a middle-of-the-road, pragmatic political philosophy.

I am asked to consider the case of a man who has worked steadily for many years and, in his fifties, is thrown out of his job because the factory closes. Why should I transfer money to him—provide him with unemployment checks and, perhaps, permanent welfare support? The answer is not difficult. I may rationalize it any number of ways, but at bottom I consent to transfer money to him because I want to. The worker has plugged along as best he could, contributed his bit to the community, and now faces personal disaster. He is one of my fellows in a very meaningful way—"There but for the grace of God . . ."—and I am happy to see a portion of my income used to help him out. (I would not be happy to see so much of my income transferred that I am unable to meet my obligations to myself and my family, however.)

A second man, healthy and in the prime of life, refuses to work. I offer him a job, and he still refuses to work. I am called upon to answer the question again: Why should I transfer money to him? Why should I not let him starve, considering it a form of suicide?

It is a question to ponder without escape hatches. I may not assume that the man can be made to change his ways with the right therapeutic intervention. I may not assume that he has some mental or environmental handicap that relieves him of responsibility. He is a man of ordinary capacities who wishes to live off my work rather than work for himself. Why should I consent?

Suppose that I decide not to let him starve in the streets, for reasons having to do with the sanctity of life (I would prevent a suicide as well). The decision does not take me very far in setting up an ideal policy. At once, I run into choices when I compare his situation (we will call him the drone) with that of the laid-off worker.

Suppose that I have only enough resources either (a) to keep both alive at a bare subsistence level or (b) to support the laid-off worker at a decent standard of living and the drone at a near-starvation level. What would be the just policy? Would it be right, would it be fair, to make the worker live more miserably so that I might be more generous to the drone?

We may put the question more provocatively: Suppose that scarce resources were not a problem—that we could afford to support both at a decent standard of living. Should we do so? Is it morally appropriate to give the same level of support to the two men? Would it be right to offer the same respect to the two men? The same discretionary choice in how to use the help that was provided?

These are not rhetorical questions nor are they questions about expedient policy. They ask about the justice and humanity of the alternatives. I submit that it is not humane to the laid-off worker to treat him the same as the drone. It is not just to accord the drone the respect that the laid-off worker has earned.

The point is that, in principle, most of us provide some kinds of assistance gladly, for intuitively obvious reasons. We provide other kinds of assistance for reasons that, when it comes down to it, are extremely hard to defend on either moral or practical grounds. An ethically ideal social policy—an *intuitively* satisfy-

ing one—would discriminate among recipients. It would attach a pat on the back to some transfers and give others begrudgingly.

We have yet to tackle the question of whether the point has anything to do with recipients in the workaday world. Who is to say that the drone has no justification for refusing to work (he was trained as a cook and we offer him a job sweeping floors)? Who is to say whether the laid-off worker is blameless for the loss of his job (his sloppy workmanship contributed to the factory's loss of business to the Japanese)? Who is to say that the income of the taxpaying donor is commensurate with his value to society—that he "deserves" his income any more than the drone deserves the gift of a part of it? But such questions define the operational barriers to establishing a social policy that discriminates among recipients according to their deserts. They do not touch on the legitimacy of the principle.

ROBBING PETER TO PAY PAUL: TRANSFERS FROM POOR TO POOR

When we think of transfers, we usually think in terms of economic transfers from richer to poorer. In reality, social policy can obligate one citizen to turn over a variety of "goods" as a donation on behalf of some other person; access to parking spaces reserved for the handicapped is a simple example.

Sometimes these noneconomic transfers, like the economic ones, are arranged so that the better-off give up something to the worse-off, and the argument about whether the transfer is appropriate follows the lines of the issues I have just raised. But in a surprising number of instances the transfers are mandated by the better-off, while the price must be paid by donors who are just as poor as the recipient.

Now suppose that the same hypothetical "I" considers the case of two students in an inner-city high school. Both come from poor families. Both have suffered equal deprivations and social injustices. They have the same intelligence and human potential. For whatever reasons—let us assume pure accident—the two students behave differently in school. One student (the good student) studies hard and pays attention in class. The other student (the mischievous student) does not study and instead creates disturbances, albeit good-natured disturbances, in the classroom.

I observe a situation in which the teacher expels the mischievous student from the classroom more or less at will. The result is that he becomes further alienated from school, drops out, and eventually ends up on welfare or worse. I know that the cause of this sequence of events (his behavior in class) was no worse than the behavior of millions of middle-class students who suffer nothing like the same penalty. They too are kicked out of class when they act up, but for a variety of reasons they stay in school and eventually do well. Further yet, I know that the behavior of the teacher toward the student is biased and unfairly harsh because the student is an inner-city black and the teacher is a suburban white who neither understands nor sympathizes with such students.

On all counts, then, I observe that the mischievous student expelled from the classroom is a victim who deserves a system that does not unfairly penalize him. I therefore protect him against the bias and arbitrariness of the teacher. The teacher cannot expel the student from class unless the student's behavior meets certain criteria far beyond the ordinary talking and laughing out of turn that used to get him in trouble.

The result, let us say, is that the student continues to act as before, but remains in the classroom. Other students also respond to the reality of the greater latitude they now have. The amount of teaching is reduced, and so is the ability of students to concentrate on their work even if they want to.

I know, however, that some benefits are obtained. The mischievous student who formerly dropped out of school does not. He obtains his diploma, and with it some advantages in the form of greater education (he learned something, although not much, while he stayed in school) and a credential to use when applying for a job.

This benefit has been obtained at a price. The price is not money—let us say it costs no more to run the school under the new policy than under the old. No transfers have been exacted from the white middle class. The transfer instead is wholly from the good student to the mischievous one. For I find that the quality of education obtained by the good student deteriorated badly, both because the teacher had less time and energy for teaching and because the classroom environment was no longer suitable for studying. One poor and disadvantaged student has been compelled (he had no choice in the matter) to give up part of his education so that the other student could stay in the classroom.

What is my rationale for enforcing this transfer? In what sense did the good student have an excess of educational opportunity that he could legitimately be asked to sacrifice? . . .

Such transfers from poor to poor are at the heart of the inequities of social policy. Saying that we meant well does not quite cover our transgressions. Even during the period of the most active reform we could not help being aware, if only at the back of our minds, of certain moral problems. When poor delinquents arrested for felonies were left on probation, as the elite wisdom prescribed they should be, the persons put most at risk were poor people who lived in their neighborhoods. They, not the elite, gave up the greater part of the good called "safety" so that the disadvantaged delinquent youth should not experience the injustice of punishment. When job-training programs were set up to function at the level of the least competent, it was the most competent trainees who had to sacrifice their opportunities to reach potentials. When social policy reinforced the ethic that certain jobs are too demeaning to ask people to do, it was those who preferred such jobs to welfare whose basis for self-respect was stripped from them. . . .

I begin with the proposition that it is within our resources to do enormous good for some people quickly. We have available to us a program that would convert a large proportion of the younger generation of hardcore unemployed into steady workers making a living wage. The same program would drastically reduce births to single teenage girls. It would reverse the trendline in the breakup of poor families. It would measurably increase the upward socioeconomic mobility of poor families. These improvements would affect some millions of persons.

All these are results that have eluded the efforts of the social programs installed since 1965, yet, from everything we know, there is no real question about whether they would occur under the program I propose. A wide variety of persuasive evidence from our own culture and around the world, from experimental data and longitudinal studies, from theory and practice, suggests that the program would achieve such results.

The proposed program . . . consists of scrapping the entire federal welfare and income-support structure of working-aged persons, including AFDC, Medicaid, Food Stamps, Unemployment Insurance, Worker's Compensation, subsidized housing, disability insurance, and the rest. It would leave the working-aged person with no recourse whatsoever except the job market, family members, friends, and public or private locally funded services. It is the Alexandrian solution: cut the knot, for there is no way to untie it.

It is difficult to examine such a proposal dispassionately. Those who dislike paying for welfare are for it without thinking. Others reflexively imagine bread lines and people starving in the streets. But as a means of gaining fresh perspective on the problem of effective reform, let us consider what this hypothetical society might look like.

A large majority of the population is unaffected. A surprising number of the huge American middle and working classes go from birth to grave without using any social welfare benefits until they receive their first Social Security check. Another portion of the population is technically affected but the change in income is so small or so sporadic that it makes no difference in quality of life. A third group comprises persons who have to make new arrangements and behave in different ways. Sons and daughters who fail to find work continue to live with their parents or relatives or friends.

Teenaged mothers have to rely on support from their parents or the father of the child and perhaps work as well. People laid off from work have to use their own savings or borrow from others to make do until the next job is found. All these changes involve great disruption in expectations and accustomed roles. . . .

Adolescents who were not job-ready find they are job-ready after all. It turns out that they can work for low wages and accept the discipline of the workplace if the alternative is grim enough. After a few years, many—not all, but many—find that they have acquired salable skills, or that they are at the right place at the right time, or otherwise find that the original entry-level job has gradually been transformed into a secure job paying a decent wage. A few—not a lot, but a few—find that the process leads to affluence.

Perhaps the most rightful, deserved benefit goes to the much larger population of low-income families who have been doing things right all along and have been punished for it: the young man who has taken responsibility for his wife and child even though his friends with the same choice have called him a fool; the single mother who has worked full time and forfeited her right to welfare for very little extra money; the parents who have set an example for their children even as the rules of the game have taught their children that the example is outmoded. For these millions of people, the instantaneous result is that no one makes fun of them any longer. The longer-term result will be that they regain the status that is properly theirs. They will not only be the bedrock upon which the community is founded (which they always have been), they will be recognized as such. The process whereby they regain their position is not magical, but a matter of logic. When it becomes highly dysfunctional for a person to be dependent, status will accrue to being independent, and in fairly short order. Noneconomic rewards will once again reinforce the economic rewards of being a good parent and provider.

The prospective advantages are real and extremely plausible. In fact, if a government program of the traditional sort (one that would "do" something rather than simply get out of the way) could as plausibly promise these advantages, its passage would be a foregone conclusion. Congress, yearning for programs that are not retreads of failures, would be prepared to spend billions. Negative side-effects (as long as they were the traditionally acceptable negative side-effects) would be brushed aside as trivial in return for the benefits. For let me be quite clear: I am not suggesting that we dismantle income support for the working-aged to balance the budget or punish welfare cheats. I am hypothesizing, with the advantage of powerful collateral evidence, that the lives of large numbers of poor people would be radically changed for the better.

There is, however, a fourth segment of the population yet to be considered, those who are pauperized by the withdrawal of government supports and unable to make alternate arrangements: the teenaged mother who has no one to turn to; the incapacitated or the inept who are thrown out of the house; those to whom economic conditions have brought long periods in which there is no work to be had; those with illnesses not covered by insurance. What of these situations?

The first resort is the network of local services. Poor communities in our hypothetical society are still dotted with storefront health clinics, emergency relief agencies, employment services, legal services. They depend for support on local taxes or local philanthropy, and the local taxpayers and philanthropists tend to scrutinize them rather closely. But, by the same token, they also receive considerably more resources than they formerly did. The dismantling of the federal services has poured tens of billions of dollars back into the private economy. Some of that money no doubt has been spent on Mercedes and summer homes on the Cape. But some has been spent on capital investments that generate new jobs. And some has been spent on increased local services to the poor, voluntarily or as decreed by the municipality. In many cities, the coverage provided by this network of agencies is more generous, more humane, more wisely distributed, and more effective in its results than the services formerly subsidized by the federal government.

But we must expect that a large number of people will fall between the cracks. How might we go about trying to retain the advantages of a zero-level welfare system and still address the residual needs?

As we think about the nature of the population still in need, it becomes apparent that their basic problem in the vast majority of the cases is the lack of a job, and this problem is temporary. What they need is something to tide them over while finding a new place in the economy. So our first step is to re-install the Unemployment Insurance program in more or less its previous form. Properly administered, unemployment insurance makes sense. Even if it is restored with all the defects of current practice, the negative effects of Unemployment Insurance *alone* are relatively minor. Our objective is not to wipe out chicanery or to

construct a theoretically unblemished system, but to meet legitimate human needs without doing more harm than good. Unemployment Insurance is one of the least harmful ways of contributing to such ends. Thus the system has been amended to take care of the victims of short-term swings in the economy.

Who is left? We are now down to the hardest of the hard core of the welfare-dependent. They have no jobs. They have been unable to find jobs (or have not tried to find jobs) for a longer period of time than the unemployment benefits cover. They have no families who will help. They have no friends who will help. For some reason, they cannot get help from local services or private charities except for the soup kitchen and a bed in the Salvation Army hall.

What will be the size of this population? We have never tried a zero-level federal welfare system under conditions of late-twentieth-century national wealth, so we cannot do more than speculate. But we may speculate. Let us ask of whom the population might consist and how they might fare.

For any category of "needy" we may name, we find ourselves driven to one of two lines of thought. Either the person is in a category that is going to be at the top of the list of services that localities vote for themselves, and at the top of the list of private services, or the person is in a category where help really is not all that essential or desirable. The burden of the conclusion is not that every single person will be taken care of, but that the extent of resources to deal with needs is likely to be very great—not based on wishful thinking, but on extrapolations from reality.

To illustrate, let us consider the plight of the stereotypical welfare mother—

never married, no skills, small children, no steady help from a man. It is safe to say that, now as in the 1950s, there is no one who has less sympathy from the white middle class, which is to be the source of most of the money for the private and local services we envision. Yet this same white middle class is a soft touch for people trying to make it on their own, and a soft touch for "deserving" needy mothers—AFDC was one of the most widely popular of the New Deal welfare measures, intended as it was for widows with small children. Thus we may envision two quite different scenarios.

In one scenario, the woman is presenting the local or private service with this proposition: "Help me find a job and day-care for my children, and I will take care of the rest." In effect, she puts herself into the same category as the widow and the deserted wife—identifies herself as one of the most obviously deserving of the deserving poor. Welfare mothers who want to get into the labor force are likely to find a wide range of help. In the other scenario, she asks for an outright and indefinite cash grant—in effect, a private or local version of AFDC—so that she can stay with the children and not hold a job. In the latter case, it is very easy to imagine situations in which she will not be able to find a local service or a private philanthropy to provide the help she seeks. The question we must now ask is: What's so bad about that? If children were always better off being with their mother all day and if, by the act of giving birth, a mother acquired the inalienable right to be with the child, then her situation would be unjust to her and injurious to her children. Neither assertion can be defended, however—especially not in the 1980s, when more mothers of all classes work away from

the home than ever before, and even more especially not in view of the empirical record for the children growing up under the current welfare system. Why should the mother be exempted by the system from the pressures that must affect everyone else's decision to work? . . .

Billions for equal opportunity, not one cent for equal outcome—such is the slogan to inscribe on the banner of whatever cause my proposals constitute. Their common theme is to make it possible to get as far as one can go on one's merit, hardly a new ideal in American thought.

NO

William Julius Wilson

THE TRULY DISADVANTAGED

THE ROLE OF WELFARE

A popular explanation for the rise of female-headed families and out-of-wedlock births has been the growth of liberal welfare policies, in particular, broadened eligibility for income transfer programs, increases in benefit levels, and the creation of new programs such as Medicaid and food stamps. Charles Murray, for example, argues that relaxed restrictions and increasing benefits of AFDC enticed lower-class women to forego marriage or prolong childlessness in order to qualify for increasingly lucrative benefits. . . .

[D]espite frequent references in the literature to rising welfare expenditures, benefit levels have fallen in real terms over the past ten years, while illegitimacy ratios have continued to rise. Both Cutright and Ellwood and Bane examined changes over time in state benefit levels and in illegitimate birth rates and found no association.

Other studies using different approaches and data sets have also yielded inconclusive, largely negative, results. Placek and Hendershot analyzed retrospective interviews of three hundred welfare mothers and found that when the women were on welfare, they were significantly *less* likely to refrain from using contraceptives, *less* likely to desire an additional pregnancy, and *less* likely to become pregnant. Similarly, Presser and Salsberg, using a random sample of New York women who had recently had their first child, reported that women on public assistance desired fewer children than women not on assistance, and were less likely to have planned their first birth. Based on a longitudinal study of low-income New York City women, Polgar and Hiday reported that women having an additional birth over a two-year period were no more likely to be receiving welfare at the start of the period than women who did not get pregnant. Moore and Caldwell reported no relationship between characteristics of AFDC programs and out-of-wedlock pregnancy and childbearing from a microlevel analysis of survey data. Ellwood and Bane examined out-of-wedlock birth rates among women likely and unlikely to qualify for AFDC if they became single mothers, and found no significant effect of welfare benefit levels; a comparison of married and unmarried birth rates in low- and high-benefit states also yielded no effects. . . .

[T]he findings from Ellwood and Bane's impressive research, and the inconsistent results of other studies on the relationship between welfare and family structure, and welfare and out-of-wedlock births, raise serious questions about the current tendency to blame changes in welfare policies for the decline in the proportion of intact families and legitimate births among the poor. As Ellwood and Bane emphatically proclaim, "Welfare simply does not appear to be the underlying cause of the dramatic changes in family structure of the past few decades. The factor that we have identified as the underlying cause is discussed in the next section.

THE ROLE OF JOBLESSNESS

Although the structure of the economy and the composition of the labor force have undergone significant change over the last forty years, the labor-force participation patterns of white men have changed little. The labor-force participation rate of white men declined from 82 percent in 1940 to 76 percent in 1980, in part because of a drop in the labor-force activity of men over the age of fifty-five (from 83.9 percent to 72.2 percent for those ages fifty-five to sixty-four). Labor-force participation of white men ages twenty-four and under actually increased over the past decade.

For blacks, the patterns are different. The labor-force participation of black men declined substantially, from 84 percent in 1940 to 67 percent in 1980. Labor-

force trends for older black men parallel those of white men of the same ages. But the decline in labor-force participation of young black men and, to a lesser extent, prime-age black men has occurred, while the participation of comparable white men has either increased or remained stable.

Economic trends for black men, especially young black men, have been unfavorable since the end of World War II. While the status of young blacks who are employed has improved with the percentage of white-collar workers among all black male workers, rising from 5 percent in 1940 to 27 percent in 1983, the proportion of black men who are employed has dropped from 80 percent in 1930 to 56 percent in 1983. Unemployment rose sharply for black male teenagers during the 1950s and remained high during the prosperous 1960s; similarly, unemployment rates for black men twenty to twenty-four years of age rose sharply during the mid-1970s and have remained high. In 1979, when the overall unemployment rate had declined to 5.8 percent, the rate for black male teenagers was 34.1 percent. In addition, while blacks have historically had higher labor-force participation levels, by the 1970s labor-force participation of black men had fallen below that of white men for all age-groups, with particularly steep declines for those ages twenty-four and younger. . . .

The adverse effects of unemployment and other economic problems of family stability are well established in the literature. Studies of family life during the Great Depression document the deterioration of marriage and family life following unemployment. More recent research, based on longitudinal data sets such as the PSID and the National Longitudinal Study or on aggregate data, shows consistently that unemployment is related to marital instability and the incidence of female-headed families. Indicators of economic status such as wage rates, income, or occupational status may also be related to marital instability or female headedness, although the evidence is not as consistent. For instance, while Cutright's analysis of 1960 census data indicates that divorce and separation rates are higher among lower-income families, Sawhill et al. find that unemployment, fluctuations in income, and lack of assets are associated with higher separation rates, but that the level of the husband's earnings has an effect only among low-income black families. However, Cohen reports that when the husband's age is controlled, the higher

Table 1.1

Employment Growth by Region

	Time Period	
Region	1950–77	1970–77
Northwest		
New England	44.6	6.3
Middle Atlantic	28.4	= 1.1
North Central		
East North Central	52.8	8.5
West North Central	71.8	15.6
South		
South Atlantic[a]	128.1	20.1
East South Central	107.5	21.9
West South Central	133.0	29.8
West		
Mountain	185.5	36.8
Pacific	155.0	21.0
U.S. Total	70.3	8.6

[a]Between 1970 and 1977, all southern states experienced job growth of at least 10 percent while the District of Columbia had a loss of 16.1 percent.

From Bernhard L. Weinstein and Robert E. Firestine, *Regional Growth and Decline in the United States: The Rise of the Sunbelt and the Decline of the Northeast.* Copyright © 1978 by Praeger Publishers. Reprinted by permission of Greenwood Publishing Group, Inc., Westport, CT.

the husband's earnings, the less likely both black and white couples are to divorce.

Nonetheless, the weight of the evidence on the relationship between the employment status of men, and family life and married life suggests that the increasing rate of joblessness among black men merits serious consideration as a major underlying factor in the rise of black single mothers and female-headed households. Moreover, when the factor of joblessness is combined with high black-male mortality and incarceration rates, the proportion of black men in stable economic situations is even lower than that conveyed in the current unemployment and labor-force figures. . . .

[Wilson discusses what he calls the "male marriageable pool index" (MMPI), which he defines as "the rates of employed civilian men to women of the same race and age-group." He presents data which, he contends, indicate a "sharp decline," beginning in the 1960s, in the nonwhite MMPI among males aged sixteen to twenty-four, "which is even more startling when compared with the rising ratios for white men."—Eds.] Clearly, what our "male marriageable pool index" reveals is a long-term decline in the proportion of black men, and particularly young black men, who are in a position to support a family. . . .

CHANGING ECONOMIC ORGANIZATION AND BLACK MALE JOBLESSNESS

If we have good reason to believe that black male joblessness is strongly related to changes in black family structure, it is also reasonable to hypothesize that the rapid contraction of the black "male marriageable pool" is related to basic changes in economic organization that have occurred in recent decades. The shift in economic activity from goods production to services has been associated with changes in the location of production: first, an interregional movement of industry from the North to the South and West; and second and more important, a movement of certain industries away from the older central cities where blacks are concentrated.

We have shown that the ratio of employed black men per one hundred black women of the same age decreased most rapidly in the two northern regions. As table 1.1 reveals, these areas have experienced substantially less employment growth than the rest of the country. Moreover, these trends are concentrated in sectors where "employment conditions typically do not require substantial education: manufacturing, retail, and wholesale trade." Between 1970 and 1980, for example, 701,700 manufacturing jobs were lost from the economies of these regions.

Data on the decrease in manufacturing, wholesale, and retail employment by region, however, do not reveal another pattern that appears especially relevant to the drop in the black MMPI ratios across the country: the decline of these jobs in the nation's largest cities, where blacks are heavily concentrated. Between 1947 and 1972, the central cities of the thirty-three most populous metropolitan areas (according to 1970 figures) lost 880,000 manufacturing jobs, while manufacturing employment in their suburbs grew by 2.5 million. The same cities lost 867,000 jobs in retail and wholesale trade at the same time that their suburbs gained millions of such positions. While the black populations of these central cities were growing substantially, white and middle-class residents migrated to the suburbs. Between 1950 and 1980, populations in these central cities lost more than 9 million whites and added more than 5 million blacks, many of them from the rural South.

The decline in demand for the designated types of unskilled labor has been most severe in the older central cities of the North. The four largest (New York, Chicago, Philadelphia, and Detroit), which in 1982 accounted for more than one-quarter of the nation's central-city poor, lost more than a million jobs in manufacturing, wholesale, and retail enterprises between 1967 and 1976 alone, at the same time that their populations were rapidly becoming minority dominant. By 1980, blacks and Hispanics accounted for virtually half of New York City's population, 57 percent of Chicago's, 67 percent of Detroit's, and 43 percent of Philadelphia's. The major portion of this minority population, especially in the latter two cities, is black.

The decline in blue-collar employment in the central city has been partly offset by expansion in "knowledge-intensive" fields such as advertising, finance, brokering, consulting, accounting, and law. For example, between 1953 and 1984 New York City lost about 600,000 jobs in manufacturing but gained nearly 700,000 jobs in white-collar service industries; Philadelphia lost 280,000 jobs in manufacturing but added 178,000 jobs in white-collar service industries; Baltimore lost 75,000 jobs in manufacturing but gained 84,000 jobs in white-collar service industries; and St. Louis lost 127,000 jobs in manufacturing but added 51,000 jobs in white-collar service industries.

However, the research on the decline of entry-level jobs in the inner city . . . provides more direct evidence that these demographic and employment trends have produced a serious mismatch between the skills of inner-city blacks and the opportunities available to them. As pointed out earlier, substantial job losses have occurred in the very industries in which urban minorities have the greatest access, and substantial employment gains have occurred in the higher-education-requisite industries that are beyond the reach of most minority workers. If one examines recent data presented by Kasarda on central-city educational attainment by race, the extent to which inner-city blacks are poorly matched for these employment trends is readily apparent. Trichotomizing attainment into less than high school, high school completion only, and some college, Kasarda finds that whereas a plurality of central-city white men (ages sixteen to sixty-four) have attended at least some college, the modal category among black men is less than high school for all regions of the country except the West. "This mismatch is one major reason why both unemployment rates and labor-force dropout rates among central city blacks are much higher than those of central city white residents," states Kasarda, "and why black unemployment rates have not responded well to economic recovery in many northern cities."

However, Kasarda's measure of "lower education requisite" jobs and "higher education requisite" jobs does not address the question of the actual relevance of levels of education to real job performance. Many jobs identified as "higher education" jobs because of the average level of education of the workforce may not really require "higher education" training. For example, a number of people have observed that the new high technology is "user friendly" and can be operated in most cases by people who have mastered the "3Rs." Nonetheless, if jobs in the high growth industry depend on a mastery of the 3Rs, and if employers tend to associate such skills with higher levels of formal education, then they will tend to favor those with more, not less, formal education, thereby institutionalizing "job requirements." Moreover, many inner-city minorities face an additional problem when access to jobs is increasingly based on education criteria. Samuel Bowles and Herbert Gintis, in a provocative study of the history of education in the United States, have argued that consignment to inner-city schools helps guarantee the future economic subordinancy of minority students. More specifically, inner-city schools train minority youth so that they feel and appear capable of only performing jobs in the low wage sector. Citing a recent study of disadvantaged workers which indicated that appearance was between two and three times as important to potential employees as previous work experience, high school diplomas or test scores, Bowles and Gintis contend that students in ghetto schools are not encouraged to develop the levels of self-esteem or the styles of presentation which employers perceive as evidence of capacity or ability. Secondly, schools adopt patterns of socialization which reflect the background and/or future social position of their students. Those schools with a high concentration of poor and minorities have radically different internal environments, methods of teaching and attitudes toward students than predominantly white, upper middle class suburban schools. Bowles and Gintis state that:

> Blacks and minorities are concentrated in schools whose repressive, arbitrary, generally chaotic internal order, coer-

cive authority structures and minimal possibilities for advancement mirror the characteristics of inferior job situations. Similarly, predominantly working-class schools tend to emphasize behavioral control and rule following, while schools in well-to-do suburbs employ relatively open systems that favor greater student participation, less direct supervision, more electives and in general a value system stressing internalized standards of control.

If the characteristics of inferior job situations are mirrored in the internal order of ghetto schools, then the transformation of the urban economy from jobs perceived to require lower education to those perceived to require higher education or the mastery of the 3Rs is even more problematic for inner-city residents.

The change in the MMPI of younger black men presents a particular problem of interpretation. Although the overall decline in the proportion of black marriageable men in the South is not nearly so great as that in the northern regions, the shrinkage in the "male marriageable pool" for ages sixteen to twenty-four is actually greater there than in the North. In a recent study of the decline in black teenage employment from 1950 to 1970, Cogan argues that "the decline in the demand for low-skilled agricultural labor" was "the driving force behind the sizable reductions in the aggregate black teenage employment ratio during the period 1950-1970." If the primary source of employment for black teenagers in the South was drastically reduced by mechanization of agricultural production, it is reasonable to assume that many southern black men aged twenty to twenty-four suffered the same fate.

The substantial decline in the MMPI for black youth outside the South cannot be explained by the mechanization of agriculture, since the vast majority of nonsouthern blacks are living in metropolitan areas. However, the changes in economic organization affecting central cities, where more than three-quarters of all metropolitan blacks reside, are likely to have had a significant impact on the employment of black youth. Research has shown that youth employment problems are concentrated among the less educated as well as among blacks. In turn, central-city and poverty-area or ghetto residence has also been found to depress youth employment. These findings are consistent with the implications of Kasarda's research: shifts in employment mix should have their greatest impact on low-skilled workers in the central cities. Finally, evidence suggests that these declines in employment of low-skilled workers accelerated during the 1970s. Decennial employment ratios of black youth show that while joblessness among southern youth increased more rapidly during the 1960s than the 1970s, among northern youth the increase was more substantial over the latter decade. The timing of these two trends is consistent with the interpretation that changes in economic organization have had an impact on the employment of black youth.

CONCLUSION: RACE, FAMILY STRUCTURE, AND PUBLIC POLICY

We have attempted . . . to show that Murray's thesis in *Losing Ground* does not begin to come to grips with the complex problem of the rising number of female-headed families and out-of-wedlock births because he overemphasizes the role of liberal welfare policies and plays down what is perhaps the most important factor in the rise of black female-headed families—the extraordinary rise in black male joblessness. We have shown here that the decline in the incidence of intact marriages among blacks is associated with the declining economic status of black men. . . . [W]e demonstrated that black women nationally, especially young black women, are facing a shrinking pool of "marriageable" (i.e., employed) black men. This finding supports the hypothesis that the sharp rise of black female-headed families is directly related to increasing black male joblessness. Regional longitudinal data on female headship and the "male marriageable pool" were presented in this chapter to provide a further test of this hypothesis.

The trends in the MMPI reveal that whereas changes in the ratios of employed men to women among whites have been minimal for all age categories and in all regions of the country from 1960 to 1980, the ratios for blacks have declined substantially in all regions except the West. On the basis of these trends, we expected the most rapid growth in the number of black female heads to be in the northern regions, followed by the South and the West. The data conformed to our expectations, except for the larger-than-expected increase in black female-headed families in the West. Our explanation of this latter finding focused on the pattern of selective black migration to the West. The smaller proportions of white women heading families varied little by region.

The MMPI can be constructed only on the basis of aggregate racial data, rather than by race and income class as we would prefer. Nevertheless, as we have shown, the rise of the female-headed family has had its major impact on the impoverished. Work cited [earlier] indicated that black female-headed families were poorer, more permanent, and more welfare-dependent than families led by white women. In a similar vein, recent work by Bane with the Michigan Panel Study of Income Dynamics showed that unlike whites, the majority of blacks experiencing a transition into a female-headed family were poor afterward. Around two-thirds of those were in poverty, however, even *before* experiencing such a transition. Such findings increase our confidence that the incidence of female-headed families among blacks, more so than among whites, is related to conditions of economic deprivation.

We conclude, therefore, that the problem of joblessness should be a top-priority item in any public policy discussion focusing on enhancing the status of families. Unfortunately, in recent years joblessness has received very little attention among policymakers concerned about the plight of families in the United States. Even the perceptive Daniel Patrick Moynihan, an early advocate of this point of view, failed to emphasize this issue in his Harvard University Godkin lectures on the family and nation. Instead he chose to focus on measures to aid poor families, such as establishing a national benefit standard for child welfare aid, indexing benefits to inflation, and enlarging personal and dependent tax exemptions. These are all constructive suggestions, but they need to be included in a more comprehensive reform program designed to create a tight labor market that enhances the employment opportunities of both poor men and women. Such an undertaking will, we believe, do far more in the long run to enhance the stability and reduce the welfare dependency of low-income black families than will cutting the vital provisions of the welfare state.

We emphasize the need to create employment opportunities for both sexes, even though our focus in this chapter is on the problem of black male joblessness. To identify black male joblessness as a major source of black family disintegration is not to suggest that policymakers should ignore the problems of joblessness and poverty among current female heads of families. Rather we underline the point that the tragic decline of intact black households cannot be divorced from the equally tragic decline in the black male "marriageable pool" in any serious policy deliberations on the plight of poor American families.

POSTSCRIPT

Does Our Welfare System Hurt the Poor?

Is the welfare problem insoluble? Murray and Wilson agree that appropriate policies can reduce poverty and that there are no easy solutions. In other respects they could not be farther apart. Where Murray concludes that the system has failed and should be abandoned, Wilson insists that the system has failed to identify and deal with the fundamental causes of poverty.

Charles Murray, in *In Pursuit of Happiness and Good Government* (Simon & Schuster, 1988), holds that social problems that persist in the face of massive government programs may yield to solutions that rely on the natural responses of individuals. What is wrong with the welfare system is the system itself, according to Murray and other conservative critics, including the essayists in Paul M. Weyrich and Connaught Marshner, eds., *Future 21: Directions for America in the 21st Century* (Devon-Adair, 1984).

Nathan Glazer takes a somewhat different tack in *The Limits of Social Policy* (Harvard, 1988). Glazer believes that a distrust of government and a greater reliance on nonpublic resources bar a fully developed national system of social welfare policy.

Liberals maintain that Americans have underfunded and undermined the welfare system. Lisbeth B. Schorr, *Within Our Reach: Breaking the Cycle of Disadvantage* (Anchor Press, 1988), concludes that social programs for poor children work, and, if pursued on a larger scale, they can lead to decline in poverty.

The position of Sar A. Levitan and Clifford M. Johnson, *Beyond the Safety Net: Reviving the Promise of Opportunity in America* (Ballinger, 1984), is that more needs to be done to enable poor people to live more productive lives. Leslie W. Dunbar, *The Common Interest: How Our Social Welfare Policies Don't Work, and What We Can Do About Them* (Pantheon, 1988), concludes that entitlement cutbacks neither save money nor stimulate enterprise, but make poverty deeper and more widespread.

Daniel T. Ellwood, *Poor Support: Poverty in the American Family* (Basic Books, 1988), rejects both conventional welfare, because it treats the symptoms and not the causes of poverty, and antiwelfare conservatism, because it lacks compassion. Ellwood proposes employment and support systems that are designed to be transitional in ending poverty and the need for welfare support.

One of the tough questions that Americans may eventually have to ask themselves is whether or not there is now in America a permanent class of dependent people who lack both the skills and aspirations to support themselves. There are many more who have not lost the desire to work, only the opportunity. The challenge is to provide the opportunity—and, somehow, to stimulate the will to work.

ISSUE 16

Should Abortion Be Considered a Basic Right?

YES: Mary Gordon, "A Moral Choice," *The Atlantic* (April 1990)

NO: John J. O'Connor, from "Abortion: Questions and Answers," *Catholic New York* (June 14, 1990)

ISSUE SUMMARY

YES: Writer Mary Gordon believes that having an abortion is a moral choice women are capable of making, involving such considerations as poverty, wanting a child, and the woman's age and circumstances.

NO: Cardinal O'Connor maintains that a fetus is an unborn child and that, whatever convictions or circumstances impel a woman to have an abortion, it amounts to taking a human life and is therefore unacceptable.

At one time, laws forbade even the publication of information regarding contraception and abortion, and it was not until 1965 that the Supreme Court declared that the law could not prohibit the dispensing of contraceptive devices to married men and women. In 1973 the Supreme Court made its landmark ruling on abortion, which has shaped the subsequent political debates. In *Roe v. Wade* the Court divided the normal pregnancy into three trimesters and ruled as follows. During the first trimester of pregnancy, women have a constitutionally protected right to secure an abortion; during the second trimester of pregnancy (that is, the fourth through sixth months), only restrictions reasonably related to a woman's health can be imposed upon her right to secure an abortion. During the final three months of pregnancy, the Court ruled that the state may prohibit abortion—but even then the abortion must be allowed if the physician believes the procedure is indicated to preserve the mother's life or health. This includes psychological as well as physical well-being.

Although illegal abortions had been widely performed before state laws forbidding abortion were invalidated, since 1973 the number of abortions has increased rapidly—current estimates are one and one-half million each year. If current trends continue, four out of every ten females will become pregnant between the ages of fourteen and twenty, and at least half of these pregnancies will be terminated by abortion.

Anti-abortion forces have mounted a political campaign for the "right to life." Federal funding for Medicaid abortions has been cut off, and federal courts have affirmed the right of Congress not to pay for abortions. Pro-abortion groups, proclaiming the "right to choose," have charged that this and similar action at the state level discriminates against poor women because it does not inhibit the ability of women who are able to pay for abortions to obtain them. Efforts to adopt a constitutional amendment or federal law barring abortion have failed, but anti-abortion forces have influenced legislation in many states.

Can legislatures and courts establish the existence of a scientific fact? Opponents of abortion believe that it is a fact that life begins at conception and that the law must therefore uphold and enforce this concept. They argue that the human fetus is a live human being, and they note all the familiar signs of life displayed by the fetus: a beating heart, brain waves, thumb sucking, and so on. Those who defend abortion maintain that human life does not begin before the development of specifically human characteristics and possibly not until the birth of a child. As Justice Harry Blackmun put it in 1973: "There has always been strong support for the view that life does not begin until live birth."

Anti-abortion forces sought a court case that might lead to the overturning of *Roe v. Wade*. Pro-abortion forces rallied to oppose new state laws limiting or prohibiting abortion. In 1989, with four new justices, the Supreme Court, in *Webster v. Reproductive Health Services* (1989), pulled back from its pro-abortion stance. In a 5 to 4 decision, the Court upheld a Missouri law that banned abortions in public hospitals, and abortions that were performed by public employees (except to save a woman's life). The law also required that tests be performed on any fetus more than twenty weeks old to determine its viability, that is, its ability to survive outside the womb.

While many Americans are uncompromising on this issue, believing either that abortion is an unqualified right or that all abortion is murder, others have taken a more modulated position. Many appear to support abortion in the case of pregnancies that result from rape or incest, or where the health of the mother may be gravely affected by childbirth.

Whatever the opinion of the public, the Congress, and state legislatures, the Supreme Court is bound once again to decide the issue after hearing the moral, constitutional, scientific, and political arguments for and against abortion. Whatever the Court's decision, it will not resolve the controversy.

In the following selections, Mary Gordon argues the morality of a woman's decision to have an abortion and Cardinal O'Connor asserts the immorality of such a decision.

YES   Mary Gordon

A MORAL CHOICE

I am having lunch with six women. What is unusual is that four of them are in their seventies, two of them widowed, the other two living with husbands beside whom they've lived for decades. All of them have had children. Had they been men, they would have published books and hung their paintings on the walls of important galleries. But they are women of a certain generation, and their lives were shaped around their families and personal relations. They are women you go to for help and support. We begin talking about the latest legislative act that makes abortion more difficult for poor women to obtain. An extraordinary thing happens. Each of them talks about the illegal abortions she had during her young womanhood. Not one of them was spared the experience. Any of them could have died on the table of whatever person (not a doctor in any case) she was forced to approach, in secrecy and in terror, to end a pregnancy that she felt would blight her life.

I mention this incident for two reasons: first as a reminder that all kinds of women have always had abortions; second because it is essential that we remember that an abortion is performed on a living woman who has a life in which a terminated pregnancy is only a small part. Morally speaking, the decision to have an abortion doesn't take place in a vacuum. It is connected to other choices that a woman makes in the course of an adult life.

Anti-choice propagandists paint pictures of women who choose to have abortions as types of moral callousness, selfishness, or irresponsibility. The woman choosing to abort is the dressed-for-success yuppie who gets rid of her baby so that she won't miss her Caribbean vacation or her chance for promotion. Or she is the feckless, promiscuous ghetto teenager who couldn't bring herself to just say no to sex. A third, purportedly kinder, gentler picture has recently begun to be drawn. The woman in the abortion clinic is there because she is misinformed about the nature of the world. She is having an abortion because society does not provide for mothers and their children, and she mistakenly thinks that another mouth to feed will be the ruin of her family, not understanding that the temporary truth of family unhappiness doesn't stack up beside the eternal verity that abortion is murder. Or she is the dupe of her husband or boyfriend, who talks her into having an abortion because a child will be a drag on his life-style. None of these pictures created by the anti-choice movement assumes that the decision to have an abortion is made responsibly, in the context of a morally lived life, by a free and responsible moral agent.

THE ONTOLOGY OF THE FETUS

How would a woman who habitually makes choices in moral terms come to the decision to have an abortion? The moral discussion of abortion centers on the issue of whether or not abortion is an act of murder. At first glance it would seem that the answer should follow directly upon two questions: Is the fetus human? and Is it alive? It would be absurd to deny that a fetus is alive or that it is human. What would our other options be—to say that it is inanimate or belongs to another species? But we habitually use the terms "human" and "live" to refer to parts of our body—"human hair," for example, or "live red-blood cells"—and we are clear in our understanding that the nature of these objects does not rank equally with an entire personal existence. It then seems important to consider whether the fetus, this alive human thing, is a *person*, to whom the term "murder" could sensibly be applied. How would anyone come to a decision about something so impalpable as personhood? Philosophers have struggled with the issue of personhood, but in language that is so abstract that it is unhelpful to ordinary people making decisions in the course of their lives. It might be more productive to begin thinking about the status of the fetus by examining the language and customs that

surround it. This approach will encourage us to focus on the choosing, acting woman, rather than the act of abortion—as if the act were performed by abstract forces without bodies, histories, attachments.

This focus on the acting woman is useful because a pregnant woman has an identifiable, consistent ontology, and a fetus takes on different ontological identities over time. But common sense, experience, and linguistic usage point clearly to the fact that we habitually consider, for example, a seven-week-old fetus to be different from a seven-month-old one. We can tell this by the way we respond to the involuntary loss of one as against the other. We have different language for the experience of the involuntary expulsion of the fetus from the womb depending upon the point of gestation at which the experience occurs. If it occurs early in the pregnancy, we call it a miscarriage; if late, we call it a stillbirth.

We would have an extreme reaction to the reversal of those terms. If a woman referred to a miscarriage at seven weeks as a stillbirth, we would be alarmed. It would shock our sense of propriety; it would make us uneasy; we would find it disturbing, misplaced—as we do when a bag lady sits down in a restaurant and starts shouting, or an octogenarian arrives at our door in a sailor suit. In short, we would suspect that the speaker was mad. Similarly, if a doctor or a nurse referred to the loss of a seven-month-old fetus as a miscarriage, we would be shocked by that person's insensitivity: could she or he not understand that a fetus that age is not what it was months before?

Our ritual and religious practices underscore the fact that we make distinctions among fetuses. If a woman took the bloody matter—indistinguishable from a heavy period—of an early miscarriage and insisted upon putting it in a tiny coffin and marking its grave, we would have serious concerns about her mental health. By the same token, we would feel squeamish about flushing a seven-month-old fetus down the toilet—something we would quite normally do with an early miscarriage. There are no prayers for the matter of a miscarriage, nor do we feel there should be. Even a Catholic priest would not baptize the issue of an early miscarriage.

The difficulties stem, of course, from the odd situation of a fetus's ontology: a complicated, differentiated, and nuanced response is required when we are dealing with an entity that changes over time. Yet we are in the habit of making distinctions like this. At one point we know that a child is no longer a child but an adult. That this question is vexed and problematic is clear from our difficulty in determining who is a juvenile offender and who is an adult criminal and at what age sexual intercourse ceases to be known as statutory rape. So at what point, if any, do we on the pro-choice side say that the developing fetus is a person, with rights equal to its mother's?

The anti-choice people have one advantage over us; their monolithic position gives them unity on this question. For myself, I am made uneasy by third-trimester abortions, which take place when the fetus could live outside the mother's body, but I also know that these are extremely rare and often performed on very young girls who have had difficulty comprehending the realities of pregnancy. It seems to me that the question of late abortions should be decided case by case, and that fixation on this issue is a deflection from what is most important: keeping early abortions, which are in the majority by far, safe and legal. I am also politically realistic enough to suspect that bills restricting late abortions are not good-faith attempts to make distinctions about the nature of fetal life. They are, rather, the cynical embodiments of the hope among anti-choice partisans that technology will be on their side and that medical science's ability to create situations in which younger fetuses are viable outside their mothers' bodies will increase dramatically in the next few years. Ironically, medical science will probably make the issue of abortion a minor one in the near future. The RU-486 pill, which can induce abortion early on, exists, and whether or not it is legally available (it is not on the market here, because of pressure from anti-choice groups), women will begin to obtain it. If abortion can occur through chemical rather than physical means, in the privacy of one's home, most people not directly involved will lose interest in it. As abortion is transformed from a public into a private issue, it will cease to be perceived as political; it will be called personal instead.

AN EQUIVOCAL GOOD

But because abortion will always deal with what it is to create and sustain life, it will always be a moral issue. And whether we like it or not, our moral thinking about abortion is rooted in the shifting soil of perception. In an age in which much of our perception is manipulated by media that specialize in the sound bite and the photo op, the anti-choice partisans have a twofold advantage over us on the pro-choice side. The pro-choice moral position is more complex, and the experience we defend is physically repellent to contemplate. None of us in the pro-choice movement would suggest that abortion is not a regrettable occurrence. Anti-choice proponents can offer pastel photographs of babies in buntings, their eyes peaceful in the camera's gaze. In answer, we can't offer the material of an early abortion, bloody, amorphous in a paper cup, to prove that what has just been removed from the woman's body is not a child, not in the same category of being as the adorable bundle in an adoptive mother's arms. It is not a pleasure to look at the physical evidence of abortion, and most of us don't get the opportunity to do so.

The theologian Daniel Maguire, uncomfortable with the fact that most theological arguments about the nature of abortion are made by men who have never been anywhere near an actual abortion, decided to visit a clinic and observe abortions being performed. He didn't find the experience easy, but he knew that before he could in good conscience make a moral judgment on abortion, he needed to experience through his senses what an aborted fetus is like: he needed to look at and touch the controversial entity. He held in his hand the bloody fetal stuff; the eight-week-old fetus fit in the palm of his hand, and it certainly bore no resemblance to either of his two children when he had held them moments after their birth. He knew at that point what women who have experienced early abortions and miscarriages know: that some event occurred, possibly even a dramatic one, but it was not the death of a child.

Because issues of pregnancy and birth are both physical and metaphorical, we must constantly step back and forth between ways of perceiving the world. When we speak of gestation, we are often talking in terms of potential, about events and objects to which we attach

our hopes, fears, dreams, and ideals. A mother can speak to the fetus in her uterus and name it; she and her mate may decorate a nursery according to their vision of the good life; they may choose for an embryo a college, a profession, a dwelling. But those of us who are trying to think morally about pregnancy and birth must remember that these feelings are our own projections onto what is in reality an inappropriate object. However charmed we may be by an expectant father's buying a little football for something inside his wife's belly, we shouldn't make public policy based on such actions, nor should we force others to live their lives conforming to our fantasies.

As a society, we are making decisions that pit the complicated future of a complex adult against the fate of a mass of cells lacking cortical development. The moral pressure should be on distinguishing the true from the false, the real suffering of living persons from our individual and often idiosyncratic dreams and fears. We must make decisions on abortion based on an understanding of how people really do live. We must be able to say that poverty is worse than not being poor, that having dignified and meaningful work is better than working in conditions of degradation, that raising a child one loves and has desired is better than raising a child in resentment and rage, that it is better for a twelve-year-old not to endure the trauma of having a child when she is herself a child.

When we put these ideas against the ideas of "child" or "baby," we seem to be making a horrifying choice of life-style over life. But in fact we are telling the truth of what it means to bear a child, and what the experience of abortion really is. This is extremely difficult, for the object of the discussion is hidden, changing, potential. We make our decisions on the basis of approximate and inadequate language, often on the basis of fantasies and fears. It will always be crucial to try to separate genuine moral concern from phobia, punitiveness, superstition, anxiety, a desperate search for certainty in an uncertain world.

One of the certainties that is removed if we accept the consequences of the pro-choice position is the belief that the birth of a child is an unequivocal good. In real life we act knowing that the birth of a child is not always a good thing: people are sometimes depressed, angry, rejecting, at the birth of a child. But this is a difficult truth to tell; we don't like to say it, and one of the fears preyed on by anti-choice proponents is that if we cannot look at the birth of a child as an unequivocal good, then there is nothing to look toward. The desire for security of the imagination, for typological fixity, particularly in the area of "the good," is an understandable desire. It must seem to some anti-choice people that we on the pro-choice side are not only murdering innocent children but also murdering hope. Those of us who have experienced the birth of a desired child and felt the joy of that moment can be tempted into believing that it was the physical experience of the birth itself that was the joy. But it is crucial to remember that the birth of a child itself is a neutral occurrence emotionally: the charge it takes on is invested in it by the people experiencing or observing it.

THE FEAR OF SEXUAL AUTONOMY

These uncertainties can lead to another set of fears, not only about abortion but about its implications. Many anti-choice people fear that to support abortion is to cast one's lot with the cold and technological rather than with the warm and natural, to head down the slippery slope toward a brave new world where handicapped children are left on mountains to starve and the old are put out in the snow. But if we look at the history of abortion, we don't see the embodiment of what the anti-choice proponents fear. On the contrary, excepting the grotesque counterexample of the People's Republic of China (which practices forced abortion), there seems to be a real link between repressive anti-abortion stances and repressive governments. Abortion was banned in Fascist Italy and Nazi Germany; it is illegal in South Africa and in Chile. It is paid for by the governments of Denmark, England, and the Netherlands, which have national health and welfare systems that foster the health and well-being of mothers, children, the old, and the handicapped.

Advocates of outlawing abortion often refer to women seeking abortion as self-indulgent and materialistic. In fact these accusations mask a discomfort with female sexuality, sexual pleasure, and sexual autonomy. It is possible for a woman to have a sexual life unriddled by fear only if she can be confident that she need not pay for a failure of technology or judgment (and who among us has never once been swept away in the heat of a sexual moment?) by taking upon herself the crushing burden of unchosen motherhood.

It is no accident, therefore, that the increased appeal of measures to restrict maternal conduct during pregnancy—and a new focus on the physical autonomy of the pregnant woman—have come into public discourse at precisely the time when women are achieving unprecedented levels of economic and political autonomy. What has surprised me is that some of this new anti-autonomy talk comes to us from the left. An example of this new discourse is an article by Christopher Hitchens that appeared in *The Nation* last April, in which the author asserts his discomfort with abortion. Hitchens's tone is impeccably British: arch, light, we're men of the left.

> Anyone who has ever seen a sonogram or has spent even an hour with a textbook on embryology knows that the emotions are not the deciding factor. In order to terminate a pregnancy, you have to still a heartbeat, switch off a developing brain, and whatever the method, break some bones and rupture some organs. As to whether this involves pain on the "Silent Scream" scale, I have no idea. The "right to life" leadership, again, has cheapened everything it touches.

"It is a pity," Hitchens goes on to say, "that . . . the majority of feminists and their allies have stuck to the dead ground of 'Me Decade' possessive individualism, an ideology that has more in common than it admits with the prehistoric right, which it claims to oppose but has in fact encouraged." Hitchens proposes, as an alternative, a program of social reform that would make contraception free and support a national adoption service. In his opinion, it would seem, women have abortions for only two reasons: because they are selfish or because they are poor. If the state will take care of the economic problems and the bureaucratic messiness around adoption, it remains only for the possessive individualists to get their act together and walk with their babies into the communal utopia of the future. Hitchens would allow victims of rape or incest to have free

abortions, on the grounds that since they didn't choose to have sex, the women should not be forced to have the babies. This would seem to put the issue of volition in a wrong and telling place. To Hitchens's mind, it would appear, if a woman chooses to have sex, she can't choose whether or not to have a baby. The implications of this are clear. If a woman is consciously and volitionally sexual, she should be prepared to take her medicine. And what medicine must the consciously sexual male take? Does Hitchens really believe, or want us to believe, that every male who has unintentionally impregnated a woman will be involved in the lifelong responsibility for the upbringing of the engendered child? Can he honestly say that he has observed this behavior—or, indeed, would want to see it observed—in the world in which he lives?

REAL CHOICES

It is essential for a moral decision about abortion to be made in an atmosphere of open, critical thinking. We on the pro-choice side must accept that there are indeed anti-choice activists who take their position in good faith. I believe, however, that they are people for whom childbirth is an emotionally overladen topic, people who are susceptible to unclear thinking because of their unrealistic hopes and fears. It is important for us in the pro-choice movement to be open in discussing those areas involving abortion which are nebulous and unclear. But we must not forget that there are some things that we know to be undeniably true. There are some undeniable bad consequences of a woman's being forced to bear a child against her will. First is the trauma of going through a pregnancy and giving birth to a child who is not desired, a trauma more long-lasting than that experienced by some (only some) women who experience an early abortion. The grief of giving up a child at its birth—and at nine months it is a child whom one has felt move inside one's body—is underestimated both by anti-choice partisans and by those for whom access to adoptable children is important. This grief should not be forced on any woman—or, indeed, encouraged by public policy.

We must be realistic about the impact on society of millions of unwanted children in an overpopulated world. Most of the time, human beings have sex not because they want to make babies. Yet throughout history sex has resulted in unwanted pregnancies. And women have always aborted. One thing that is not hidden, mysterious, or debatable is that making abortion illegal will result in the deaths of women, as it has always done. Is our historical memory so short that none of us remember aunts, sisters, friends, or mothers who were killed or rendered sterile by septic abortions? Does no one in the anti-choice movement remember stories or actual experiences of midnight drives to filthy rooms from which aborted women were sent out, bleeding, to their fate? Can anyone genuinely say that it would be a moral good for us as a society to return to those conditions?

Thinking about abortion, then, forces us to take moral positions as adults who understand the complexities of the world and the realities of human suffering, to make decisions based on how people actually live and choose, and not on our fears, prejudices, and anxieties about sex and society, life and death.

NO

John J. O'Connor

ABORTION: QUESTIONS AND ANSWERS

Over the course of the years I have been asked many questions about life and abortion by many well-meaning people. Today I still find that many good people are confused. They really believe they are doing the right thing—or, at least, the best thing—when they support, or encourage, an abortion. Such is certainly the case with some parents who love a daughter and, as they put it, "don't want to see her life ruined by an unintended pregnancy." I believe the same is true of a number of social workers and other advisers of the young, who believe that in promoting abortions they are performing a truly humane service, to the mothers of the unborn, to unborn babies whose lives they feel will not be happy (especially if they will be poor), and to society at large.

I received a letter recently, for example, from a set of anguished parents. Their talented young daughter is all set for college, but she has become pregnant. They tell me they are encouraging her to have an abortion because they don't want to see her career ruined. They say they are afraid abortion is a "sin," but that it would be a worse sin if their daughter couldn't go to college, "just because she made a mistake and got pregnant." I know many people feel that way.

Then there are those who honestly believe it is only "fair" to permit pregnant girls or women to decide for themselves whether to carry or to abort a baby. They say: "A woman should have control over her own body. Nobody has the right to invade her privacy." They see free choice in all things as an essential characteristic of the American way of life, and regardless of how they, themselves, see abortion, they do not feel they have the right "to impose their beliefs on others."

There are at least three other kinds of people who consider abortion acceptable. There are those who believe that a baby in the womb is not really fully human, that only with birth does the baby achieve this status. Others believe that because the law permits abortion, it must be morally acceptable. Then there are those—and I believe they are many—who simply don't think about the subject at all. They don't see it as a serious issue. It has never personally touched their lives. Or perhaps they deliberately refuse to think about it because they would only become further confused.

While one finds a certain number of Catholics holding various of these positions, it's probably necessary to add another category altogether for those who argue that they are good Catholics, but believe the Church is wrong in its position on abortion, or that the Church has no right to "dictate" to them on this matter. I would distinguish this group from those Catholics who simply don't know or don't understand what the Church teaches or why.

One can be compassionate and understanding about all these positions, but sadly nothing changes the objective reality: abortion kills babies in their mothers' wombs. It pains me to say that, as I know it pains all people of good will, but it is the tragic reality. And there is another tragic reality that has nothing whatever to do with compassion, and that is that abortion is big business, netting hundreds of millions of dollars for abortionists.

I know that many are offended by the use of the word "killing." Actually, it is the word used in a famous editorial published in 1970 in the California Medical Association Journal:

"Since the old ethic has not yet been fully displaced it has been *necessary to separate the idea of abortion from the idea of killing*, which continues to be socially abhorrent. *The result has been a curious avoidance of the scientific fact which everyone really knows, that human life begins at conception and is continuous whether intra- or extra-uterine until death.* The very considerable semantic gymnastics which are required to rationalize abortion as anything but taking a human life would be

ludicrous if they were not often put forth under socially impeccable auspices. It is suggested that this schizophrenic sort of subterfuge is necessary because while a new ethic is being accepted the old one has not yet been rejected." (Emphasis added.) (From California Medicine, 113:67, 1970.)

This editorial was not written to oppose abortion. It was simply an exceptionally frank warning to doctors that they had better adopt the new ethic and gear up for the brave new world of abortion ahead of them. As the editorial pointed out, some real twisting of words would be required to make people forget that abortion is the taking of human life. In other words, they would have to come up with another word for "killing," if they were ever to make abortion socially acceptable. But a change in words, unfortunately, does not change the reality.

In any event, it seems to me time to list some of the questions I have been asked about abortion, and to try to suggest some answers, recognizing that some may require lengthier and more complicated answers than space permits, and that there are many other questions that might be asked. Following that, I would like to propose some ways of helping to restore a sense of sacredness about the life of the unborn and, indeed, of all human life.

What Is Abortion?
This can sound like a foolish question. But it is my experience that there are a number of young people who undergo abortions and do not understand what is happening to them. As a matter of fact, doctors who perform abortions generally prevent the woman or girl from seeing what is happening, and pro-abortion organizations have consistently resisted

any legislation which would require that a young girl be told what an abortion is, or be required to wait even 24 hours before having an abortion.

The important thing, perhaps, is to emphasize what abortion is not. Abortion is not merely the removal of some tissue from a woman's body. Abortion is not the removal of a living "thing" that would become human if it were allowed to remain inside the woman's body. Abortion is the destruction of an unborn baby.

A new human life begins as soon as the egg has been fertilized. Science reveals without question that once the egg is fertilized every identifying characteristic of a brand-new human being is present, even the color of the eyes and the hair, the sex and everything else. Pregnancy is the period for this new human life to mature, not to "become human"— it already is. This is why the Church considers abortion the killing of a human being, and why the Second Vatican Council called it an "unspeakable crime."

The World Medical Association adopted in September 1948 the Declaration of Geneva: "I will maintain the utmost respect for human life, from the time of conception; even under threat I will not use my medical knowledge contrary to the laws of humanity." In October 1969 the International Code of Medical Ethics stated: "A doctor must always bear in mind the importance of preserving human life from the time of conception until death." Again in 1970 the World Medical Association reaffirmed its position by way of the Declaration of Oslo: "The first moral imposed upon the doctor is respect for human life as expressed in the Declaration of Geneva: 'I will maintain the utmost respect for human life from the first moment of conception.' "

In 1974 the Declaration on Procured Abortion (by the Congregation for the Doctrine of the Faith) stated: "Respect for human life is called for from the time that the process of generation begins. From the time that the ovum is fertilized, a life is begun which is neither that of the father nor of the mother; it is rather the life of a new human being with its own growth. It would never be made human if it were not human already . . ." This declaration was ratified by Pope Paul VI, who confirmed it and ordered it to be promulgated.

When the Church uses the phrase "procured abortion" it means, in nontechnical terms, deliberately terminating a pregnancy at any stage before the child in the womb can live outside the womb.

Don't the Majority of Americans Support Abortion?

Based on my experience, the majority of Americans do not support abortion on demand. For example, most Americans would not support abortion in cases where a woman does not want a baby of a particular sex. The majority of those who support abortion seem to limit that support to cases of rape, incest or when the life of the mother is in jeopardy.

Certainly there are polls which seem to suggest that the majority do favor abortion and abortion funding. Many who feel that if they are a minority they must be wrong can feel intimidated by these findings. We must remember, however, that the timing of a poll, the kinds of questions asked, who asks the questions, and who is asked, all influence the results. This has been demonstrated frequently in relation to polls on abortion.

Polls, however, whatever the results, do not determine what is morally right or wrong. If abortion is the taking of innocent life, it is wrong, no matter what the polls might say, or how many people might vote for it.

Despite some recent reports of psychological studies, I personally receive letters from all over the United States from women who have suffered the pain of an abortion, or who, in the moments shortly before having an abortion, came to see that abortion is the killing of a baby. These letters are deeply moving, and most end by encouraging me to continue to speak out, and to do whatever I can to help restore a sense of sacredness of the child in the womb.

Some feel that the right to be born is dependent on being *wanted*. They suggest that if a mother does not want her baby, the baby will be deprived of love, care and nurturing and may even be subject to abuse. Yet, how many unplanned children have been born to parents who initially did not want them, but whose attitudes changed completely to total acceptance and love? How many unwanted children have made enormous contributions to the world, as musicians, writers, doctors, entertainers, teachers, parents, or in other capacities?

Is an unborn baby to be denied the right to life because it is not wanted? Candidates for political office spend much campaigning time and often a great deal of money in trying to convince voters who *don't* want them to vote for them. Is an unborn baby to be denied even the opportunity to have someone plead with a mother to let the baby live, wanted or not? Is the unwanted baby to be denied the opportunity given to millions of refugees who have been admitted to the United States?

Mother Teresa of Calcutta is world famous for her concern for the poor, the abandoned, the dying, the homeless, the institutionalized, the forgotten. Far from seeing a solution to the problems of such in abortion, however, she startled the world by her address when she received the Nobel Peace Prize in 1979. One of the most important statements she made is, "Today the greatest destroyer of peace is abortion."

For Almighty God there is no such thing as an "unwanted baby." Every one is made in His image and likeness and is uniquely part of the Divine Plan. If there is a woman *anywhere* who does not "want" her baby, I plead with her to nevertheless let that baby live. A great number of people want that baby as does the Church—we love that baby from the moment it is conceived.

> For it was you who created my being,
> Knit me together in my mother's womb,
> I thank you for the wonder of my being,
> for the wonders of all your creation.
> *(Psalm 139)*

Why Do People in the Pro-Life Movement Want to Change the Law?

Some people argue that changing laws will not eliminate abortions. It is certainly true that a change of heart is more important than a change of law. What is forgotten, however, is that the law is the great teacher. Children grow up believing that if a practice is *legal*, it must be *moral*. Adults who live in a society in which what was illegal and believed to be immoral is suddenly declared legal, soon grow accustomed to the new law, and take the "new morality" for granted. In fact, many people seem to fear that if they don't support the new law and the "new morality" it has introduced, they will be considered undemocratic and "unAmerican."

It is amazing, for example, how smoking habits have been turned around.

With the deluge of media advertising and the strict legal limitations put on smoking in places like New York City, many people now even feel embarrassed to smoke in public. Suddenly, with new laws in jurisdiction after jurisdiction, smoking is seen as less acceptable than ever before—actually immoral and irresponsible in the eyes of many. Now a law is being proposed that a state should divest itself of all investments in tobacco companies. There is no question: law and changes in law constitute a mighty force if there is a determination to enforce it.

I have no doubt that a change in the law would go a long way toward changing the attitude of Americans toward the rights of the unborn, at least over the long haul. It is effective regarding virtually every other issue. For example, in 1966 at the White House Conference on Civil Rights, then Solicitor General of the United States Mr. Thurgood Marshall (now a Justice of the Supreme Court) had this to say about the effect a change in law can bring about:

"Of course law—whether embodied in acts of Congress or judicial decision—is, in some measure, a response to national opinion, and, of course, non-legal, even illegal events, can significantly affect the development of the law. But I submit that the history of the Negro demonstrates the importance of getting rid of hostile laws and seeking the security of new friendly laws . . .

"Provided there is a determination to enforce it, law can change things for the better. There's very little truth in the old refrain that one cannot legislate equality. Laws not only provide concrete benefit, they can even change the hearts of men, some men anyway, for good or evil . . . The simple fact is that most people will obey the law and some, at least, will be converted by it."

There are those who argue that we can not legislate morality, and that the answer to abortion does not lie in the law. The reality is that we do legislate *behavior* every day. Our entire society is structured by law. We legislate against going through red lights, smoking in airplanes and restaurants, selling heroin, committing murder, burning down peoples' homes, stealing, child abuse, slavery and a thousand other acts that would deprive other people of their rights. And this is precisely the key: law is intended to protect us from one another regardless of private and personal moral or religious beliefs. The law does not ask me if I personally believe stealing to be moral or immoral. The law does not ask me if my religion encourages me to burn down homes. As far as the law is concerned, the distinction between private and public morality is quite clear. Basically, when I violate other peoples' rights, I am involved in a matter of public morality, subject to penalty under law.

Is it outlandish to think that laws against abortion might have *some* protective effect? It is obvious that law is not the entire answer to abortion. Nor is it the entire answer to theft, arson, child abuse, or shooting police officers. Everybody knows that. But who would suggest that we repeal the laws against such crimes because the laws are so often broken?

If Abortion Were Again Declared Illegal, Wouldn't Many Women Risk Their Lives in Back Alley Abortions?

It should not be taken for granted that merely because an abortion is performed legally, it is performed under medically favorable circumstances, in sterile operating rooms, by expert physicians. Stories of "botched" abortions are sadly plentiful. That many abortions are carried out by highly competent doctors under clinical conditions as physically safe for the mother as in other forms of surgery cannot be questioned. But legality is not guarantee of safety or concern.

The question itself suggests that a pregnant woman must have an abortion for one reason or another. Obviously, there will always be people who will take their own route to try to solve their problems, but legalizing abortion has encouraged many women to follow the abortion route because it now seems respectable. They would never have considered an illegal abortion.

Who can do more than speculate about what might happen? If we turn to the pre-1973 record, even the highest estimates of abortions annually were but a tiny fraction of the million-and-a-half a year since 1973, the year abortions were legalized for the nation.

I quote Dr. Bernard Nathanson, M.D., once the hero of the abortion movement, now firmly committed to the right to life of every unborn. In his book, "Aborting America," Dr. Nathanson addresses the question of "back alley" abortions:

"The favorite button of the pro-abortionists is the one showing the coathanger, symbol of the self-induced abortion and the carnage that results from it, or the similar problem of botched illegal abortions done by 'back-alley butchers' . . .

"How many deaths were we talking about when abortion was illegal? In NARAL (National Association for the Repeal of Abortion Laws) we generally emphasized the drama of the individual case, not the mass statistics, but when we spoke of the latter it was always

'5,000 to 10,000 deaths a year.' I confess that I knew the figures were totally false, and I suppose the others did too if they stopped to think of it. But in the 'morality' of our revolution, it was a useful figure, widely accepted, so why go out of our way to correct it with honest statistics? The overriding concern was to get the laws eliminated, and anything within reason that had to be done was permissible. Statistics on abortion deaths were fairly reliable . . . but not all these deaths were reported as such if the attending doctor wanted to protect a family by listing another cause of death. In 1967 . . . the federal government listed only 160 deaths from illegal abortion. In . . . 1972, the total was only 39 deaths. Christopher Tietze estimated 1,000 maternal deaths as the outside possibility in an average year before legalization; the actual total was probably closer to 500."

Are 1,000 deaths meaningless? Are 39? Of course not. One death is meaningful. But once again, the mothers involved could have chosen not to abort. Moreover, there is no guarantee that they would have survived legal abortions either.

Can there really be any doubt that legalization has multiplied the number of abortions almost infinitely beyond anyone's expectations? I go back to what I said above about smoking. Who would ever have believed that the day would come that smoking, such a widespread habit, would be so severely restricted by law—and in relatively such a brief period of time? Have the advertising campaigns and the governmental regulations reduced smoking? Remarkably.

God forbid that making abortion illegal would result in the death of even one woman. It seems to me that the way to avoid such is to help make life livable for every pregnant woman and help make her bringing her baby into the world a socially desirable event, in which she is praised rather than condemned.

But Do Catholics Have the Right to Impose Their Beliefs on Others?

Life is a right which must be acknowledged by a civil society as a given; it is never the concession of the state. Indeed, the state has as its primary purpose the defense of the lives of its citizens; Thomas Jefferson called it, "the first and only legitimate object of good government—the care of human life, and not its destruction." Those who are weakest or most defenseless have traditionally been given even higher degrees of protection. As former Speaker of the House Thomas P. O'Neill Jr. said, quoting the truly noble words of Senator Hubert Humphrey, "The moral test of government is how it treats those who are in the dawn of life, the children; those who are in the twilight of life, the aged; and those who are in the shadows of life, the sick, the needy, the handicapped." Human life must be protected from its inception until natural death; any other point which is determined by law is purely arbitrary and wrongly allows the state to take upon itself mastery over human life.

Those who accuse the Church of imposing its beliefs on others assume that the Church's teaching on human life has been created by the Church. Not so. All who accept the Ten Commandments, that is, Divine Law, know that it is never lawful, under any circumstances, deliberately or directly to take the life of any innocent human being. (This is one of the key principles, for example, in the tradition of "Just War"—it is never "just" to attack innocent civilians.) Unborn babies are innocent of any aggression against anyone.

Abortion is also forbidden, however, by Natural Moral Law, which governs all peoples, of all religions. The Greek playwright Sophocles and the Roman official Cicero spelled out the universal character of Natural Law long before Christ. Our own Declaration of Independence was declared, not on the basis of a particular religion, but on the basis of Natural Moral Law. It appealed to "the Laws of nature and of Nature's God," and on this basis declared it self-evident that all are endowed by their Creator with certain unalienable rights, and that the first of these is the right to life.

To argue on the basis of Natural Moral Law takes us back to the question of whether the unborn is human. If it is human, it is in the very nature of things that we should not deliberately destroy it, just as it is in the very nature of things that we have no right to go around killing children already born. No one ever hears a woman who learns she is pregnant say: "I am going to have a fetus." She says: "I am going to have a baby." It would be "unnatural" for a mother to put her baby to death after birth. It goes against the very nature of things. If the baby is a baby before birth, to destroy it is equally unnatural. Yet science today, and not only religion, reveals without reasonable doubt that an unborn baby is a baby. The other night I heard a woman arguing on television that it is "unnatural" to take the skin off an animal in order to make a fur coat. The program went on to talk about how cruel we are to raise foxes and minks for that purpose. Is it only the destruction of an unborn human being that is considered "natural"?

Don't Some Catholics Claim That They "Personally Oppose" Abortion But That They Cannot "Impose" That Belief on Others?

A peculiar problem has arisen over the past three decades, particularly involving Catholics in political life. The problem stems from the positions, "I am personally opposed to abortion, but cannot impose my morality on others," or "I cannot permit my personal beliefs to deprive a woman of her right to choose." The "personally opposed" phrase says, in effect: "In public life I will act indistinguishably from someone who sees abortion as a positive social good, but please know that I will do so with personal regret." This regret is hardly effective, since, whatever its intention, it serves the agenda of those who actively favor abortion. It seems to me that the "personally opposed, but" position is equivalently a "pro-choice" position. In November of 1989, the bishop of the United States unanimously resolved that "No Catholic can responsibly take a 'pro-choice' stand when the 'choice' in question involves the taking of innocent human life."

Pope Leo XIII, remembered as the great champion of the labor movement, repudiated such a position over a hundred years ago when he taught:

"Further, it is unlawful to follow one line of conduct in private and another in public, respecting privately the authority of the Church, but publicly rejecting it: for this would amount to joining together good and evil, and to putting man in conflict with himself; whereas, he ought always to be consistent, and never in the least point nor in any condition of life to swerve from Christian virtue." (Immortale Dei, November 1, 1885)

The Congregation for the Doctrine of the Faith addressed the question of political action related to abortion in its "Declaration on Procured Abortion" (November 18, 1974). This declaration not only condemns the immorality of all direct abortion (n. 7), it commends all positive efforts to combat its causes "including political action, which will be in particular the task of law." (n. 26) Further, the declaration is most explicit that one can never obey a law which is in itself immoral, "nor can one take part in a propaganda campaign in favor of such a law, or vote for it," nor can one "collaborate in its application." (n. 22) On the contrary, "it is at all times the task of the State to preserve each person's right to protect the weakest." (n. 21)

It seems to me that those who say, "I am personally opposed to abortion but I will not impose my moral or religious beliefs on others" have the obligation to demonstrate that their position is not rooted simply in political expediency.

I cannot judge anyone's conscience, but surely I may ask if a public official is being morally consistent if he or she personally believes abortion is killing, but simultaneously believes his or her office requires supporting it, funding it, or refusing even to work for legislation opposed to it. While it is true that there are varying political strategies for changing any law which allows the unborn to be killed, in my view, it cannot be seriously debated that the law *must* be changed.

As much as I want to be understanding of the complexities of political life and its responsibilities and pressures, and not jump to harsh conclusions, I simply can not find anything in authentic Catholic teaching that can support a "personally opposed, but" position. Nor can I find it consistent with Catholic teaching or the Natural Moral Law to support abortion in any way, by legislation, a call for funding, or silence born of a refusal to seek a reversal of legislation supporting abortion. It does not seem harsh to suggest that if we are to call ourselves Catholic, we should be acting in consistence with Catholic teaching. I would think that to be simply a matter of integrity. I would think it a requirement, as well, for those who are not Catholic, at least to think through the real meaning of abortion and how it violates nature and the Natural Moral Law, which is not a question of religious faith.

St. Thomas More, who was an accomplished statesman and an exemplary Catholic, had the courage to withstand the pressure of "privatizing" his conscience. And while he remained committed to his king, his first obligation was to Almighty God. What greater thing could be said of a statesman than what Thomas More said prior to his death, "I die the king's good servant, but God's first." Catholics in political office must also have this commitment to serve the state; but service to God must always come first.

What About Abortion in Cases of Rape or Incest?
Some evils are what we call intrinsic evils, that is, evil in themselves, so that no circumstances can justify them. Direct abortion is such an evil. For example, a mother of a pregnant teenager does not want her daughter to have an abortion because of the emotional and spiritual damage it will cause her daughter. At the same time the mother does not want her daughter to have a baby and perhaps have to give up her future dreams. Is there a legitimate choice here?

Can abortion be considered a "lesser evil"? No, it is an *intrinsic* evil. It simply cannot be morally justified.

This principle holds even in regard to rape or incest. An unborn baby is an innocent human being who has committed no crime, regardless of how conception came about. It is never morally right to destroy an innocent human being.

It is true that many in the pro-life movement temporarily settle for "imperfect" law, that is, law which permits abortion under severely limited circumstances, such as in cases of rape or incest. Such legislation is "supported" only as the lesser of evils and those who support it will continue to work toward legislation which prohibits the killing of any unborn, for any reason.

This does not imply that abortion in cases of rape or incest is less of an "intrinsic" evil than in other cases, or that pro-life people accept it as a *morally* lesser evil. One might call it a *legally* lesser evil. It implies that at a particular point the political reality may be that it is impossible to bring about *legislation* that prohibits all abortion. In such circumstances, moral theologians point out that it is better to achieve "imperfect" legislation that may save the lives of a great many unborn babies now, while continuing to work strenuously for "perfect" legislation that may save the life of every unborn baby at some future date. In my judgment, it is unfair to accuse those who fight for imperfect legislation, as the best they can get at a given time, of "sacrificing the lives" of those unborn they know they can not protect at the same time. I personally know public officials who have spent their entire political lives fighting to protect *all* unborn children. To date they have not been successful, but I thank God that they have succeeded in protecting huge numbers. Moreover, they have helped keep alive in our country the belief that all abortion is evil. They have helped keep the entire pro-life movement alive. Many of them have consistently risked their political futures to do this, and have taken bitter abuse from the pro-abortion movement. For anyone in the pro-life movement to accuse them of "trading off" babies conceived by rape or incest, as though they were callous to the sacredness of human life, or simply trying to protect themselves politically, would be unjust, uncharitable and terribly counterproductive to the cause of life.

The conflict over imperfect law has definitely been divisive to the pro-life movement. It seems to me that our goal must always be to advance protection for the unborn child to the maximum degree possible. It certainly seems to me, however, that in cases in which perfect legislation is clearly impossible, it is morally acceptable to support a pro-life bill, however reluctantly, that contains exceptions if the following conditions prevail:

A. There is no other feasible bill restricting existing permissive abortion laws to a greater degree than the proposed bill;

B. The proposed bill is more restrictive than existing law, that is, the bill does not weaken the current law's restraints on abortion; and

C. The proposed bill does not negate the responsibility of future, more restrictive laws.

In addition, it would have to be made clear that we do not believe that a bill which contains exceptions is ideal and that we would continue to urge future legislation which would more fully protect human life.

I recognize that some in the pro-life movement may consider it politically or strategically unwise to take the course outlined above, but that is a matter of prudential judgment. It is not a matter of supporting intrinsic evil as such.

I agree with and strongly encourage the following from the Joint Committee on Bio-Ethical Issues of the Catholic Bishops' Conference of Great Britain:

"In a society which widely permits and procures abortion (e.g. by publicly funding it), some may judge that justice and the common good are most fittingly served by campaigning uncompromisingly for the 'politically impossible': full equal legal protection for the unborn. Others may judge it right to concentrate on pressing for a measure of protection which is less than complete but which is greater than that accorded by today's unjust law and has, they consider, a better prospect of being soon enacted and brought into force.

"Those who chose the stricter course should not adversely judge those who promote imperfect legislation, provided that the actions and attitudes of the latter are consistent with all other guidelines . . . Nor should those who promote imperfect legislation make adverse judgments on those whose preference for the stricter course seems to hinder the pursuit of the politically possible. Either group's adverse criticism of the other may undermine the common effort—to extend the equal protection of the law to all." (Briefing 89, Vol. 19, No. 14, July 7, 1989.)

Church and State Are Separate in America. Aren't The Bishops Interfering in Politics?

Bishops have every right and duty to be involved in public policy, which is a different thing altogether from politics, both because they are bishops and because they are American citizens.

All citizens should express themselves on the moral dimensions of public policy issues. Those citizens who are generally perceived as "moral leaders," such as the bishops, have a special obligation to do so. People expect bishops to denounce unjust war and aggression, to plead for the homeless, to denounce drug traffic, racism and so on. Bishops are criticized if they remain silent about such issues.

Why are bishops criticized only when the public policy question involves abortion? Why would I be praised for encouraging the mayor, the governor, the Congress and the president to intensify the war on drugs, but criticized if I urge the same regarding abortion?

Actually, many bishops find that local political leaders want to involve them, the bishops, in various public policy matters, rather than vice versa. Political leaders want bishops involved in community action. It is, again, only when abortion is involved that some political leaders complain about bishops.

This brings up the "single issue" question. Bishops are told they should not criticize a political candidate for simply being "pro-abortion," or favor a candidate simply for being "pro-life." It is argued that a candidate's entire record, his or her entire set of attitudes must be considered.

There are several things to be said about this. First, with the staggering increase in abortion in less than 20 years, other issues, important as they are, are secondary to this direct taking of human life.

Secondly, in regard to many other issues, the question is one of public policy strategy, a question of the best way to do

things. But abortion is not a question of mere strategy, or of how best to accomplish a particular public policy objective. Abortion—every abortion—is the destruction of human life. There is no "best way" of destroying human life. That is an absolute.

For example, everyone can argue that we need a stronger police force. How is that achieved? That's a matter of strategy. For example, some might recommend raising taxes. Others believe that higher taxes will ruin the economy and result in a very high rate of unemployment. Are they right or wrong? That's an economic judgment more than it's a moral judgment. Many such examples could be given.

In reality, aren't "single issues" always driving forces in American political life? Doesn't the state of the economy or employment strongly influence thinking? Could any candidate win office today who favored a return to slavery, even if he had a wonderful record in regard to all other issues? Could a candidate win who supports drug traffic? Suppose a candidate said the vote should be withdrawn from women? Clearly, these are "single issues" which many people consider serious enough that no other qualities of a candidate would compensate. Why is it wrong, then, to look at abortion in this light, if one believes that abortion is the taking of innocent life?

As a matter of fact, an interesting development has taken place since the famous Webster decision of the United States Supreme Court, which gave states new latitude in restricting abortions. The very day the decision was announced, leaders of the pro-abortion movement were threatening political office holders on national television: "Take away our right (to abortion), and we will take away your job." That is certainly a "single issue" approach! We have seen a boycott threatened against a potato crop, then against an entire state because of proposed legislation restricting abortion. On May 28, 1990, *The New York Times* reported that the National Abortion Rights Action League "has jumped into" a certain state's gubernatorial race, vowing to defeat the only candidate who opposes abortion. This was generally perceived as a call for "single issue" voting. This phenomenon has clearly swept the country in the 1990 primaries.

In a day in which it can prove very embarrassing to a candidate if it is learned that he belongs to a country club that excludes blacks or women, it should be reasonable enough to ask a candidate if he excludes the right to life to the unborn. Strange. He cannot be "prochoice" about a country club, but he can be "pro-choice" about human life.

Obviously, it would be a grave and foolish error to vote in favor of a candidate only because he or she opposes abortion, if such a candidate favors some other gross immorality, or is incompetent to serve.

The bishops have repeatedly stated publicly that they do not encourage the development of a "religious bloc" of voters. They try to urge people to discern the morality of positions and vote their conscience, recognizing that some moral problems are more important than others. It is not for the bishops, however, to recommend particular candidates.

POSTSCRIPT

Should Abortion Be Considered a Basic Right?

Mary Gordon and Cardinal O'Connor come to different conclusions in considering the question: When does human life begin and have the right to be protected by the state? At the moment of conception, at a defined stage of fetal development? When a live child could be delivered? At the moment of biological birth?

Anti-abortionists ask: Do abortions cause pain to fetuses? Are pregnant women psychologically scarred by abortion? Does legalized abortion produce insensitivity to human life? Pro-abortionists in their turn ask: What harm is done to an unmarried teenage girl in bearing a baby? Who will raise and care for all the unwanted children? Will not prohibition produce, as it always has, countless unsafe back-alley abortions?

Dozens of books have dealt with these questions since the Supreme Court's decision in *Roe v. Wade* in 1973. A comprehensive selection ranging from the pro-abortion views of Dr. Alan Guttmacher to the anti-abortion position of Daniel Callahan can be found in J. Douglas Butler and David F. Walbert, eds., *Abortion, Medicine, and the Law*, 3rd ed. (Facts on File, 1986).

More briefly, most of the legal, ethical, and medical issues are considered in Hyman Rodman, Betty Sarvis, and Joy Walker Bonard, *The Abortion Question* (Columbia University, 1987).

Vigorous defense of the right to abortion will be found in Nanette J. Davis, *From Crime to Choice: The Transformation of Abortion in America* (Greenwood Press, 1985); Rosaline Petchesky, *Abortion and Woman's Choice* (Longman's, 1984); and Beverly Wildung Harrison, *Our Right to Choose: Toward a New Ethic of Abortion* (Beacon Press, 1983).

The opposition to abortion is thoughtfully expressed in James T. Burtchaell, *Rachel Weeping and Other Essays* (Andrews and McMeel, 1981) and in John Noonan's *A Private Choice* (Free Press, 1979). Former president Ronald Reagan, who was strongly identified with this position, summarized his views in "Abortion and the Conscience of the Nation," *Human Life Review* (Spring 1983).

The passion that these authors express in articulating their thoughtful analyses makes clear that no other moral issue that has become the subject of political debate in modern America arouses such deep and irreconcilable feelings.

ISSUE 17

Should We Have a "Wall of Separation" Between Church and State?

YES: Edd Doerr, from "Does Religion Belong in Our Public Schools?" *USA Today Magazine,* a publication of the Society for the Advancement of Education (September 1987)

NO: George Goldberg, from *Reconsecrating America* (Eerdmans, 1984)

ISSUE SUMMARY

YES: Edd Doerr, executive director of Americans for Religious Liberty, believes that public schools, like other public institutions, should promote and reflect shared values, leaving religious instruction and celebration to the home and place of worship.

NO: George Goldberg, a writer and lawyer, holds that government may not favor one religion over another but school prayer and the teaching of religion are permissible as long as all religions are accorded equal treatment.

The United States has more members (well in excess of 100 million) of more churches (more than 300,000) than any other country in the world. More than 95 percent of all Americans profess a belief in God. Recently, the growth of so-called cult religions and the increasing visibility of born-again Christians remind us that religion remains a powerful force in American society.

Because religious tolerance was a compelling issue when the United States was founded, the first clauses of the First Amendment to the Constitution deal with the relationship between the nation and religion. The Supreme Court now interprets these clauses to be binding upon the states as well as the national government.

The actual words are: "Congress shall make no law respecting an establishment of religion, or prohibiting the free exercise thereof." With some notable exceptions (involving such issues as textbooks and blood transfusions), the "free exercise" clause does not pose many constitutional controversies. The "establishment" clause does.

For the past forty years, the U.S. Supreme Court has been examining and resolving church-state controversies. Sometimes it has appeared as if the Supreme Court supports the view of those who invoke Thomas Jefferson's famous metaphor about the necessary "wall of separation" between church and state. This appears to be the case in what has proven to be the most controversial church-state issue, the right of children and teachers to start their school day with a prayer.

In the case of *Engel v. Vitale* (1962), a twenty-two word prayer, recited daily in a number of public schools throughout the state of New York, became the center of a national controversy:

> Almighty God, we acknowledge our dependence upon Thee, and we beg Thy blessings upon us, our parents, our teachers, and our country.

This prayer, composed by the New York State Board of Regents (the governing body of the school system), was intended to be nondenominational. It was also voluntary, at least in the sense that the children were not required to recite it and could leave the room when it was recited. Nevertheless, the Court declared it unconstitutional, and in subsequent cases it also outlawed Bible reading and reciting the Lord's Prayer.

Other Supreme Court decisions have defended the right of the state to accommodate differing religious views. The Court has upheld a state's reimbursement of parents for the cost of sending their children to church-related schools on public buses, the loan of state-owned textbooks to parochial school students, and grants to church colleges for the construction of religiously neutral facilities. Public acknowledgement of religion is supported by such long-standing practices as chaplains in the armed forces, tax exemptions for churches, and the motto "In God We Trust" on coins.

The Supreme Court has sought to define the constitutional boundaries of state support of religion by forbidding religious instruction in a public school class but permitting "release time" programs, which allow a student to be absent from public school in order to attend a religious class elsewhere. In 1990 the Supreme Court upheld the right of religious clubs to meet in public schools under the same conditions as other voluntary student organizations.

Those who advocate an impregnable wall of separation would forbid direct or indirect aid to religious bodies or religious causes. In direct opposition are those who have proposed a constitutional amendment to declare that the United States is a Christian nation and who would rewrite the laws and textbooks to reflect that conviction. Between these two extremes are a variety of accommodations made by legislatures and courts, compromises which probably fail to satisfy any of the advocates of absolutist views on the relations between church and state in America.

The irreconcilable conflict is posed here between Edd Doerr's support for stricter separation of church and state and George Goldberg's plea for government's increased accommodation to the needs of all religious groups.

YES

Edd Doerr

DOES RELIGION BELONG
IN OUR PUBLIC SCHOOLS?

Why can't children pray in school? Isn't creationism just as scientific as evolution and shouldn't it also be taught in public schools? If students can meet during school hours for other clubs, why can't they have a Bible discussion club? Aren't our public schools teaching "secular humanism," and isn't that why schools and textbooks rarely mention anything about Christianity?

These questions sum up much of the constant barrage of charges against American public schools, made mainly by such "New Religious Right" or "Radical Right" television evangelists as Jerry Falwell and Pat Robertson and their followers. Although the annual Gallup/Phi Delta Kappa polls of public attitudes toward public schools have not registered measurable popular support for the charges, they need to be examined because they have been put forth so vehemently and so extensively. The U.S. Supreme Court and lower courts have been and are being asked to rule on cases involving school prayer, "creationism," Bible clubs, and "secular humanism." The issues continually are being raised in Congress in proposed legislation and proposed constitutional amendments. Pres. Reagan, his administration, and his party's platforms have taken positions on these issues. Televangelists and columnists have made careers out of pressing the charges.

Tensions over religion have haunted public education in America since its humble beginnings in Massachusetts in the mid-17th century. Back when communities were more homogeneous than now, it was natural that the religion of the majority would permeate the curriculum, and there was little that minorities could do about it other than move to another community or start private schools. That is what many Catholics did in the 19th century, when the public schools tended to reflect a generalized, nondenominational Protestantism. However, over the generations, the growing pluralism of our society gradually smoothed over the religious rough edges in the schools, rendering them increasingly neutral with regard to religion and increasingly acceptable to families of nearly all religious persuasions.

From Edd Doerr, "Does Religion Belong in Our Public Schools?" *USA Today Magazine* (September 1987). Copyright © 1987 by the Society for the Advancement of Education. Reprinted by permission.

It is significant that nonpublic school enrollment, a concrete measure of dissatisfaction with public education, peaked in the mid-1960's (at about 13% of total enrollment), both absolutely and proportionally. When Pres. Nixon's commission on nonpublic school finance, a body predisposed to favor tax aid to nonpublic schools, hired two Catholic universities to study the causes of enrollment decline in Catholic schools, which enrolled about nine-tenths of nonpublic students, the researchers concluded that the enrollment shift had little to do with ability to afford nonpublic schools and much to do with growing Catholic acceptance of public education. Between 1965 and the present, the proportion of Catholic students in nonpublic schools declined from about half to about one-quarter.

The increase in Protestant fundamentalist school enrollment in recent years has not equalled the decline in Catholic school enrollment. Primarily a response to racial integration of public schools originally, fundamentalist school enrollment now seems largely religiously motivated, a phenomenon related to the growth of what might be termed the "moral majoritarian" movement begun during the late 1970's.

The downturn in nonpublic enrollment began shortly after the Supreme Court's 1962 and 1963 school prayer rulings, which sharply punctuated a process of secularization that, before 1962, already had eliminated school-sponsored devotional activities from most schools. Critics of the Supreme Court's 1960's prayer rulings failed to grasp that Catholics had challenged Protestant prayers in public schools in the midwest at least two generations earlier.

Let us look at the specific problem areas cropping up in the courts:

School Prayer

Until 1962 and 1963, eastern and southern states tended to require and sponsor daily group prayers and/or Bible readings to open the school day. Lawsuits in New York, Pennsylvania, and Maryland brought by a variety of parents and students resulted in Supreme Court rulings to the effect that government-mandated or -sponsored devotions are incompatible with the religious neutrality required of public schools by the First Amendment clause barring laws "respecting an establishment of religion." That clause, like most of the Bill of Rights, is made applicable to state and local government by the Fourteenth Amendment.

Many people can't or won't understand that the Supreme Court in the *Engel* and *Schempp* rulings did not prevent individual students from praying or reading the Bible privately in the classroom; it only proscribed government-mandated, -sponsored, or -regimented devotions. Powerful movements of religious conservatives began pressuring Congress to amend the Constitution to allow government - sponsored group prayer in school. Civil libertarians and mainstream religious leaders rallied behind the Supreme Court, however, and all the proposed amendments were defeated, though not without many anxious moments for defenders of church-state separation. Perhaps the closest battle occurred in the House of Representatives in 1971, when a discharge petition brought a prayer amendment to the floor. Defeat of the amendment was largely due to the efforts of Rep. Robert Drinan, a Catholic priest who represented a mainly Catholic district in Massachusetts.

Advocates of school prayer amendments cite opinion polls which seem to show strong public support for their campaign. Nearly all of these polls, however, conveyed to respondents the false notion that students are denied the right to voluntary prayer, so the results are of questionable validity.

Preceding and setting the stage for the prayer rulings was a 1948 Supreme Court ruling (*McCollum*) holding that religious instruction could not be offered in public schools on a "released time" basis. Four years later, the Court ruled that schools could release students for up to an hour per week of religious instruction off the schools' grounds if there was no school pressure to get the students to attend. "Released time" religious instruction is no longer very common, though instances of *McCollum* violations continue to turn up in rural school districts.

TEACHING ABOUT RELIGION

In its school prayer rulings, the Supreme Court said that schools could and should offer objective, neutral instruction *about* religion. Yet, not a great deal of such instruction is taking place, for a variety of reasons. There is little demand for it from parents, educators, or religious groups, and there is some fear, partially justified, that such instruction could be converted too easily into proselytizing. Few states have any provision for training or certificating teachers to deal with a subject more complex and fraught with problems than any other. There is little agreement among educators, parents, scholars, and religious leaders about what should be taught and at what grade levels. Finally, those who are most concerned about getting some sort of religion into public education are not interested in objective, neutral education

so much as in promoting their own particular viewpoints.

Related to this topic is the furor over a recent U.S. Department of Education study which shows that mention of religion is infrequent in textbooks, so infrequent as to lead to charges that the schools and textbook publishers are somehow hostile to religion. It is true that textbooks tend to overlook religion, but the reasons for this seldom are discussed. Textbook publishing is a highly profitable and competitive business. Our school populations are highly pluralistic, and religion is one of the touchiest subjects. In order to sell books, publishers have to avoid offending or making nervous the people responsible for selecting textbooks for local schools.

Can a textbook mention one religion or denomination without giving some sort of equal treatment to all? Should a textbook present only the positive side of religion and ignore the dark side? One critic bemoans texts which fail to discuss the reasons for the first Thanksgiving and the religious motives of the Puritan and Pilgrim settlers. Yet, a balanced treatment of religion in early New England would have to discuss the intolerance which led to the Salem witch trials, the execution of Mary Dyer for being a Quaker, and the exile of Anne Hutchinson for holding unauthorized religious meetings in her home. The Great Awakenings may be left out, but so too is the mention of religious support for slavery and religious insensitivity to other forms of social injustice. Schools and publishers evidently have found from generations of experience in hundreds, if not thousands, of communities that neglecting religion is safer than paying much attention to it.

Prof. Richard C. McMillan spoke for many experts in his excellent book, *Religion in the Public Schools*, in stating that, even though schools should offer objective instruction about religion, "it would be wise to restrict courses in religion studies to adolescents," and even then they should be electives. McMillan also puts the ball in the critics' court when he says that "A religious community should not request any form of religious instruction in the public schools until it may take pride in the quality of religious education provided by its own religious institutions."

Creationism and Evolution
In December, 1986, the Supreme Court heard an argument in the case involving a challenge to the Louisiana law which requires "balanced treatment" for "creationism" whenever evolution is taught in public schools. The lower Federal courts had found the law to violate the First Amendment's establishment clause. Advocates of "balanced treatment" contend that "creationism" and evolution are equally scientific, or equally unscientific, and therefore merit equal treatment. The scientific and educational communities, however, are in fairly solid agreement that "creationism" is essentially a fundamentalist religious doctrine, no matter how lawmakers might try to camouflage it. That was the view of the lower Federal courts when they struck down both Louisiana and Arkansas' "balanced treatment" laws.

The religious community is split on the issue, with fundamentalists supporting "balanced treatment" and mainstream Christianity and Judaism opposing it. Indeed, the plaintiffs in the Arkansas case were Catholic, Episcopal, United Methodist, Presbyterian, Baptist, Jewish, and Unitarian Universalist leaders and clergy.

("Creationism" follows a literal reading of Genesis and holds that our planet is not over 10,000 years old, that the fossil record was laid down by the biblical flood, that a deity created different "kinds" of plants and animals, and that humans were created separately from other animals. The consensus in science, however, is that the Earth is several billion years old, that all life forms evolved from earlier forms, that the fossil record was laid down over a vast span of time, and that humans evolved from primate ancestors and thus are related to other animals, most closely to the great apes. Scientists find little of scientific value in the writings of creationists. Many scientists are religious, while mainstream religious leaders do not find science hostile to religious values.)

Scientists, educators, and mainstream religious leaders believe that, if "balanced treatment" laws are upheld as constitutional, science education will be seriously damaged and American education will decline sharply in comparison with other advanced countries.

"Secular Humanism"
In mid-1986, an Alabama Federal judge presided over a trial in which a group of fundamentalist parents charged that public schools and textbooks teach the "religion of secular humanism." There are humanist or "secular humanist" organizations—such as the American Humanist Association, the Council for Democratic and Secular Humanism, the American Ethical Union, and the Society for Humanistic Judaism—but the charge that humanism or secular humanism is taught in public schools generally is accepted only by people of various funda-

mentalist persuasions. Whether humanism and secular humanism are religions or philosophies or "life stances" is irrelevant. What is relevant is whether what is distinctive about humanism is taught in the schools.

A typical argument of the accusers is that, since humanists believe in evolution and since schools teach evolution, therefore the schools teach humanism. Humanists also believe in democracy, but teaching democracy does not mean that the schools teach humanism. In the real world, the various currents of mainstream religion favor democracy and generally are not offended by evolution.

Whether humanism or secular humanism are religions or philosophies or life stances, their positions generally track Humanist Manifestoes I and II of 1933 and 1973 and the Secular Humanist Declaration of 1980. Apart from humanists' strong emphasis on philosophical naturalism, as contrasted with the supernaturalism of most forms of Christianity, for example, humanist views of moral and social issues are shared widely by Christian, Jewish, and other Americans.

In brief, humanism as a distinct philosophical or religious viewpoint is not taught in public schools. After all, our 16,000 public school districts are run by elected boards of local parents and voters. Our teachers and board members are a cross section of our population. To imagine that these tens of millions of voters, school board members, teachers, administrators, and parents are allowing humanism to be taught or promoted in their schools is to engage in paranoid fantasizing.

Nevertheless, it is becoming ever clearer that what fundamentalist critics call "secular humanism" is only a list of features of public education to which "moral majoritarian" critics object, such as evolution, sex and family education, critical thinking, books containing thoughts or words offensive to the critics, and materials which do not consign women to "traditional" roles.

"Opting Out"

"Religious Right" attacks on public education took a new form in *Mozert v. Hawkins County Public Schools*, decided by a Tennessee Federal court in October, 1986. Finding for the fundamentalist plaintiffs, the judge held that their children should be allowed to "opt out" of an elementary reading program which allegedly conflicted with their "sincerely held" religious beliefs. Since no reading textbook series could satisfy the parents without raising establishment clause problems, the judge ordered that the children be allowed to study reading at home with the parents, subject to testing by school officials.

Critics of the ruling, now on appeal, point out that, if the ruling is not overturned, large numbers of fundamentalist and other parents may opt their children out of reading, social studies, science, and other classes to avoid having them exposed to any idea or utterance they regard as inconsistent with their religious beliefs. The resulting opt-outs would render much of public education chaotic and would put severe pressure on school administrators, teachers, and textbook publishers to exercise prior censorship over reading material and the content of class discussion. This in turn would render education sterile and very dull. The "moral majoritarians" who want public school curricula censored seem also to have a hidden agenda: They would like to create enough dissatisfaction with public education to generate popular support, now lacking, for tax support of sectarian private schools, which are free to permeate a curriculum with a particular sectarian point of view.

"Equal Access"

The early 1980's saw a sudden squall over whether "student - initiated" religious clubs could meet in public schools during or immediately before or after class hours. After several lower Federal courts held the practice unconstitutional, pressure was put on Congress to pass legislation to require all public schools accepting any Federal funds (as virtually all do) to allow religious groups "equal access" if schools allowed chess clubs or Young Democrats or Young Republicans to meet. Advocates of "equal access" held that it was discriminatory and a violation of free exercise for schools to allow all clubs except religious ones to operate.

Opponents replied that religion is singled out in the Constitution as special, that allowing religious clubs to operate in schools would be so close to government sponsorship as to violate the establishment clause, and that such clubs would generate sectarian divisiveness in schools. At one Congressional hearing on an "equal access" bill, I pointed out that "equal access" groups already were proselytizing and converting students, and doing so without the knowledge or consent of the parents of the targeted students. I urged defeat of the bill, or, failing that, that amendments be added to limit participation to older students (say, 16 or older), to require written parental permission for participation, and to prohibit "equal access" clubs from bringing in outside professional proselytizers. None of the safeguards was added to the bill and it was approved by Congress in

1984. While there seems to be no great expansion of religious clubs in public schools, no data exist to show just how extensive they are.

"INVASION OF THE SOUL SNATCHERS"

The most overlooked problem in our public schools is what I have termed the "invasion of the soul snatchers." In 1983, an *Education Week* survey showed that some 4,500 adult professional missionaries were operating in public schools. Young Life had over 400 paid missionaries; Campus Life, the high school program of Youth for Christ, 800 missionaries; Bill Bright's Campus Crusade, 120 missionaries; Fellowship of Christian Athletes, 168 paid missionaries and 3,200 volunteer leaders and coaches, etc.

The problem only can have worsened after passage in 1984 of the "equal access" legislation, which specifically allows school religious clubs to bring in adult professionals. During the Congressional debate on "equal access," Moral Majority leader Rev. Jerry Falwell told *The Philadelphia Inquirer* that "We knew we couldn't win on school prayer [Pres. Reagan's proposed school prayer amendment had been defeated in the Senate in March, 1984] but equal access gets us what we wanted all along." What Falwell wanted was made clear in his *Fundamentalist Journal* in September, 1984, in a lead article describing the public schools as "a larger mission field than many countries."

The most successful single public school evangelist is probably Jerry Johnston, a 28-year-old preacher from Shawnee Mission, Kans., who claims to have spoken to over 2,000,000 students in more than 2,000 public schools. In a promotion piece for his

"Life Public School Assembly" program, he states: "In the public junior and senior high school age bracket there are approximately 40,000,000 teenagers in the United States. This large group of young people represents one of the greatest virgin mission fields existent today and yet by and large, they are unreached by the Christian community." In the same promotion piece, Johnston urges fundamentalist "youth pastors" to use the "equal access" legislation to gain entry to public schools.

No one knows how successful these public school missionaries are, as there are no statistics on conversions. Astonishingly, the practice of allowing missionaries into schools has not been challenged in court, though it is unquestionably unconstitutional.

Holiday Observances
In New England before the American Revolution, Christmas observance, in school or anywhere else, was frowned upon as unbiblical and as too "high church" or "too papist." By the 20th century, however, Christmas and other observances became quite common. With the growth of pluralism and increased sensitivity toward the rights of religious minorities, sectarian activities began to recede. Yet, many holiday observances remain, and controversies continually flare up over school sanctioning of what religious minorities—including many Christians—regard as improper sectarian practices. Incidentally, many conservative Christians do not celebrate Dec. 25 religiously since they regard it as unbiblical.

Certainly, public schools may educate students *about* the traditions and festivals of various religions and cultures, but this should be done in an academic context. School-sponsored religious exhibits and ceremonies tend to be divisive, to slight whatever children in a school do not belong to the majority or plurality tradition, and raise not inconsequential First Amendment issues. The wisest course for public schools to follow is to provide religiously neutral education. They may and should promote the common democratic, civic, and civilized values shared by virtually all religious traditions, but religious instruction and celebration are best left to the home and to the church, synagogue, or mosque.

The best way to end this all too sketchy survey of the problems on the interface between religion and public education is to cite Justice William J. Brennan's remarks in his concurring opinion in the 1963 *Schempp* school prayer case:

> The public schools are supported entirely, in most communities, by public funds—funds exacted not only from parents, nor alone from those who hold particular religious views, nor indeed from those who subscribe to any creed at all. It is implicit in the history and character of American public education that the public schools serve a uniquely public function: the training of American citizens in an atmosphere free of parochial, divisive, or separatist influence of any sort—an atmosphere in which children may assimilate a heritage common to all American groups and religions. This is a heritage neither theistic nor atheistic, but simply civic and patriotic.

NO
George Goldberg

RECONSECRATING AMERICA

The current controversy over church-state relations in America, in particular the issues of prayers in public schools, governmental support of parochial schools, and displays of religious symbols in public places, is unfortunate and unnecessary. A constitutional amendment to resolve these issues would be worse.

The United State Supreme Court, whose decisions beginning in 1940 gave rise to the current controversy, seems at last to be aware of the mistake it made. Recent decisions of the Court have gone a long way to rectifying the problems and defusing the controversy. But the Court, which earned much of the public disapproval it received in recent years, now needs informed public support for its efforts to repair the damage it did in its series of misguided and confusing decisions involving the religion clauses of the First Amendment. Such support has not been forthcoming, neither from public officials issuing resounding calls for a constitutional amendment which would only usher in another generation of conflict over interpretation and application, nor from "strict separationists" demanding, with cool disdain for the desires of the overwhelming majority of Americans and with a sorry ignorance of American history, the complete exclusion of all forms of religious expression from public life.

The great mass of American people has watched the emotional debate with anxiety. They see the admirable and precious interfaith amiability of recent years disturbed by completely unnecessary lawsuits over issues as divisive as they are irrelevant to true religious freedom. To me, a Jew living in a country where almost everybody else is Christian, there is only one religious issue: equal treatment. If the New Testament is read in public schools, I want the Old Testament too. If Catholic parochial schools receive financial aid, I want yeshivas to get their fair share. If public employees get time off for Good Friday, I want them to get time off for Yom Kippur. If a crèche is displayed during the Christmas season on the lawn of the public library, I want to see a menorah nearby.

My position is hardly unduly modest. Imagine in almost any other country of the world a member of a religious group representing less than 3 percent of the population *demanding*, and with a fair chance of receiving, equal treatment with the dominant religion. And yet there are Americans—Jews, Unitarians, "humanists," atheists, even some Protestants—who believe I do not demand enough. They do not want equal time with their neighbors, they want absolute veto power over their neighbors' actions. As they do not wish to say prayers in public school, they insist that nobody else be permitted to do so. As they do not send their children to parochial schools, they insist that no public aid be given such schools, although the parents of parochial school children are assessed for public school taxes at the same rate as everyone else. They are offended by any form of religious symbol in a public place and cannot be consoled with the right to erect their own there—especially if they do not have any.

We are a free country and there is no reason, apart from good taste and respect for the sensitivies of others, why a person so disposed should not lobby against the provision at public expense of textbooks to parochial schools. But to raise such a personal preference to constitutional status is wrong and dangerous. It invites a change in the Constitution, and we already have the most liberal constitution in the world, with greater protections for minorities than most nations dream of. We would be crazy to tamper with it.

But we cannot expect the vast majority of Americans to be willing to be governed by a document which a small minority is able to manipulate for its own benefit. Moreover, the supposed benefit is nonexistent, except for those who make their living conducting wasteful litigation. Barring Handel's *Messiah* from the public schools will have far less im-

pact on the Christian child who can sing it in church than on the Jewish child who will thereby be "protected" from exposure to an important and enriching part of the culture of the Western world; and if crèches and menorahs are given comparable prominence in public displays the prime beneficiary will be the menorah. FCC equal-time rules primarily benefit minority candidates. . . .

CONCLUSION

The essence of religious freedom in a multisectarian society is, as our Founding Fathers perceived, twofold: (1) freedom from governmental compulsion to worship in any particular way, and (2) freedom to worship in one's own particular way. It was in recognition of this dual aspect of religious freedom that the federal government was explicitly forbidden to establish or disestablish any religion or to interfere with anyone's exercise of his faith. . . .

There is little question but that to the Founding Fathers "religion" did essentially have one meaning: the beliefs and practices associated with the worship of God, whether the Christian God, the Jewish God, nature's God, or Divine Providence. With that broad definition, and with the concomitant understanding, which the Founding Fathers also shared, that the only thing prohibited by the establishment clause of the First Amendment was *compulsion* of worship or the *preferential* treatment of one religion over competing religions, there would be little trouble today over interpretation and application of the establishment clause, and little "tension" between it and the free exercise clause.

But the Supreme Court greatly expanded both the definition of "religion" and the scope of the prohibitions of the establishment clause, with the result that an impasse, the classical irresistible force meeting immovable object, was created. As phrased by the Court, "tension inevitably exists between the Free Exercise and the Establishment clauses." But there was nothing inevitable about it.

There are good reasons for expanding the definition of "religion" to include virtually anything anybody deems sacred. The alternative puts the courts in the business of defining and assessing professed religious beliefs, a business for which they are neither equipped nor suited. If Henry David Thoreau occupies a place in a person's life comparable to that occupied by God in the life of a believer (the Supreme Court's phraseology in the conscientious objector cases), there seems no good reason why *Walden* should not enjoy all the protections accorded sacred scripture. But this special status extended to a writing under the free exercise clause will be a cruel joke if *as a consequence* it ends up on the establishment clause index.

Actually, if establishment continued to be defined as compulsion or preferential treatment, religion could be defined as broadly as might be desired. The "tension" only appears when the definition of religion is broadened for free exercise purposes *and* it is held that any governmental aid of religion, no matter how evenhanded, is prohibited by the establishment clause. *Then* it is inevitable that there will be tension between what the free exercise clause *requires* and what the establishment clause *forbids*.

The courts have become, if rather late in the day, fully aware of this dilemma. When in 1973 the Supreme Court struck down a New York plan to reimburse low-income families for parochial school tuition, it admitted that "it may often not be possible to promote the [free exercise clause] without offending the [establishment clause]." Similarly, when in 1980 the United States Court of Appeals for the Second Circuit held that the establishment clause required a public high school to deny the request of students to be allowed to hold prayer meetings on school grounds before the beginning of the school day, it conceded that the denial would violate their free exercise rights.

The preference of the courts for the establishment clause over the free exercise clause has given rise to much comment. It has been observed that free exercise is the goal of *both* of the religion clauses, the prohibition of establishment merely constituting a necessary means by which to realize it. According to this interpretation, whenever tension appears between the clauses, free exercise should prevail. . . .

That brings us to the central questions: (1) What is an establishment of religion? and (2) What is the free exercise thereof? It seems to me, after reading what Jefferson and Madison wrote on the subject, studying the cases, state and federal, and considering the observations of legal scholars of varying predilections, that there really should be no serious disagreement over the meaning of either of the religion clauses of the First Amendment.

The free exercise clause is perhaps the simpler one to understand, so I will consider it first. In essence it means that, consistent with public morals and an orderly society, every person should be allowed, and wherever possible helped, to worship whatever it is he deems sacred in whatever manner he deems appropriate. The qualifying phrase, "consistent with public morals and an orderly society," should and usually has been interpreted to require a showing of significant public harm to justify inhibiting a religious practice. Thus an Indian tribe was permitted to use an hallucinatory drug in its rituals despite its general proscription as a "controlled substance," Old Order Amish were permitted to remove their children from school at fourteen despite a law requiring school attendance until sixteen, and Jehovah's Witness children were permitted to abstain from pledging allegiance to the flag, which their religion held was a graven image, but no exemptions from the general laws were granted to polygamists or to Amish employers who did not wish to pay social security taxes for their employees. . . .

The free exercise clause, then, interpreted broadly and applied with common sense and goodwill, should not give rise to serious problems. Establishment clause cases are inherently more difficult; yet they too could be decided with relative ease with the application of a bit more common sense and goodwill than has been in evidence in judicial decisions striking down nondiscriminatory public assistance programs.

. . . The Supreme Court in 1983 upheld a state statute providing reimbursement of parochial school tuition. But the Court was obliged to accomplish this result by means of a disingenuous acceptance of a farfetched rationale of universality. But why shouldn't a nondiscriminatory program of public support of all schools within a jurisdiction, public, secular private, and church-sponsored, be allowed? In other words, let us consider the extreme case where a state offers its citizens educational vouchers redeemable at any school meeting state accreditation requirements. Such a system has been advocated, notably by Milton and Rose Friedman, and has been opposed with great vehemence by the educational establishment. Should the political processes by which such a program could be adopted or rejected be short-circuited by a judicial holding that it would be unconstitutional under the establishment clause because aid would be given to parochial schools along with public and secular private schools?

The issue of *compulsion* can be quickly disposed of. No one under a voucher program would be obliged to attend a parochial school. Indeed, the issue of school prayers, usually considered under the rubric of compulsion, would be significantly defused if children could attend any school they desired. If prayers were important, then, a child could be sent to a school which said them; and [an atheist's child] probably could go, with children of similarly minded parents, to a school which didn't.

The issue of *preferential treatment* of one religion over others would seem as easily disposed of. In a scheme of vouchers redeemable at any accredited school, no issue of preference could arise. The argument that such a scheme would primarily benefit the Catholic Church, because most parochial schools are Catholic, completely misconstrues the purpose of the establishment clause. It might as well be argued that maintaining the roads favors Catholics because they use them to go to church more often than Protestants, Jews, or Madalyn Murray O'Hair, or that lowering postal rates for books supports Southern Baptists who mail so many Bibles. As long as equal benefits are available to all religions, a scheme is not rendered unconstitutionally preferential because one or more religious groups choose not to take equal advantage of it.

There would thus appear to be *no* establishment clause reason why an educational voucher system should not be sponsored by a state. (There might be an equal protection clause reason if such a system tended to result in racially segregated schools, but that could be dealt with, as it was in the tuition reimbursement scheme allowed by the Court, by requiring that beneficiary schools agree to adhere to civil rights legislation.) Yet I fear that the Court, even as constituted today, would have difficulty in allowing such a program.

Why? Because of Justice Black's formulation of the establishment clause thirty-seven years ago:

> The "establishment of religion" clause of the First Amendment means at least this: Neither a state nor the Federal Government can set up a church. Neither can pass laws which aid one religion, *aid all religions*, or prefer one religion over another.

The answer to Justice Black is that he was wrong, and that thirty-seven years of adherence by the Supreme Court to a wrong theory is enough. As stated by a leading American legal scholar:

> The historical record shows beyond peradventure that the core idea of "an establishment of religion" comprises the idea of *preference*; and that any act of public authority favorable to religion in general cannot, without manifest falsification of history, be brought under the ban of that phrase.

There remains but one church-state issue to consider: religious activities in public schools—prayers, Bible recitations, hymn singing, Christmas and Hanukkah pageants, grace before milk and cookies. No discussion of church-state relations in America can be complete without a candid discussion of this difficult issue, and it should be noted at the outset that there are men and women of goodwill on both sides, and that reference to the Founding Fathers is of limited assistance since the first public school was founded in 1821 (in Boston) and public schools were not widespread in the United States until after the Civil War.

The arguments in favor of school religious exercises boil down to a belief that "spiritual" values must be inculcated in our children and that the home and the church are unequal to the job. The principal argument against is that religion in our pluralistic society is essentially divisive and must be kept out of the public schools which have been a major vehicle for creating a cohesive society. . . .

. . . It is fascinating how the same people who on certain occasions profess great sympathy for minorities and poor people turn into Marie Antoinette when confronted with school prayers: let them go to private school, or let their parents teach them religion. How can a person who in the context of aid to dependent children cites statistics of broken homes, rodent-infested apartments crowded beyond imagination, and children roaming the streets untended, in the context of school prayers conjure up warm families sitting around the fireside listening to the paterfamilias (50 percent of minority children in the United States live in fatherless homes) recite verses from the Bible with appropriate commentary?

But middle-class children from two-parent families may not receive much more religious training at home than ghetto children. For the image of the patriarchical family reading the Bible (or anything else) around the hearth is nearly as fanciful in the suburbs as in the central city. Only judges of venerable age and advanced myopia can suppose that there is time and occasion in the modern middle-class home for morning prayers. In the real world the weekday morning is a paradigm of chaos—of father racing about shaving, searching for the one tie he really likes with this suit, gulping a Danish and coffee, grabbing his briefcase, and rushing off to catch the 7:07; of mother trying to feed everyone (maybe even herself), dress herself and the five-year-old, search for the ten-year-old's math paper, assure the thirteen-year-old that she did not hide his sneakers, drive the children to school(s) and/or bus stop(s), and perhaps also get to her job on time (half of American mothers hold jobs outside the home). In this frenetic, frantic atmosphere, the possibility of stopping everything for three minutes to calm the spirit and give thanks to something beyond ourselves . . . is remote.

After-school opportunities for familial contemplation of eternity are even fewer. Extracurricular activities consume most of the children's time before dinner, shopping and cooking and perhaps her job consume all of mother's, and father is lucky if he makes it home for dinner. And then there is the ubiquitous television set by means of which the children will be taught that happiness may be found, may *only* be found, through the acquisition of nonessentials—a toy, a vacation, a car capable of going 120 mph in a country with a 55 mph speed limit. They see grown men and women exploding with joy because they guessed the price of an appliance they do not need and now will be given; they see fairytale children playing blissfully in an enchanted land and are told that their palpable joy derives from chewing a certain brand of gum; they see portrayals of

camaraderie, of intimacy and sharing among handsome men and lovely women untouched by sickness or human frailty in a pastoral idyll based solely on the consumption of a certain brand of beer. . . .

That, your Honor, is what children learn at home. Perhaps religious faith is a sham, "a chronic disease of the imagination contracted in childhood," the opium of the people. Perhaps Charlie's angels have more to offer than those Billy Graham writes about. But if you think so, why not say so? To pay lip service to the "spiritual needs of our young people" and then tell them that they must seek their fulfillment at home and only at home, is ignorant or dishonest or both.

Sex must be taught in the schools because parents are unequal to the task, but religious instruction is held to be within their competence. Surely the evidence compels the opposite conclusion.

The argument that, like Sergeant Friday in the old *Dragnet* series, schools are only concerned with *facts*, is equally untenable. The selection and presentation of the limitless supply of available observations, theories, and opinions determine the direction and meaning of the educational process. George Washington was born in 1732. So was Haydn. So, no doubt, were many other people, including saints and sadists and blasphemers and traitors. All *facts*, but which will you disinter and teach? Obviously it depends upon your animating principles. The Founding Fathers were animated by a belief in Divine Providence, a faith broad enough to take in theism and even, perhaps, pantheism, along with traditional religions. Some of us are still animated by similar beliefs, others are busy looking out for "Number 1," and still others are totally immersed in the beliefs and rituals of ancient religions. The one thing we should all be able to agree upon is that the courts should not take sides in the ongoing debate.

But *what about prayers?* The Court has now held that prayers may be said at the beginning of legislative and judicial sessions . . . [but] prayers are still banned from all public elementary and high schools in the country.

It should be understood that the ban is virtually total. For example, in 1982 the Tennessee legislature was considering a bill to allow (not require) public schools to set aside time for—well, for whatever the courts would allow. It had before it a statute drawn up by the Georgia legislature according to which a school could set aside up to three ten-minute periods a day—before school, after school, or during the lunch break—when students who so desired could use an empty classroom for prayers or silent meditation. The attorney general of Tennessee advised the legislature that the statute was unconstitutional. After several tries the legislature finally agreed on one minute of silence at the beginning of the school day and included in the statute a warning that teachers were not to suggest what the students should be thinking about during that minute. Even this statute was submitted to the attorney general for an opinion. He reviewed the cases, noted that "It is well-settled that the Establishment Clause forbids the state from requiring or even condoning perceptible religious exercises in public schools," and said that as long as the teachers did not encourage the students to say prayers during the minute of silence, the statute was constitutional.

Isn't that ridiculous? Any attempt to restrict the availability of obscene, racist novels in public school libraries is immediately attacked as Nazism in the making; public school students are held to have a constitutional right to select their dress and hairstyles and to demonstrate in class against governmental policies of which they disapprove; but *God* has become so terrible a word that all the legal talent in the country must be mustered to exclude it absolutely from the public schools.

It is true that America's religions did not always live together in peace and harmony. The Puritans were not known for their tolerance of dissenters, anti-Catholic agitation once disfigured a large part of our public life, and no one named Goldberg is unaware of the history of anti-Semitism in America. But it is equally true that the tables have turned 180 degrees, and shields have been transformed into swords. . . .

Intolerance is ugly, no matter who practices it. When a minority practices it, it is also foolhardy, for intolerance breeds more intolerance, and minorities naturally suffer the most from an atmosphere of intolerance. With tolerance for the beliefs and practices of others, however foolish they may seem, and enlisting the aid of the courts not to prevent others from doing what they want but only to enforce one's own right to equal time, the issue of prayers in public school can be resolved without amending the Constitution.

POSTSCRIPT

Should We Have a "Wall of Separation" Between Church and State?

Few issues in American politics arouse such deep feelings as those relating to moral and religious convictions, and those deep feelings find expression in the preceding essays. Edd Doerr is convinced that American public education can perform its function only if free of the parochial and divisive influence of opposing creeds. George Goldberg is equally persuaded that this neutrality in theory is anti-religion in practice, often effectively denying the exercise of religious belief.

Those on opposing sides of this issue freely and frequently invoke the Founding Fathers when making their arguments, finding appropriate quotations to establish—at least to their own satisfaction—the continuity of tradition. However, it should be obvious that many of the specific issues raise points of intersection between church and state that the framers of the Constitution could not have imagined.

When the Supreme Court invalidated prayers in the public schools, critical reaction was so strong that many school districts simply disregarded the Court's decrees. Thoughtful consideration of this and other issues is best undertaken in the larger context of church-state relations.

Recent judicial decisions and legislative actions are considered in Richard P. McBrien's *Caesar's Coin: Religion and Politics in America* (Macmillan, 1987), a study that is sympathetic to, but not uncritical of, religious interests. A strongly separatist position is argued in Robert L. Maddox's *Separation of Church and State: Guarantor of Religious Freedom* (Crossroad, 1987).

What happens when religious views affect political policies? Richard G. Hutcheson, Jr., author of *God in the White House: How Religion Has Changed the Modern Presidency* (Macmillan, 1988), examines the impact of former president Jimmy Carter, a born-again Sunday-school-teaching Southern Baptist, and former president Ronald Reagan, who received strong support from religious conservatives for his anti-abortion views and his views favoring school prayer.

The impact of religion on politics is not new. The influence of church policy on slavery, women's suffrage, Prohibition, and the civil rights movement is described in A. James Reichley's book, *Religion in American Public Life* (Brookings, 1985). Church-state relations and religious attitudes on abortion and nuclear disarmament are examined in Kenneth D. Wold's *Religion and Politics in the United States* (St. Martin's Press, 1987).

PART 4

America and the World

What is the role of the United States in world affairs? More particularly, what is the current state of affairs between the United States and the Soviet Union? And how does U.S. foreign policy impact on our resources and development? American government does not operate in isolation from the world community, and the issues in this section are crucial ones indeed.

Should the United States Support *Perestroika* in the Soviet Union?

———————

Should Idealism Be the Basis of American Foreign Policy?

———————

Is America Declining?

ISSUE 18

Should the United States Support *Perestroika* in the Soviet Union?

YES: John Lewis Gaddis, from "Coping With Victory," *The Atlantic* (May 1990)

NO: Z, from "To the Stalin Mausoleum," *Daedalus* (Winter 1990)

ISSUE SUMMARY

YES: Historian John Lewis Gaddis argues that aid, at least on a conditional basis, will benefit not only the Soviet Union but the West as well.
NO: Z, an anonymous author identified only as "a sometime observer of the Soviet scene," sees no point in trying to prop up a system that belongs in the scrap heap of history.

"While capitalism and socialism exist side by side, they cannot live in peace. One or the other will triumph—a funeral dirge will be sung over the Soviet Republic or over world capitalism." Thus wrote the chief founder of the Soviet Union, Vladimir Ilyich Lenin, in his 1920 essay *On Peaceful Coexistence*. In this decade, Lenin's prophecy appears to be coming to pass, although not in the way he hoped or intended. In the years from 1985 to 1990, the Soviet Union has undergone some extraordinary changes.

In 1985 Mikhail Gorbachev became the new leader of the Soviet Union, and within months he was heralding his new policies of *glasnost* (openness) and *perestroika* (restructuring). In a sense, the policies worked all too well. Critics of all persuasions took full advantage of the new openness by openly denouncing all the ills of Soviet society, from shoddy consumer goods and food shortages to the long history of political oppression in the U.S.S.R. *Glasnost* also lifted the lid on a number of ethnic and national feuds that had been contained during the long years of centralized tyranny. Gorbachev's *perestroika*, the restructuring of the Soviet economy, opened still another Pandora's box. Gorbachev managed to weaken the hold of the centralized planning apparatus, throwing out many of the party hacks who had been running it, but the Soviet Union continues to lack an efficiently functioning economic system. The result: longer and longer lines at Soviet stores, serious shortages of essential goods, hoarding, and a general loss of confidence in the economy.

In 1990, revolts against Soviet rule took place inside and outside of the Soviet Union. In the closing months of 1989, one after another of the former

Soviet satellites in Eastern Europe—Poland, East Germany, Hungary, Czechoslovakia, Bulgaria, Romania—got rid of their old-line Communist rulers and instituted some form of democracy. By 1990 the spirit of secessionism had entered the Soviet Union itself. Lithuania, one of the three Baltic states absorbed into the Soviet Union in 1940, declared itself independent, and only by heavy-handed tactics (fuel cutoffs and military pressure) was Gorbachev able to get Lithuania to back away from immediately implementing its independent status. The two other Baltic republics, Estonia and Latvia, also moved toward secession, as did the Ukraine, one of the largest Soviet republics. Meanwhile, the Communist party, which Lenin had designated the vanguard of the people, suffered a catastrophic loss of popularity. The once dominant Communist parties in Eastern Europe changed their names to "Socialist" in a desperate attempt to compete with other parties at the polls, and within the Soviet Union some of the most popular leaders, such as Russian president Boris Yeltsin, turned in their party cards.

For better or for worse, then, the Soviet Union is experiencing dizzying changes. Politically, it is becoming freer and more pluralistic than it has ever been since the revolution of 1917 brought it into being. Economically, the deadening grip of centralized planning seems to be loosening, and some degree of free enterprise now exists. The Soviet Union is tolerating changes in Eastern Europe that it never would have contemplated a decade ago, and its relationship to the West has never been more cordial. It has abandoned the triumphalist rhetoric of Lenin and his successors. To the dismay of Kremlin hardliners, Soviet foreign minister Eduard Shevardnadze in 1988 openly repudiated the Leninist line about the inevitable struggle between communism and capitalism, and, in 1990, Gorbachev dropped his objection to a reunified Germany belonging to NATO. But together with these promising developments in Soviet domestic and foreign policy are the troubling accompaniments to *glasnost* and *perestroika:* economic chaos, ethnic strife, racism, anti-Semitism, and political instability—all of which could throw into reverse the more positive changes and launch the Soviet Union into a dangerous, unpredictable course.

The issue is whether the United States should do anything to help the Soviet Union during this crisis. The help might be as modest as giving advice on how to set up profitable enterprises, or as ambitious as a new Marshall Plan (the aid program that the United States extended to Western Europe after World War II). On the other hand, there are those who argue that it is better to let events take their course in the Soviet Union. If the very foundation of the Soviet system is built on lies and self-deception, can anything we do really help it survive? These are some the questions debated by historian John Gaddis and Z, the anonymous author and observer of the Soviet scene. Gaddis argues for some sort of aid, at least on a conditional basis, whereas Z sees no point in trying to prop up a system that belongs in the scrap heap of history.

YES

John Lewis Gaddis

COPING WITH VICTORY

One day in September of 1946 an as yet little-known George F. Kennan found himself trying to explain to State Department colleagues what it was going to be like to deal with the Soviet Union as the other great power in the postwar world. Traditional diplomacy would not impress Stalin and his subordinates, Kennan insisted: "I don't think we can influence them by reasoning with them, by arguing with them, by going to them and saying, 'Look here, this is the way things are.' " They weren't the sort to turn around and say, "By George, I never thought of that before. We will go right back and change our policies."

But by last year leaders of the Soviet Union and Eastern Europe were saying something very much like that. Once confident of having mastered the "science" of politics and history, the successors to Lenin and Stalin have had to acknowledge that the system those "founding fathers" imposed on Russia after the First World War and on its neighbors after the Second World War simply has not worked. They have now in effect turned to the West and said, "Tell us what to do. We will go right back and change our policies."

We have witnessed one of the most abrupt losses of ideological self-confidence in modern history. The once impressive façade of world communism no longer impresses anyone: those who lived for so long under that system have at last, like Dorothy in *The Wizard of Oz*, looked behind the curtain; they have found there, frantically pulling the levers, pumping the bellows, and pontificating into the speaking tubes, a few diminutive and frightened humbugs. As a result, Eastern Europe has come to resemble the stage set for *Les Misérables*, but with the revolutionaries this time winning. And most remarkably of all, it is the leader of the Soviet Union itself—the current chief wizard, if you will—who seems to be playing simultaneously the roles of Dorothy and Jean Valjean.

The resulting situation leaves the United States and its allies—preoccupied so recently with visions of American decline—in a position of great and unexpected influence. For not only have we prevailed, by peaceful means, over our old Cold War adversaries; it is also the case that for the first time inmore than a century there is no clear challenger to the tradition of liberal

From John Lewis Gaddis, "Coping With Victory," *The Atlantic* (May 1990), pp. 49–51, 56–57, 60. Copyright © 1990 by John Lewis Gaddis. Reprinted by permission of the author.

democratic capitalism according to which this country and much of the rest of the West organizes itself. We are at one of those rare points of leverage in history when familiar constraints have dropped away; what we do now could establish the framework within which events will play themselves out for decades to come.

Unfortunately we are almost certainly not up to this task. There exists in the West something we might call the dog-and-car syndrome: the name refers to the fact that dogs spend a great deal of time chasing cars but very little time thinking about what they would actually *do* with a car if they were ever to catch one. Our leaders are not all that different: they pour their energy vigorously into the pursuit of victory, whether in politics or in war, but when victory actually arrives, they treat it as if it were an astonishing and wholly unforeseen development. They behave like the senator-elect in Robert Redford's movie *The Candidate* when he takes an aide aside at the victory celebration and asks incredulously, "What do we do now?"

If history is any guide, what we will probably do is fritter away the fruits of victory by failing to think through what it is we want victory to accomplish. The Athenians defeated the Persians in the fifth century B.C. only to defeat themselves through their own subsequent ambition and arrogance. The Turks spent centuries trying to take Constantinople for Islam only to see world power passing at the moment of their triumph, in 1453, to secular European states for whom the question of which faith ruled the "Eastern Rome" meant very little. The British drove the French from North America in 1763 but then alienated their own colonists, who in turn drove them out of their most valuable possessions on that continent. Victory in the First World War brought only dissension and disillusionment among the victors, and a purposeful urge for revenge among the vanquished. An even more decisive victory in the Second World War produced a long, costly, and nerve-wracking Cold War for those who won, and the mutually reinforcing benefits of peace and unprecedented prosperity for those who lost.

This depressing pattern of victories gone awry is almost enough to make one wish we were commemorating Cold War defeat. It certainly ought to make us think seriously, and rather quickly, about how not to squander the opportunities that now lie before us.

We should begin by recalling that the Cold War was a new kind of great-power rivalry, one in which the possibility of going to war always existed, but in which the necessity for doing so—at least in a form that would pit the Soviet Union and the United States *directly* against each other—never arose. As a result, that conflict took on the paradoxical character we associate with the name history has given it: the Cold War contained most of the anxieties, animosities, and apocalyptic exhortations that one tends to find in "hot" wars, but without the rubble or the body count. In time people became so used to this situation that some, myself included, began using the equally paradoxical term "long peace" to characterize it. Whatever the merits of the label, the importance of what it describes ought not to be minimized: a great-power competition carried on without great-power war is a distinct improvement over the way most such rivalries have been handled in the past.

But we also need to remember that the long peace grew out of a relationship between two superpower adversaries. If they are no longer to be adversaries—or if one of them is no longer to be a superpower—then the conditions that gave us the long peace will change. We need to make sure as we put the Cold War behind us that we do not also jettison those principles and procedures that allowed it to evolve into the longest period of great-power rivalry without war in the modern era. If a long peace was in fact the offspring of the Cold War, then the last thing we should want to do, in tossing the parent onto the ash heap of history, is to toss the child as well.

We will need a strategy that does not waste time and energy trying to turn back irreversible changes, but also one that is imaginative enough to find ways, within the limits of what is possible, to preserve the stability the Cold War has given us. The very concepts we employ in thinking about international affairs grew out of the now antiquated circumstances of superpower rivalry: if all we do is to apply old categories of thought to the new realities we confront—if we limit ourselves to trying to teach new dogs old tricks—we could find our approach to world politics to be as outdated as was the approach that certain now-defunct Marxist regimes took toward their own internal affairs prior to 1989.

The following are some new issues we will face as we seek to extend the long peace beyond a Cold War the West has now won. Old answers will not suffice in dealing with them.

SHOULD WE WELCOME THE DECLINE AND POSSIBLE BREAKUP OF THE SOVIET UNION?

The most astonishing fact facing us as the 1990s begin is that we can longer take

for granted the continued existence of the USSR as the superpower we have known throughout the Cold War. Its economy is in ruins; its government is unsure of its own authority; its leaders confront nationalist pressures far more deeply rooted than the "socialist" values the Soviet state has been trying to implant for more than seven decades. There are those in the West who welcome these developments as the consummation of a wish long and devoutly held. Second thoughts, one hopes, will produce more-mature reflections.

Among them should be the realization that it takes two to tango, and that the United States has no particular reason to want to conclude the bipolar superpower dance that has been going on since 1945. For by comparison with the multipolar international systems that preceded it, Cold War bipolarity has served the cause of peace remarkably well: the First and Second World Wars arose from failures of communication, cooperation, and common sense among several states of roughly equal strength, not from situations in which two clear antagonists confronted each other. The relative simplicity of postwar great-power relations may well have made possible their relative stability, and a situation in which the Soviet Union is no longer such a power would mean an end to that arrangement. War might not result, but instability, volatility, and unpredictability almost certainly would.

It is also worth noting that military hardware does not simply vanish into thin air as a nation's position in the world declines, or as its internal authority crumbles. The means by which a new war could start—and indeed, with nuclear weapons, the means by which we ourselves could be destroyed—will remain in the hands of whoever rules the Soviet Union. If that country should break apart, these lethal instruments might well come under the control of competing factions whose caution with respect to their use might not exceed the intensity of the rivalries that exist among them.

We confront, then, an apparent paradox: now that we have won the Cold War, our chief interest may lie in the survival and successful rehabilitation of the nation that was our principal adversary throughout that conflict. But a historian would see nothing odd in this: Napoleon's conquerors moved quickly to reintegrate France into the international community after 1815; Germany and Japan received similar treatment after their defeat in 1945. It was the failure to arrange for Germany's reintegration after the First World War, some scholars have argued, that led to the Second World War. Power vacuums are dangerous things. Solicitude for a defeated adversary, therefore, is not just a matter of charity or magnanimity; it also reflects the wise victor's calculated self-interest, as confirmed by repeated historical experience.

But to say that the United States should seek the survival and rehabilitation of the Soviet Union is not to say that we should do so in its present form. That country's future is in question today not because anyone has attacked it but because its own internal structure has proved unworkable. If the USSR is to recover, it will have to change that structure; the only question is how. And although the Soviet people themselves will, in the end, decide that question, we in the West are not without influence in the matter: consider the regularity with which Soviet officials now solicit our advice.

Americans have long questioned the wisdom of trying to maintain multinational empires against the will of their inhabitants. The collapse of the Russian, Ottoman, and Austro-Hungarian empires during the First World War vindicated that skepticism, as did the dismantling of the British, French, Dutch, and Portuguese empires after the Second World War. Soviet officials have argued, of course, that the analogy is imperfect, that their non-Russian republics are not colonies at all but rather constituent parts of the USSR, linked to it by their own free will. But the French used to insist, with equal lack of credibility, that Algeria was part of France itself and content to remain so. A mother country's claims of filial devotion do not establish its existence.

The French experience also shows how close a state can come to destroying itself by trying to hang on to an empire for too long. It would hardly strengthen the Soviet Union to have several simultaneous insurgencies going on within its borders; just one, in Algeria, was enough to persuade that most imperious of modern statesmen, Charles de Gaulle, that imperial devolution had its advantages. France's position in the world has hardly declined since then, and many of its former colonies have chosen to maintain economic, linguistic, and cultural ties with their former ruler—as have many of Great Britain's—even as they have broken political ties. Denying autonomy ensures the absence of allegiance; allowing it at least leaves possibilities open.

A Russia that embraced a De Gaulle solution would remain a great power: even if the Russian federal republic alone were all that survived under Moscow's rule, it would still control 76 percent of the land area and 52 percent of the population of the present USSR. Bloated boundaries have never provided very much security in a nuclear age in any event, but with nationalism rampant and with the means of suppressing it no longer effective, they are certain in the future to provide even less.

It would appear to make sense, therefore, for the United States to favor as much of a breakup of the Soviet Union as would be necessary to leave it with a reasonably contented as opposed to a disaffected population, *precisely because we should want to see that state survive as a great power*. And who knows: in a post-Cold War world Kremlin leaders might actually acknowledge the sincerity of our motives in taking such a position (although we should probably not count on that). . . .

SHOULD WE HELP TO REPAIR THE DAMAGE MARXISM HAS CAUSED?

Economic distress obviously encourages political instability: as Paul Kennedy, the Yale historian, has pointed out, uneven rates of economic and technological development are what cause great powers to rise and fall. If one accepts the argument that the United States and its allies should want Russia to remain a great power, then it would hardly make sense to welcome an economic collapse there or in Eastern Europe, however misguided the policies were that produced that prospect.

But the West has an ideological as well as a material interest in wanting to see *perestroika* succeed: the cause of democracy throughout the world can only prosper if that ideology—and not Marxist authoritarianism—provides the means by which the USSR and its neighbors at last achieve economies capable of satisfying the needs of their peoples. And if the emergence of even partly democratic institutions inside the Soviet Union makes the prospect of war less likely—there is strong historical evidence that democracies tend not to fight each other—then that would be an important reinforcement for the role nuclear deterrence has already played in discouraging the incautious use of military force.

Few people today remember that a similar combination of geopolitical and ideological motives impelled Secretary of State George C. Marshall in 1947—at Kennan's suggestion—to offer to include the Soviet Union and Eastern Europe in the plan for economic assistance that came to bear Marshall's name. Stalin, with characteristic shortsightedness, rejected the idea, and the Marshall Plan went on to become a program for the rehabilitation of Western Europe—one that was so successful that editorial pages ever since have resounded with calls for its revival, however dissimilar the circumstances might be to those that existed at the time of its creation.

Now, though, the way is open to implement Marshall's original vision. For although it lies beyond the power of anyone in the West to ensure the success of economic reforms in either the Soviet Union or Eastern Europe, those countries are already asking the United States to provide much of the training and technology without which failure will be certain. We will need to think carefully about just what we can do, and how we should do it.

One thing is apparent at the outset: any new aid program for the Soviet Union and Eastern Europe will have to be multinational in character. The United States is well beyond the point at which it can take on a burden of this magnitude by itself, as it did in 1947. Fortunately, though, it can now enlist the very considerable resources and skills of former recipients of Marshall Plan aid in Europe, notably West Germany, and also those of Japan, another past beneficiary of American assistance. All these states have cause to welcome an integration of Soviet and Eastern European economies with those of the rest of the world; none of them has any good reason to want to see *perestroika* fail.

A multinational aid program would have several advantages over older, unilateral forms of aid. It would maximize the resources available while minimizing the burden on an already overstretched American economy. It would be less susceptible than past foreign-aid programs to the charge that it serves the political interests of a particular state; it would also be less vulnerable to the volatility of domestic politics in any one state. It would soak up surplus products and capital from two large-scale exporters of these commodities—Germany and Japan—whose success in exporting has periodically strained their relationship with the United States. And such a program might also help to heal political differences that still exist between Japan and the Soviet Union and that might well exist between a reunified Germany and the Soviet Union.

We might also consider encouraging corporate rather than government sponsorship for at least a major portion of this assistance, where profitability and propriety make it feasible. Corporate management could provide faster action and greater efficiency than would otherwise occur; it might also be more sensitive than official initiatives to those market forces in the Soviet Union and Eastern Europe whose emergence we want to encourage. Some such activity is already

under way, most conspicuously with a project that surely marks a turning point of some kind in the history of our times: I refer to the recent and long-awaited opening of McDonald's in Moscow, a project that will be particularly interesting to watch because of the corporation's decision to develop its own network of farms, processing plants, and training centers inside the USSR. The resulting contest is sure to be a titanic one, and whether Russia will overwhelm McDonald's or McDonald's will overwhelm Russia is far from clear. But the fact that it is taking place at all can only warm the heart of anyone who has ever been to the Soviet Union and felt the urge to shout, out of sheer exasperation: "What this country needs is a good service economy!"

WHAT HAPPENS AFTER GORBACHEV?

No one, not even the current leader of the Soviet Union, is indispensable (although he comes about as close as any person in recent memory). The frailties that flesh—or a political career—is heir to can only increase with the passage of time; we in the West must be prepared for the moment when the most imaginative Soviet leader since Lenin is no longer on the scene. To fail to do this—to assume that everything that is happening hinges on Gorbachev alone—would in itself be to fall into an outmoded way of thinking.

There is at least one reason to think that the post–Cold War era will continue into the post-Gorbachev era: it is the fact that the roots of the long peace were in place well before Gorbachev came to power. Whatever their dissimilarities, neither Stalin nor Khrushchev nor Brezhnev wanted a war with the United States; the likelihood of such a conflict has declined steadily over the years, regardless of whether tyrants, reformers, or stagnationists ruled in the Kremlin. It is true that Soviet domestic and foreign policies are harder to separate today than they once were: an abandonment of *perestroika* or a crackdown on dissent would obviously undermine Moscow's improved relations with the West, just as the Tiananmen Square massacre undermined Beijing's. But a return to all-out Cold War seems unlikely, if for no other reason than that today's Soviet Union would have to compete in it from a severely weakened geopolitical, ideological, and economic position.

The West's strategy, therefore, ought to be to do nothing to undermine Gorbachev's authority, but not to be wholly dependent upon it either. Because the forces that have ended the Cold War are deeply rooted—and because the problems that beset the Soviet Union will remain after Gorbachev leaves the scene—we have some basis for confidence that the initiatives he has taken to deal with both domestic and foreign-policy issues are not going to disappear after he does.

The names that we attach to things—which in turn determine the categories we use in thinking about them—are only representations of reality; they are not reality itself. Reality can shift, sometimes more rapidly than the names we have devised to characterize it. Concepts like "communism," "capitalism," "deterrence," "credibility," and "security" only approximate the conditions we confront; but words like these tend to take on a life of their own, thereby constraining imagination. One sees the argument made even today that Communist parties running command economies will never give up power, despite overwhelming evidence that this is exactly what is happening. We need to avoid letting the categories that exist in our minds blind us to what our eyes are seeing.

At the same time, though, there is at least one thing to be said in favor of retaining old names, even as one accommodates to new realities. Cloaking change in the appearance of continuity is a time-honored technique of political leadership, for it allows those at the top to alter their thinking and shift their policies without seeming to be inconsistent. Cloaking change in the garb of continuity eases transitions; it can be a way of making revolution look like evolution, which is sometimes a useful thing to do. We should not, therefore, do away entirely with the terminology of the Cold War, or even with all the institutions that reflect that terminology; but we should welcome the opportunity slowly but steadily to shift the meanings we attach to them.

Who is it that we have defeated in the Cold War? It is not the Russian people, whom we never saw as enemies, and toward whom we bear no ill will. It is not the Soviet Union, for we should want to see that state survive as a great power. It is not communism, because that doctrine has proved so malleable over the years that it has long since lost any precise meaning. It is certainly not Gorbachev and the current Soviet government, who have had the wisdom to recognize reality and the courage to adjust to it. It is not even the Cold War, because that experience brought us the long peace. Indeed, it is odd that there should be so much talk of victory and so little specificity as to at whose expense it actually came.

It might help clarify things if we recall what appears to be a recurring competition in human affairs between coercive authority and individual autonomy, between what the sociologist John A. Hall has referred to as the forces of power and those of liberty. The tension is as old as recorded history, and it will no doubt be with us as long as history continues. But power and liberty are rarely precisely balanced: one or the other predominates most of the time, with only occasional shifts back and forth.

The century has not, on the whole, been kind to liberty. The forces of authoritarianism overcame those of autonomy in most parts of the world most of the time during this period: witness the respective triumphs of facism, communism, and all the varieties of dictatorship that lay between. It appeared until quite recently to be the fate of most people to have most of their lives managed for them, to lack the means of controlling their own affairs.

What happened in the revolutionary year 1989 was that liberty suddenly found itself pushing against an open door. The balance swung away from power with breathtaking speed; the authoritarian alternatives that have dominated so much of twentieth-century history were revealed to be, for the most part, hollow shells. We have good reason to hope that liberty will flourish in the next few years as it has not in our lifetime; and it is in that context that the real nature of the West's "victory" in the Cold War becomes clear. For it was authoritarianism that suffered the real defeat, and in that sense all of us—including our old Cold War adversaries—have won.

But history will not stop with us, any more than it did with all the others—Marx and Lenin among them—who thought they had mastered its secrets. The triumph of liberty will almost certainly be transitory; new forces will eventually arise that will swing the balance back to power once again. It is not clear at the moment, though, where they will come from, or when they will arrive. It would be prudent to be on the lookout for them; it would be wise to be prepared for their effects. But the fact that the forces of resurgent power are not yet in sight—that we have the luxury of at least some time to savor the liberties that all of us, Russians included, have won—ought to be an occasion for ecumenical, if wary, celebration.

NO

TO THE STALIN MAUSOLEUM

While the world is much preoccupied with Gorbachev, his successes and his prospects, fundamental questions about the capabilities of the Soviet political and economic system to achieve the structural reforms promised by perestroika *are ignored. Z reports on what the expectations of* glasnost *and* perestroika *have been, why the accomplishments fall so far short of the much-heralded intentions. With respect to democratization, economic restructuring, and growth, and the complex and diverse nationality issues, the historical record of seventy years of Sovietism permits only great skepticism about the possible outcomes of* perestroika; *the internal contradictions of the system are simply too overwhelming.*

> The most dangerous time for a bad government is when it starts to reform itself.
> —Alexis de Tocqueville, anent Turgot and Louis XVI

The Soviet socialist "experiment" has been the great utopian adventure of our century. For more than seventy years, to millions it has meant hope, and to other millions, horror; but for all it has spelled fascination. Nor does age seem to wither its infinite allure.

Never has this fascination been greater than since Mikhail Gorbachev launched *perestroika* in the spring of 1985: a derivative painting in the Paris manner of 1905, a Beatles' vintage rock concert, or a *Moscow News* article revealing some dark episode from the Soviet past known to the rest of the planet for decades could send tremors of expectation throughout the West if it were datelined Moscow. So conservative-to-centrist Margaret Thatcher and Hans-Dietrich Genscher have vied with the liberal-to-radical mainstream of Anglo-American Sovietology in eulogizing Gorbachev's "modernity." Even though after seventy years, the road to the putative "radiant future" of mankind no longer leads through Moscow, the road to world peace still does. And who is against world peace?

But this is not the whole explanation: Moscow is still the focus of a now septuagenarian ideological fixation. On the Right there is the hope that communism may yet repent of its evil totalitarian ways and evolve into a market democracy of sorts (into the bargain putting down the Western Left).

From Z, "To the Stalin Mausoleum," *Daedalus*, vol. 19, no. 1 (Winter 1990). Reprinted by permission of *Daedalus*, Journal of the American Academy of Arts and Sciences. Some notes omitted.

On the Left there is the wish that the "experiment" not turn out to be a total loss (if only so as not to comfort the Western Right) and yet acquire something approximating a human face. So on all sides alleged connoisseurs of the *res sovietica* are anxiously asked: Are you optimistic or pessimistic about the chances for perestroika? Can Gorbachev succeed? Will he survive? Should we help him?

These questions, however, presuppose answers with diverse ideological intonations. To what is no doubt a majority in Western opinion, Gorbachev's reforms mean that Stalinism and the Cold War are over and that democracy is at hand in the East, bringing with it the end of global conflict for all. For a smaller but vocal group, the Cold War is indeed over and the West has won, a victory that presages the global triumph of capitalism, the end of communism, indeed even the "end of history."[1] A third group, once large but now a dwindling phalanx, holds that communism remains communism for all Gorbachev's glitter, and that *glasnost* is simply a ploy to dupe the West into financing perestroika until Moscow recovers the strength to resume its inveterate expansionism.[2]

Yet the two dominant Western perspectives on Gorbachev have one element in common: the implication that our troubles with the East are over, that we are home free, at the "end of the division of Europe" and on the eve of the Soviet Union's "reintegration into the international order," a prospect first advanced by Gorbachev but eventually taken up by a hesitant President Bush. So in an odd way the perestroika pietism of the Gorbophiles and the free-market triumphalism of the Gorbophobes converge in anticipation of a happy dénouement of a half-century of postwar polarization of the world. . . .

Gorbachev's economic program has thus far consisted of two main components, both formulated in 1987. The first of these is the creation of small "cooperatives," in reality private ventures, in the service sector. But the impact of this cooperative sector has been derisory, since its services are priced far above the purchasing power of the 200-rouble-per-month average wage of the majority of the population. These enterprises have therefore become the focus of popular hostility to economic reform in general, since any form of marketization is perceived by "the people"—as the miners made clear during their strike—to benefit only "speculators" and the privileged—a reaction quite in conformity with the socialist egalitarianism the regime inculcated in the population for decades. Moreover, the cooperatives are harassed by the state bureaucracy, whose monopoly they threaten, and are often either taken over by, or made to pay protection money to, various Mafias from the "black" economy.

The second component of Gorbachev's economic reform is the Law on State Enterprises, providing for "self-management" and "self-financing." If actually applied, these provisions would significantly reduce the role of Gosplan and the central ministries by using self-interest to correct the predominance of administrative directives. This reform is thus an effort to return to the spirit, if not the precise institutions, of the NEP, and to its policy of *khozraschyot*, or businesslike management and accountability under a regime of state enterprise. In other words, it is a variant of the half-measures of soft communism, put forth periodically in Soviet history from Bukharin to Eugene

Varga just after World War II to Kosygin, but never really implemented because they threaten the Party apparat's "leading role." And, indeed, this time too, the Law on State Enterprises has remained a dead letter ever since it took effect in January 1988, because the silent resistance of legions of apparatchiki has kept industry operating at 90 percent on "state orders"—that is, on the old Plan.

In still other domains, Gorbachev's economic perestroika has met with failure, but this time without his having really tried to produce a program. In agriculture Gorbachev has spoken repeatedly of long-term leases of land, indeed up to fifty years, for the peasantry. But this proposal has gone nowhere, in part because of the resistance of the huge kolkhoz bureaucracy, in part because the peasantry has seen so many different agrarian reforms imposed from above that it will not trust the regime to respect leases of any duration and hence will not take up the government's half-offer. . . .

Another such block is financial monetary policy. Heavy state subsidies to hold retail prices low, to keep unprofitable factories running, to maintain full employment, and to secure the safety net in place—what some Western specialists call the social contract between regime and people—cannot be abolished without unleashing inflation and thus igniting a social explosion. But unless these subsidies are abolished, or at least reduced, the economy cannot move to real prices; and without real prices there can be no dilution of the Plan by marketization or privatization; nor can there be convertibility of the rouble to reintegrate Russia into the international order. And without movement in these directions, there can be no revival of the economy. So the alternative before Gorbachev is either economic stagnation through subsidies or social upheaval through real prices.

And perestroika faces other problems as well: the infrastructure and the capital stock created by decades of extensive development are now approaching exhaustion. In a nationally televised address in October 1989, Prime Minister Ryzhkov warned that the overburdened railway system (Russia still lives basically in the railroad age) was on the verge of collapse. The country's enormous metallurgical plant is outmoded and unprofitable. Housing and administrative buildings are in a state of disrepair often bordering on disintegration. The extraordinary number of industrial "accidents," from Chernobyl to the gas-line and train explosions of June 1989 are usually due to functional breakdown or criminal neglect. All this exhausted equipment must be restored or replaced, and much of the work force retrained and remotivated.

Then, too, the stores must be filled again. Under the present conditions of collapse and penury, available goods are either siphoned off legally by state enterprises to supply their workers, or they disappear illegally into the black economy. But short of massive imports of foreign goods, stocking the shelves is an impossible task, since decades of wasteful investments and subsidies, and of printing money to finance both, have now created an enormous budget deficit and rapid inflation—both "discovered," or admitted, by the government only in late 1988. As a result of this, a movement away from the rouble to the dollar or to barter is well under way, a phenomenon that presages the collapse of the consumer market.

Under such conditions of near breakdown, any transition to real prices, self-management, and self-financing are quite out of the question for the forseeable future; and the old reflexes of the command-administrative system are sure to persist, if only to ensure a modicum of order. Thus, active consideration of real market reform has been postponed time and again and is now slated, more or less, for the mid-1990s. Indeed, economic perestroika of any type has been stalled since early 1988.

Overall, then, the balance sheet of more than four years of perestroika has been that the half-reforms introduced so far have unsettled the old economic structures without putting new ones in their place. And in this, perestroika resembles earlier failed halfway-house reforms in Central Europe: General Jaruzelski's reforms of self-management in 1982 and of self-financing in 1987 in Poland, and earlier still the failed, halfway New Economic Mechanism in Hungary. Yet, despite this accumulated evidence of failure, Gorbachev intends to stick to the unnatural hybrid of "market socialism," as his chief economic advisor, Leonid Abalkin, made clear in November 1989 in launching an updated plan of alleged "transition" away from statism. . . .

In the midst of all this, what of Gorbachev, on whose person the West concentrates its attention and hopes? To the outside world, he passes for a bold and decisive leader, a mover and a shaker of major stature, especially in international affairs. When seen from Moscow, however, after his first initiative in unleashing the perestroika deluge, he has come to look more like a reactive than an active figure, a man increasingly incapable of staking out strong policy positions on the two make-or-break domestic issues of his reign, the economy and the nationalities. Instead, he appears essentially as a polit-

ical tactician, fully at home only in Party maneuvering, now pruning the Politburo of conservative foes such as the former KGB chief, Chebrikov, or the Ukrainian Party boss, Shcherbitsky, as in the fall of 1989, now tacking from left to right and back again in the debates of the new Supreme Soviet. Indeed, by giving way totally and immediately to the miners' demands in July 1989, he appeared downright weak. And in all things he acts as if his economic problems could be solved by political means. Yet, since the direct road to economic perestroika is closed to him by structural blockage, this easier political route of glasnost and democratization is the only one left open to him.

Nor does he seem to be able to make up his mind whether he is head of state or head of the opposition. As one Soviet commentator put it, he is trying to be both Luther and the pope at the same time. But in such a contradictory situation, for all his political prowess, he may yet turn out to be no more than the ultimate sorcerer's apprentice of Sovietism. . . .

Let us return now to the questions with which this inquiry began: Can Gorbachev succeed? Should we help him? It is now the official United States position, to quote President Bush, that Gorbachev is a "genuine reformer" and that we all "wish perestroika to succeed," a stance that implies at least moral help. But to answer these questions meaningfully, we must, as with the questions of Stalin's necessity, rephrase them first. Succeed at what? Help him to do what?

If by perestroika's success we mean producing a communist system that is economically effective and politically democratic, then the answer must be no: the empirical record of seventy years shows that the fundamental structures of the Leninist system reached an inextricable impasse at the end of the 1970s; and the mounting contradictions of perestroika indicate that the system cannot be restructured or reformed, but can only either stagnate or be dismantled and replaced by market institutions over a long period of time. In this case, any aid the West might render to the Soviet state to save or improve the existing system would be futile: on this score, Gorbachev is beyond our help. Such aid would also work against the real interests of the restive Soviet peoples and thus of international stability. Like Western credits to Eduard Gierek and the Polish Party-state in the 1970s, aid to the Soviet government would simply prolong the agony of everyone concerned.

Yet if by perestroika's success we mean effecting a transition from a Party-state and a command economy to democracy and the market, then the answer, unfortunately, must still be no. First of all, such a transition is not the aim of Gorbachev's perestroika; its aim, rather, is to salvage what can be saved of the existing system by halfway-house concessions to economic and human reality, concessions moreover that are constantly being revised as new sections of the system give way and as the regime improvises frantically in the hope that something might turn the situation around. Second, and even more important, such a transition would bring the end of the cardinal leading role and hence would amount to the self-liquidation of communism, something Gorbachev clearly does not intend to do.

Still, events are pressing toward the eventual dwindling away of the system, whatever the Soviet leadership's intentions and whoever that leader might be

in the future. And here Western help could play a constructive role. First, reducing the mutual burden of armaments, if carried out with due attention to legitimate security concerns, would ease the severity of the Soviet crisis (though it would not alter its structural causes). And Gorbachev has clearly indicated his willingness to engage in arms reductions, while at the same time taking care that the Soviets' international retreat does not turn into a rout.

Second, although Western aid should not go to shoring up Soviet economic institutions in the state sector, it could be usefully applied to the piecemeal development of parallel structures in a private sector operating on market principles so as to promote economic and, eventually, political pluralism. This could take the form, say, of free economic zones operating under IMF conditions in such places as the Baltic states, Armenia, or the Soviet Far East. In this case, the expectation would be that such a parallel sector, perhaps with its own convertible currency, would eventually spread across the Soviet Union.

Such a policy is, indeed, the approach that the Mazowiecki government and its finance minister, Leszek Balcerowicz, are now attempting to inaugurate in Poland. But what Gorbachev is prepared to accept for his outer empire in Central Europe (where he effectively lost control over events sometime in 1988) would be much more difficult for him to accept for the inner empire of the Soviet Union itself, since foreign investment would imperil national sovereignty. So Western investment, in joint or other enterprises in Russia, would have to be handled without triumphalism about capitalism's superiority, and with due sensitivity to Soviet national pride. The West's aim should be to encourage the change of Soviet realities, while leaving the old labels intact—in a kind of socialist-emperor-of-Japan arrangement.

Yet, however the Soviet Union edges toward its particular exit from communism, this unchartered process can only be a long and painful one. Nor will it be a unilinear or an incremental progress toward integration in some "common European house." Instead, further crises will most likely be necessary to produce further, and more real, reforms. And a last-ditch attempt to stave off ruin by curtailing destabilizing reform altogether could lead to that military reaction so feared by Moscow liberals. And who knows, in this scenario Gorbachev might be agile enough to become his own successor, or if perestroika ends in another eighteenth of Brumaire, to be his own Bonaparte. Gorbachev would be hard to replace because his international reputation is now the Soviet Union's chief capital asset; yet he could not afford to be a very tough Bonaparte, since he has become the prisoner of his foreign policy successes.

Obviously, none of these prospects is a cheering one, and none would be easy for the West to live alongside. But it is better to look realistically at the genuine options in the East as they have been molded by seventy years of failed utopia than to engage in fantasies about Gorbachev as a demiurge of instant democracy or about the end of conflict in history. Nor should we forget that communism, though a disaster in almost every creative domain, has always been supremely successful at one thing: resourcefulness and tenacity in holding on to its monopoly of power. So the Soviet world's transition to normality will be a long time coming, for the Party, though

now dyed with the hues of glasnost and democratization, will cling to the bitter end, like some poisoned tunic of Nessus, around the bodies of nations it has enfolded in its embrace for so many decades.

NOTES

1. Francis Fukuyama, "The End of History?" *The National Interest* (Summer 1988).
2. See, for example, Judy Stone, *The Coming Soviet Crash: Gorbachev's Desperate Pursuit of Credit in Western Financial Markets* (New York: The Free Press, 1989)—a bad title for an otherwise good book. The threat of financial crash is quite real, but until now Gorbachev has steadfastly refused to use foreign credit extensively for fear of compromising national independence.

POSTSCRIPT

Should the United States Support *Perestroika* in the Soviet Union?

Z's attitude toward the Soviet Union today is that it is doomed to collapse, and that the best course for this country is to stand clear of the wreckage. Gaddis, on the other hand, suggests that it is in the interest of the United States to try to prevent a collapse, for such a catastrophe could have consequences harmful to the world. What remains unclear in both essays is what exactly threatens the Soviet Union today. Famine? A new revolution? Some sort of fascist coup? Independence for all of the Soviet "constituent republics"? These are vastly different outcomes; some are extremely unlikely, others may not be catastrophic at all. The debate would be enhanced by a clearer understanding of what is meant by a collapse of the Soviet Union.

Mikhail Heller and Aleksandr Nekrich's *Utopia in Power: A History of the Soviet Union From 1917 to the Present* (Summit Books, 1986) is an important recent work which attempts to reexamine the course of events that brought the Soviet Union to its present state. Jerry Hough's *Russia and the West* (Simon and Schuster, 1988) is an absorbing account of the circumstances that brought Gorbachev to power. Moshe Lewin's *The Gorbachev Phenomenon: A Historical Interpretation* (University of California, 1988) is a more academic treatment of the forces that brought Gorbachev into prominence. Gorbachev's own work, *Perestroika: New Thinking for Our Country and the World* (Harper & Row, 1988), is an attempt to explain and justify his new departures.

Whatever the future of the Soviet Union, its present condition and its relationship to the West seems to be changing daily. Even the most hard-line critics of the Soviet system now agree that real and profound changes have occurred in the U.S.S.R. since 1985. The remaining questions seem to stem from the basic issue of whether we can now consider that nation a possible friend and ally. If so, the case for extending some kind of aid to it becomes a strong one. On the other hand, we might do well to ponder the quotation from Alexis de Tocqueville that Z uses at the top of his article: "The most dangerous time for a bad government is when it starts to reform itself."

ISSUE 19

Should Idealism Be the Basis of American Foreign Policy?

YES: Stanley Kober, from "Idealpolitik," *Foreign Policy* (Summer 1990)

NO: Arthur Schlesinger, Jr., from "In the National Interest," *Worldview Magazine* (December 1984)

ISSUE SUMMARY

YES: Writer Stanley Kober believes that the ultimate objective of American foreign policy should not be a narrow view of its self-interest or the balance of power but the spread of freedom and democracy.
NO: Historian Arthur Schlesinger, Jr., worries that moralism may lead to fanaticism, and he suggests that rational self-interest benefits not only the United States but also the rest of the world.

A revolution of democracy has resulted in the sudden disappearance of the Soviet empire and the communist ideology which saw the world divided into opposing camps. Within the Soviet Union, President Mikhail Gorbachev has defined *perestroika* (restructuring) not as economic reform but as a legal revolution designed to prevent the concentration of power. American foreign policymakers have come far from their initial skepticism of the sincerity of Gorbachev's professions of reform to later considering the possibility of assisting his political survival.

Circumstances in international relations change, although rarely so radically as they did in 1989 and 1990 with the collapse of the Soviet empire and its sphere of influence. These changes inspire very different responses from "realists," whose perspective is that of national interest, and "idealists," who affirm a vision of world interest. Put simply, idealists ask "what is good?" and realists ask "what is good for us?": both profess that in answering their question they have also answered the other.

After World War I and the collapse of the idealist impulses of President Wilson's crusade to prosecute a "war to end wars" in order to make the world safe for democracy, realists emphasized the importance of military land and sea dominance. For realists, what really counted was control of economic resources and production. This was seen as the object of military power and the source of conflict among nations.

After World War II, it was the realist logic that led to the policy of containment, whereby America and its allies sought to restrict Soviet power within a confined sphere by military preparedness and, if necessary, the use of military power. This was in the tradition of balance of power politics, whose shifting alliances had sustained peace or, when it failed to do so, erupted into war.

Realists interpreted the Cold War between the Soviet bloc and the Western alliance in familiar terms. It was a fear of nuclear war that maintained the peace between the superpowers, and that fear required ever-escalating levels of conventional and nuclear weapons. It was a strategy sometimes formulated as a doctrine of Mutually Assured Destruction (MAD). Realists did not consider it "mad" at all. What could be saner or more realistic than the West's awareness—and the awareness of the Soviet Union—that if either side struck with great force, the other side would retain sufficient retaliatory power to strike a comparable devastating blow?

Idealists argued that the policy was truly mad; it risked an accidental war, ignored nuclear proliferation among smaller nations with demagogic leaders, and diverted and diminished economic resources that could be used to make the great power stronger internally. Fundamentally, the idealist approach to international politics rejects the notion that nations act rationally in pursuit of self-interest. Hitler's Nazi Germany was not animated by the quest of national self-determination, but by the ambition of a dictator who was capable of destroying the too fragile democratic German constitution.

The events of the past few years—the expanding economic power of Japan, the growth of the European Community, the unification of Germany, and the disintegration of the Communist bloc—have transformed world politics. It is necessary to reexamine the realist and idealist approaches to foreign policy in the light of these changes.

Should the United States maintain its vigilance in the form of powerful armed forces, or should it engage in general disarmament? Should it extend military and economic support to all nations which support it, or should it deny aid to governments that violate democratic principles? Should America's economy be safeguarded with tariffs and other economic barriers, or should it embrace free trade?

In the following selections, Stanley Kober argues that moral principles in foreign relations are in America's best interest. Arthur Schlesinger, Jr., believes that personal morality is not applicable to international relations, and that a realistic view of national interest will produce the most enlightened foreign policy.

YES

Stanley Kober

IDEALPOLITIK

A revolution is sweeping the world—a revolution of democracy. The success of this democratic revolution has shaken Europe to its foundations and shattered the strategic guideposts used to chart American foreign policy for more than 40 years. Groping through this new landscape, foreign policy specialists are struggling to develop policies to encourage democratic change while safeguarding strategic stability.

The failure to anticipate these changes, however, has understandably introduced a note of caution into the American response. The events were unexpected but they should not have been if the policy framework had been correct. Throughout the postwar era, American foreign policy has been dominated by a philosophy of realism, which views international politics as a struggle for power in which the interests of the great powers must be in conflict. This was a natural vision of foreign policy during a time in which then Soviet Foreign Minister Andrei Gromyko declared that "the world outlook and the class goals of the two social systems are opposite and irreconcilable."

It is precisely this "realistic" approach to foreign policy that is now being challenged, however, as Soviet President Mikhail Gorbachev and his allies in the Soviet leadership explicitly repudiate Gromyko's position. "Coexistence," proclaimed Foreign Minister Eduard Shevardnadze in July 1988, "cannot be identified with the class struggle." Instead, it "should have universal interests as a common denominator." The realignment of the Soviet Union's foreign policy has been accompanied by an even more fundamental transformation of its domestic political structure. . . .

At the end of World War I, President Woodrow Wilson traveled to Europe to help develop a structure assuring that "the war to end wars" would be just that. Wilson's approach consisted of two main parts. First, the Central European empires were dismantled and new states based on the principle of national self-determination were established. Second, Wilson proposed the creation of the League of Nations to handle future threats to international security.

From Stanley Kober, "Idealpolitik," *Foreign Policy*, no. 79 (Summer 1990). Copyright © 1990 by the Carnegie Endowment for International Peace. Reprinted by permission of *Foreign Policy*.

Wilson's ideas were immediately challenged by the great British geopolitician Sir Halford Mackinder. In *Democratic Ideals and Reality*, which was first published in 1919, Mackinder argued that Wilson's democratic idealism might be noble but failed to deal with world realities. "Idealists are the salt of the earth," he wrote condescendingly; but, he warned, "democracy is incompatible with the organization necessary for war against autocracies." Mackinder asserted that "political moralists" like Wilson "refused to reckon with the realities of geography and economics." Mackinder defined these realities in his famous formulation: "Who rules East Europe commands the Heartland: Who rules the Heartland commands the World-Island: Who rules the World-Island commands the World." Given the importance of Eastern Europe, the prevention of another world war would depend on the establishment of "a tier of independent states between Germany and Russia." The political structure of these states did not concern him; what interested him was the balance of power. . . .

POSTWAR REALISM

Mackinder's "realistic" critique of Wilson's idealism found an echo in U.S. policy in the late 1940s. . . .

"The main signpost that helps political realism to find its way through the landscape of international politics is the concept of interest defined in terms of power," wrote Hans Morgenthau, probably the foremost exponent of the realist school. Morgenthau's book, *Politics Among Nations: The Struggle for Power and Peace* (1948), helped provide the intellectual basis for America's engagement in power politics. "Politics, like society in general, is governed by objective laws that have their roots in human nature," observed Morgenthau. Since these laws are objective, they are necessarily universal, and consequently it is futile and deceptive to examine foreign policy exclusively by looking at the motives of government officials. . . .

By acknowledging that the effective functioning of international politics depends on the existence of "shared values," Morgenthau admitted that the "laws" of power politics are not so objective after all. Yet if Morgenthau grieved for a world order that was no more, former Secretary of State Henry Kissinger insists that it still exists and is irreplaceable. "To have stability," he wrote in a recent *Washington Post* article, "an international system must have two components: a balance of power and a generally accepted principle of legitimacy." . . .

Similarly, Kissinger shares Morgenthau's conviction that the realities of power politics compel the subordination of a nation's ideology to more basic interests. "National security concerns should be in harmony with traditional American values," he explained in a 1986 article, but "this ideal cannot always prevail, imposing the necessity to strike a balance." Underlying this view is Kissinger's assessment, expressed at a 1977 lecture at New York University, that "the United States is now as vulnerable as any other nation." Not only is it subject to the danger of nuclear annihilation, but American "prosperity is to some extent hostage to the decisions on raw materials, prices, and investment in distant countries whose purposes are not necessarily compatible with ours." Thus, although "our morality and our power should not be antithetical," in the final analysis "all serious foreign policy must begin with the need for survival."

THE NEW IDEALISM

In contrast to geopolitics and realism, idealism has never had a distinct line of philosophical development. The German philosopher Immanuel Kant wrote that the rule of law would result in "perpetual peace," but he provided little guidance on how governments should behave until that day arrives. . . .

Unfortunately, idealism is still seen as a naive philosophy that fails to understand the realities of power politics. Because of the uncompromising moralism with which it is endowed by its opponents, idealism is viewed as leading either to withdrawal from an imperfect world or to unrestrained interventionism to right all the world's wrongs. It is time for a new, more rigorous idealist alternative to realism.

A proper understanding of idealism, therefore, begins with the recognition that ideologies matter, and that the foreign policy of a state is an outgrowth of the values embodied in its domestic institutions. In the idealist view, the structure of a government determines how aggressive it can be. Specifically, dictatorships will be more aggressive than parliamentary democracies, since dictators can undertake military actions on their own initiative without having to obtain prior consent from popularly elected legislatures.

In taking this position, idealists recognize that democracies have behaved aggressively in the past but add that they are also evolving institutions. Democracy embodies strict criteria for majority rule and minority rights. Majority rule means that all the people are entitled to vote, and that those elected are accountable to the voters at frequent and regular intervals. The idealist views a democracy in which women, minorities, or other groups are excluded as more likely to be aggressive, since those making the decisions for war or peace are not accountable to everyone affected. In order to be accountable, representatives must provide the voters with the information they need to exercise their authority properly, and the people must have some mechanism for obtaining this information if it is being improperly withheld.

Minority rights are widely regarded as contradictory to majority rule, but this view is misguided. As recent ethnic conflicts demonstrate, majorities can change over time, and majority rule in the absence of guaranteed minority rights is a prescription for catastrophe. More to the point, however, guarantees of minority rights, which can be enforced only by the voluntary consent of the majority, signify respect for the weak by the strong. This value system of respect for law rather than for power is the best assurance of order and stability, both domestically and internationally.

Thus, the idealist is an unabashed proponent of democracy, seeing democracy as the best guarantee of world peace. While admitting that there is little historical experience of democracies of the sort described, the idealist would point to the relationship between the United States and Canada as instructive. Although these two countries were at war with each other at the beginning of the nineteenth century, they now share the longest undefended border in the world. The idealist would attribute this outcome to their mutual development of democratic institutions and would challenge the realist to explain why, if the balance of power is so important, Canadians do not tremble in fear at the prospect of an American invasion. The realist might reply that although there is an imbalance of power between the United States and Canada, they share an accepted principle of legitimacy. This answer is incomplete, for what is the source of that accepted principle of legitimacy if it is not the democratic values and respect for law both countries share?

In short, if it is democratic values that bring peace, one should say so forthrightly and not pretend that one principle of legitimacy is as good as another so long as it is generally accepted. If the balance of power cannot explain the peaceful U.S.–Canadian relationship, neither can it explain the outbreak of World War II. No geopolitical arrangement achievable at the time could have deterred Adolf Hitler because he saw war as the glorious means for achieving his objective, the occupation and subjugation of lands to the east. "No one will ever again have the confidence of the whole German people as I have," Hitler observed in August 1939. "All these favorable circumstances will no longer prevail in two or three years' time. No one knows how much longer I shall live." Whereas normal people are afraid of war, Hitler was afraid he would die before he could start a war.

The cause of World War II, therefore, must be sought not in the geopolitics of Europe, but in the domestic politics of Germany. . . .

Idealist analysis provides criteria for assessing whether a military buildup is the result of perceptions of insecurity or the product of a drive for military supremacy to achieve political objectives by the threat or use of arms. The difference is crucial in determining the proper response. If the former, policy should focus on alleviating the political causes of insecurity. In this case, arms control has its

greatest effect by building confidence. In the latter case, however, political measures are of limited, if any, use since there is no insecurity to alleviate. On the contrary, policy here should focus on countervailing arms buildup, both to safeguard one's own security and to convince the arming power that it cannot achieve its objective. Arms control in this case can play a modest role by directing the competition away from the most destabilizing weapons, but it cannot achieve its ultimate objective of building confidence.

Faced with the need to choose between these two causes of an arms race, realism is helpless, since either cause might be rational depending on the policy objectives of a country's leaders. Unwilling to trust policy statements and rejecting the connection between domestic and foreign policy, realists ultimately base their assessments on their own value biases with no independent test. The idealist, on the other hand, insists that policy statements, particularly those designed for domestic officials, are revealing. More to the point, the idealist believes that even if such statements are too ambiguous to be a guide for formulating a response, the values embodied in a country's domestic policy and institutions provide invaluable insight into its purposes in foreign policy.

It is incorrect, therefore, to say that idealism rejects the balance of power. In fact, idealism recognizes that in the face of a military threat, there is no alternative to maintaining a balance, or even a preponderance, of power. What idealism rejects is the idea that international peace is solely the product of a balance of power. For the idealist, a country can have friends as well as interests. The ultimate objective of idealism is to broaden the circle of friendship by fostering the spread of democratic values and institutions. In the meantime, recognizing the dangers of the world as it exists, idealism provides a mechanism for assessing the degree of threat posed by hostile regimes, in particular the threat posed by a military buildup. . . .

REVOLUTION IN THE '90s

It is no longer possible to dismiss idealists as utopian dreamers who do not understand the harsh reality of power. On the contrary, idealists can respond that it is realists and geopoliticians who have oversimplified the concept of power and misunderstood the lessons of history. The debate between them is of critical importance in formulating policy to respond to the revolutionary changes now confronting the world.

Of all the momentous changes now occurring, the most dramatic is the transformation of the Soviet bloc. It is worth noting that the Soviets have always accepted some principles of idealism. Unlike realists, the Soviets have always stressed the importance of ideology and insisted that it is impossible to understand the foreign policy of a country without appreciating its domestic values and institutions. Similarly, like idealists, the Soviets professed to see the ultimate guarantee of world peace in the domestic structure of states. However, they saw that domestic structure in the communist principles of Karl Marx and V. I. Lenin, rather than in the democratic institutions of Thomas Jefferson and James Madison.

What is so revolutionary about the current changes in the Soviet Union is that they are based on the acknowledgement that the guarantee of world peace

lies not in the spread of socialism, but in parliamentary control over war-making power. According to a January 1988 article in *Kommunist*, the theoretical journal of the Soviet Communist party, "there are no politically influential forces in either Western Europe or the U.S." that contemplate "military aggression against socialism." But even if there were, America's democratic institutions would make such large-scale aggression impossible. The article emphasizes that "bourgeois democracy serves as a definite barrier in the path of unleashing such a war. . . . The history of the American intervention in Indochina clearly demonstrated this. . . . The Pentagon now cannot fail to recognize the existence of limits placed on its actions by democratic institutions." By formulating the question of war and peace in this way, the authors posed, albeit implicitly, an extremely profound question: If it is democratic institutions like those in the West that prevent war, then where is the threat to peace? Logically, it must come from those countries without such democratic institutions—countries like the Soviet Union. Astonishing as it may seem, this realization is one of the foundations on which *perestroika* is being built.

"The use of armed forces outside the country without sanction from the Supreme Soviet or the congress is ruled out categorically, once and for all," Gorbachev affirmed in assuming his new powers as president in March 1990. This statement reflects the fundamental nature of the changes taking place in the Soviet Union, which have little, if anything, to do with Marxism-Leninism. Indeed, as the former head of the Soviet Institute of State and Law, Vladimir Kudryavtsev, has forthrightly acknowledged, "Marxists criticized the 'separation of powers' theory which drew a clear dividing line between legislative and executive power." Now Soviets are recognizing their mistake and embracing the separation of powers and the rule of law. The philosophical basis for these changes can be found in the writings of Kant. "The philosophical foundation of the rule-of-law state was formulated by Kant," Kudryavtsev and Yelena Lukasheva, a doctor of juridical science, flatly stated in a *Kommunist* article following the June-July 1988 19th party conference, which established the rule of law as a major objective of *perestroika*. Soviet officials from Gorbachev on down now routinely refer to Kant, and Shevardnadze has specifically identified Kant's 1795 booklet *Perpetual Peace* as a work deserving special attention.

Perpetual Peace was a major contribution to idealist philosophy. An admirer of the principles behind the American Revolution, Kant saw perpetual peace as a product not of the balance of power, but of republican government. Similarly, he rejected economic mercantilism, which is the foundation of geopolitics, in favor of Adam Smith's promotion of free trade. These themes are now commonplace in the Soviet media.

Viewed from the realist perspective, Gorbachev's actions, particularly in Eastern Europe, are puzzling; viewed from an idealist position, however, they are easily explicable. Since it is commerce rather than control of resources that is the source of wealth, better to abandon the territory where people are resentful of occupation. Free trade will provide more economic benefits than occupation. Nor is there any security risk; Soviet security is, in the final analysis, assured not by the territorial glacis or even by the might of the Soviet armed forces,

but by the institutions of Western democracy. . . .

The changes in Eastern Europe go to the heart of the debate between realism and idealism. Since realists maintain that it is power rather than ideology that matters, they view Gorbachev's changes with suspicion. Realists are concerned that if Gorbachev is successful, the result could be a stronger Soviet Union and thus an even greater threat to the United States. Realists do not see a necessary link between the Soviet Union's domestic changes and its foreign policy. "*Glasnost* [openness] and *perestroika* represent attempts to modernize the Soviet state," Kissinger wrote in a January 1988 article in the *Washington Post*. "That is an internal Soviet matter, relevant to the democracies only if accompanied by a change in Soviet foreign policy." Indeed, Kissinger worries "whether Americans can be brought to see foreign policy in terms of equilibrium rather than as a struggle between good and evil." In his view, this was the problem with former President Ronald Reagan's policy toward the Soviet Union, which in a few years went from denunciations of an evil empire to an embrace of Gorbachev. "Such an approach," Kissinger stressed in another *Washington Post* article in February 1989, "neglects the realities of power, ambition and national interest."

For the idealist, on the other hand, there are no immutable "realities of power, ambition and national interest." All these must be viewed through the prism of policy, which changes as people change. Policy will be affected by a society's values, which in turn are embodied in its domestic institutions. Thus, the idealist rejects the notion that there is no connection between *perestroika* and Soviet foreign policy. Whereas the realist is in perpetual pursuit of a stabilizing equilibrium—believing, in former President Richard Nixon's words, that "the only time in the history of the world that we have had any extended periods of peace is when there has been balance of power"—the idealist seeks the spread of freedom, which ultimately would eliminate the need for a balance of power.

The difference between the two approaches is manifest in the way their adherents assess current developments in Europe. According to President George Bush, "the enemy is instability." But although instability can be dangerous if it is a prelude to chaos, stability by itself cannot be the highest American value. "Those who won our independence by revolution. . . . did not fear political change," Justice Louis Brandeis wrote in 1927. "They did not exalt order at the cost of liberty." Affirming this idealist view, President Vaclav Havel of Czechoslovakia told the American people in February 1990 that "the best guarantee against possible threat or aggressivity is democracy," and, accordingly, he told Congress that the United States should "help the Soviet Union on its irreversible but immensely complicated road to democracy."

Safeguarding and spreading democracy in Eastern Europe means, above all, fostering the demilitarization of the Soviet Union and accelerating the withdrawal of its armed forces from foreign territory. Arguments that Gorbachev's position is too uncertain to be a basis for security decisions are unconvincing because arms control agreements are one of the best ways to bolster Gorbachev's position against hardline rivals. The more the USSR disarms and the more troops it withdraws from Eastern Europe, the more difficult it will be for any regime that might overthrow Gorbachev to reconstitute a significant military threat. In such a situation, moreover, violations of agreements will provide warning of the change in Soviet intentions, thereby further protecting American security. . . .

Two hundred years ago, the Enlightenment produced one of the great eras of human civilization. Its spirit, the spirit of tolerance, was captured by Voltaire: "Every individual who persecutes a man, his brother, because he does not agree with him, is a monster. . . . We should tolerate each other because we are all weak, inconsistent, subject to mutability and to error." This spirit was one of the inspirations for the American form of government. In the words of George Washington, "the Citizens of the United States of America have a right to applaud themselves for having given to mankind examples of an enlarged and liberal policy: a policy worthy of imitation. All possess alike liberty of conscience and immunities of citizenship."

Today, Americans are witnessing the reaffirmation of these principles of the Enlightenment and the power of the American example. For too long Americans have compromised their principles in the name of geopolitics. By doing so, they gave rise to a perception of moral equivalence between the United States and the Soviet Union, which undermined American interests. More to the point, they betrayed their special heritage. "Let us be diverted by none of those sophistical contrivances wherewith we are so industriously plied and belabored," Lincoln urged the American people in 1860 on the eve of their greatest test. "Let us have faith that right makes might, and in that faith, let us, to the end, dare to do our duty as we understand it." . . .

The realist perspective has gone unchallenged long enough. Idealism is not naive utopianism but a rigorous approach to the conduct of foreign policy. Moreover, it is idealism that is the great American tradition. As Washington declared in his Farewell Address:

Observe good faith and justice toward all nations. Cultivate peace and harmony with all. Religion and morality enjoin this conduct. And can it be that good policy does not equally enjoin it? It will be worthy of a free, enlightened, and at no distant period a great nation to give mankind the magnanimous and too novel example of a people always guided by an exalted justice and benevolence. Who can doubt that in the course of time and things the fruits of such a plan would richly repay any temporary advantages which might be lost by a steady adherence to it?

Americans should not fear that the spread of the democratic system created by the founders of their republic could present a threat to their security. They should instead follow Washington's advice and reject the realist's compromises as leading only to those "temporary advantages" of which he spoke. The long-term interests of the United States are fulfilled when it is true to its ideals, thus setting an example for the rest of the world. "We shall be as a City upon a Hill, the Eyes of all people are upon us," John Winthrop proclaimed in 1630. More than 350 years later, our revolutionary world demonstrates that it is the power of America's ideals, and not the might of its armies, that is the real source of U.S. influence in the world.

NO

Arthur Schlesinger, Jr.

IN THE NATIONAL INTEREST

William James used to say that temperaments determined philosophies. People who respond to international affairs divide temperamentally into two schools: those who see policies as wise or foolish, and those who see them as good or evil. One cannot presume an ultimate metaphysical antagonism here. No person can escape perceptions of good and evil—even Machiavelli counseled the Prince not to forget, when circumstances impelled him to do a bad thing, that he *was* doing a bad thing—and no policy can wholly divorce political from moral principles. Nor in the impenetrability of human motives can we easily know when the moral reasons are political reasons in disguise (very often the case) or when political reasons are moral reasons in disguise (more frequent than one might think).

That moral values should control foreign policy decisions was not particularly the view of the Founding Fathers, who saw international affairs in the light of the balance of power. But in the century after 1815, as Americans turned their backs on the power struggles of Europe, they stopped thinking about power as the essence of international politics. The moralization of foreign policy became a national penchant; and the subsequent return of the republic to the world power game has not much enfeebled that cherished habit. In our own day both Right and Left yield with relish to the craving for moral judgment. Ronald Reagan, Jimmy Carter, Philip Berrigan, and Noam Chomsky disagree over the substance of such judgment, but they agree that moral principles should dominate or at least pervade foreign policy decisions.

Let us not overstate the moral argument. Many foreign policy decisions are self-evidently questions of prudence and adjustment, not of good and evil. Most moralizers would readily join with their acute critic George Kennan in doubting that "it matters greatly to God whether the free trade area of the Common Market prevails in Europe, whether the British fish or do not fish in Icelandic territorial waters, or even whether Indians or Pakistanis run Kashmir. It might matter, but it is hard for us, with our limited vision, to know." The raw material of foreign affairs is, a good deal of the time, morally neutral or ambiguous. Consequently, moral principles cannot be decisive for the great majority of foreign policy transactions.

But these, it may be said, are technical transactions. On the great issues, surely, moral principles should be controlling. Yet how are right and wrong to be defined in dealings among sovereign states? Here the moralist of foreign affairs has recourse to the moral code most familiar to him: the code that governs dealings among individuals. His contention is that states should be judged by principles of individual morality. As Woodrow Wilson put it in his address to Congress on the declaration of war in 1917: "We are at the beginning of an age in which it will be insisted that the same standards of conduct and of responsibility for wrong done shall be observed among nations and their governments that are observed among the individual citizens of civilized states." John Foster Dulles said it even more directly, in the midst of World War II: "The broad principles that should govern our international conduct are not obscure. They grown out of the practice by the nations of the simple things Christ taught."

The argument for the application of simple moral principles to questions of foreign policy is, thus, that there is, or should be, an identity between the morality of individuals and the morality of states. The issues involved here are not easy. One cannot doubt that there are cases in foreign affairs where moral judgment is possible and necessary. But one may also suggest that these are extreme cases and do not warrant the routine use of moral criteria in making foreign policy decisions. It was to expose such indis-

criminate moralism that Reinhold Niebuhr wrote *Moral Man and Immoral Society* forty years ago.

Niebuhr insisted that a distinction had to be drawn between the moral behavior of individuals and that of social groups. The obligation of the individual is to obey the law of love and sacrifice; "from the viewpoint of the author of an action, unselfishness must remain the criterion of the highest morality." But nations cannot be sacrificial. Governments are not individuals. They are trustees for the happiness and interest of their nation. Niebuhr quotes Hugh Cecil's argument that unselfishness "is inappropriate to the action of a state. No one has a right to be unselfish with other people's interest." Alexander Hamilton had made the same point in the early years of the American republic:

The rule of morality . . . is not precisely the same between nations as between individuals. The duty of making its own welfare the guide of its actions is much stronger upon the former than upon the latter. Existing millions, and for the most part future generations, are concerned in the present measures of a government; while the consequences of the private action of an individual ordinarily terminate with himself, or are circumscribed with a narrow compass.

This is not to say that might makes right. It is to say that the morality of states is inherently different from the morality of individuals. Saints can be pure, but statesmen must be responsible. As trustees for others, they must defend interests and compromise principles. In consequence, politics is a field where practical and prudential judgment must have priority over simple moral verdicts.

LIMITS AND SUBSTANCE

Against this view it may be urged that the question between individual morality and political necessity has been, to a considerable degree, bridged within national societies. This takes place when the moral sense of a community finds embodiment in positive law. But the shift of the argument from morality to law only strengthens the case against the facile intrusion of moral judgment into foreign affairs.

A nation's law can set down relatively clear standards of right and wrong individual behavior because domestic law is the product of an imperfect but nonetheless authentic moral consensus. International life has no such broad or deep areas of moral consensus. It was once hoped that modern technology would create a common fund of moral imperatives transcending the concerns of particular nations—common concepts of interest, justice, and comity—either because the revolution in communications would increase mutual understanding or because the revolution in weaponry would increase mutual fear. Such expectations have been disappointed. Until nations come to adopt the same international morality, there can be no world law to regulate the behavior of states as there is law within nations to regulate the behavior of individuals. Nor can international institutions—the League of Nations or the United Nations—produce by sleight of hand a moral consensus where none exists. World law must express world community; it cannot create it.

This is not to say we cannot discern the rudiments of an international consensus. Within limits, humanity has begun to develop standards for conduct among nations—defined, for example, in the Hague Conventions of 1899 and 1907, in the Geneva Protocol of 1925 and the Geneva Conventions of 1949, in the Charter and Covenants of the United Nations, in the Charter, Judgment, and Principles of the Nuremberg Tribunal, and so on. Such documents outlaw actions that the civilized world has placed beyond the limits of permissible behavior. Within this restricted area a code emerges that makes moral judgment in international affairs possible up to a point. And within its scope this rudimentary code deserves, and must have, the most unflinching enforcement.

But these international rules deal with the limits rather than with the substance of the policy. They seek to prevent abnormalities and excesses in the behavior of states, but they do not offer grounds for moral judgment on normal international transactions (including, it must be said sorrowfully, war itself, so long as war does not constitute aggression and so long as the rules of warfare are faithfully observed). These international accords may eventually promote a world moral consensus. But, for the present, national, ideological, ethical, and religious divisions remain as bitterly intractable as ever.

Not only are simplistic moral principles of limited use in the making of foreign policy decisions, they may actually impede the intelligent conduct of foreign affairs. For many Americans the "moral" element in foreign policy consists in the application to the world of a body of abstract precepts, a process to be accompanied by lectures to others and congratulations to ourselves. The assumption is that we are the anointed custodians of the rules of international behavior, and that the function of United States policy is to mark other states up and down, according to their obedience to our rules.

Laying down the moral law to erring brethren from our seat of judgment no doubt does wonders for our own sense of virtue. But it fosters misconceptions about the nature of foreign policy. Moralizers tend to prefer symbolic to substantive politics. They tend to see foreign policy as a means of registering attitudes, not of producing hard results in a hard world. Moralistic rhetoric, moreover, often masks the pursuit of national advantage—a situation we recognize at once when other states hide their selfish objectives under a cloak of moral universalism. Should we be surprised that those other states are just as skeptical about American claims to moral disinterestedness?

The moralization of foreign policy creates still graver problems. Moral reasons offered cynically may indeed do the world less harm than moral reasons fervently believed. The compulsion to see foreign affairs in moralistic terms often has, with the noblest intentions, the most ghastly consequences, for the person who converts conflicts of interest and circumstance into conflicts of good and evil necessarily invests himself with moral superiority. Those who see foreign affairs as made up of questions of right and wrong begin by supposing they know better than other people what is right for them. The more passionately they believe they are right, the more likely they are to reject expediency and accommodation and seek the final victory of their principles. Little has been more pernicious in international politics than excessive righteousness.

The moralizing fever may, as noted, strike at any point along the political spectrum. From the standpoint of those who mistrust self-serving ethical poses, there is little difference between moralists on the Right who see the Soviet Union as the focus of all evil and moralists on the Left who ascribe all sin to the United States. They are all victims of the same malady. Both regard foreign policy as a branch of theology. They end as mirror images of each other. In the process of moral self-aggrandizement, each loses the humility that is the heart of human restraint. All nations, said Gladstone—a Christian statesman if ever there was one—are equal,

and you have no right to set up a system under which one is to be placed under moral suspicion or espionage, or made the subject of constant invective. If you do that, and especially if you claim for yourself a pharisaical superiority . . . you may talk about your patriotism as you please, but you are a misjudging friend of your country and are undermining the basis of esteem and respect of others for it.

Moralism in foreign policy is likely to conclude in fanaticism; and a fanatic, Mr. Dooley reminds us, "does what he thinks th' Lord wud do if he only knew th' facts in th' case." At home, moralism perceives mistakes in political judgment as evidence of moral obliquity: The issue becomes not self-delusion or stupidity but criminality and treason; it ends in ferreting out the reprobates as traitors or war criminals. Abroad, moral absolutism leads to crusades and the extermination of the infidel. Religion, the ultimate absolutist sanction, is in the 1980s the main cause of most of the killing taking place in the world: in the Middle East, in the Persian Gulf, in Ireland, in India, in Cyprus, in the Philippines, throughout Africa—not to mention the havoc wrought by the totalitarian religions of the twentieth century. Those whose view on foreign policy arise from convictions of their own superior righteousness should recall the warning of Chekhov: "You will not become a saint through other people's sins."

THE MAGNETIC COMPASS

If moral principles have only limited application in foreign affairs, and if moral absolutism breeds intolerance and fanaticism, is the world therefore condemned to moral anarchy in international relations? No necessarily. The argument moves, rather, to the conclusion that foreign policy decisions must generally be taken on other than moralistic grounds. It is necessary to consider what these other grounds are.

The men "who act upon the Principles of disinterestedness," wrote George Washington, "are, comparatively speaking, no more than a drop in the Ocean." He recognized, Washington continued, the power of patriotism. "But I will venture to assert that a great and lasting War can never be supported on this principle alone. It must be aided by a prospect of Interest. . . . We must take the passions of Men as Nature has given them." What was true for men, Washington believed, was even more true for nations. He called it "a maxim founded on the universal experience of mankind, that no nation is to be trusted farther than it is bound by its interest." In short, where the embryonic international community cannot regulate dealings among nations, the safest basis for decision in foreign policy lies not in attempts to determine right or wrong but in attempts to determine the national interest.

The idea of national interest sees international politics as, in the end, a struggle for power. The realist rejects cant and

sentimentality. He is honest about his motives and takes life as history and experience reveal it to be. In reaction against soft Wilsonian righteousness, national interest seemed for a season a hard doctrine, the analytic key to the foreign policy riddle. For Washington was obviously right in saying that every nation *must* respond to some conception of national interest. No nation that abandons self-preservation as the mainspring of its policy can survive; nor, indeed, can any nation be relied upon in international dealings that acts against its national interest. Without the magnetic compass of national interest there would be no order or predictability in international affairs.

Moreover, every nation has a set of fairly definite strategic interests. One has only to recall the continuities of Russian foreign policy, whether directed by czars or by commissars. When one moves on to politics and economics, identification of national interest becomes more debatable. Still, even here nations often retain, through changes of government and ideology, an impressive amount of continuity: Consider France from De Gaulle to Mitterrand.

National interest is obviously not a fiction. But, as critics soon pointed out, neither is it a self-executing formula providing an automatic answer to every international perplexity. In practice, citizens quarrel endlessly about the content of national interest. The idea is dangerously stretchable and subject to much abuse. Almost as many follies have been committed in the name of national interest as in the name of national righteousness. The national interest, critics conclude, is not easily identified or objectively ascertained.

Hans Morgenthau, the great theoretician of national interest, thus argued that

German leaders had twice in one generation betrayed Germany's national interest;
but that is hardly what the kaiser and
Hitler thought they were doing. In the
United States in the 1960s, the prominent
realists—Morgenthau, Kennan, Niebuhr,
Walter Lippmann—condemned American participation in the Vietnam war as
wholly unwarranted in terms of national
interest. The advocates of American participation argued with equal vehemence
that the national interest demanded the
Americanization of the war. History, it is
true, has vindicated the realists; but who
could *prove* at the time where the national interest truly lay? When indeed
have statesmen ever supposed that they
were betraying the national interest of
their countries? National interest, while
not an altogether phantasmagoric concept, clearly does not offer unequivocal
policy guidance in specific situations.

There are still deep objections. Moralizers consider national interest an unworthy if not a wicked idea on which to
found national policy. It nourishes a nation's baser self. It becomes, they say, a
license for international aggrandizement.
The pursuit of exclusively national goals
leads ineluctably to aggression, imperialism, war. National interest, in short, is a
mandate for international amorality.

In practice, this is often so. In principle, however, national interest prescribes
its own morality. After all, the order and
predicability in international affairs valued
by Washington constitute the precondi-
tion for international moral standards.
More important, national interest, consistently construed, is a self-limiting motive. Any rigorous defender of the idea
must accept that other nations have their
legitimate interests too. The recognition
of equal claims sets abounds on aggression. Unless transformed by an injection

of moral righteousness, the idea of national interest cannot produce ideological
crusades for unlimited objectives.

This self-limiting factor does not rest
only on the perception of other nations'
interests. It is reinforced by self-correct-
ing tendencies in the power equilibrium—tendencies that prevent national
interest, at least when the disparity of
power is not too great, from billowing up
into unbridled national egoism. History
has shown how often the overweening
behavior of an aggressive state leads to
counteraction on the part of other states
determined to restore a balance of power.
This means that uncontrolled national
egoism generally turns out to be contrary
to long term national interest. State that
throw their weight around are generally
forced to revise their notions as to where
national interest truly lies. This has happened to Germany and Japan. In time it
may even happen to the Soviet Union
and the United States.

For these reasons, it may be suggested
that national interest, realistically construed, will promote enlightened rather
than imperial policy. So it was that a
realist like Hamilton could say that his
aim was not "to recommend a policy
absolutely selfish or interested in nations; but to show that a policy regulated
by their own interest, as far as justice and
good faith permit, is, and ought to be,
their prevailing one."

POSTSCRIPT

Should Idealism Be the Basis of American Foreign Policy?

As the essays by Kober and Schlesinger demonstrate, the choice between idealism, the primacy of moral principles, and realism, the perception of national interest, is not always clear-cut. Kober clearly believes that idealism is ultimately more realistic, and Schlesinger is persuaded that national interest is more moral.

Nevertheless, foreign policy decisions frequently pose a clear choice between these approaches to international relations. Such was the case with President Bush's renewal of trade benefits to China in 1990. "Realists" defended his actions as being in America's interests in protecting U.S. investments and supporting reform-minded Chinese, whereas "idealists" were critical because the action did not indicate disapproval of China's continued denial of human rights.

Kober and Schlesinger both cite the works of Hans Morgenthau for providing the most influential defense of realist foreign policy. William Appleman Williams, in *The Tragedy of American Diplomacy* (Delta, 1959, revised 1962), has presented the classic critique of Morgenthau's position.

Leading policymakers from the administrations of presidents Kennedy to Bush have contributed informed essays to Edward K. Hamilton, ed., *American's Global Interests: A New Agenda* (W. W. Norton, 1989). These essays largely subscribe to a realist approach to foreign policy-making.

Most analyses written before 1990 appear badly outdated as a result of the extraordinary changes that have taken place in international relations. Bogdan Denitch, author of *The End of the Cold War* (University of Minnesota, 1990), anticipates that European democratic socialism will present new challenges to American influence. William G. Hyland, *The Cold War Is Over* (Times Books, 1990), is not certain that the danger has passed. Perhaps the best contemporary discussions of American policy are to be found in *Foreign Affairs* and *Foreign Policy*, as well as *Harper's Magazine*, *Commentary*, and other nonspecialized periodicals.

The questions to be answered were unimaginable only a few years ago. The Cold War is over—or is it? How does the United States refashion its foreign policy to take into account the changing conditions in Europe, the Soviet Union, and Asia? Does military might matter less and economic productivity more in the relations between nations? At bottom, of course, the broad question is the enduring one: Should American foreign policy be guided by moral principles or by the concept of national interest?

ISSUE 20

Is America Declining?

YES: Paul Kennedy, from *The Rise and Fall of the Great Powers* (Random House, 1987)

NO: Samuel P. Huntington, from "The U.S.—Decline or Renewal?" *Foreign Affairs* (Winter 1988–89)

ISSUE SUMMARY

YES: Historian Paul Kennedy believes that the United States, like other great powers before it, has developed an imbalance between international military commitments and domestic economic development, which will inevitably result in America's decline in power.

NO: Political scientist Samuel P. Huntington maintains that American decline is exaggerated, temporary, and reversible. Because America possesses the major sources of national power, it has the capacity to renew itself.

The United States emerged after World War II as the most powerful nation in the world. In part this was the result of the cumulative economic costs of World Wars I and II for England, Germany, the Soviet Union, and Japan. America escaped the physical devastation of the wars that these nations suffered, and America's economy boomed during the war years and continued to grow in the post-war periods. Having become the most prosperous and powerful of nations, the United States assumed international leadership in armaments, investments, and aid.

Critics now argue that the costs of maintaining this leadership role have surpassed the nation's willingness to pay. In less than a decade the national debt has more than doubled. A nation that was long the world's greatest creditor is now the largest debtor nation in history.

It is difficult for Americans living today to accept the view that this nation's power and influence will not endure. Yet historians have always noted the "rise and fall of great powers," as does Paul Kennedy in his book. Kennedy's book has attracted great interest because it is an impressive survey of the past that also ventures to peer ahead to the near future, with direct relevance to the United States.

Kennedy summarized his thesis: "The historical record suggests that there is a very clear connection *in the long run* between an individual Great

Power's economic rise and fall and its growth and decline as an important military power (or world empire)." Nations must spend to create the armies and navies that protect their wealth and security; but if they spend too much, they weaken their economic competitiveness. "Imperial overstretch" is Kennedy's term for the tendency of great powers to commit too much wealth to overseas commitments and too little to domestic economic growth.

Kennedy identifies the loss of power with the decline of economic competitiveness. In his account, the most powerful nations in the last five centuries—successively, Spain, the Netherlands, France, and England—were unable or unwilling to tax themselves sufficiently to pay for their armed forces and empires, and the United States now finds itself in a comparable position. The greater the power of a state, the greater the expenditure that must be made to support it.

There is an almost instinctive American rejection of any theory that even suggests that historical forces determine our fates independent of our wills. Public rhetoric expresses a conviction that there is little that Americans cannot achieve, if they will it and work to achieve it. The qualities that made it possible for earlier American generations to settle a subcontinent and make it prosper—idealism, dedication to a common purpose, a willingness to sacrifice for significant long-range goals—can enable this generation to keep America prosperous and powerful into the future.

A further objection is that Kennedy's generalizations confuse different cases. After all, the United States has not created an international empire similar to those established by Spain, France or England. Far from trying to become the dominant nation in the world, the United States since World War I has sought to strengthen its allies to create an effective balance of power vis-à-vis the Soviet Union and its allies. To be sure, the United States, by virtue of its military and economic power, has exercised leadership; but that is very different from domination. American support for the United Nations, economic aid to rebuild war-torn Europe, and mutual security acts with the non-communist nations of Europe and Asia are the acts of an ally, not a conqueror.

The collapse of the Soviet Union and its communist allies would appear to leave the United States as the only superpower, rebutting predictions of America's decline. However, if the measure of power is now economic and not military, Japan and a newly united Europe emerge as formidable challengers to American dominance and leadership.

In the following selections, Paul Kennedy applies his historical analysis of inevitable decline to the United States, while Samuel P. Huntington argues that such a decline has taken place and can be reversed, and America can continue to be both powerful and influential.

YES
Paul Kennedy

THE UNITED STATES: THE PROBLEM OF NUMBER ONE IN RELATIVE DECLINE

Although the United States is at present still in a class of its own economically and perhaps even militarily, it cannot avoid confronting the two great tests which challenge the *longevity* of every major power that occupies the "number one" position in world affairs: whether, in the military/strategic realm, it can preserve a reasonable balance between the nation's perceived defense requirements and the means it possesses to maintain those commitments; and whether, as an intimately related point, it can preserve the technological and economic bases of its power from relative erosion in the face of the ever-shifting patterns of global production. This test of American abilities will be the greater because it, like Imperial Spain around 1600 or the British Empire around 1900, is the inheritor of a vast array of strategical commitments which had been made decades earlier, when the nation's political, economic, and military capacity to influence world affairs seemed so much more assured. In consequence, the United States now runs the risk, so familiar to historians of the rise and fall of previous Great Powers, of what might roughly be called "imperial overstretch": that is to say, decision-makers in Washington must face the awkward and enduring fact that the sum total of the United States' global interests and obligations is nowadays far larger than the country's power to defend them all simultaneously. . . .

[T]he United States today has roughly the same massive array of military obligations across the globe as it had a quarter-century ago, when its shares of world GNP, manufacturing production, military spending, and armed forces personnel were so much larger than they are now. Even in 1985, forty years after its triumphs of the Second World War and over a decade after its pull-out from Vietnam, the United States had 520,000 members of its armed forces abroad (including 65,000 afloat). That total is, incidentally, substan-

From Paul Kennedy, *The Rise and Fall of the Great Powers* (Random House, 1987). Copyright © 1987 by Paul Kennedy. Reprinted by permission of Random House, Inc.

tially more than the overseas deployments in peacetime of the military and naval forces of the British Empire at the height of its power. Nevertheless, in the strongly expressed opinion of the Joint Chiefs of Staff, and of many civilian experts, it is simply not enough. Despite a near-trebling of the American defense budget since the late 1970s, there has occurred a "mere 5 percent increase in the numerical size of the armed forces on active duty." As the British and French military found in their time, a nation with extensive overseas obligations will always have a more difficult "manpower problem" than a state which keeps its armed forces solely for home defense; and a politically liberal and economically laissez-faire society—aware of the unpopularity of conscription—will have a greater problem than most.

Possibly this concern about the gap between American interests and capabilities in the world would be less acute had there not been so much doubt expressed—since at least the time of the Vietnam War—about the *efficiency* of the system itself. Since those doubts have been repeatedly aired in other studies, they will only be summarized here; this is not a further essay on the hot topic of "defense reform." One major area of contention, for example, has been the degree of interservice rivalry, which is of course common to most armed forces but seems more deeply entrenched in the American system—possibly because of the relatively modest powers of the chairman of the Joint Chiefs of Staff, possibly because so much more energy appears to be devoted to procurement as opposed to strategical and operational issues. In peacetime, this might merely be dismissed as an extreme example of "bureaucratic politics"; but in actual wartime operations—say in the emergency dispatch of the Rapid Deployment Joint Task Force, which contains elements from all four services—a lack of proper coordination could be fatal.

In the area of military procurement itself, allegations of "waste, fraud and abuse" have been commonplace. The various scandals over horrendously expensive, *under*performing weapons which have caught the public's attention in recent years have plausible explanations: the lack of proper competitive bidding and of market forces in the "military-industrial complex," and the tendency toward "gold-plated" weapon systems, not to mention the striving for large profits. It is difficult, however, to separate those deficiencies in the procurement process from what is clearly a more fundamental happening: the intensification of the impacts which new technological advances make upon the art of war. Given that it is in the high-technology field that the USSR usually appears most vulnerable—which suggests that American *quality* in weaponry can be employed to counter the superior Russian *quantity* of, say, tanks and aircraft—there is an obvious attraction in what Caspar Weinberger termed "competitive strategies" when ordering new armaments. Nevertheless, the fact that the Reagan administration in its first term spent over 75 percent more on new aircraft than the Carter regime but acquired only 9 percent more planes points to *the* appalling military-procurement problem of the late twentieth century: given the technologically driven tendency toward spending more and more money upon fewer and fewer weapon systems, would the United States and its allies really have enough sophisticated and highly expensive aircraft and tanks in reserve after the early stages of a ferociously fought conventional war?

Does the U.S. Navy possess enough attack submarines, or frigates, if heavy losses were incurred in the early stages of a *third* Battle of the Atlantic? If not, the results would be grim; for it is clear that today's complex weaponry simply cannot be replaced in the short times which were achieved during the Second World War.

This dilemma is accentuated by two other elements in the complicated calculus of evolving an effective American defense policy. The first is the issue of budgetary constraints. Unless external circumstances became much more threatening, it would be a remarkable act of political persuasion to get national defense expenditures raised much above, say 7.5 percent of GNP—the more especially since the size of the federal deficit . . . points to the need to balance governmental spending as the first priority of state. But if there is a slowing-down or even a halt in the increase in defense spending, coinciding with the continuous upward spiral in weapons costs, then the problem facing the Pentagon will become much more acute.

The second factor is the sheer variety of military contingencies that a global superpower like the United States has to plan for—all of which, in their way place differing demands upon the armed forces and the weaponry they are likely to employ. This again is not without precedent in the history of the Great Powers; the British army was frequently placed under strain by having to plan to fight on the Northwest Frontier of India *or* in Belgium. But even that challenge pales beside the task facing today's "number one." If the critical issue for the United States is preserving a nuclear deterrent against the Soviet Union at *all* levels of escalation, then money will inevitably be poured into such weapons as the MX missile, the B-1 and "Stealth" bombers,

Pershing IIs, cruise missiles, and Trident-bearing submarines. If a large-scale conventional war against the Warsaw Pact is the most probable scenario, then the funds presumably need to go in quite different directions: tactical aircraft, main battle tanks, large carriers, frigates, attack submarines and logistical services. If it is likely that the United States and the USSR will avoid a direct clash, but that both will become more active in the Third World, then the weapons mix changes again: small arms, helicopters, light carriers, an enhanced role for the U.S. Marine Corps become the chief items on the list. Already it is clear that a large part of the controversy over "defense reform" stems from differing assumptions about the *type* of war the United States might be called upon to fight. But what if those in authority make the wrong assumption? . . .

The final question about the proper relationship of "means and ends" in the defense of American global interests relates to the economic challenges bearing down upon the country, which, because they are so various, threaten to place immense strains upon decision-making in national policy. The extraordinary breadth and complexity of the American economy makes it difficult to summarize what is happening to all parts of it—especially in a period when it is sending out such contradictory signals. . . .

The first of these is the country's relative industrial decline, as measured against world production, not only in older manufactures such as textiles, iron and steel, shipbuilding, and basic chemicals, but also—although it is far less easy to judge the final outcome of this level of industrial-technological combat—in global shares of robotics, aerospace, automobiles, machine tools, and computers.

Both of these pose immense problems: in traditional and basic manufacturing, the gap in wage scales between the United States and newly industrializing countries is probably such that no "efficiency measures" will close it; but to lose out in the competition in future technologies, if that indeed should occur, would be even more disastrous. In late, 1986, for example, a congressional study reported that the U.S. trade surplus in high-technology goods had plunged from $27 billion in 1980 to a mere $4 billion in 1985, and was swiftly heading into a deficit.

The second, and in many ways less expected, sector of decline is agriculture. Only a decade ago, experts in that subject were predicting a frightening global imbalance between feeding requirements and farming output. But such a scenario of famine and disaster stimulated two powerful responses. The first was a massive investment into American farming from the 1970's onward, fueled by the prospect of ever-larger overseas food sales; the second was the enormous (western-world-funded) investigation into scientific means of increasing Third World crop outputs, which has been so successful as to turn growing numbers of such countries into food *exporters*, and thus competitors of the United States. These two trends are separate from, but have coincided with, the transformation of the EEC into a major producer of agricultural surpluses, because of its price-support system. In consequence, experts now refer to a "world awash in food," which in turn leads to sharp declines in agricultural prices and in American food exports—and drives many farmers out of business.

It is not surprising, therefore, that these economic problems have led to a surge in protectionist sentiment throughout many sectors of the American economy, and among businessmen, unions, farmers, and their congressmen. As with the "tariff reform" agitation in Edwardian Britain, the advocates of increased protection complain of unfair foreign practices, of "dumping" below-cost manufactures on the American market, and of enormous subsidies to foreign farmers—which, they maintain, can only be answered by U.S. administrations abandoning their laissez-faire policy on trade and instituting tough countermeasures. Many of those individual complaints (e.g., of Japan shipping below-cost silicon chips to the American market) have been valid. More broadly, however, the surge in protectionist-sentiment is also a reflection of the erosion of the previously unchallenged U.S. manufacturing supremacy. Like mid-Victorian Britons, Americans after 1945 favored free trade and open competition, not just because they held that global commerce and prosperity would be boosted in the process, but also because they knew that they were most likely to benefit from the abandonment of protectionism. Forty years later, with that confidence ebbing, there is a predictable shift of opinion in favor of protecting the domestic market and the domestic producer. And, just as in that earlier British case, defenders of the existing system point out that enhanced tariffs might not only make domestic products *less* competitive internationally, but that there also could be various external repercussions—a global tariff war, blows against American exports, the undermining of the currencies of certain newly industrializing countries, and a return to the economic crisis of the 1930s.

Along with these difficulties affecting American manufacturing and agriculture there are unprecedented turbulences in

368 / 20. IS AMERICA DECLINING?

the nation's finances. The uncompetitiveness of U.S. industrial products abroad and the declining sales of agricultural exports have together produced staggering deficits in visible trade—$160 billion in the twelve months to May 1986—but what is more alarming is that such a gap can no longer be covered by American earnings on "invisibles," which is the traditional recourse of a mature economy (e.g., Great Britain before 1914). On the contrary, the only way the United States can pay its way in the world is by importing ever-larger sums of capital, which has transformed it from being the world's largest creditor to the world's largest debtor nation *in the space of a few years.*

Compounding this problem—in the view of many critics, *causing* this problem—have been the budgetary policies of the U.S. government itself. Even in the 1960s, there was a tendency for Washington to rely upon deficit finance, rather than additional taxes, to pay for the increasing cost of defense and social programs. But the decisions taken by the Reagan administration in the early 1980s—i.e., large-scale increases in defense expenditures, plus considerable decreases in taxation, but *without* significant reductions in federal spending elsewhere—have produced extraordinary rises in the deficit, and consequently in the national debt, as shown in Table 1.1.

The continuation of such trends, alarmed voices have pointed out, would push the U.S. national debt to around $13 *trillion* by the year 2000 (fourteen times that of 1980), and the interest payments on such debt to $1.5 *trillion* (twenty-nine times that of 1980). In fact, a lowering of interest rates could bring down those estimates, but the overall trend is still very unhealthy. Even if federal deficits could be reduced to a "mere" $100 billion

Table 1.1

U.S. Federal Deficit, Debt, and Interest, 1980–1985
(billions of dollars)

	Deficit	Debt	Interest on Debt
1980	59.6	914.3	52.5
1983	195.4	1,381.9	87.8
1985	202.8	1,823.1	129.0

annually, the compounding of national debt and interest payments by the early twenty-first century will still cause quite unprecedented totals of money to be diverted in that direction. Historically, the only other example which comes to mind of a Great Power so increasing its indebtedness in *peacetime* is France in the 1780s, where the fiscal crisis contributed to the domestic political crisis. . . .

[G]iven the worldwide array of military liabilities which the United States has assumed since 1945, its capacity to carry those burdens is obviously less than it was several decades ago, when its share of global manufacturing and GNP was much larger, its agriculture was not in crisis, its balance of payments was far healthier, the government budget was also in balance, and it was not so heavily in debt to the rest of the world. In that larger sense, there is something in the analogy which is made by certain political scientists between the United States' position today and that of previous "declining hegemons."

Here again, it is instructive to note the uncanny similarities between the growing mood of anxiety among thoughtful circles in the United States today and that which pervaded all political parties in Edwardian Britain and led to what has been termed the "national efficiency" movement: that is, a broad-based debate within the nation's decision-making, business, and educational elites over the various measures which could reverse what was seen to be a growing uncompetitiveness as compared with other advanced societies. In terms of commercial expertise, levels of training and education, efficiency of production, standards of income and (among the less well-off) of living, health, and housing, the "number one" power of 1900 seemed to be losing its position, with dire implications for the country's long-term *strategic* position; hence the fact that the calls for "renewal" and "reorganization" came at least as much from the Right as from the Left. Such campaigns usually do lead to reforms, here and there; but their very existence is, ironically, a confirmation of decline, in that such an agitation simply would not have been necessary a few decades earlier, when the nation's lead was unquestioned. A strong man, the writer G. K. Chesterton sardonically observed, does not worry about his bodily efficiency; only when he weakens does he begin to talk about health. In the same way, when a Great Power is strong and unchallenged, it will be much less likely to debate its capacity to meet its obligations than when it is relatively weaker. . . .

A quite different problem, but one equally important for the sustaining of a proper grand strategy, concerns the impact of slow economic growth upon the American social/political consensus. To a degree which amazes most Europeans, the United States in the twentieth century has managed to avoid ostensible "class" politics. This is due, one imagines, to the facts that so many of its immigrants were fleeing from socially rigid circumstances elsewhere; that the sheer size of the country allowed those who were disillusioned with their economic position to "escape" to the West, and simultaneously made the organization of labor much more difficult than in, say, France or Britain; and that those same geographical dimensions, and the entrepreneurial opportunities within them, encouraged the development of a largely unreconstructed form of laissez-faire capitalism which has dominated the political culture of the nation (despite occasional counterattacks from the left). In consequence, the "earnings gap" between rich and poor in the United States is significantly larger than in any other advanced industrial society; and, by the same token, state expenditures upon social services form a lower share of GNP than in comparable countries (except Japan, which appears to have a much stronger family-based form of support for the poor and the aged).

This lack of "class" politics despite the obvious socioeconomic disparities has obviously been helped by the fact that the United States' overall growth since the 1930s offered the prospect of individual betterment to a majority of the population; and by the more disturbing fact that the poorest *one-third* of American society has not been "mobilized" to become regular voters. But given the differentiated birthrate between the white ethnic groups on the one hand and the black and Hispanic groups on the other—not to mention the changing flow of immigrants into the United States, and given also the economic metamorphosis which is leading to the loss of millions of relatively high-earning jobs in manufacturing, and the creation of millions of poorly paid jobs in services, it may be unwise to assume that the prevailing norms of the American political economy (low governmental expenditures, low taxes on the rich) would be maintained if the nation entered a period of sustained economic difficulty caused by a plunging dollar and slow growth. What this also suggests is that an American polity which responds to external challenges by increasing defense expenditures, and reacts to the budgetary crisis by slashing the existing social expenditures, may run the risk of provoking an eventual political backlash. . . .

This brings us, inevitably, to the delicate relationship between slow economic growth and high defense spending. The debate upon "the economics of defense spending" is a highly controversial one, and—bearing in mind the size and variety of the American economy, the stimulus which can come from large government contracts, and the technical spin-offs from weapons research—the evidence does not point simply in one direction. But what is significant for our purposes is the comparative dimension. Even if (as is often pointed out) defense expenditures formed 10 percent of GNP under Eisenhower and 9 percent under Kennedy, the United States' relative share of global production and wealth was at that time around *twice* what it is today; and, more particularly, the American economy was not then facing the challenges to either its traditional or its high-technology manufactures. Moreover, if the United States at present continues to devote 7 percent or more of its GNP to defense spending while its major economic rivals, especially Japan, allocate a far smaller proportion, then *ipso facto* the latter have potentially more funds "free" for civilian investment; if the United States continues to invest a massive amount of its R&D activities into military-related production while the Japanese and West Germans concentrate upon commerical R&D; and if the Pentagon's spending drains off the majority of the country's scientists and engineers from the design and production of goods for the world market while similar personnel in other countries are primarily engaged in bringing out better products for the civilian consumer, then it seems inevitable that the American share of world manufacturing will steadily decline, and also likely that its economic growth rates will be slower than in those countries dedicated to the marketplace and less eager to channel resources into defense.

It is almost superfluous to say that these tendencies place the United States on the horns of a most acute dilemma over the longer term. Simply because it is *the* global superpower, with far more extensive military commitments than a regional Power like Japan or West Germany, it requires much larger defense forces—in just the same way as imperial Spain felt it needed a far larger army than its contemporaries and Victorian Britain insisted upon a much bigger navy than any other country. Furthermore, since the USSR is seen to be the major military threat to American interests across the globe and is clearly devoting a far greater proportion of *its* GNP to defense, American decision-makers are inevitably worried about "losing" the arms race with Russia. Yet the more sensible among these decision-makers can also perceive that the burden of armaments is debilitating the Soviet economy; and that if the two superpowers continue to allocate ever-larger shares of their national wealth into the unproductive field of armaments, the critical question might soon be: "Whose economy will decline *fastest,* relative to such expanding states as Japan, China, etc.?" A low investment in armaments may, for a globally overstretched Power like the United States, leave it feeling vulnerable everywhere; but a very heavy investment in armaments, while bringing greater security in the short term, may so erode the commercial competitiveness of the American economy that the nation will be *less* secure in the long term.

Here, too, the historical precedents are not encouraging. For it has been a common dilemma facing previous "number-one" countries that even as their relative economic strength is ebbing, the growing foreign challenges to their position have compelled them to allocate more and more of their resources into the military sector, which in turn squeezes out productive investment and, over time, leads to the downward spiral of slower growth, heavier taxes, deepening domestic splits over spending priorities, and a weakening capacity to bear the burdens of defense. If this, indeed, is the pattern of history, one is tempted to paraphrase Shaw's deadly serious quip and say: "Rome fell; Babylon fell; Scarsdale's turn will come."

In the largest sense of all, therefore, the only answer to the question increasingly debated by the public of whether the United States can preserve its existing position is "no"—for it simply has not been given to any one society to remain *permanently* ahead of all the others, because that would imply a freezing of the differentiated pattern of growth rates, technological advance, and military developments which has existed since time immemorial. On the other hand, this reference to historical precedents does *not* imply that the United States is destined to shrink to the relative

obscurity of former leading Powers such as Spain or the Netherlands, or to disintegrate like the Roman and Austro-Hungarian empires; it is simply too large to do the former, and presumably too homogeneous to do the latter. Even the British analogy, much favored in the current political-science literature, is not a good one if it ignores the differences in *scale.* This can be put another way: the geographical size, population, and natural resources of the British Isles would suggest that it ought to possess roughly 3 or 4 percent of the world's wealth and power, *all other things being equal;* but it is precisely because all other things are *never* equal that a peculiar set of historical and technological circumstances permitted the British Isles to expand to possess, say, 25 percent of the world's wealth and power in its prime; and since those favorable circumstances have disappeared, all that it has been doing is returning down to its more "natural" size. In the same way, it may be argued that the geographical extent, population, and natural resources of the United States suggest that it ought to possess perhaps 16 or 18 percent of the world's wealth and power, but because of historical and technical circumstances favorable to it, that share rose to 40 percent or more by 1945; and what we are witnessing at the moment is the early decades of the ebbing away from that extraordinarily high figure to a more "natural" share. That decline is being masked by the country's enormous military capabilities at present, and also by its success in "internationalizing" American capitalism and culture. Yet even when it declines to occupy its "natural" share of the world's wealth and power, a long time into the future, the United States will still be a very significant Power in a multipolar world, simply because of its size.

The task facing American statesmen over the next decades, therefore, is to recognize that broad trends are under way, and that there is a need to "manage" affairs so that the *relative* erosion of the United States' position takes place slowly and smoothly, and is not accelerated by policies which bring merely short-term advantage but longer-term disadvantage. This involves, from the president's office downward, an appreciation that technological and therefore socioeconomic change is occurring in the world faster than ever before; that the international community is much more politically and culturally diverse than has been assumed, and is defiant of simplistic remedies offered either by Washington or Moscow to its problems; that the economic and productive power balances are no longer as favorably tilted in the United States' direction as in 1945; and that, even in the military realm, there are signs of a certain redistribution of the balances, away from a bipolar to more of a multipolar system, in which the conglomeration of American economic-cum-military strength is likely to remain larger than that possessed by any one of the others individually, but will not be as disproportionate as in the decades which immediately followed the Second World War. This, in itself, is not a bad thing if one recalls Kissinger's observations about the disadvantages of carrying out policies in what is always seen to be a bipolar world . . . ; and it may seem still less of a bad thing when it is recognized how much more Russia may be affected by the changing dynamics of world power. In all of the discussions about the erosion of American leadership, it needs to be repeated again and again that the decline referred to is relative not absolute, and is therefore perfectly natural; and that the only serious threat to the real interests of the United States can come from a failure to adjust sensibly to the newer world order.

NO

Samuel P. Huntington

THE U.S.—DECLINE OR RENEWAL?

In 1988 the United States reached the zenith of its fifth wave of declinism since the 1950s. The roots of this phenomenon lie in the political economy literature of the early 1980s that analyzed the fading American economic hegemony and attempted to identify the consequences of its disappearance. These themes were picked up in more popular and policy-oriented writings, and the combination of the budget and trade deficits plus the October 1987 stock market crash produced the environment for the spectacular success of Paul Kennedy's scholarly historical analysis in early 1988. Decline has been on everyone's mind, and the arguments of the declinists have stimulated lively public debate.[1]

Although predominantly of a liberal-leftist hue, declinist writings reflect varying political philosophies and make many different claims. In general, however, they offer three core propositions.

First, the United States is declining economically compared to other market economy countries, most notably Japan but also Europe and the newly industrializing countries. The declinists focus on economic performance and on scientific, technological and educational factors presumably related to economic performance.

Second, economic power is the central element of a nation's strength, and hence a decline in economic power eventually affects the other dimensions of national power.

Third, the relative economic decline of the United States is caused primarily by its spending too much for military purposes, which in turn is the result, in Kennedy's phrase, of "imperial overstretch," of attempting to maintain commitments abroad that the country can no longer afford. In this respect, the problems the United States confronts are similar to those of previous imperial or hegemonic powers such as Britain, France and Spain.

Declinist literature sets forth images of a nation winding down economically, living beyond its means, losing its competitive edge to more dynamic peoples, sagging under the burdens of empire, and suffering from a variety of intensifying social, economic and political ills. It follows that American

From Samuel P. Huntington, "The U.S.—Decline or Renewal?" *Foreign Affairs*, vol. 67, no. 2 (Winter 1988/89). Copyright © 1989 by the Council on Foreign Relations, Inc. Reprinted by permission of *Foreign Affairs*.

leadership must recognize and acquiesce in these conditions and accept the "need to 'manage' affairs so that the *relative* erosion of the United States' position takes place slowly and smoothly, and is not accelerated by policies which bring merely short-term advantage but longer-term disadvantage."

Before one accepts the policy conclusions of the declinists, however, their basic propositions should be critically examined. Does their argument hold water? Is the United States fundamentally a nation in decline? Or is it a nation in the midst of renewal?

The declinists point to many urgent if transitory American problems and other serious if long-standing American weakness. Overall, however, their argument fails; it is seriously weak on both the extent and causes of decline. The image of renewal is far closer to the American truth than the image of decadence purveyed by the declinists.

II

With some exceptions, declinist writings do not elaborate testable propositions involving independent and dependent variables. With a rather broad brush, they tend to paint an impressionistic picture of economic decline, mixing references to economic trends and performance (economic growth, productivity), educational data (test scores, length of school year), fiscal matters (deficits), science and technology (R&D expenditures, output of engineers), international trade and capital flows, savings and investment, and other matters. In general, however, they point to three bodies of evidence to support their argument for decline:

- first, mounting U.S. trade and fiscal deficits which, to date, the U.S. political system has shown no signs of being able to correct;
- second, continuing and even accelerating declines in U.S. shares of global economic power and in U.S. rates of growth in key areas of economic performance;
- third, sustained systemic weaknesses, including research and development practices, primary and secondary education, production of scientists and engineers, and most seriously, savings and investment patterns.

Each body of evidence requires separate examination.

Deficits. Escalating current account and budgetary deficits have been the most important changes affecting the U.S. position in the world in the 1980s. They furnish dramatic immediacy to the declinist argument. In a few short years the United States was transformed from the principal creditor nation in the world to its largest debtor. The current account balance, which had a surplus of $6.9 billion in 1981 and a small deficit of $8.7 billion in 1982, plunged to deficits of almost $140 billion in 1986 and about $160 billion in 1987. In 1981 the United States had a net credit in its international investment position of $141 billion; by 1987 it was a net debtor to the tune of $400 billion. Assets in the United States owned by foreigners roughly doubled between 1982 and 1986 to $1.3 trillion.

Coincidental with this growth of U.S. international deficits and a major cause of them was the burgeoning of the U.S. budget deficit. The annual deficit had fluctuated in the vicinity of $50 billion to $75 billion in the Ford and Carter Administrations. In 1982 it began to increase rapidly, reaching a peak of $221 billion in

FY 1986. It dropped back to $150 billion in FY 1987 and was modestly higher at about $155 billion in FY 1988.

Declinists see these deficits as evidence of fundamental weaknesses in the American economic position. They correctly point out that the massive influx of foreign funds has largely gone not for investment but for private consumption and governmental spending for defense. Such borrowing will not generate revenues with which it can be liquidated. The United States is living in a style it cannot afford and is imbued with an "eat, drink and be merry" psychology. . . .

Several points must be made to disentangle the valid from the invalid elements of these declinist arguments.

First, trade and budget deficits were not a major problem before 1982. They then mushroomed. This development may in some small measure flow from underlying weaknesses in productivity, savings and investment, but it cannot primarily result from such causes. If the deficits did come from these causes, they would have developed slowly rather than rapidly and very probably would have manifested themselves before the advent of the Reagan Administration. Instead, the deficits are overwhelmingly the result of the economic policies of the Reagan Administration: reduction in tax rates, expansion of defense spending, a strong dollar. These policies were premised on the assumption that domestic governmental spending could be curtailed and that lower tax rates would stimulate investment, growth and revenues. These assumptions did not prove to be valid, and the policies that were based on them produced the surging deficits. A different Administration with different fiscal and economic policies would have produced different results.

The deficits stem from the weaknesses, not of the American economy, but of Reagan economics. Produced quickly by one set of policies, they can be reversed almost as quickly by another set of policies.

Second, that reversal has begun and is likely to intensify. The reversal results partly from changes in policy by the Reagan Administration, partly from policies adopted by other governments and partly from the workings of the international economy, which naturally generates equilibrating tendencies. President Bush will probably move to reinforce U.S. policies designed to reduce the deficits. Through tight controls on spending, promotion of economic growth, "revenue enhancements" and, at some point, new taxes (luxury taxes, gasoline taxes and a general value-added tax are most frequently mentioned), the budget deficit is likely to be brought down to a sustainable level at which it does not pose a threat to long-term economic growth. As it is, the deficit in 1988 is only about half of what it was in 1983 as a percent of gross national product (3.1 percent versus 6.3 percent).

The trade deficit began to decrease with the rapid expansion of American exports in 1988. Its further reduction will be facilitated by budget deficit reduction, increases in manufacturing productivity (which rose significantly in the 1980s), ceilings on the exchange rate of the dollar and pressure which the U.S. government will—and must—apply under the new trade law to open up foreign markets. Cutting the trade deficit will be further enhanced, of course, to the extent that oil prices do not increase, American wage levels remain below those of the principal U.S. competitors, the developing countries' debt problem is contained and foreign economies grow at healthy rates. The trade deficit, some analysts predict, will become a trade surplus in the coming decade.

Third, both the deficits and the processes of curing them impose significant costs on the American economy. The substantial increase—absolute and net—in American foreign indebtedness means that a larger portion of U.S. GNP will be paid to foreigners in debt service. These funds will not be available for either personal consumption or savings and domestic investment. The future American standard of living will be less than it would have been otherwise. . . .

In the coming years both deficits will probably be reduced to sustainable and nonmalign proportions. Their effects, however, will be around for some while to come. But it is a mistake to view them as open sores that will continue to bleed away American strength. They are wounds that will heal, although their scars will remain.

Declining Shares. This argument has been put most explicitly by Paul Kennedy. "The U.S.A.'s share of total GNP," he says, "of world manufacturing output, and of many other indices of national efficiency has steadily declined." The United States has suffered "relative industrial decline, as measured against world production, not only in older manufactures such as textiles, iron and steel, shipbuilding, and basic chemicals, but also—although it is far less easy to judge the final outcome of this level of industrial-technological combat—in global shares of robotics, aerospace, automobiles, machine tools, and computers." American agriculture has also declined. The decline in the U.S. share of world GNP was "natural" after 1945, but it "has declined much more quickly than it should have

over the last few years" and the decline has become "precipitous."

These propositions need serious qualification. Various estimates exist of global and national gross products for various times. All have to be used with caution. Virtually all, however, show a common pattern.

The United States produced 40 to 45 percent of the gross world product in the late 1940s and early 1950s. That share declined rapidly, reaching the vicinity of 20 to 25 percent of gross world product by the late 1960s. That is roughly where it has remained.

It certainly has not declined more rapidly in the past two decades than it did during the previous two decades. Figures of the U.S. Council on Competitiveness (whose mission is to voice alarm about declining U.S. competitiveness) and from other sources show, for instance, that:

• between 1970 and 1987 the U.S. share of the gross world product varied between 22 and 25 percent and most recently was 23 percent;

• the U.S. share of world exports was 12 percent in 1970 and ten percent in 1987, and varied between nine and 14 percent in the years between;

• the U.S. share of the exports of the seven economic summit countries was 24 percent in 1970 and 23 percent in 1987, varying between 20 and 25 percent in the intervening years;

• in 1965 the United States accounted for 27.5 percent of world exports of technology-intensive products; this dropped to a low of 22.9 percent in 1980 and was back at 25.2 percent in 1984.

Overall, the United States accounts for 22 to 25 percent of the major forms of global economic activity and has done so fairly consistently for twenty years or more. The declinists are clearly right in saying that this is much less than the U.S. shares according to the same indices during the decade after World War II. A situation in which one country accounted for up to 50 percent of the global economic action was clearly a temporary product of the war. The ending of that imbalance was a major and successful goal of U.S. policy. The shift from 40–45 percent of global economic activity to 20–25 percent had generally occurred by the late 1960s. It is an increasingly remote historical event. For about a quarter-century U.S. shares in global economic activity have fluctuated within a relatively narrow range. . . .

In short, if "hegemony" means having 40 percent or more of world economic activity (a percentage Britain never remotely approximated during its hegemonic years), American hegemony disappeared long ago. If hegemony means producing 20 to 25 percent of the world product and twice as much as any other individual country, American hegemony looks quite secure.

Systemic Failures. A third set of phenomena cited by declinists consists of what might be termed systemic failures. These involved the sustained inability of America's society and its economy to function either at the levels of comparable societies or at levels presumed necessary to sustain the American role in the world. Since systemic characteristics have, by definition, been present for a long period of time, their contributions to American decline presumably stem from their cumulative impact. Among other deficiencies, declinists point to the poor quality of American primary and secondary education (manifested, for instance, in the low scores of American students in comparative tests of mathe-

matics and reading skills), the small numbers of scientists and engineers produced in the United States (particularly compared to the high production of lawyers), and the complexity and inefficiency of American governmental policymaking processes. The most heavily emphasized systemic weakness, however, concerns low savings and investment rates.

Americans clearly save less than most other people. During the 1970s and 1980s U.S. gross savings as a proportion of GDP varied between 14.8 and 19.1 percent. During this period Japanese savings varied between 27.1 percent and 32.9 percent of GDP. In 1970 the Japanese savings rate was more than twice that of the United States (32.9 versus 16.1 percent); in 1987 it was almost twice the U.S. rate (28.2 versus 14.8 percent). Throughout these years U.S. savings lagged behind those of the other major industrialized democracies. . . .

As one might expect, similar patterns across countries exist with respect to investment. Between 1965 and 1984 U.S. gross fixed capital formation varied between 17 percent and 19.8 percent of GNP. That for Japan varied between 27.8 percent and 35.5 percent of GNP. The OECD average, less the United States, varied between 21.6 and 26 percent. Other measures of investment yield comparable results: the U.S. rates tend to be slightly more than half those of Japan and perhaps 75 percent of those of the other major industrialized democracies.

The significance of these differences in savings and investment can be debated, and mitigating factors may explain and compensate for some low U.S. rates. In addition, the poor U.S. performance seems not to have noticeably affected U.S. economic growth as yet. Nonetheless, clearly the declinists are right in highlighting savings and investment as long-term systemic weaknesses that require correction if economic growth is to be maintained.

Many, although not all, declinists go wrong, however, when they identify the reasons for poor U.S. performance. They argue that overexpenditure for military purposes crowds out investment for economic growth and hence leads to economic decline. Decline flows from imperialism and militarism.

This argument has little to support it, especially as applied to the United States. Kennedy's historical examples themselves suggest that the burden of empire usually becomes onerous when it amounts to ten percent or more of the society's product. Defense, however, takes only six to seven percent of American GNP. The declinists' thesis is clearly more relevant to the Soviet Union, which apparently (Soviet officials themselves claim they do not know for sure) spends 17 to 18 percent or more of its GNP for military purposes. Is this, however, a cause of Soviet decline? Its military sector is widely held to be the most technically efficient sector of the Soviet economy, and it is the only sector that is able to compete internationally. More generally, there is little comparative evidence to suggest that military expenditures are necessarily a drag on economic development. Some analysts, indeed, have argued that defense spending stimulates economic growth. One does not necessarily have to buy that argument in order to reject its opposite.

In fact, of course, how much a country invests is influenced by, but not determined by, how much it spends on defense. The Soviet Union spends close to three times as much of its GNP on defense as does the United States. It also invests more of its GNP than does the United States. This occurs at the expense of Soviet consumption. In theory, a country can allocate its resources as it wishes among consumption, defense and investment. In fact, countries make different choices, and the countries with the three largest economies in the world do exactly that. It is difficult to get comparable figures for the Soviet Union and market economy countries, and the portions of government spending which are in fact investment do not always show up in national accounts. Nonetheless, a rough prototypical allocation of GNP for the three largest economies might be as follows:

- U.S. consumption (private and public) at about 78 percent of its GNP, Japan's at 67 percent, and the Soviet Union's 56 percent;
- U.S. defense spending at about seven percent of its GNP, Japan's about one percent, and the Soviet Union's 18 percent;
- U.S. investment at roughly 17 percent of GNP, Japan's at about 30 percent of its GNP, and the Soviets' about 26 percent.

In short, the Soviets arm, the United States consumes, Japan invests. . . .

In any event, even if half the resources the United States uses for defense were shifted to investment, the American investment ratio would still lag behind the ratios of Japan and the Soviet Union. If the United States is to increase its investment ratio significantly, that increase will have to come primarily from the 75 percent or more of the GNP devoted to consumption, not from the less than seven percent committed to defense. If the United States falters economically, it will not be because U.S. soldiers, sailors and airmen stand guard on the Elbe, the Strait of Hormuz and the 38th parallel; it will be because U.S. men, women and children overindulge themselves in the comforts of the good life. Consumerism, not militarism, is the threat to American strength. The declinists have it wrong; Montesquieu got it right: "Republics end with luxury; monarchies with poverty."

III

The predominant view among declinists points to external expansion rather than internal stagnation as the principal cause of the decline of nations. This argument runs counter to a tradition of political thought going back to Plato and Aristotle which focuses on the internal ability of a society to renew itself. According to modern formulations of this view, a society declines when bureaucratic stagnation, monopoly, caste, hierarchy, social rigidity, organizational obesity and arteriosclerosis make innovation and adaptation difficult or impossible. As societies age, these characteristics tend to become more predominant.

In his sophisticated theoretical analysis which departs from the declinist mainstream, Mancur Olson argues this point persuasively, explaining the decline of nations by the development of vested interests or "distributional coalitions" that reduce economic efficiency and constrain economic growth. Societies whose social, economic and political structures are substantially destroyed through war, revolution or other upheaval grow rapidly. Over time, however, distributional coalitions develop and economic dynamism wanes. Although Olson does not discuss it in his book, the prototypical contemporary case of an economy grinding to a halt because of the constrictions imposed by distributional coalitions is, of course, the Soviet Union under Brezhnev.

Successful societies, in contrast, are those that find ways short of their own destruction to sustain the dynamism of their youth. The structure of such societies will presumably encourage competition, mobility, fluidity, pluralism and openness—all qualities that prevent a society from becoming mired in a network of collusive deals in which everyone benefits to everyone's disadvantage.

Viewed from this perspective, the United States is less likely to decline than any other major country. It is distinguished by the openness of its economy, society and politics. Its engines of renewal are competition, mobility and immigration.

Competition and opposition to monopoly, both public and private, are hallmarks of American society. The United States led the way in the modern world in attempting to institutionalize antitrust and antimonopoly practices in business. Government bureaucracy in the United States is weaker and more divided against itself than bureaucracies in most other countries. State-owned enterprises are rare. New companies are created—and go bankrupt—on a scale unknown in European societies. Small, new companies have been responsible for the bulk of the twenty million new jobs created in the past decade.

Labor unions have never been strong and are declining. American universities, it has been argued, are the best in the world because of the intense competition among them for faculty, students and money. Secondary education, it might be noted, is, in contrast, overwhelmingly a public monopoly and is inferior as a result; widely considered proposals for improving it are to introduce competition among schools for students and state support.

In comparison to other societies, individual mobility, both horizontal and vertical, is extremely high. Far more rapidly than elsewhere, American workers shift from job to job, up and down the income scale, in and out of the poverty brackets. People move from region to region at about three times the rate they do in European countries. With the notable exception of race, ascriptive obstacles to upward mobility have been relatively minimal compared to other societies.

The continuing flow of immigrants into American society reflects the opportunities it offers and contributes to its renewal. Historically, first- and second-generation immigrants have been a dynamic force in American society. Under the Immigration Act of 1965, about 600,000 legal immigrants enter the United States each year. Thousands more enter illegally. These newcomers renew the pools of cheap labor, entrepreneurial skill, intellectual talent and driving ambition to succeed. Thirty-six of the 114 American citizens who won Nobel prizes in science and medicine between 1945 and 1984 were born elsewhere. In the 1940s and 1950s American scientific and intellectual life was tremendously enriched by Jewish refugees from Hitler and the children of East European Jewish immigrants before World War II. Today Asian-Americans sweep the intellectual honors. (About two percent of the total population, they make up 14 percent of the 1988 freshman class at Harvard.) In the coming decades, immigration also means that the American population will continue to grow, unlike those of many European countries and will remain relatively young, unlike that of Japan.

IV

The ultimate test of a great power is its ability to renew its power. The competition, mobility and immigration characteristic of American society enable the United States to meet this test to a far greater extent than any other great power, past or present. They are the central sources of American strength. They are supplemented by three aspects of the American position in international affairs.

First, in comparison to other major countries, American strength is peculiarly multidimensional. Mao Zedong reportedly said that power grows out of the barrel of a gun; the declinists see power coming out of a belching smokestack. In fact, power comes in various forms and international influence can stem from very different sources. The Soviet Union, it has often been said, is a one-dimensional superpower, its international position resting almost exclusively on its military might. Whatever influence Saudi Arabia has in international affairs flows from its oil reserves. Japan's influence has come first from its manufacturing performance and then from its control of financial resources. . . .

In contrast to other countries, the United States ranks extraordinarily high in almost all the major sources of national power: population size and education, natural resources, economic development, social cohesion, political stability, military strength, ideological appeal, diplomatic alliances, technological achievement. It is, consequently, able to sustain reverses in any one arena while maintaining its overall influence stemming from other sources. At present, no country can mount a multidimensional challenge to the United

States, and with one conceivable exception no country seems likely to be able to do so in the relevant future.

Second, U.S. influence also flows from its structural position in world politics. The United States benefits from being geographically distant from most major areas of world conflict, from having a past relatively free of overseas imperialism, from espousing an economic and political philosophy that is antistatist and, hence, less likely to be threatening to other peoples, from being involved in a historically uniquely diversified network of alliances and from having a sense, stronger in the past than more recently, of identification with universal international institutions.

These factors pull the United States into a leadership role in dealing with international problems and disputes. They help create a demand for the American presence overseas. Slogans of "U.S. go home!" may command headlines, but in many regions the underlying fear is that the United States might just do that. Neither Germans, French, Dutch nor (some say) the Soviets are eager for the United States to pull out of Europe. Many Filipinos act as if they wished the bases removed from their country, and some may actually want that to happen, but many others worry deeply that an American withdrawal from Southeast Asia would leave them to the tender mercies of the Soviets and the Japanese. Long before diplomatic relations existed between Washington and Beijing, China supported the American presence in Japan and Korea. . . .

Finally, no alternative to hegemonic power, with one possible exception, seems likely to emerge in the coming century. A short while ago, of course, it was widely thought that the Soviet Union would perform that role. Mr. Khrushchev talked confidently about the U.S.S.R. overtaking the United States economically and the grandchildren of Western capitalists playing under red flags.

These seem not just forlorn but bizarre hopes. The Soviet Union still has the resources, size and military strength of a superpower, but it has lost economically, ideologically and diplomatically. Conceivably, the Gorbachev reforms could start a process that would put the Soviet Union back into competition to become the number-one actor on the world stage, but at the moment the success of his efforts is in doubt and the impact of the reforms, if they are successful, will not necessarily enhance Soviet power.

Currently, the popular choice—and the choice of the declinists—for the country that will supersede the United States is, of course, Japan. "The American Century is over," a former U.S. official has said. "The big development in the latter part of the century is the emergence of Japan as a major superpower." With all due respect to Clyde Prestowitz, this proposition will not hold up. Japan has neither the size, natural resources, military strength, diplomatic affiliates nor, most important, the ideological appeal to be a twentieth-century superpower.

In a world of instant communication, widespread literacy and social mobilization, a superpower has to stand for an idea with appeal beyond its borders. In recent history the United States and the Soviet Union have done this. Today the message of the Soviet Union is tattered and apparently rejected, in part by its own leadership. The appeal of the American message of political democracy and economic liberalism has never been stronger. Conceivably, Japan could also develop a message to the world, but that would require fundamental changes in Japanese culture and society. . . .

The declinists play an indispensable role in preventing what they are predicting. Contrary to Professor Kennedy, the more Americans worry about the health of their society, the healthier they are. The current wave will serve a useful historical function if it encourages the new president and Congress to take prompt and effective actions on the deficits and to inaugurate longer-term policies designed to promote saving and investment.

"If Sparta and Rome perished," asked Rousseau, "what State can hope to endure forever?" The obvious answer is "no state" and that may be the right answer. The United States is not immortal and American preeminence is not inevitable. Yet, some states endure for extraordinary lengths of time, and little reason exists to assume that recent prophecies of American decline are more accurate than earlier ones. Every reason exists, however, to encourage belief in such prophecies in order to disprove them. Happily, the self-renewing genius of American politics does exactly that.

NOTES

1. Apart from the more academic international political economy literature, declinist works that have been widely discussed in policy debates and the general media include: Walter Russell Mead, *Mortal Splendor*, Boston: Houghton Mifflin, 1987; David P. Calleo, *Beyond American Hegemony*, New York: Basic Books, 1987; and, of course, Paul Kennedy, *The Rise and Fall of the Great Powers: Economic Change and Military Conflict from 1500 to 2000*, New York: Random House, 1987. In discussing declinist ideas, I will rely primarily on Kennedy's writings and statements, since they have had the greatest impact on public debate in the United States.

POSTSCRIPT

Is America Declining?

Despite disagreement over whether or not the United States is declining, it is inescapable that other nations are growing and are likely to continue to grow in productivity, military power, and international influence. These nations include the Soviet Union, those of the European Economic Community and, most impressively, those of Asia. Even if America continues to prosper, it is likely to represent a decreasing share of world productivity.

Does the United States strive to be *the* dominant power in the world? Or is the United States a powerful leader in an alliance of nations arrayed against another bloc in arrangements akin to traditional balance-of-power politics? Those who see an America in decline believe that our policymakers hold the former view. Walter Russell Mead urges cutback in American commitments in *Mortal Splendor: The American Empire in Transition* (Houghton Mifflin, 1987). Like Kennedy, Mead traces parallels with past empires and concludes that decline is inevitable, but he maintains that America can shape its post-imperial future. David P. Calleo, in *Beyond American Hegemony: The Future of the Western Alliance* (Basic Books, 1987), argues that Europe must bear a greater share of military costs.

Steven Schlosstein, *The End of the American Century* (Congdon and Weed, 1989), concludes that the United States has declined economically because it has become inferior to Japanese society with respect to the quality of education, the stability of family life, the balance between personal and collective welfare, and other social and economic factors.

Pessimism regarding America's power and influence in the post–cold war world is rejected by analysts who believe that the nation has the ability and the will to continue to play a leading role under changing conditions. This is the position of Joseph S. Nye, Jr., *Bound to Lead: The Changing Nature of American Power* (Basic Books, 1990). Nye argues that only the United States possesses great resources of land, population, military power, economic capacity, scientific discovery, and technology.

Kennedy's decline thesis is also rejected by Richard McKenzie, "The Decline of America: Myth or Fate?" *Society* (November/December 1989), and Owen Harries, "The Rise of American Decline," *Commentary* (May 1988). For Norman Podhoretz, the issue is not overstretching or overspending but national will. In *The Present Danger* (Simon & Schuster, 1980), he posed the question: "Do we have the will to reverse the decline of American power?"

Whatever our conclusions, the debate prompted by the theory of decline compels us to examine the nature and consequences of American values and goals in relation to the rest of the world.

CONTRIBUTORS
TO THIS VOLUME

EDITORS

GEORGE McKENNA was born in Chicago in 1937 and attended public schools in the city. He received a bachelor's degree from the University of Chicago in 1959, a master's degree from the University of Massachusetts in 1962, and a Ph.D. from Fordham University in 1967. He has been teaching at City College of New York since 1963. Professor McKenna is currently chairman of the Department of Political Science. He is the author of several books and articles, including *American Politics: Ideals and Realities* (McGraw-Hill, 1976) and *A Guide to the Constitution: That Delicate Balance* (Random House, 1984). His most recent textbook is *The Drama of Democracy: American Government and Politics* (Dushkin Publishing Group, 1990).

STANLEY FEINGOLD was born in New York City in 1926. He attended high school in the city and received his bachelor's degree from the City College of New York. He received his graduate education at Columbia University and taught political science at City College. From 1970 to 1974, he was given a special appointment as Visiting Professor of Politics at the University of Leeds, England. At present he is Visiting Professor at Westchester Community College, a unit of the State University of New York.

STAFF

Marguerite L. Egan   Program Manager
Brenda S. Filley   Production Manager
Whit Vye   Designer
Libra Ann Cusack   Typesetting Supervisor
Juliana Arbo   Typesetter
Shawn Callahan and Meredith Scheld   Graphics
Diane Barker   Editorial Assistant

384

AUTHORS

HERBERT E. ALEXANDER is director of the Citizens Research Foundation in Los Angeles, California and professor of political science at the University of Southern California.

WALTER BERNS is John M. Olin Professor of Government at Georgetown University in Washington, D.C.

ROBERT H. BORK is the John M. Olin Scholar in Legal Studies at the American Enterprise Institute. He is a former U.S. Court of Appeals judge for the District of Columbia Circuit.

WILLIAM J. BRENNAN, Jr., recently retired as U.S. Supreme Court justice after serving for 34 years. He was appointed in 1956 by then-President Eisenhower.

NOAM CHOMSKY is the Institute Professor in the Department of Linguistics and Philosophy at the Massachusetts Institute of Technology.

BARRY CRICKMER is the manager of editorial services at the Edison Electric Institute in Washington, D.C. He is a former editor of *Nation's Business*, a monthly magazine published by the U.S. Chamber of Commerce.

DONNA A. DEMAC is a lawyer, writer, educator, and board member of the National Coalition Against Censorship. She teaches law at New York University and is the author of *Keeping America Uninformed: Government Secrecy in the 1980s* (Pilgrim Press, 1984).

JAMES C. DOBSON was a member of the Meese Commission on Pornography, which delivered its report in 1986. He is the founder and president of Focus on the Family, an organization dedicated to preserving traditional values.

EDD DOERR is executive director of Americans for Religious Liberty in Silver Spring, Maryland.

THOMAS R. DYE is professor of political science and director of the Policy Sciences Program at Florida State University.

GREGG EASTERBROOK is a writer who contributes regularly to *The Atlantic*, *Newsweek*, and other publications.

JOHN LEWIS GADDIS is a professor of history at Ohio University. He is the author of *Russia, the Soviet Union, and the United States: An Interpretive History.*

BENJAMIN GINSBERG is a professor of government at Cornell University. He is director of the Cornell in Washington Program.

GEORGE GOLDBERG is an author and member of the New York State

Bar. His book, *Church, State and the Constitution*, examines church-state relations in the United States.

MARY GORDON is a novelist and short-story writer. She is the author of *Men and Angels, Temporary Shelter*, and *The Other Side*. Currently, she is working on a collection of essays.

ANDREW M. GREELEY is a Roman Catholic priest and an adjunct professor of sociology at the University of Arizona.

EDWARD S. HERMAN is professor emeritus of finance at the University of Pennsylvania's Wharton School of Business.

HERBERT HILL is a professor of Afro-American studies and a professor of industrial relations at the University of Wisconsin at Madison. He is the former labor director of the National Association for the Advancement of Colored People.

SAMUEL P. HUNTINGTON is professor of government and director of the John M. Olin Institute for Strategic Studies at Harvard University.

PAUL KENNEDY is the J. Richardson Dilworth Professor of History at Yale University and the author of several books on contemporary international relations.

STANLEY KOBER is an adjunct scholar at the Cato Institute in

Washington, D.C. He is currently writing a book about democracies.

EVERETT CARLL LADD is a professor of political science at the University of Connecticut. He is president and executive director of the University of Connecticut's Roper Center for Public Opinion Research.

LEONARD W. LEVY is a professor in the Department of History at the Claremont Graduate School. He is the author of *Essays on the Making of the Constitution*.

GLENN C. LOURY is professor of political economy at the John F. Kennedy School of Government at Harvard University.

DONAL E. J. MACNAMARA is professor of criminology and director of corrections programs at the John Jay College of Criminal Justice in New York City. He is the author of *Corrections* and other books and articles.

CHARLES MURRAY is a senior fellow at the Manhattan Institute for Policy Research.

ETHAN A. NADELMANN is assistant professor of politics and public affairs at Princeton's Woodrow Wilson School.

ROBERT NISBET is a historian and sociologist. He is a professor emeritus at Columbia University.

JOHN J. O'CONNOR is archbishop of New York and chairman of the Committee on Pro-Life Activities of the National Conference of Catholic Bishops.

THEODORE B. OLSON is a Washington, D.C., attorney. He is a former assistant attorney general in the Office of Legal Counsel at the U.S. Department of Justice.

GARY ORFIELD is a professor of political science at the University of Chicago. He is a former staff member of the Brookings Institution.

WILLIAM H. REHNQUIST is chief justice of the U.S. Supreme Court. He was appointed to the Court in 1972 by then-president Nixon.

LINDA ROCAWICH is the managing editor of *The Progressive*. She is a former staff member of the National Council on Crime and Delinquency.

WILLIAM A. RUSHER is a senior fellow at the Claremont Institute. He is a former publisher of the *National Review.*

ARTHUR SCHLESINGER, Jr., is a historian and political observer. He is the author of *The Cycles of American History* and *Robert Kennedy and His Times.*

MARTIN SHEFTER is a professor in the Department of Government at Cornell University. He is the author of *Patronage and Its Opponents: A Theory and Some European Cases.*

MARTIN TOLCHIN is a congressional correspondent for the *New York Times.*

SUSAN TOLCHIN is a professor of public administration at George Washington University.

FRED WERTHEIMER is president of Common Cause, a citizen's lobbying organization.

JAMES Q. WILSON is the Collins Professor of Management and Public Policy at UCLA. Previously, he was the Henry Lee Shattuck Professor of Government at Harvard University for many years. He has published several successful books on crime and American government.

WILLIAM JULIUS WILSON is the Lucy Flower Distinguished Service Professor of Sociology and Public Policy at the University of Chicago.

Z is a sometime observer of the Soviet scene. The identity of Z has not been made public by the author or the editors of the journal *Daedalus,* where the article "To the Stalin Mausoleum" first appeared.

INDEX